THE VARIETIES
OF METAPHYSICAL
POETRY

By T. S. Eliot

THE COMPLETE POEMS AND PLAYS OF T. S. ELIOT

verse

COLLECTED POEMS 1909–1962

FOUR QUARTETS

THE WASTE LAND *and* OTHER POEMS

THE WASTE LAND
A Facsimile and Transcript of the Original Drafts
Including the Annotations of Ezra Pound
Edited by Valerie Eliot

SELECTED POEMS

ANABASIS, BY ST.-JOHN PERSE
Translated by T. S. Eliot

children's verse

OLD POSSUM'S BOOK OF PRACTICAL CATS

GROWLTIGER'S LAST STAND AND OTHER POEMS

plays

MURDER IN THE CATHEDRAL

THE FAMILY REUNION

THE COCKTAIL PARTY

THE CONFIDENTIAL CLERK

THE ELDER STATESMAN

THE COMPLETE PLAYS OF T. S. ELIOT

literary criticism

SELECTED ESSAYS

THE USE OF POETRY *and* THE USE OF CRITICISM

TO CRITICIZE THE CRITIC

ON POETRY AND POETS

ESSAYS ON ELIZABETHAN DRAMA

FOR LANCELOT ANDREWES

SELECTED PROSE OF T. S. ELIOT
Edited by Frank Kermode

social criticism

THE IDEA OF A CHRISTIAN SOCIETY
Edited by David Edwards

NOTES TOWARDS THE DEFINITION OF CULTURE

Theresa Garrett Eliot's pencil drawing of T. S. Eliot
delivering his final Clark Lecture in the Hall of
Trinity College, Cambridge, 9 March 1926

THE VARIETIES
OF METAPHYSICAL
POETRY
by T. S. Eliot

THE CLARK LECTURES
at Trinity College, Cambridge, 1926

and

THE TURNBULL LECTURES
at The Johns Hopkins University, 1933

Edited and introduced by

RONALD SCHUCHARD

A HARVEST BOOK
HARCOURT BRACE & COMPANY
San Diego   New York   London

First published in 1993 by Faber and Faber Limited.
All texts by T. S. Eliot © 1993 by SET Copyrights Limited
Editorial matter and annotations © 1993 by Ronald Schuchard

The Harvest edition corrects the printer's errors
and inconsistencies of the first edition.

Library of Congress Cataloging-in-Publication Data
Eliot, T. S. (Thomas Stearns), 1888–1965.
The varieties of metaphysical poetry: the Clark lectures at
Trinity College, Cambridge, 1926, and the Turnbull lectures at the
Johns Hopkins University, 1933/by T. S. Eliot; edited and
introduced by Ronald Schuchard.—1st U.S. ed.
p.   cm.
Includes indexes.
ISBN 0-15-100096-4
ISBN 0-15-600256-6 (pbk.)
1. English poetry—Early modern, 1500–1700—History and criticism.
2. Donne, John, 1572–1631—Criticism and interpretation.
3. Metaphysics in literature. I. Schuchard, Ronald. II. Title.
III. Title: Clark lectures. IV. Title: Turnbull lectures.
PR545.M4E39   1994
821'.309—dc20   94-2959

Printed in the United States of America
First Harvest edition 1996
A C E F D B

CONTENTS

THE CLARK LECTURES
On the Metaphysical Poetry of the Seventeenth Century with Special Reference to Donne, Crashaw and Cowley

THE TURNBULL LECTURES
The Varieties of Metaphysical Poetry

[vii]

ACKNOWLEDGEMENTS

I wish to express my deepest thanks to Mrs Valerie Eliot for her confidence and encouragement during the preparation of this edition of her husband's Clark Lectures and Turnbull Lectures. The volume would not have been possible without her personal interest, assistance and hospitality.

I am indebted to the following persons for help and advice: the late William Arrowsmith, Boston University; Joseph C. Baillargeon, Seattle, Washington; George Bornstein, University of Michigan; Jewel Spears Brooker, Eckerd College; William C. Charron, Saint Louis University; Robert Crawford, University of Glasgow; Denis Donoghue, New York University; Donald Gallup, Yale University; Warwick Gould, Royal Holloway and Bedford New College, University of London; John S. Kelly, St John's College, Oxford; Frank Kermode, King's College, Cambridge; Mrs Frances Kidder, Cockeysville, Maryland; Joseph Kronik, Louisiana State University; A. Walton Litz, Princeton University; James B. Longenbach, University of Rochester; Roger H. Lonsdale, Balliol College, Oxford; Richard A. Macksey, Johns Hopkins University; Louis L. Martz, Yale University; Lawrence Rainey, Yale University; Christopher Ricks, Boston University; John Paul Riquelme, Boston University; Philip Rusche, Yale University; John Paul Russo, University of Miami; Herman J. Saatkamp Jr, Texas A & M University; Craig A. Simmons, Yale University; Stephano Tani; Deirdre Toomey, London; Anne Varty, Royal Holloway and Bedford New College, University of London; George Watson, St John's College, Cambridge; and my colleagues at Emory University: Mark Bauerlein, Jerome Beaty, Martine W. Brownley, Josué Harari, John Johnston, Dalia Judowitz, Paul Kuntz, Judy Raggi Moore, Walter Reed, Harry Rusche, John Sitter.

I am grateful to the following librarians and archivists for research assistance: Rodney Dennis and Elizabeth A. Falsey, Houghton Library, Harvard University; Jacqueline Cox and Michael Halls, King's College, Cambridge; Richard Luckett, Magdalene College, Cambridge; Eric R. Nitschke and Greta Boers, Robert W. Woodruff Library, Emory University; David J. McKitterick, Trinity College Library, Cambridge; Julia B. Morgan and James Stimpert, The Ferdinand Hamburger Jr Archives, Johns Hopkins University; Michael Plunkett, Alderman Library, University of Virginia; Cynthia H. Requardt, The Milton S. Eisenhower Library, Johns Hopkins University; Margery Sly, College Archives, Smith College;

Susan D. Weinandy, Maryland Historical Society; Howard Gerwing and the staff of the McPherson Library, University of Victoria.

Special thanks to my wife, Keith Schuchard, for critical and judicious readings of the manuscript at various stages of preparation. Jewel Spears Brooker, Louis L. Martz, A. Walton Litz and Christopher Ricks read the manuscript generously and closely in a late stage, and I am indebted to them for their corrections and suggestions. I am further indebted to David Bradshaw of Worcester College, Oxford, for providing his bibliographical list of eleven previously unrecorded reviews that TSE published in *TLS* from 1927–30, and to John Bodley of Faber and Faber for editorial assistance and for skilfully seeing the volume through the press.

For permission to quote from translations I am indebted to the following: Keith Bosley, *Mallarmé The Poems* (Harmondsworth, Middlesex: Penguin Books, 1977); John Cairncross, Racine's *Phaedra*, in *Masterpieces of the Drama*, 5th edition, ed. Alexander W. Allison, Arthur J. Carr, Arthur M. Eastman (New York: Macmillan, 1986); Michael Collie, *Laforgue* (Edinburgh and London: Oliver and Boyd, 1963); Alfred Allinson, *Down There [Là-bas]*, by J.-K. Huysmans (London: Fortune Press, 1930); G. P. Goold, *Catullus* (London: Duckworth, 1983); C. F. MacIntyre, *One Hundred Poems from Les Fleurs du Mal* (Berkeley: Univ. of California Press, 1947), and *Selections from Les Amours Jaunes* (Berkeley: Univ. of California Press, 1954); Geoffrey Wagner, *Selected Writings of Gérard de Nerval* (London: Peter Owen, 1958); *The Penguin Book of French Verse*, ed. Brian Woledge, Geoffrey Brereton and Anthony Hartley (Harmondsworth, Middlesex: Penguin Books, 1977); Grover A. Zinn, *Richard of St. Victor* (New York: Paulist Press, 1979). Unacknowledged translations in the notes are by the editor.

Drawings by Theresa Garrett Eliot are reproduced by permission of the Houghton Library, Harvard University, and Mrs Valerie Eliot.

I am grateful to the Emory University Research Committee for a grant that provided partial support for the research of this edition.

ABBREVIATIONS AND SHORT FORMS
Principal sources cited or quoted

PUBLISHED

BY T. S. ELIOT

ASG (UK/US)	*After Strange Gods.* London: Faber and Faber, 1934. New York: Harcourt, Brace & Company, 1934.
Criterion	*The Criterion.* Collected edition, 18 vols, ed. T. S. Eliot. London: Faber and Faber, 1967.
CPP (UK/US)	*The Complete Poems and Plays.* London: Faber and Faber, 1969. *The Complete Poems and Plays 1909–1950.* New York: Harcourt, Brace & Co. 1952.
FLA (UK/US)	*For Lancelot Andrewes.* London: Faber and Gwyer, 1928. New York: Doubleday, Doran, 1929.
KEPB	*Knowledge and Experience in the Philosophy of F. H. Bradley.* London: Faber and Faber, 1964. New York: Farrar, Straus, 1964.
L1	*The Letters of T. S. Eliot*, vol. 1, ed. Valerie Eliot. London: Faber and Faber, 1988. New York: Harcourt Brace Jovanovich, 1988.
L2	*The Letters of T. S. Eliot*, vol. II, ed. Valerie Eliot. London: Faber and Faber; New York: Harcourt Brace & Company (in preparation).
OPP (UK/US)	*On Poetry and Poets.* London: Faber and Faber, 1957. New York: Farrar, Straus & Cudahy, 1957.
SE (UK/US)	*Selected Essays*, third enlarged edition. London: Faber and Faber, 1951. *Selected Essays*, new edition. New York: Harcourt, Brace & Co., 1950.
SW	*The Sacred Wood*, second edition. London: Methuen & Co., 1928. New York: Alfred Knopf, 1930.

[xi]

TCC   *To Criticize the Critic*. London: Faber and Faber, 1965.
New York: Farrar, Straus & Giroux, 1965.

UPUC (UK/US)   *The Use of Poetry and the Use of Criticism*, second
edition. London: Faber and Faber, 1964. Cambridge:
Harvard University Press, 1986.

WLF   *The Waste Land: A Facsimile and Transcript of the
Original Drafts*, ed. Valerie Eliot. London: Faber and
Faber, 1971. New York: Harcourt Brace Jovanovich,
1971.

OTHER WORKS

CFQ   Helen Gardner, *The Composition of Four Quartets*.
London: Faber and Faber, 1978.

Gosse I   Edmund Gosse, *The Life and Letters of John Donne*,
vol. I. London: William Heinemann, 1899.

Gosse II   – *The Life and Letters of John Donne*, vol. II. London:
William Heinemann, 1899.

Grierson I   *The Poems of John Donne*, vol. I. Oxford: Clarendon
Press, 1912.

Grierson II   *The Poems of John Donne*, vol. II. Oxford: Clarendon
Press, 1912.

LMEP   Samuel Johnson, *Lives of the Most Eminent English
Poets*. Chandos Classics, new edition. London:
Frederick Warne, 1872.

MLPSC   *Metaphysical Lyrics and Poems of the Seventeenth
Century: Donne to Butler*, ed. H. J. C. Grierson.
Oxford: Oxford University Press, 1921.

OBEV   *The Oxford Book of English Verse 1250–1900*, ed.
Arthur Quiller-Couch. Oxford: Clarendon Press,
1918.

PBFV   *The Penguin Book of French Verse*, ed. Brian Woledge,
Geoffrey Brereton and Anthony Hartley.
Harmondsworth, Middlesex: Penguin Books, 1977.

Ser   *The Sermons of John Donne*, ed. G. R. Potter and
Evelyn M. Spearing, 10 vols. Berkeley, Univ. of
California Press, 1953–62.

TC I   *The Inferno of Dante*. Temple Classics edition.
London: J. M. Dent, 1909.

TC II   *The Purgatorio of Dante*. Temple Classics edition.
London: J. M. Dent, 1910.

TC III   *The Paradiso of Dante*. Temple Classics edition.
London: J. M. Dent, 1910.

PERIODICALS

RES I   Ronald Schuchard, 'T. S. Eliot as an Extension
Lecturer, 1916–1919', Part I, *Review of English
Studies*, n.s. 25 (May 1974), pp. 163–73.

RES II   – 'T. S. Eliot as an Extension Lecturer', Part II, *Review
of English Studies*, n.s. 25 (August 1974), pp. 292–304.

All other published sources are cited in full at the first mention.

UNPUBLISHED

Berg	The Berg Collection, New York Public Library
Hopkins	The Ferdinand Hamburger, Jr Archives, The Johns Hopkins University
Houghton	The Houghton Library, Harvard University.
King's	Modern Archive Centre, King's College Library, Cambridge University
MS VE	Private collection, Mrs Valerie Eliot, London
Nottingham	University of Nottingham Library
Princeton	Princeton University Library
Smith	College Archives, Smith College
Texas	Harry Ransom Humanities Research Center, University of Texas at Austin
Trinity	Trinity College Library, Cambridge University
Victoria	University of Victoria, British Columbia
Virginia	Alderman Library, University of Virginia

THE VARIETIES
OF METAPHYSICAL
POETRY

EDITOR'S INTRODUCTION

T. S. Eliot's immersion in the poetry of Dante, Donne and Laforgue at Harvard University led him to formulate a major theory of metaphysical poetry during his first decade as a poet and critic in London. Though its development was the driving force behind his critical reading and poetic practice, the theory remained fragmented in his literary reviews until it found sustained expression in his unpublished Clark Lectures, originally entitled 'ON THE METAPHYSICAL POETRY OF THE SEVENTEENTH CENTURY with special reference to Donne, Crashaw and Cowley'. The eight lectures were delivered at Trinity College, Cambridge, in 1926, and though he planned to revise them as a book to be entitled *The School of Donne*, the project was gradually and reluctantly abandoned. Some scholars have had the privilege of reading the 184-page typescript at King's College, Cambridge, or the carbon copy at Harvard. Others have quoted from or paraphrased parts of the lectures in critical studies of his work, but most of Eliot's readers have had no access to this extraordinary exposition of learning in the year that preceded his religious conversion. Written under intense pressure during a period of great personal difficulty, the unrevised text survives as a crucial document of his intellectual life: much of his reading and writing for the twenty years preceding the lectures went into them; much of his critical activity in the twenty years following the lectures drew upon them. They were drafted and delivered at the turning point of his career: *The Sacred Wood* (1920) and *The Waste Land* (1922) were behind him; with all that lay before him as poet and playwright, he would never again find occasion to write at such length about the historical currents of poetry and philosophy that determined the shape of his work. It may be that the publication of Eliot's Clark Lectures on metaphysical poetry will have as much impact on our revaluation of his critical mind as did the facsimile

[1]

edition of *The Waste Land* (1971) on our comprehension of his poetic mind.

I

Eliot began to exercise his nascent theory of metaphysical poetry in his earliest reviews from 1917 to 1920, drawing upon Donne and Chapman to show the dissociation of object, feeling and thought in nineteenth- and twentieth-century poetry. The critical preoccupation first appears in 'Reflections on Contemporary Poetry' (1917), where he compares the relation of Donne, Wordsworth and the Georgian poets to their poetic objects, arguing that whereas the others derive their emotion from the object, in Donne the emotion and the object 'preserve exactly their proper proportions'[1]. In 'Observations' (1918) he tried his criterion on a contemporary poet, tentatively comparing the relation of thought and feeling in the poetry of Marianne Moore and Jules Laforgue: 'Even in Laforgue there are unassimilated fragments of metaphysics and, on the other hand, of sentiment floating about. I will not assert that Miss Moore is as interesting in herself as Laforgue, but the fusion of thought and feeling is perhaps more complete.'[2] Though Eliot was the first critic to point out the metaphysical strain in Chapman, he took pains in 'Swinburne and the Elizabethans' (1919) to assert that 'the quality in question is not peculiar to Donne and Chapman . . . In common with the greatest . . . they had some quality of sensuous thought, or of thinking through the senses, or of the senses thinking, of which the exact formula remains to be defined. If you look for it in Shelley or Beddoes . . . you will not find it, though you may find other qualities instead' (*SW* 23). In his first essay on Dante, originally entitled 'Dante as a "Spiritual Leader" ' (1920), he drew upon a book that he had read and mastered at Harvard, a book that had stimulated his theory and that was to become a central document in his Clark Lectures – George Santayana's *Three Philosophical Poets* (1910). Reacting to Santayana's study of Lucretius, Dante and Goethe as poets who give expression to a philosophical system, Eliot makes the distinction that what the philosophical poet really endeavours to find is 'the concrete poetic equivalent for this system – to find its complete equivalent in vision' (*SW* 161). He then declares that Dante's poetry contains 'the most comprehensive, and the

1–*Egoist* (September 1917), p. 118.
2–*Egoist* (May 1918), p. 70.

most *ordered* presentation of emotions that has ever been made' (*SW* 168). Dante was thus already in place as Eliot's distant point of reference for exploring what constitutes the 'metaphysical' in poetry, but his immediate fascination lay in working out the 'exact formula' of sensuous thought in Donne, Chapman and Laforgue for his own poetry and criticism.

By 1921 the resurgence of interest in metaphysical poetry had flooded the London literary world as critics 'rediscovered' Donne, Crashaw, Cowley and other poets of their school, and Eliot immediately plunged into the swell of commentary. The appearance of the third volume of George Saintsbury's *Minor Poets of the Caroline Period* was but one of several publishing events in 1921 that focused Eliot's mind on all things metaphysical. In these volumes he discovered new matter in the lesser-known metaphysicals – Bishop King, Edward Benlowes and Aurelian Townshend. On 22 April, he wrote to John Middleton Murry, who had recently reviewed *The Sacred Wood*, that he now envisaged 'A seventeenth Century volume to Pope with a *Nachblick* [glance] at Collins and Johnson' (*L1* 447). A tercentenary tribute to Andrew Marvell had afforded him the first of three major reviews in *TLS* between March and October. 'A poet like Donne . . . or Laforgue,' he wrote in 'Andrew Marvell', 'may almost be considered the inventor of an attitude, a system of feeling or of morals' (*SE* 292/251), but as he formulated these tentative statements the publication of Herbert Grierson's comprehensive anthology – *Metaphysical Lyrics and Poems of the Seventeenth Century* – pushed Eliot to 'a brief exposition of a theory' (*SE* 288/248), as he described it in his famous review, 'The Metaphysical Poets'. He looked upon Grierson's anthology as 'a provocation of criticism' (*SE* 281/241), and thus provoked he made his well-known declaration: 'In the seventeenth century a dissociation of sensibility set in, from which we have never recovered; and this dissociation . . . was aggravated by the two most powerful poets of the century, Milton and Dryden' (*SE* 288/247). There was, however, recognizably a small pocket of recovery in nineteenth-century France: 'Jules Laforgue, and Tristan Corbière', he declared, 'are nearer to the "school of Donne" than any modern English poet . . . they have the same essential quality of transmuting ideas into sensations, of transforming an observation into a state of mind' (*SE* 290/249).

These declarations were yet to be developed, but Eliot had begun to outline a theory based on three metaphysical moments – Dante in Florence in the thirteenth century; Donne in London in the seventeenth century; Laforgue in Paris in the nineteenth century. Implicitly, there was a fourth moment at hand – Eliot in London in the twentieth century. Meanwhile, the

[3]

appearance of Mark Van Doren's *John Dryden* allowed Eliot to probe the alleged dissociation in a poet he deeply admired, Dryden, 'the ancestor of nearly all that is best in the poetry of the eighteenth century' (*SE* 305/264). So buoyed up was Eliot's mind by these metaphysical deliberations that it is startling to remember that he was then on the verge of an emotional collapse. In October 1921, after his doctor prescribed three months of rest, Eliot went off to the Albemarle Hotel in Margate, and then to a sanatorium near Lausanne, where he completed *The Waste Land*. During this unsettled period he wrote to his friend Richard Aldington not only about his '*aboulie* and emotional derangement' (*L1* 486), but about his discoveries of King, Cowley, Waller, Denham and Oldham. Moreover, in the pages of *TLS* he engaged Professor Saintsbury in spirited debate about the alleged presence of metaphysical qualities in Swinburne. On 15 November 1922, a month after the publication of *The Waste Land*, he wrote again to Aldington, who had become Eliot's assistant editor on the *Criterion*, and who had published an article on Cowley the previous year: 'Have you studied with any care Bishop King in Saintsbury's collection? He seems to me one of the finest and I have long desired to write a short paper about him. I want to write something about Cowley also, undeterred by the fact that you preceded me and probably know a great deal more about him' (*L1* 596–7).

During the next three years, the increasing distress of his personal life broke the momentum of Eliot's deliberations on metaphysical poetry. His work at Lloyds Bank, his editing of the *Criterion*, his wife's chronic illness and increasing dependence, together with his own frequent bouts of illness, were taking their physical and psychic toll. By the time the Woolfs persuaded him to collect and publish his three *TLS* reviews as *Homage to John Dryden* at the Hogarth Press in October 1924, he had assumed a weary, exhausted outlook on his work: 'Some apology' was called for, he wrote in his dispirited Preface to the volume, and he announced resignedly that the piecemeal theory represented here had since been abandoned:

> My intention had been to write a series of papers on the poetry of the seventeenth and eighteenth centuries; beginning with Chapman and Donne, and ending with Johnson. This . . . might have filled two volumes . . . the series would have included Aurelian Townshend and Bishop King, and the authors of 'Cooper's Hill' and 'The Vanity of Human Wishes,' as well as Swift and Pope. That which dissipation interrupts, the infirmities of age come to terminate . . . I have abandoned this design in the pursuit of other policies. I have long felt that

the poetry of the seventeenth and eighteenth centuries . . . possesses an elegance and a dignity absent from the popular and pretentious verse of the Romantic Poets and their successors. To have urged this claim persuasively would have led me indirectly into considerations of politics, education, and theology which I no longer care to approach in this way. I hope that these three papers may in spite of and partly because of their defects preserve in cryptogram certain notions which, if expressed directly, would be destined to immediate obloquy, followed by perpetual oblivion.[3]

Eliot's new friends at Cambridge, however, particularly I. A. Richards, would accept no apologies or pleas of infirmity from the author of *The Sacred Wood* and *The Waste Land*. Richards, who had enjoyed Eliot's poetry and friendship since he read *Ara Vos Prec* in 1920, had in 1922 become a lecturer for the new Cambridge School of English. Established in 1917, the School allowed students to opt for a course of modern English studies over traditional Anglo-Saxon, philological and editorial studies. To Richards, Eliot was '*the one hope*' for the school.[4] In the hope of luring him away from the bank to Cambridge, he had invited him up on several occasions to lecture or to attend his 'protocols' on Practical Criticism. Richards had also directed to Eliot's work the attention of E. M. W. Tillyard, Secretary of the Faculty Board of English, who was greatly impressed with *The Sacred Wood* and helped prepare the way for Eliot. 'Eliot's unconventional ideas irritated or delighted in the right way', wrote Tillyard. 'They were fresh and stirred people up and some of the people who were stirred up looked a bit more closely on account of the stirring.'[5] To Basil Willey, who became a lecturer for the School in 1923, Eliot 'was only one of many intruders into pre-lapsarian Cambridge. Yet I date the beginning of the climatic change from the day when Tillyard casually

3 – *Homage to John Dryden* (London: Hogarth Press, 1924), p. 9. F. R. Leavis was to recall that '*The Sacred Wood . . .* had very little influence or attention before the Hogarth Press brought out *Homage to John Dryden . . .*. It was with the publication in this form of those essays (the Hogarth Press had recently published *The Waste Land*) that Eliot became the important contemporary critic. It was the impact of this slender new collection that sent one back to *The Sacred Wood* and confirmed with decisive practical effect one's sense of the stimulus to be got from that rare thing, a fine intelligence in literary criticism.' *Anna Karenina and Other Essays* (London: Chatto & Windus, 1967), pp. 177–8.
4 – 'On TSE', in *T. S. Eliot: The Man and His Work*, ed. Allen Tate (New York: Dell, 1966; London: Chatto & Windus, 1967), p. 3.
5 – *The Muse Unchained: An Intimate Account of The Revolution in English Studies at Cambridge* (London: Bowes & Bowes, 1958), p. 98.

observed, to me, at the end of a walk round Grantchester, that there was a new chap called T. S. Eliot for whom one should be on the look-out.'[6] Both Tillyard and Willey would testify to the immediate impact that the essays in *Homage to John Dryden* had on English studies, and in November 1924 – his apologetic Preface ignored, his wife temporarily in a sanatorium in Paris – Eliot was back at Cambridge lecturing on George Chapman. He now had a student following, and the editor of the undergraduate magazine, *Granta*, noted on 7 November that 'the most discussed of contemporary highbrows' would appear before the Cam Literary Club the following evening at the Tea Shop:

> Mr. Eliot is notorious for his poem 'The Waste Land,' which has occasioned nearly as many disputes as Prohibition . . . many a home has been broken up owing to a difference of opinion as to its poetic merits! The Secretary says that he had hoped to obtain larger premises, but he has not yet been able to. Members or guests are therefore advised to appear fairly punctually, unless they want to sit on the floor.[7]

It happened that Eliot's London friend and intellectual antagonist, John Middleton Murry, now editor of the *Adelphi*, had been elected Clark Lecturer for 1924–5, and in the autumn and winter of that academic year he gave ten lectures on 'Keats and Shakespeare'. In an act of intellectual generosity, Murry, the apologist for Romanticism, nominated Eliot, the apologist for Classicism, to succeed him as Clark Lecturer the following year. On 20 February, while Eliot nursed Vivien through a dreadful illness, he wrote in excited gratitude to Murry:

> £200 would make a vast just all the difference to my inclination to jump out into the world this year – and the appointment is very attractive. Meanwhile could you let me know the terms and conditions – i.e. *subject* of lectures, expenses whether one is put up at Trinity, whether fares paid etc – and anything else – whether it is definitely during the winter term? . . . You must have realised that your proposal of my name, and the hope of this job, would come as a ray of hope just at the *blackest moment of my life*. I think there is no doubt I should accept. (*L*2)

Murry's thoughtful and encouraging reply brought even more light to Eliot's darkened life. 'The subject you suggest was of course an intuition on

6 – *Cambridge and Other Memories 1920–1953* (New York: W. W. Norton, 1968), p. 26.
7 – 'The Waste-Landers', *Granta* (7 November 1924), p. 70.

your part', Eliot wrote on 22 February. 'What I am aching to do if acceptable is to take the 17th C. metaphysicals (not only the poets, but the Cambridge platonists) and compare and contrast them with Dante and his school (Guido, Cino etc.) and this would be a big job – and primarily for the "hypothetical". What you say merely convinces me that I want to do this' (*L2*). Eliot was immensely grateful to Murry for what he saw as an act of genuine friendship. 'Other people have offered things, gifts, but no one, except you, has ever come with them exactly at the right moment. What is this except friendship?'

'Murry's star sank as Eliot's rose', wrote Murry's biographer, 'rather ironically, since it was due to his own exertions, in the face of staunch opposition to an American, that Eliot was offered the next series of Clark Lectures.'[8] In fact, the Trinity College Council had initially nominated its own Fellow, A. E. Housman, who prudently declined the burden. His letter to the Master of Trinity, Sir Joseph Thomson, was read to the Council on 27 February 1925:

> If I devoted a whole year (and it would not take less) to the composition of six lectures on literature, the result would be nothing which could give me, I do not say satisfaction, but consolation for the wasted time; and the year would be one of anxiety and depression, the more vexatious because it would be subtracted from those minute and pedantic studies in which I am fitted to excel and which give me pleasure. I am sorry if this explanation is tedious, but I would rather be tedious than seem thankless and churlish.[9]

Housman's declination opened the way for Eliot's supporters: at the next meeting on 6 March, 'It was agreed that the lectureship for 1925–26 be offered to Mr. T. S. Eliot' (Trinity). Recovering from a protracted bout of flu, Eliot was exhilarated by this gesture of intellectual acceptance, however controversial he knew the invitation must have been. Here was the chance and the challenge to flesh out his theory, to consider the transformations in metaphysical literature from Dante to Laforgue in relation to the political, philosophical and theological forces that had become central to his intellectual life. At a special meeting convened on 24 April, the minutes record that 'Mr. T. S. Eliot was appointed Lecturer . . . and the subjects proposed for his Lectures approved' (Trinity).

8–F. A. Lea, *The Life of John Middleton Murry* (London: Methuen, 1959), p. 130.
9–*The Letters of A. E. Housman*, ed. Henry Maas (Cambridge, MA: Harvard Univ. Press, 1971), p. 228.

II

The Clark Lectures had been endowed by a bequest of £300 a year from William George Clark (1821–78), a Fellow of Trinity College who in 1868 had become the founder-editor of the *Journal of Philology* and who, in addition to his travel writing, had edited the Globe Shakespeare (1864) and the Cambridge Shakespeare (1863–6). The Master and current members of the College Council would elect the lecturers, who were to receive a stipend of £200. Thus, the Clark Lectures were duly inaugurated in the Lent term of 1884 by Leslie Stephen, editor of the *Dictionary of National Biography*. Pressed for time to publish the first volume that year, and convinced that he had no talent as a literary critic, he wrote to C. E. Norton to express his dismay at having let himself be persuaded to take the lectureship: 'I shall have to go to Cambridge three times a week to talk twaddle about Addison and Pope to a number of young ladies from Girton and a few idle undergraduates and the youthful prince, and feel down to the soles of my shoes that I am making an ass of myself'.[10] He was followed by Sir Edmund Gosse and a string of distinguished scholars and writers that included Edward Dowden, Sir Sidney Lee, W. P. Ker, Walter de la Mare and Lascelles Abercrombie (see Appendix 11).[11] Only two Americans had been Clark Lecturers: Professor Barrett Wendell of Harvard in 1902, and William Everett – a Trinity College graduate, the first American elected to the Cambridge Apostles, a Harvard Latin professor, a Unitarian minister and a US congressman – in 1907. Thus the election in 1925 of a thirty-six-year-old American, who lived in London as a banker, editor and controversial poet with limited academic credentials and no college affiliation, was, by Cambridge standards, extraordinary. In common with his fellow-American predecessors, he was at least a Harvard man. 'Even by 1925', as his new friend Frank Morley recalled, 'Eliot's reputation as a literary man had not

10–See Frederic William Maitland, *The Life and Letters of Leslie Stephen* (London: Duckworth, 1906), p. 380.
11–The early Clark Lecturers filled a void in the curriculum before the establishment of the Cambridge School of English. After Dowden's first series of lectures on 'The Influence of the French Revolution on English Literature', in which he discussed Burns, Godwin, Mary Wollestonecraft, Wordsworth, Southey, Landor, Byron and Shelley, an editor of the *Cambridge Review* noted (10 May 1894, p. 315) that 'Few who attended this course could help regretting that the only work sanctioned by the University in connection with modern English literature was limited to six short lectures a term delivered by a professor borrowed for the occasion. All must have regretted that no Cambridge Professor of English should exist in any more tangible form than in the figments of the minds of enthusiastic writers to the *Times* and other papers'.

spread very far. His literary judgments were commanding only to a few. Some of the few were in high places, but for the most part those who followed Eliot were a ragged battalion.'[12]

Eliot had eight months to prepare eight lectures for a stipend of £200, unchanged after forty-two years, and payable, the Council had recently determined, at the end of the course. In late July, as he sought to expand the historical context of his theory, he wrote with some anxiety to Richard Aldington: 'When you write, can you suggest any bibliography of Marino / Marinism / Gongora / Gongorism for my lectures on XVII C poets (English). I must be well fortified' (L2). Aldington's response is lost, but Eliot wrote thankfully on 31 July: 'The information about Marino is most useful' (L2). However, when Tillyard wrote in October to request an outline of the lectures, Eliot had made little progress. Not surprisingly: Vivien, suffering from acute neuralgia, rheumatism and shingles, had needed constant attention through the summer; a painful infection of his teeth and gums compelled him to have an operation on his jaw in September, the month he assumed his new position as editor at Faber & Gwyer; his new volume, *Poems 1909–1925*, had to be prepared for publication in November; difficult negotiations over the future of the *Criterion* had become time-consuming. He replied apologetically on 26 October:

> I cannot give you an outline of my lectures, which have not yet taken definite shape. But I shall deal specially with Donne, Crashaw and Cowley (3 different types); only touching Marvell lightly, and shall mention Benlowes & Cleveland. I shall make no attempt to be *comprehensive*. I only take representatives. An acquaintance with Waller & Denham ('Cooper Hill') [sic] would be useful. Cowley's 'Mistress'; Crashaw's 'Weeper' 'St. Theresa' – it is impossible to select any one poem of Donne's. (L2)

Ten days later, on 5 November, Eliot wrote to Ottoline Morrell that he had arranged for Vivien to go to the country until Christmas. 'And I am going tomorrow morning for a short sea voyage – (have never quite got over that operation) . . . This Cambridge business will make it difficult for me to get out of London again until the Spring' (L2). On his doctor's advice, Eliot sailed to the South of France with no lectures, a few books, and a strong

---

12–'T. S. Eliot as a Publisher', in *T. S. Eliot*, ed. Richard March and Tambimuttu (London: Editions Poetry, 1948; New York: Tambimuttu & Mass, 1965), pp. 61–2.

reliance on his memory of the poems and prose passages that informed his critical point of view. Settling at the Savoy Hotel, La Turbie, in the Alpes Maritimes, he recuperated in the sunshine and worked assiduously on the Clark Lectures, determined to have four lectures drafted before his return to London late on Christmas Eve.

Eliot was arranging his early lectures on Donne to counter Mary Paton Ramsay's thesis in *Les Doctrines médiévales chez Donne* (1917) that Donne's sensibility was essentially medieval; he would argue that Donne represented the transition from the sixteenth to the seventeenth century. But what finally got him going was the unexpected arrival of a new book for review from *TLS*, Mario Praz's *Secentismo e marinismo in Inghilterra*. This ground-breaking study of Donne and Crashaw made the lectures coalesce, and on 23 November Eliot wrote to Praz, then a senior lecturer at Liverpool University, about his enthusiasm for the book:

> I shall make copious reference to it in some lectures which I am to give during the winter at Trinity College, Cambridge, *on the metaphysical poetry of the XVII century in England*. I am writing to tell you that I have found nothing by any of our scholars – even by Saintsbury or Grierson or Gosse, which can challenge comparison with your book for critical taste and judgment and for width (*envergure*) of learning. I am a little jealous indeed that you have forestalled me on several points: in your criticism of Miss Ramsay, in your comparison and contrast of Donne and Guido Cavalcanti, and in your insistence on the importance of the Society of Jesus in England at that time. All of these points had occurred to me, but you have spoken first. (*L2*)

No notes or drafts from this saving retreat in France survive, but by 11 December he had begun to write and could describe his thesis to Herbert Read with some conviction:

> The idea is briefly this: to take the XIII century – in its literary form, Dante – as my *point de repère*, to treat subsequent history as the history of the disintegration of that unity – disintegration inevitable because of the increase of knowledge and consequent dispersion of attention, but bringing with it many undesirable features. Disintegration, which, WHEN the world has crystallised for another moment into a new order, can be treated as a form of generation; but which the historian at the present time, who does not anticipate, must regard partly as the history of corruption. That is to say, to consider and criticise the poetry

of the XVII century from the point of view of the XIII. It seems to me that such an examination should bring out some curious things. I am far from sure that I have succeeded. (L2)

After his return to London, Eliot regularly sent requests to the London Library for the books and editions he needed, and he continued to work on and revise each lecture up to the date of delivery. Two weeks after the lectures had begun, having received a dinner invitation from his friend Mary Hutchinson, he was quick to explain that 'for the next fortnight, until I have finished my Cambridge lectures, I am anxious to avoid evening engagements' (L2).

III

When Eliot arrived in Cambridge for the first lecture on 26 January 1926 he faced an imposing pantheon of Fellows at Trinity College, many of whom had played major roles in his intellectual life: Sir James George Frazer, author of *The Golden Bough*; Alfred North Whitehead, co-author with Bertrand Russell of the *Principia Mathematica*; Francis Cornford, author of *The Origins of Attic Tragedy*, which Eliot had studied intensively when writing *Sweeney Agonistes*; the Revd Hugh Fraser Stewart, the eminent Pascal scholar who would later escort Eliot to Little Gidding; the poet and classical scholar A. E. Housman; the philosopher G. E. Moore, and others. Housman sat in the front row for all the lectures, and though there is no evidence that his fellow luminaries were in attendance, the younger dons of the English School were there in allied support for some or all of the lectures: Richards, Tillyard, Willey, H. S.[Stanley] Bennett and his wife Joan Bennett, Mansfield Forbes, Aubrey Attwater and F. R. Leavis, the last of whom had joined the faculty of Emmanuel College the previous autumn. When Eliot asked Richards to meet him the morning after his third lecture, Richards, who was writing his review of Eliot's *Poems 1909–1925* for the *New Statesman*, wrote on 8 February that 'I should be going to all your lectures in any case'.[13] Happily elected Fellow of Magdalene College the following week, he was keen to see that Eliot met all members of the English School. On 15 February he invited him to come round to his rooms after the fourth lecture: 'I want you to meet Margaret Gardiner, who has I think *very* good

13—*Selected Letters of I. A. Richards*, ed. John Constable (Oxford: Clarendon Press, 1990), p. 41.

natural judgment in poetry besides being intelligent and attractive . . . Later on you ought to see the remainder of the English lecturers (Faculty folk), e.g. Tillyard, Attwater, Forbes. That last is amusing, the others dullish; but Forbes is busy just now' (p. 42).

Eliot's detractors were represented by T. R. Henn, newly appointed at St Catharine's College, who was later to lecture on 'the vulgarity of most of Eliot's work, all the more pernicious since cloaked by an austere and pseudo-learned style',[14] and by F. L. ('Peter') Lucas, a Fellow and librarian of King's who was about to publish his *Authors Dead and Living* (1926), a collection of essays on metaphysical and modern poets. Lucas was 'openly hostile' to Eliot, wrote Tillyard,[15] so much so, confirmed T. E. B. Howarth, that he 'would not even allow Eliot's work to be bought for the library'.[16] Eliot was to write to Aldington after the third lecture that it 'was not at all boring to me but I cannot speak for the audience' (*L2*). But Lucas readily presumed to speak for the audience that evening to Virginia Woolf, declaring that Eliot had 'thrown intellect to the winds; given up the ghost'. Woolf, describing Lucas as 'a bony rosy little austere priest', wrote in her diary that night: 'Tom has been down lecturing, & not creating a good impression at Cambridge, I fancy. He tells the young men, in private, how they cook fish in Paris: his damned selfconsciousness again, I suppose.'[17]

Eliot may indeed have discussed the shortcomings of College-cooked fish with undergraduates at the Wednesday morning coffee-circles that followed his Tuesday afternoon lectures. Moreover, the undergraduates took more notice of Eliot than the senior Fellows and the Cambridge papers. While the *Cambridge University Reporter* dutifully noted the fact and the dates of the lectures, for which academic dress was required, the *Cambridge Review* –

---

14 – From a lecture read before a literary society at St John's in 1933, quoted in T. E. B. Howarth, *Cambridge Between Two Wars* (London: Collins, 1978), p. 166.

15 – *The Muse Unchained*, p. 98.

16 – *Cambridge Between Two Wars*, p. 166. The intellectual antagonism between TSE and Lucas was widely known, and in his two lengthy reviews of Lucas's edition of *The Complete Works of John Webster* (1927), TSE was to reveal the core of conflict: Lucas's 'fanciful' attitude towards the Renaissance, which leads him to generalities and judgments in which 'he seems to lose his head entirely', and his confusion of literary and moral values, which leads to his 'tendency to assume moral weakness as artistic strength' (*TLS*, 26 January 1928, p. 59). 'If I have insisted upon one or two principles of Elizabethan criticism where it seems to me that Mr. Lucas has gone astray', wrote TSE of their larger-than-personal disagreements, 'it is because they are divagations which he shares with other critics, and which are of some importance' (*Criterion*, June 1928, p. 446).

17 – *The Diary of Virginia Woolf*, vol. III, ed. Anne Olivier Bell (London: Hogarth Press, 1980), p. 65.

the discerning recorder of intellectual events at Cambridge – failed to mention them. After the first lecture, however, the student editor of *Granta* noted with satiric glee that the women's colleges were out early and in overwhelming force, leaving precious little room at the back for male undergraduates:

> The whole of both Newnham and Girton Colleges, with a fair sprink-ling of dons, undergraduates and Bachelors of Arts, assembled in the Hall of Trinity College to hear Mr. T. S. Eliot deliver the first of his Clark Lectures . . . The hall was full, so that undergraduates were sitting about on the tables at the back, diligently taking notes of the distant sounds that reached their ears. Next week we shall have to arrive at least a quarter of an hour early.[18]

The Wednesday morning coffee-circles were arranged by the College specifically for undergraduates, who were invited to meet Eliot after breakfast. On one particular morning, however, six promising students were chosen to have breakfast with him, including John Davy Hayward, an Exhibitioner at King's College and a precocious editor whose edition of the *Collected Works of John Wilmot, Earl of Rochester* was to appear from the Nonesuch Press later in the year. Hayward had actually written to Eliot the previous autumn, unsuccessfully inviting him to lecture to the Heretics. Though he suffered from muscular dystrophy, at this time he got about with a rubber-tipped cane. Known for his mixture of learning, banter and parody, he was a vocal participant in numerous undergraduate activities. 'He sang with musical societies', wrote his college biographer, 'in a fine bass voice. In the theatre, behind the scenes, he enacted the part of a bevy of prisoners under torture, producing some of the most blood-curdling Grand

---

18–'Metaphysicians', *Granta* (29 January 1926), p. 203. The Cambridge tradition of mocking women students who eagerly attended lectures had been intact since Leslie Stephen reported impatiently that the audience for his Clark Lectures consisted 'chiefly of young women from the ladies' colleges', chiding them for taking 'ornamental lectures seriously, not understanding with her brother students that the object of study is to get a good place in an examination, and that lectures are a vanity and a distraction' (*The Life and Letters of Leslie Stephen*, p. 382). The *Cambridge Review* observed from time to time that 'the Clark Lectures attracted a large number of ladies with note-books, and a fair number of members of the University, without' (30 November 1899, p. 116). Only when the popular lecturer and classicist Arthur Woollgar Verrall gave the Clark Lectures in 1909 did male undergraduates outnumber the women, 'a fact', observed the *Cambridge Review*, 'most rare in the history of Cambridge lectures on English Literature or on Art' (quoted in Verrall's *Collected Literary Essays: Classical and Modern* [Cambridge: Cambridge Univ. Press, 1913], p. lxxxv).

Guignol noises ever heard in Cambridge; and many still remember the brilliant brochure which he delivered in the Reading Room after Founder's Feast in 1926, enlivened by his Rabelaisian wit.'[19] In the following decades he was to become one of Eliot's closest friends, to share a flat with him in London after the war, and, ironically, to become the eventual recipient of the typescript of the Clark Lectures. 'At this early morning meeting,' as T. S. Matthews recounts, 'everyone was so gripped by shyness that no one spoke for a full minute. Finally Hayward said, "Mr. Eliot, have you read the last volume of Proust?" Eliot replied, "No, I'm afraid I have not." Again, silence. This was the beginning of a notable friendship.'[20]

Another undergraduate present at the breakfast, William Empson, a first-year student at Magdalene under the tutelage of I. A. Richards, had his own recollection of the exchange: 'At the first of these very awed gatherings someone asked him what he thought of Proust. "I have not read Proust" was the deliberate reply. How the conversation was picked up again is beyond conjecture, but no one cared to plumb into the motives of his abstinence. It was felt to be a rather impressive trait in this powerful character.' Empson evidently misheard or misremembered the dialogue: Eliot may not have read 'the last volume' of Proust, but he had certainly read and formed an impression of earlier work before the Cambridge visit. When Empson returned to the circle the following week, a new member unawares asked Eliot 'what he thought of the translation of Proust by Scott Moncrieff, and Eliot delivered a very weighty, and rather long, tribute to that work . . . We were startled by so much loquacity from the silent master rather than by any disagreement with what he had said before'.[21] Forty years later, Empson revealed to George Watson, a Fellow of St John's who canvassed his colleagues for their memories of Eliot's Clark Lectures, that he never actually attended any of the lectures, 'on the single and sufficient ground, as he thought, that in his undergraduate days he attended no lectures. But he went to the coffee-circle and met Eliot there for the first time, remaining

---

19—*King's College Annual Report* (November 1965), p. 31.

20—*Great Tom: Notes Towards the Definition of T. S. Eliot* (London: Weidenfeld and Nicolson, 1974; New York: Harper & Row, 1974), p. 124.

21—'The Style of the Master', in *T. S. Eliot*, pp. 36–7. Charles Kenneth Scott-Moncrieff (1889–1930), translater of the first seven volumes of Proust's eight-volume *A la recherche du temps perdu*, had published three translations: *Swann's Way* (1922), *Within a Budding Grove* (1924) and *The Guermantes Way* (1925). TSE had published Scott-Moncrieff's translation of Proust's 'The Death of Albertine' in the July 1924 issue of the *Criterion*, and he was to write in 'A Note on the Criterion' (1966): 'I am proud to have introduced to English readers the work of Marcel Proust'.

impressed to the end of his life by the seriousness with which he listened to questions and arguments, and the earnestness of his answers'.[22]

At the coffee-circle following Lecture VI, Empson also listened well to Eliot's discussion of Shelley's careless use of imagery in 'To a Skylark' and in a chorus of *Hellas*. Four years later, the attentive Empson reconstructed the discussion in his *Seven Types of Ambiguity* (1930). To illustrate the fifth type of ambiguity, in which, 'for instance, there is a simile which applies to nothing exactly, but lies half-way between two things when the author is moving from one to the other', he returned to the fifth stanza of 'To a Skylark', 'about which Mr. Eliot started a discussion. I am afraid more points were brought out than I remembered'.[23]

> Keen as are the arrows
> Of that silver sphere
> Whose intense lamp narrows
> In the white dawn clear,
> Until we hardly see, we feel that it is there.

'Mr. Eliot claimed not to know what the *sphere* was', Empson recalled as he began his own analysis of the ambiguities, and Eliot 'complained that Shelley had mixed up' night and day in the poem (p. 157). Further, pointing to lines from the chorus of *Hellas* ('The earth doth like a snake renew / Her winter weeds outworn'), 'Mr. Eliot said that *snakes* do not *renew* their cast skins, and do not cast them at the end of *winter*; and that a seventeenth-century poet would have known his own mind on such points' (p. 159). Empson, in his attempt to justify Shelley's 'bad natural history', was moved to 'agree very heartily with what Mr. Eliot was saying at the time . . . this muddle of ideas clogging an apparently simple lyrical flow may be explained, but is not therefore justified; and it is evident that a hearty appetite for this and the following type of ambiguity would apologise for, would be able to extract pleasure from, very bad poetry indeed' (p. 160). Thus did Eliot unwittingly impress his critical imagination on Richards' dauntless student during the coffee meetings.

T. R. Henn wrote to George Watson, however, that 'Eliot was not a lecturer of any technique', recalling that 'the discourses were (a) difficult to

---

22 – See George Watson, 'The Cambridge Lectures of T. S. Eliot', *Sewanee Review* (Fall 1991), p. 579.

23 – Second edition (London: Chatto & Windus, 1947), pp. 155–6. Empson did not attribute the discussion to Eliot so directly in the first edition (London: Chatto & Windus, 1930), writing more obliquely that Shelley's poem 'has received much discussion recently. I am afraid more points will have been brought out than I have noticed' (p. 197).

hear because of a very low voice; (b) extremely dull to listen to; (c) too *nachgesucht* [recondite] for the temper of the young men.' Joan Bennett remembered that the lectures 'began with a very large audience, dwindling by about the third lecture. They were difficult to hear and rather difficult to follow. Stanley thinks he remembers a good deal of quotation from medieval Latin.' Henn, too, seemed to remember 'that he read or chanted long passages of medieval Latin poetry?'.[24] Their memories served them well after four decades, for in his third lecture Eliot did indeed read – apologizing for his 'somewhat Italianated pronunciation of Latin' – a substantial passage from Richard of St Victor in Migne's *Patrologia Latina* and from the *Summa Theologica* of Aquinas. Eliot may have been difficult to hear in the large, cold, non-acoustical hall in January, but his recondite allusions and Latin quotations were balanced by playful remarks and personal jabs at D. H. Lawrence, H. G. Wells, John Middleton Murry, I. A. Richards, Lytton Strachey, Bertrand Russell, Frank Harris, and others who served as contemporary targets for historical contrasts.

Among Eliot's supporters in the audience were his brother, Henry Ware Eliot, and his sister-in-law, the artist Theresa Garrett Eliot, who came over in late February at the beginning of a five-month honeymoon in England, France and Italy. At Eliot's final lecture on 9 March, Theresa made from her seat a sketch of Eliot reading before the portraits and panelling at the rear of the hall (frontispiece). Henry noted on the back of the drawing that Eliot was introduced by A. E. Housman, and that the smaller picture overlooking Eliot's right shoulder was Watts's portrait of Tennyson. As David Mc-Kitterick, the Trinity librarian, describes the drawing:

> It shows Eliot standing in the hall, on the east side of the dais, with the oriel window to his left, facing down the hall. One of the gowned figures in the foreground has his elbow on one of the ordinary dining tables, left in place with the benches beside them for people to make themselves comfortable as best they could. Theresa Eliot was, presumably, sitting on a bench on the other side. The chairs towards the front were rather few in number. Such an arrangement was of course quite normal for most lectures in the humanities before the construction of specialist lecture rooms.

Theresa later noted on a negative copy of the drawing (Houghton) that at dinner that evening 'Housman sat at high table, an honor to T.S.E.' Several weeks after the lectures, Eliot joined the honeymooning couple in Rome, where, Theresa later revealed, he fell to his knees in front of the Pietà in St Peter's Cathedral, the first sign of his imminent conversion.[25]

While the lectures were in progress at Cambridge, Eliot's new friend and employer, Geoffrey Faber, nominated him for a Research Fellowship at All Souls College in Oxford, hoping thereby to provide Eliot with the means of transforming his lectures into a book. Eliot submitted his essays on Elizabethan literature to All Souls for consideration, but it was a copy of *Poems 1909–1925* that doomed his election. 'I was the only person in college to possess a volume of his poems', wrote A. L. Rowse, the Shakespearean scholar who was then a Junior Fellow. 'I had no sense at all, or I would have hidden it or burned it. For someone asked to borrow it, and when the Scotch professors read some of the episodes of *The Waste Land* (the typist's tea-time hour, in Part III, for example), or "Lune de Miel" . . . they were horrified.'[26] Though Rowse could not divulge the proceedings of the meeting, he always felt that his 'fatal' possession of the poems was responsible for Eliot's non-election. The episode was so indelibly imprinted in Eliot's memory that it became the primary anecdote in his eulogy for Faber in 1961:

> Only those who are aware of Faber's intense devotion to the College will realise what a great honour he wished to do me, and what generous feeling inspired him. It was a distinction for which my qualifications were not obvious either to myself or to the College. I am happy to say that the College was spared the ignominy of electing an unscholarly member and I was spared the waste of energy involved in pretending to a scholarship which I did not possess.[27]

The loss of the Fellowship obviously affected Eliot's planned revisions – few, if any, were actually made after the lectures were delivered. By June 1926 a fair copy, with a carbon, had been typed from Eliot's original script – possibly by his secretary at Faber & Gwyer, Miss Irene P. Fassett, though he more likely hired a professional typist, as he had done on previous occasions. The original script, which served as his reading copy for the lectures, was apparently discarded at that time. Eliot then added an

25–Theresa Garrett Eliot, interview in BBC production, 'The Mysterious Mr Eliot', televised 3 January 1971.
26–*A Cornishman at Oxford* (London: Jonathan Cape, 1965), p. 314.
27–*Geoffrey Faber 1889–1961* (London: Faber & Faber, 1961), p. 15.

epigraph page and a preface, typed on Miss Fassett's office typewriter on different paper, to both the top and carbon copies before they were punched and placed in folders with long metal clamps, the outlines of which would eventually be imprinted by rust marks on the title pages. As had become his custom, he sent the carbon to his mother for safe-keeping. The epigraph page was lost from the top copy when it circulated among selected friends and scholars for review.

IV

It was only logical that Eliot should ask Herbert Read to be one of his first readers. Read, then Assistant Keeper of the Victoria and Albert Museum, had become one of Eliot's closest advisors and confidants in a group of *Criterion* 'regulars' that included F. S. Flint, Frank Morley and Bonamy Dobrée. He was himself intensely interested in metaphysical poetry, and after the appearance of Eliot's 'The Metaphysical Poets' he proposed to write his own essay for the *Criterion*. Eliot made numerous queries and suggestions on Read's two-page outline (Victoria) and published the completed essay, 'The Nature of Metaphysical Poetry', in the issue for April 1923. As an intellectual ally and supporter, Read went up to Cambridge for Eliot's second Clark Lecture on 2 February 1926, and when he later received the full fair copy for commentary he felt free to make pencilled comments and corrections in the margins. Read did not write to Eliot about the lectures because, as he later pointed out, from 1926 'we were seeing each other so frequently that the correspondence is sparse'.[28] What their existing letters do reveal, however, is that Eliot was in continuous dialogue with Read as he worried over revisions. On 18 January 1927, after Read's essay was reprinted in his *Reason and Romanticism* (Faber & Gwyer, 1926), Eliot wrote to say that he was re-reading 'The Nature of Metaphysical Poetry' – 'carefully (for my own vile purposes)' (*L*2) – and that he wanted to discuss several points with him when they next met, especially the evidence for his assertion that 'The philosophical spirit in both Donne and Chapman was . . . derived directly from Dante and the early Italian poets, rather than from more immediate forerunners in Spain and France' (p. 44). When Read stood his ground, Eliot wrote on 28 January to reaffirm his conviction that 'Donne and Chapman have certainly more relation to Spain, (in contrast to Crashaw) but I should question both their knowledge and their sympathy

28–'T.S.E. – A Memoir', in *T. S. Eliot: The Man and his Work*, p. 22.

with the Guidos and Cino etc. and with Dante himself. And it is just this "philosophical spirit" in Donne and Chapman and Shakespeare that I am at present bothered about!' (*L2*).

As the typescript circulated among friends, Eliot determined that it should also be read by the scholars he most admired. On 21 June he wrote apprehensively to Professor Grierson, who had agreed to give him a reading, that he would send it along as soon as the present reader returned it: 'At the same time, I must say emphatically that I *dread* your inspection of my manuscript in its present form. It represents lectures as they were delivered and most of it was written in circumstances of great difficulty; it is full of hasty generalisations unsubstantiated statements and unverified references: there are great gaps in my knowledge which ought to be filled; and the style is abominable' (*L2*). Grierson's comments do not survive, nor do those of the probable readers in Eliot's circle who would have replied orally at their frequent meetings – Aldington, Faber, Morley, Flint and Dobrée.[29] Eliot's most attentive reader, however, was to be Mario Praz.

Eliot did not send the typescript to Praz at the University of Liverpool until mid-January 1927. Praz spent several nights reading and taking notes on the lectures before writing to Eliot about them on 31 January. His main concern was whether Eliot would be able to illustrate his theory about the disintegration of the intellect with sufficient detail and forcefulness. Stating that he knew from the preface that Eliot was himself fully aware of the problems, Praz suggested that Eliot reconsider some of his interpretations, historical assertions and 'second-hand authorities', particularly his use of Remy de Gourmont as an authority on Dante and Provençal literature. An avid admirer of Eliot's poetry, Praz had the most praise for lectures v, vii and viii, primarily because 'they throw light on your own verse, apart from the interest of the theories as such'. He concluded his remarks by saying that he looked forward to reading the completed work, generally entitled 'The Disintegration of the Intellect' and described in the preface as a trilogy to be comprised of '*The School of Donne*', '*Elizabethan Drama*', and '*The Sons of Ben*':

> it will be a book of criticism which will read like fiction, perhaps, and so much better for it, if it does: history is, after all, as somebody said, always contemporary history, and in writing your book, you will be

29 – TSE nominated Dobrée to succeed him as Clark Lecturer for 1927, but the Council appointed E. M. Forster after their first choice, Percy Lubbock, declined.

writing the history of your own mind. And your mind, I am afraid, interests me even more than Donne, Crashaw and all the dead worthies. (MS VE)[30]

Praz returned the lectures by hand to Eliot's secretary when he came down to London on 9 February to give a lecture. Eliot had hoped to discuss them with Praz over lunch, but Praz dashed out of Eliot's office for another engagement under the mistaken belief that he was out of town. Eliot wrote to express his regret at having missed him and to thank him for his comments. But Eliot was evidently somewhat discouraged by Praz's criticism, and he replied in a lost letter that the whole of his trilogy would probably take years to research and write properly. Praz, apologetic for a hasty letter that had led to 'exaggeration, as usual', wrote back to alter his pedantic tone and to encourage Eliot to publish the lectures straight away with only minor modifications:

> If I were you I would publish as soon as possible the lectures: it would help very much the development of your thoughts on the subject, through the discussions that might ensue. But of course, if you brood over them a long time, you will get sick of them. Besides, you have more important things to do than to work in the British Museum! (MS VE)

Praz had in fact taken more interest in Eliot's theories than he let on, and he began to search for materials that would be of use to Eliot in revising the manuscript, unaware that Eliot was privately preparing for his baptism and confirmation in the Church of England.[31] On 8 March he wrote to inform Eliot that he would find 'considerable support' for his views in the *Saggio Critico sul Petrarca* (new edition, 1921), of the famous Italian critic Francesco de Sanctis (1817–83), and he appended a list of recommended books and articles on Donne and other metaphysical poets (King's). Though they had no further correspondence on the matter, Praz continued to anticipate the work and to refer to it in his essays. In 'Donne and the Poetry of his Time' (1931), Praz not only quoted and discussed Eliot's definition of metaphysical poetry in Lecture VIII but pointed to the overall importance of the lectures. Eliot, wrote Praz, 'spoke of three metaphysical periods in European poetry: a medieval period, a baroque period, and a modern one

---

30—Praz accidentally transposed the numbers in mistyping the date of the letter, 13 January for 31 January 1927.
31—Eliot was baptized into the Church on 29 June 1927 in Finstock Church, Oxfordshire, and confirmed the following day at Cuddesdon, the theological college near Oxford.

with Jules Laforgue as its chief representative.'[32] Praz had taken careful notes on the lectures, and when his increasing interest in Eliot's criticism led him to write 'T. S. Eliot and Dante' (1937), he returned to those notes once again to illustrate his discussion of Eliot's views:

✗ In the VIIIth of his Clark Lectures (not published) Eliot defined metaphysical poetry as 'that in which what is ordinarily apprehensible only by thought is brought within the grasp of feeling, or that in which what is ordinarily only felt is transformed into thought without ceasing to be feeling'. In the VIIth Lecture Eliot stressed the difference between Dante and Donne, which I had tried to define myself in *Secentismo e marinismo in Inghilterra.*[33]

Years after his initial criticism of the Clark Lectures, Praz frequently recognized Eliot as an important, first-hand authority on Dante and Donne.

Though Herbert Read pencilled a few comments in the margins, Eliot did not himself take note of his readers' suggestions in the typescript. On one occasion, however, he pencilled an outline of his projected enlargement of the book (see p. 303). This included conflating lectures II and III into one chapter; the possible expansion of Chapter V: '(D[onne]'s relation to Elizabethan Drama? / Chapman)'; the addition of a new chapter to be inserted between the chapters on Crashaw and Cowley: 'A note on Geo. Herbert / Vaughan and Traherne'; and an Appendix: 'The ultra-conceited: Cleveland and Benlowes'. None of these additions was actually undertaken, but Eliot continuously seized opportunities to express his thoughts on these subjects in reviews, essays and broadcasts, as when he described Vaughan as 'in some ways the most original and difficult of all the followers of Donne' and as 'really the most various of all our metaphysical poets'.[34]

V

Eliot formally announced his preparation of *The School of Donne* in the preface to *For Lancelot Andrewes*, published on 20 November 1928, but by then the other titles of the ambitious trilogy had been replaced by *The*

---

32 – In *A Garland for John Donne*, ed. Theodore Spencer (Cambridge, MA: Harvard Univ. Press, 1931; Oxford: Oxford Univ. Press, 1932), pp. 58–9.
33 – *Southern Review* (September 1937), p. 547.
34 – 'Mystic and Politician as Poet: Vaughan, Traherne, Marvell, Milton', *Listener* (2 April 1930), p. 590.

Outline of Royalism and *The Principles of Modern Heresy*. The new titles, never published, reflected a shift of interest and ambition after his conversion and were closely tied to his declaration that the point of view behind his new essays was 'classicist in literature, royalist in politics, and anglo-catholic in religion' (*FLA* ix/vii). The first book to go was the last conceived, *The Sons of Ben*, mentioned for the first time in the preface of the Clark Lectures and meant to cover 'the development of humanism, its relation to Anglican thought, and the emergence of Hobbes and Hyde'. His abiding interest in the subject surfaced again in 'Hooker, Hobbes and Others' (*TLS*, 11 November 1926), and in 'Archbishop Bramhall' (*Theology*, July 1927), but the proposed title was never mentioned again.

The book on Elizabethan drama must have been the most difficult to let go, for it had been linked in his mind with *The School of Donne* since 1922, when he described to John Middleton Murry that his plans also included 'An Elizabethan volume' (*L1* 447). When his 'Four Elizabethan Dramatists' appeared in the *Criterion* in 1924, it was strategically subtitled 'A Preface' in anticipation of the larger work to come. But when, two years after the Clark Lectures, Tillyard inquired about such a book, Eliot's motivation had escaped him. He wrote to Tillyard on 22 March 1928: 'It is true that I had often thought of writing a critical book on Elizabethan drama, although the older I get the more ignorant I feel myself to be. If you ever have any suggestions as to what form you would like such a book to take to fill in the gap which you find, your suggestions might be very helpful' (*L2*). When Eliot included 'Four Elizabethan Dramatists' in *Selected Essays* (1932), the subtitle was permanently expanded: 'A Preface to an Unwritten Book'. After Praz's somewhat deflating criticism of the Clark Lectures, Eliot seems gradually to have realized that his mode of living and writing could sustain neither the luxury nor the burden of the exhaustive scholarship that such books demanded. The exploratory essay was to remain his critical forte.

Eliot's abandonment of *The School of Donne* was slower to come. That it was still on his agenda in 1929 is clear in his letter of 21 May to I. A. Richards regarding the effect of certain remarks on poetry and belief in the draft of his essay on Dante: 'The only other effect is that having put these remarks in connection with Dante will alter the form of my Donne, and I think improve it'.[35] He was, however, sharply aware that the momentum of the book had begun to dissipate. On 12 August, after having successfully

---

35—See John Constable, 'I. A. Richards, T. S. Eliot, and the Poetry of Belief', *Essays in Criticism* (July 1990), p. 233.

nominated Herbert Read as Clark Lecturer for 1929, he sent Read a parenthetical admonition: '(And don't follow my cunctative example; get your lectures ready for the book immediately after you deliver them, or delay will undermine conviction)' (L2). By the spring of 1930 Eliot's conviction was fading rapidly, evidenced by his raids on the Clark Lectures to extract material for a series of six broadcasts on seventeenth-century poetry for the BBC.[36] His energy for the book was also siphoned away by his detailed attention to the work of others. John Hayward, in completing his edition of Donne's *Complete Poetry and Selected Prose* for the Nonesuch Press (1929), wrote a 'brief tribute of thanks' to Eliot for his assistance in preparing the edition. In the following year, George Williamson, a young American scholar inspired by Eliot's poetry and criticism, stole some of his thunder in *The Donne Tradition: A Study in English Poetry from Donne to the Death of Cowley*. Williamson, too, was quick to honour his debt to Eliot: 'His critical thinking on the "metaphysical poets" has so influenced my own that I can only express my deep obligation to him, without trying to define its limits. To him also I owe the courtesy of reading part of my book in manuscript.'[37] Thus, when Eliot came to write 'Donne in our Time' (1931), he felt that the metaphysical surge had passed him by: 'I know that by 1926, when I gave some lectures on Donne, the subject was already popular, almost topical; and I know that by 1931 the subject has been so fully treated that there appears to me no possible justification of turning my lectures into a book.'[38] He took the lectures with him, possibly with a renewed intention to revise them, when he sailed to America in September 1932 as Charles Eliot Norton Professor of Poetry at Harvard for the academic year. Under pressure to present a number of lectures at American universities, he there abbreviated and partially revised the eight lectures into three lectures entitled 'The Varieties of Metaphysical Poetry' for the Turnbull Lectures at Johns Hopkins University in January 1933. Upon his return to London, the Clark Lectures were shelved once again. The carbon copy, meanwhile, was changing hands.

36 – The uncollected essays appeared in successive issues of the *Listener*, III (1930): 'Thinking in Verse: A Survey of Early Seventeenth-century Poetry' (12 March, pp. 441–3); 'Rhyme and Reason: The Poetry of John Donne' (19 March, pp. 502–3); 'The Devotional Poets of the Seventeenth Century: Donne, Herbert, Crashaw' (26 March, pp. 552–3); 'Mystic and Politician as Poet: Vaughan, Traherne, Marvell, Milton' (2 April, pp. 590–1); 'The Minor Metaphysicals: From Cowley to Dryden' (9 April, pp. 641–2); 'John Dryden' (16 April, pp. 688–9).
37 – (Cambridge, MA: Harvard Univ. Press, 1930), p. ix.
38 – *A Garland for John Donne*, p. 4.

VI

✦ Eliot's appointment as Norton Professor had been announced on 15 December 1931. Anticipating his brother's arrival, Henry Ware Eliot, who lived in New York, wrote on 17 April 1932 to his cousin Henry (Harry) Eliot Scott, proposing to donate to Eliot House at Harvard his complete set to date of the *Criterion*: 'I should also like to give them in memory of my mother, Charlotte C. Eliot, who would have been so happy could she have lived to enjoy his stay in Cambridge and the honor conferred by his appointment' (Houghton).[39] Upon her death in September 1929, her collection of Eliot's writings – including the carbon copy of the Clark Lectures – went to Henry, who placed them in his own collection and kept a detailed catalogue of all additions.[40] On 22 April 1932, the Master of Eliot House, Roger B. Merriman, wrote to Henry to say that the library 'would be proud to possess all of your brother's work which you feel inclined to give it' (Houghton). On 27 April Henry shipped to Eliot House his initial contribution: forty-four issues of the *Criterion*, the second edition of *The Sacred Wood*, a copy of his mother's book, *Savonarola*, which Eliot had introduced, Eliot's college copy of Chaucer's poems, the June 1915 issue of *Poetry*, which contained the first appearance of 'Prufrock', and copies of *Homage to John Dryden* and *For Lancelot Andrewes*. Eliot himself began to donate inscribed copies of his works to the library during and after his residence at Eliot House in 1932–3, but Henry made no further donations from his collection until he moved from New York to Cambridge in 1936 to become a research fellow in anthropology at the Peabody Museum.

In late November 1936, after settling into his new position, Henry transported the carbon copy of the Clark Lectures and other items to the Eliot House librarian, J. McG. Bottkol, but within days he became uneasy about unauthorized use of the material. On 5 December he wrote to his brother about the new location of the copy and urged him to write to Bottkol about any restrictions.[41] On 15 December, before Eliot had a

---

39 – Eliot House, opened in the autumn of 1931 under the mastership of Roger B. Merriman, was named after Charles W. Eliot (1834–1926), President of Harvard from 1869 to 1909. Though they were distantly related (he was a third cousin once removed of TSE's grandfather), TSE was not sympathetic to the left-wing Unitarianism that guided his presidency.

40 – 'It was T.S.E.'s custom', Henry wrote parenthetically in his catalogue (Houghton), beneath a list of manuscripts which included the carbon copy of the Clark Lectures, 'to send carbons or proofs of forthcoming works to his mother. Such are the above'.

41 – This letter, and the following letter of 4 February 1937 to Bottkol, the carbon of which is in the possession of Mrs Valerie Eliot, have been mislaid in the Houghton Library.

chance to reply, Henry wrote to Bottkol himself: 'It occurs to me that I had better caution you against allowing anyone who may have occasion to read any unpublished manuscripts that there may be in the T. S. Eliot collection, to make any excerpts for publication without first getting permission from T. S. Eliot himself. This applies particularly to his series of Cambridge (England) lectures of 1926, entitled *The Metaphysical Poetry of the Seventeenth Century*' (Houghton). Henry's anxiety over the lectures was borne out in Eliot's reply to him on 30 December. After ten years of brooding on them, Eliot, as Praz had prophesied, no longer had a stomach for his lectures:

> I have one copy of my Trinity Lectures. I will write to Bottkol as you suggest about permission to quote from them. I used some of the material when I lectured in Baltimore (but that hasnt been published either). I dont want these lectures ever to be published. They are pretentious and immature. One of them, on Cowley, I am supposed to be revising to publish in a presentation volume of essays to Grierson. (Houghton)

Eliot eventually wrote to Bottkol on 4 February 1937 to 'make it clear that I do not want anyone to quote in print from my unpublished Clarke [sic] Lectures at Trinity College without obtaining my written consent for the specific passage to be quoted. I have no intention of publishing these lectures in their present form, and the time has long since passed when it was possible to think of revising them for publication; so I hope that you will take note of my request for the benefit of yourself and your eventual successors.'

Thus, scholars who became aware of the Clark Lectures in the 1930s could but report the fact of their existence. F. O. Matthiessen, who had conversations with Eliot at Harvard in 1932–3 while preparing *The Achievement of T. S. Eliot* (1935), reported with a modicum of hope that the lectures 'on the metaphysical poetry of the seventeenth century in comparison and contrast with that of the Italian thirteenth century have not yet been published'.[42] When Henry deposited the carbon typescript at Eliot House in 1936, it immediately caught the eye of Harvard Professor Theodore Spencer, who had recently presented Eliot's manuscript lecture notes for his course in modern literature, English 26, notes given to Spencer by Eliot before his departure in June 1933. Spencer and Mark Van Doren of

42–Third edition (Oxford: Oxford Univ. Press, 1958), p. 26, n. 9.

Columbia University were compiling a bibliography of research on meta-physical poetry, and they listed Eliot's Clark Lectures among important 'General Studies' in their *Studies in Metaphysical Poetry* (1939).[43] The listing went unnoticed, however, and the lectures languished undisturbed until the autumn of 1944, when the US Navy took over Eliot House and transferred the Eliot Collection to the Houghton. Henry died in 1947 before his prized collection could be returned to Eliot House on 22 January 1948. It was a short-lived homecoming: in the summer of 1951 the Eliot Collection was permanently transferred to the Houghton, where the carbon copy of the Clark Lectures, removed from its original folder, remained boxed and unbound among restricted materials.

Meanwhile, Eliot's revision of the penultimate lecture on Cowley appeared as 'A Note on Two Odes of Cowley' in *Seventeenth Century Studies Presented to Sir Herbert Grierson*, published at the Clarendon Press in January 1938. Soon after sending in his contribution to the volume, Eliot, in what must have seemed an act of closure, turned his top copy of the Clark Lectures over to John Hayward's 'Archives'.

During the 1930s Eliot and Hayward had become close friends, and in 1935, three years after Eliot had separated from Vivien, Hayward had even suggested that they share lodgings. By the end of the decade Hayward was living alone at 22 Bina Gardens, a regular gathering place for Eliot, Morley, Faber and other friends. Now confined to a wheelchair, his removal from London became imperative as the war approached. At the end of August 1939 he was evacuated by Victor Rothschild and taken to Merton Hall, on the Backs in Cambridge, where he remained for the duration of the war. It was here that Hayward began to collect and preserve Eliot's manuscripts in earnest. On 27 June 1940 he confirmed in a letter to Eliot that the drafts of *East Coker* 'have been carefully placed with the Archives (the most important of which I've got here) for safe keeping. Or rather, they will be as soon as Mr. Gray has bound them together to match "Burnt Norton" ' (*CFQ* 8). The Clark Lectures, removed from the metal-clamp binder, were among the manuscripts bound in light green boards for Hayward by John P. Gray & Sons of Cambridge. On one of his several war-time trips to Cambridge, or possibly after the war, Eliot inscribed the front flyleaf in blue ink 'to | John Hayward | privately, confidentially | and in humility' and relinquished them permanently to his keeping.

In February 1946 Eliot and Hayward took a flat in Chelsea and lived there

43–(New York: Columbia Univ. Press, 1939), p. 36.

together until Eliot's marriage to Valerie Fletcher in January 1957. During this eleven-year period it is difficult to say that Eliot did not harbour a future for his Clark Lectures in the back of his mind. Indeed, in the preface to the 1950/51 editions of *Selected Essays*, in which he announced the addition of new essays, he disclosed that 'There remain several uncollected papers which I am disposed to preserve, as well as a number of unpublished lectures, on matters connected with the art of poetry, which await their final form' (*SE* 7–8/[ix]). Not until 1961, in correspondence with the critic Alfred Alvarez, did Eliot finally release his hold on the lectures. As Alvarez explained in his book, *The School of Donne* (1961), 'Mr. Eliot has now kindly given me his permission to use this title . . . I would not have used the title had there been any hope of Mr. Eliot's own work appearing in the near future.'[44] The following year, in his last major essay, a pamphlet on *George Herbert* (1962), Eliot distantly declared that 'we must exercise caution in our interpretation of the phrase "the school of Donne". The present writer once contemplated writing a book under that title . . . The phrase is legitimate and useful to designate that generation of men younger than Donne whose work is obviously influenced by him, but we must not take it as implying that those poets who experienced his influence were for that reason lesser poets.'[45] That said, the lectures were put to rest in Eliot's mind.

Hayward retained the Eliot Archives at 19 Carlyle Mansions after Eliot's precipitous departure in 1957. Upon Hayward's death on 17 September 1965, nine months after Eliot's death on 5 January, the Clark Lectures became part of the Hayward Bequest to King's College, Cambridge, where they remain in the Modern Archives today.

VII

The odysseys of the two copies of Clark Lectures, their departures and returns, are fittingly symbolic of Eliot's long relationship with the two Cambridges. But it was in England rather than in America that his theory of metaphysical poetry was to have its immediate impact, and his Clark Lectures were to seal his identification with Cambridge in the 1930s rather than with Oxford, where the English Literature curriculum stopped in 1832. Muriel Bradbrook, who went up to Girton in the autumn of 1927, testifies that Eliot's critical essays 'were canonized in the Cambridge of the

44–(London: Chatto & Windus, 1961), pp. 9–10.
45–(London: for the British Council, Longmans, Green & Co., 1962), p. 16.

time' and 'quite dazzlingly set the fashion'.[46] In 1927, at Tillyard's behest, Eliot served as outside examiner for a doctoral dissertation on Emerson by an American Jesuit, Father Francis Joseph Yealey of Christ's College, who had himself attended the Clark Lectures. Eliot's periodic presence in Cambridge for such academic matters would lead to important opportunities: on the afternoon of 25 May 1936, after participating in a *viva voce* that morning at the request of John Maynard Keynes, Eliot was taken to Little Gidding for the first time by the Revd Hugh Fraser Stewart and his wife Jessie.

Thus, Eliot rapidly became both a participant in and an object of discussion in the academic and intellectual life of the University, especially among the students and younger faculty, who had much to do with the rapid spread of his reputation in the 1930s. Richards, who had already attached his review of *Poems 1909–1925* as an appendix to the second edition of *Principles of Literary Criticism* (1926), continued his lectures on Eliot's criticism and poetry, and the two kept up their dialogue on the problem of poetry and belief well into the 1930s. Leavis, at this time one of Eliot's strongest supporters and defenders, declared unabashedly in his review of *Cambridge Poetry, 1929* that Eliot's influence 'of course, predominates'.[47]

If by the end of the 1920s Eliot had taken a commanding place in Cambridge letters, that place was not without controversy. As James Reeves, who went up to Jesus College as a young poet in 1928, put it, 'Eliot's influence was paramount, though not altogether unchallenged'.[48] When Jacob Bronowski, the undergraduate polymath at Jesus, reviewed Eliot's *For Lancelot Andrewes* in the *Cambridge Review*, his admiration was tempered by his fervent hope that 'by the time Mr Eliot finishes *The School of Donne* he will have become less self-conscious of his faith'.[49] And where Empson included with impunity passages from 'Whispers of Immortality' and *The Waste Land* as additional examples in *Seven Types of Ambiguity*, Leavis was ostracized by an older don for his 'worse than imprudent' praise of Eliot in *New Bearings in English Poetry* (1932). When the book

---

46–See *T. S. Eliot: A Study of his Writings by Several Hands*, ed. Balachandra Rajan (London: Denis Dobson, 1947), pp. 119–20.

47–*Cambridge Review* (1 March 1929), p. 317. Three weeks earlier, in response to snobbish and condescending reviews that regarded Eliot as less than a critic of 'the first trenchancy', Leavis replied: 'There could be no more effective awakener of the intellectual conscience than Mr. Eliot: he has made it less easy to shirk'. *Cambridge Review* (8 February 1929), p. 256.

48–'Cambridge Twenty Years Ago', in *T. S. Eliot*, p. 40.

49–(30 November 1928), p. 176.

appeared, Leavis wrote in retrospect, 'the advanced academic intellectual of the day declined (or so the gloating whisper ran) to have anything to do with it, and *The Cambridge Review* could find no reviewer for it in Cambridge.'[50] Further, Tillyard set out to correct Eliot's alien views of Milton, first in *Milton* (1930): 'Some sort of dissociation of sensibility in Milton . . . has to be admitted; but that he was responsible for any such dissociation in others . . . is untrue';[51] secondly in *The Miltonic Setting* (1938): 'I admire Mr Eliot's best criticism so much that I may the better be excused for attacking what I think his worst, that of Milton.'[52] When Eliot responded to his give-and-take criticism in 'Milton II' (1947), he cordially conceded after twenty-five years that Milton should not be saddled with his infamous charge:

> the general affirmation represented by the phrase 'dissociation of sensibility'. . . retains some validity; but I now incline to agree with Dr. Tillyard that to lay the burden on the shoulders of Milton and Dryden was a mistake. If such a dissociation did take place, I suspect that the causes are too complex and too profound to justify our accounting for the change in terms of literary criticism. (*OPP* 152–3/173)

Eliot did, of course, believe that a dissociation of thought and feeling took place; unfortunately, his extra-literary analyses of the causes lay embedded in his unfinished *The School of Donne*.

After delivering his Clark Lectures, Eliot had kept up an infrequent correspondence with A. E. Housman, to whom he sent an inscribed advance copy of *Journey of the Magi*: 'A. E. Housman respectful homage of T. S. Eliot 17.8.27'. Housman, of course, was one of the dons (if not the older refusing don, above) antagonistic to the 'Practical Criticism' of Richards and Leavis, and he was particularly hostile to the writing in *Scrutiny*, which Leavis founded in 1932. When, in advancing age and declining health, Housman grudgingly agreed to give the Leslie Stephen Lecture in May 1933, his lecture was widely taken to be an oblique attack ('Meaning is of the intellect, poetry is not') on Leavis and his 'doctrinaire teachers of youth', as

---

50–New edition (London: Chatto & Windus, 1950), p. 219. In 'The Triumph of T. S. Eliot' (*Critical Quarterly*, Winter 1965, pp. 328–37), George Watson has argued that Leavis's account of the reception of *New Bearings* at Cambridge is mythical: 'I find it inconceivable that so conservative a work should have been felt to be alarming as late as 1932. It is not now possible to discover why the *Cambridge Review* omitted to review it; but, after all, journals omit to review books all the time, and if for some inconceivable reason it found the book outrageous it only had to say so' (p. 335).
51–(London: Chatto & Windus, 1930; sixth impression, 1956), p. 356.
52–(Cambridge: Cambridge Univ. Press, 1938), p. 90.

he called them.[53] When Eliot favourably reviewed the published lecture, *The Name and Nature of Poetry* (1933), in the *Criterion*, Housman found the review amusing, 'because its author, T. S. Eliot, is worshipped as a god by the writers in the paper [*Scrutiny*] which had the only hostile review' (p. 344). Eliot was not uncritical: he was 'more than doubtful' about Housman's view of the relation of poetry and wit in metaphysical poetry, but he was surprisingly sympathetic to some of Housman's harshest remarks about English poetry from Donne to Dryden: 'I feel a certain sympathy with Mr. Housman's acid comments on the poetry of the seventeenth and eighteenth centuries, because I suspect that both have lately been for some amateurs a fashion rather than a taste'.[54] But a larger sympathy informed Eliot's review: he was painfully aware that Housman's theory of the relation of intellect, emotion and meaning in poetry was too complex for the lecture, that he as reviewer must affirm 'the extraordinary complexity of the problem, and the mazes of intellectual subtlety into which it is bound to lead the conscientious enquirer' (p. 154). The frustrated Clark Lecturer was writing in full sympathy with the Stephen Lecturer who had been so courteous and attentive to him seven years earlier. Eliot's caveat to Housman's readers might stand as a caveat to readers of the Clark Lectures:

> We must keep in mind that this essay is a lecture; and the exigencies of a popular lecture require the author to select his points very carefully, to aim at form and proportion rather than connected profundity, and to avoid going too deeply into anything which is, for the purposes of the moment, another problem. We must not, in short, judge a lecture on Poetry as if it was a book on Aesthetics. The author may himself walk the straight line, but if he is to say anything at all in the time it is difficult for him, if not impossible, not to make assertions which, if pressed firmly and indefatigably by an unfriendly critic, will not yield a concentrated drop of heresy. (p. 152)

The strength of Eliot's reputation and friendships at Cambridge overcame rearguard antagonisms of younger and older dons. As his reputation grew in the 1930s, so did the University's recognition of his achievements. On 9 June 1938 the dubious Clark Lecturer of 1926 was recalled to Cambridge to receive an honorary Doctorate of Letters. As reported in *The Times* the following day, 'Mr. Eliot's distinction as poet and critic was proclaimed by

---

53 – *The Letters of A. E. Housman*, p. 355.
54 – *Criterion* (October 1933), p. 153.

the Orator as symbolic of a new order in which the antagonism between poetry and philosophy has disappeared, and we ask the philosophers to decide what the Muses may do.'[55] Appropriately for Eliot, the recipients were guests for dinner that evening at Trinity College, where the toast was given by his former host, the Master, Sir Joseph Thomson, OM. In twelve short years, few had come so far, or been so taken up, as this occasional visitor to Cambridge.

Shortly after Eliot's death, as the contents of the Hayward Bequest slowly became known, students and scholars from around the world began seeking permission to read his Clark Lectures at King's College, as did this editor in 1974. The sense of scholarly privilege that came with turning the pages in a corner of the Old Library was surpassed only by the delight of learning that it was permissible to take some treasured notes. Generously, Valerie Eliot has determined that an annotated edition of the text should now be made available to a larger reading audience. The sense of historical privilege that came with editing the volume is now surpassed by the pleasure of knowing that the Clark Lectures will be read by many new readers in a new century of Eliot studies.

Emory University,
Atlanta, Georgia

55–(10 June 1938), p. 8.

Note on the text and editorial principles

Eliot's original typescript and reading copy of his Clark Lectures is lost. The copy-text for this edition is the top copy of the fair copy (King's) that was prepared with a single carbon (Houghton) shortly after the lectures were delivered. They were not typed by Eliot on his typewriter; they were evidently typed by a professional speed-typist on two separate, unidentified machines with black ribbons: lectures I, III, V and VII were typed on machine A, lectures II, IV, VI and VIII on machine B. All lectures were typed on 'Plantagenet / British Make' paper, a commercial-grade paper commonly found in typing offices. An inexpensive, unmarked paper was used for the carbon. The preliminary pages for the lectures were subsequently typed on a different paper, 'Colindia Parchment', which was also used for the carbon. These pages were typed on the purple-ribboned office machine of Eliot's secretary, Miss Irene P. Fassett. It is doubtful that she typed the lectures after-hours on other machines at Faber & Gwyer, or at home, for her typing habits were more meticulous and professional than those evidenced in the typescript. Since the epigraph page for the top copy was lost in circulation, the carbon has been used in this single instance.

The typist sacrificed textual accuracy to speed: there was seldom an erasure, and the carbon shows very few single-letter erasures. In the typescript of each lecture many lines were carried to the last space of the extreme right margin. No time was given to proofreading; consequently, a wide spectrum of typographical errors abounds: transposed letters, misspellings, dropped words, misread words and names, garbled words and phrases, accidental capitalization, mispunctuation, unitalicized words and titles, and so forth. No accentual or diacritical marks were provided for foreign quotations. Eliot and his various readers later corrected some of these errors and added some accents, but most were passed over or ignored.

Eliot occasionally placed an insertion mark at the place of an omission, followed by a question mark in the margin, uncertain of the missing word or phrase after the event. In some instances an unidentified reader supplied or suggested the missing word. Thus, the typist's obvious errors, including grammatical oversights (subject–verb agreement), have been silently corrected, though some of possible interest are recorded in the textual notes. The typist's numerous punctuation slips have also been silently corrected: where no punctuation was intended, it has been deleted; where it was clearly intended, or where the omission would interrupt the readability of the text, it has been supplied; where the punctuation is in error, frequently a comma for a semicolon, the correct punctuation has been supplied. Word omissions in the text have been supplied in square brackets; foreign words and phrases have been italicized.

The typist also followed some of the typing habits, short-cuts and abbreviations characteristic of Eliot's letters and first drafts, particularly his use of capital roman numerals for numerical adjectives ('the XVII century'). For readability, all such numerical abbreviations have been written out; except for line, stanza and page numbers, typed numbers under one hundred have been written out; abbreviated names (E. Gosse) and places (Cambridge, Mass.) have been expanded; the abbreviation (p.) for page has been expanded in those instances where it was clearly spoken in the text. Eliot's inconsistent use of titles ('The Extasie', 'The Ecstasy') is made to conform to the text he used for the lectures, Grierson's *Metaphysical Lyrics and Poems of the Seventeenth Century* ('The Extasie'). Vague or confusing references to book titles have been emended ('Walton's life' to 'Walton's *Life*'); variant spellings ('almanacks', 'experimentors') and obsolete usage ('to confer' for 'to compare') are unchanged; inconsistencies of usage and convention have been made to conform to that in Eliot's published writings of the period; singular editorial problems are described in the textual notes.

Eliot made revisions in the text on at least four separate occasions, physically identifiable by the grades of pencils and the colours of ink in his hand. All of his marginal comments related to the text are identified and quoted in the footnotes, as are the written remarks and queries of his readers, except in the Turnbull Lectures, where the singular remarks of Frank Morley are described in the textual notes. One interest of Eliot in each instance of editing was arbitrarily to remove traces of the informal lecturer in preparation for more intensive revisions prior to publication. Since these revisions were never made, the editor's aim has been to preserve the lectures as delivered. Hence, all cancelled phrases, sentences and paragraphs read to his Trinity College audience have been restored to the text and recorded in the textual notes. His later stylistic emendations for clarity and precision (diction, word order, etc.) are similarly recorded.

There are numerous misquotations, mistranscriptions and slips in the typescript. When W. P. Ker died before he could edit his contribution to an early number of the *Criterion*, 'Byron: An Oxford Lecture', Eliot wrote in a rare editorial note that Ker's manuscript 'has been faithfully followed, except that the quotations, obviously made from memory, have been altered to coincide with the standard text of Byron' (October 1923, p. 15). In spite of Eliot's own practice in this instance, the editor has preserved Eliot's misquotations from memory and corrected them in the footnotes. In some instances the misquotations affect the commentary, and in every instance it is of interest to observe how Eliot held certain passages of poetry and criticism in memory and summoned them spontaneously for use in illustration. Frank Kermode, the editor of Eliot's *Selected Prose* (1975), took pains to point out the misquotations in Eliot's collected essays, 'not from pedantry, but from a conviction that in the poet Eliot misquotation is sometimes creative'.[1] Christopher Ricks, in a provocative essay, 'Walter Pater, Matthew Arnold and Misquotation' (1977), went on to place Eliot squarely in the modern 'genre of misquotation' and to discuss 'the way in which this "misquotation as re-creation" is intimate with Eliot's profoundest sense of what creation is: the creation of one's self, and the creation of others' selves, in society and in procreation and through or within art's imaginings'.[2] We now know that the 'genre of misquotation' was endemic in modernist writers. As Richard Aldington ironically observed, 'Unlike most poets, Eliot is not only a competent but a brilliant lecturer. Pound on the other hand, relies chiefly on a faulty memory, an almost non-existent power of improvisation and a cough.'[3]

Ricks also points out the prevalence of 're-creative mistranscriptions' in the genre: 'For the simplest way to become something else than a transcriber is to mistranscribe.'[4] Accordingly, Eliot's slips and his mistranscriptions from the texts at hand are also preserved in the text and corrected in the footnotes. Because it is seldom clear whether a mistranscription is Eliot's or the typist's, all quotations, except for obvious typographical errors, are

---

1—(London: Faber & Faber, 1975), p. 307.
2—In *The Force of Poetry* (Oxford: Clarendon Press, 1984), p. 414.
3—*Ezra Pound & T. S. Eliot* (New York: Oriole Chapbooks, 1954), p. 7.
4—*The Force of Poetry*, p. 405.

printed as typed, unless noted. Dropped words from transcribed lines of poetry are inserted in square brackets; mistranscribed words in prose passages are followed by a bracket correction ('which it deigns [*for* designs] to represent'). Eliot wrote the lectures under weekly pressure for the sole purpose of delivery: he modernized the texts liberally, and he had little concern for the faithful transcription of old spellings, elisions, line indentations, italicized and capitalized words, and end-line punctuation. Thus, his transcriptions are integral to the visual and typographical character of the lectures as he prepared them.

Eliot was reluctant to publish the Clark Lectures in their present form because, as he says in his preface, many of his remarks needed qualification, clarification, and details of fact and authority. The editor has thus attempted to annotate the lectures in the larger intellectual context of Eliot's writings, drawing upon his own earlier and later comments on a subject to help provide the qualification or clarification that he desired. Eliot makes hundreds of oblique allusions and references as his mind moves rapidly over complex literary, historical, philosophical and theological periods. The lectures were originally prepared for and delivered to a general academic audience of Cambridge dons and undergraduates and were perceived to have been in part too 'recondite' for much of that audience. Thus, the annotations aim on the one hand to keep the general reader in the text by providing the identifications, characterizations, relationships, contexts and translations that serve to enhance the clarity and accessibility of Eliot's highly referential discourse: when he refers, for example, to 'Sappho's famous ode', the ode is not only identified but printed in a translation that he may have known; on the other hand, the annotations aim to send the specialist reader beyond the text: the Clark and Turnbull lectures open significant new areas of Eliot studies, and the reader is directed to the vast store of Eliot's uncollected writings, unpublished manuscripts, letters and other documents that further illuminate the sources and extensions of his intellectual interests. When the editions that Eliot used for the lectures have been determined, they are identified and cited in the footnotes, as are editions in his personal library. The larger aim of the annotations, however, is to reveal beneath the difficult surface of the lectures the breadth of Eliot's learning, the richness of his mind at the time of composition, and the unplumbed depths of allusion in this long-unpublished typescript, which became a veritable watershed for the great work to come.

THE CLARK LECTURES

to / John Hayward
privately, confidentially
and in humility

T. S. Eliot

LECTURES ON
THE METAPHYSICAL POETRY
OF THE SEVENTEENTH
CENTURY

with special reference to
Donne, Crashaw and Cowley

delivered at Trinity College
Cambridge 1926

T. S. ELIOT

Madonna, lo fine del mio amore fu già il saluto di questa donna, forse de cui voi intendete; ed in quello dimorava la beatitudine, ch'e il fine di tutti li miei desiri.

La Vita Nuova[1]

I want someone to treat me rough.
Give me a cabman.

Popular song[2]

1 – Misquoted from section XVIII: 'Madonne, lo fine del mio amore fu già il saluto di questa donna, di cui voi forse intendete; ed in quello dimorava la mia beatitudine, chè era fine di tutti i miei desiderii.' ['Ladies, the end and aim of my Love was but the salutation of that lady of whom I conceive that ye are speaking; wherein alone I found that beatitude which is the goal of desire.' Trans. Dante Gabriel Rossetti, *Early Italian Poets* (London: George Newnes, 1904), p. 195.]
2 – Untraced; possibly remembered from a music-hall or ragtime lyric.

[Author's Preface]

It is the intention of the author to rewrite these lectures as a book. Beyond the obvious alterations – the conversational style and the constant repetitions to be removed – the whole argument is to be reformed; assertions must be proved; much detail of fact and authority must be added. The divers parts must be made more coherent; I am aware that in the present form my fundamental ideas remain quite obscure. In particular, the whole of my case turns upon my interpretation of the *Vita Nuova*, which is only hinted at in Lecture III, and my interpretation of the childhood of Dante. This must be developed very fully.

The completed book on *The School of Donne* will be very much longer than these lectures, and will include detailed examination of the work of other poets of the epoch who have here been only casually mentioned. It is intended as one volume of a trilogy under the general title of "The Disintegration of the Intellect": the other two volumes will deal with *Elizabethan Drama*, its technical development, its versification, and its intellectual background of general ideas; and with *The Sons of Ben* – the development of humanism, its relation to Anglican thought, and the emergence of Hobbes and Hyde. The three together will constitute a criticism of the English Renaissance.

LECTURE I

{Introduction: On the Definition
of Metaphysical Poetry}

My purpose in these lectures is to arrive if possible at a systematic description of the common characteristics of the poetry of the Seventeenth Century in England commonly known as metaphysical, and further to seek for a definition of the nature of metaphysical poetry in general. It suits my purpose if the subject has, as I believe it has, a certain actuality and contemporary bearing. We have seen in the present century and increasingly within the last few years, an awakening of interest in this seventeenth-century poetry. However this arose, it undoubtedly contains besides pure literary appreciation, a consciousness or a belief that this poetry and this age have some peculiar affinity with our own poetry and our own age, a belief that our own mentality and feelings are better expressed by the seventeenth century than by the nineteenth or even the eighteenth. Donne is more frequently used as a critical measure than ever before. Even the obscurer poets receive recognition: last year the Nonesuch Press, which is a pretty good index of popular cultivated taste, produced a sumptuous edition of the poems of Bishop King.[1] Contemporary poets are by their admirers likened to Donne or to Crashaw; some of them no doubt study these writers deliberately and elect to receive their influence; there are not wanting voices to declare that the present age is a metaphysical age.

This actuality of the subject does not merely make it fashionable; it is a subject upon which it is vital to have clear and distinct ideas. If the likeness exists, then it is valuable to understand the poetry of the seventeenth century, in order that we may understand that of our own time and understand ourselves.

1 – The Nonesuch edition of *The Poems of Bishop Henry King*, edited by John Sparrow, had appeared in May 1925.

[43]

If the likeness is only fancied, then it is worth the trouble to clear up the misconception, for the same reason. And if as is antecedently probable, the likeness exists in certain particulars along with utter dissimilarity in other particulars, then it will still more usefully clear up our notions about the seventeenth century and our own, if we can arrive at a proper analysis. It may reveal to us tendencies and attitudes in ourselves and our age of which we were conscious and which we must make up our minds either to forward or oppose. But in any case we should be able to find good reasons for our likes and dislikes in this age or any other.

And here it is necessary for me to point out, both in guidance towards the method to be adopted and in common modesty, that these lectures will not continue or develop the work of scholarship. I shall make use, with due sense of obligation, of the work of scholars, such as Mr. Saintsbury and Mr. Grierson, who have done so much to make the material available and to make possible a proper understanding of it.[2] But my point of view is not that of scholarship, but that of literary criticism, and particularly that of one type of literary criticism. My attitude is that of a craftsman who has attempted for eighteen[3] years to make English verses, studying the work of dead artisans who have made better verses. The interest of a craftsman is centred in the present and the immediate future: he studies the literature of the past in order to learn how he should write in the present and the immediate future; and no matter how profound and disinterested his studies, they will always so to speak come out at the finger tips, and find their completion in the action of the chisel, the brush or the typewriter.

What I have just said is really a reservation: for the difference between the two kinds of pure literary criticism is more evident in the defects and

2 – George Edward Bateman Saintsbury (1845–1933), English man of letters and historian of French literature, was formerly Professor of Rhetoric and English Literature at Edinburgh (1895–1915), where he prepared the first two volumes (1903, 1905) of his monumental *Minor Poets of the Caroline Period*, the third and final volume of which appeared in September 1921. TSE wrote earlier that 'his services to literature have been great: had he done nothing but his edition of Caroline poets . . . he would still have earned our perpetual gratitude' (*Dial*, July 1922, p. 95). TSE also dedicated his *Homage to John Dryden* (1924) to Saintsbury.

Herbert John Clifford Grierson (1866–1960; knighted 1936) published his two-volume *Poems of John Donne* (1912) before assuming Saintsbury's professorship at Edinburgh (1915–35), and his standard anthology, *Metaphysical Lyrics and Poems of the Seventeenth Century: Donne to Butler*, was published in August 1921. TSE's review, 'The Metaphysical Poets', appeared in *TLS* on 20 October of that year and had been included in *Homage to John Dryden* and would be in *Selected Essays* (1932).

3 – Writing late in 1925, before the lecture was delivered on 26 January 1926, TSE dates his career from his first publications in the *Harvard Advocate* in 1907–8.

limitations of individual critics than it is in theory. You can distinguish but you cannot dissect; the end of criticism is both practical and theoretic. The speculative critic refines and intellectualises our enjoyment, heightens, not destroys, the keenness of our immediate and irreflective apprehension; establishes standards which create a demand for the highest form of art, and so affects production. And the artisan critic, whose aim is production and novelty, production of the *best* possible, and novelty because we can only capture the enduring by perpetual movement and adaptation, must also adopt disinterestedness in the pursuit of such kind of truth as exists in his material. My interest in enquiring after a definition of metaphysical poetry is that I wish to know what value the term "metaphysical" as applied to verse can have for the present day; whether it is a will-of-the-wisp formed by the combustion of confused and irreconcilable ideas, or whether it represents a legitimate and possible ideal. And now, as Mr. George Herbert would say, let us tune our instruments.[4]

I am of opinion that the failure to arrive at a satisfactory definition of metaphysical poetry – and we shall presently examine two or three definitions of this poetry and some of its elements – is due to a preliminary misconception of the nature of the problem. As a consequence, most of the definitions have destroyed that which they attempted to define. We have on the one hand an idea, or a term which by being a term claims to represent some idea; and on the other hand we have a considerable mass of literature which appears to embody this idea. Nothing, at first sight, more easy. We have only to evolve from our insides a definition of what metaphysical poetry *must* be, then apply it, separate the metaphysical authors from the non-metaphysical, and if we are inclined to be a little more analytical, the metaphysical from the non-metaphysical portions and passages of their works. But consider the idea and the material more closely. This term "metaphysical", used by Dryden, adopted by Johnson, was first used as a

4 – An allusion to an anecdote in Izaak Walton's *Life of Herbert* (1670). On his way to meet musical friends in Salisbury, Herbert had stopped to render assistance to and bestow blessings upon a poor man and his overburdened horse. Arriving uncharacteristically soiled and dishevelled, he was rebuked by one of the musicians for engaging in 'so dirty an employment'. Herbert replied piously before turning to the interest at hand: 'And though I do not wish for the like occasion every day, yet let me tell you, I would not willingly pass one day of my life without comforting a sad soul, or shewing mercy; and I praise God for this occasion. And now let's tune our instruments' (*The Complete Angler & The Lives of Donne, Wotton, Hooker, Herbert & Sanderson* [London: Macmillan, 1906], p. 409). TSE recounted this favourite anecdote in full to illustrate his portrayal of Herbert as an 'exemplary parish priest' in a later pamphlet, *George Herbert* (1962).

convenient term, and as much *defined* by the material in hand, as defining it.[5] It was used by persons who were not themselves metaphysicians, or of a philosophical cast of mind, and they certainly did not employ the term with any thought of Lucretius or Dante in their heads. The more metaphysical branches of philosophy were neither much practised, nor in high repute in England, either in the age of Dryden or in the age of Johnson. Incidentally, there is room to examine whether the meaning of the term had not somewhat altered between Dryden and Johnson. We have first therefore to consider how much community of intension may be found between the term as thus used and the term as we can use it; whether the term can be retained at all for the poets to whom it was originally applied. Second, we must remember that we use the term not only for a larger number of poets than did Dryden or Johnson, but also for these poets seen in a different order. Both these differences are important. We stretch the term to include virtually all of the poets flourishing under James I and Charles I who can be called lyric poets (though we include many who were not). There is no evidence that Johnson had in mind, or would have included, or would have thought worthy to include, many poets who seem to us to belong more or less to this category: Crashaw, Marvell,[6] King, George and Edward Herbert, Vaughan, Carew, Stanley, Benlowes, Chamberlayne and of course Traherne pass unmentioned.[7] Johnson is indeed far from giving satisfaction: he speaks of Donne and of Ben Jonson as setting the fashion (he makes a vague allusion to Marino) and enumerates as their "immediate successors" who still possessed some shreds of honour in his own time, Suckling, Waller, Denham, Cowley, Cleveland and Milton. Waller, Denham and Milton he presents only to withdraw instantly: Suckling he

5 – As TSE knew, Dryden did not actually use the term 'metaphysical' to describe Donne and his school, but in 'A Discourse Concerning the Original and Progress of Satire' (1693), he wrote that Donne 'affects the metaphysics, not only in his satires, but in his amorous verses, where nature only should reign'. Johnson probably adopted Dryden's passage as his source for the term in his *Life of Cowley* (1779), where he established the usage: 'About the beginning of the seventeenth century appeared a race of writers that may be termed the metaphysical poets . . . The metaphysical poets were men of learning, and to show their learning was their whole endeavour'.

6 – 'Lovelace' was later pencilled in TSE's hand in the top margin, with a line to insert after Marvell.

7 – The primary works of Henry King, Bishop of Chichester (1592–1669), Thomas Stanley (1625–78), Edward Benlowes (1603–76) and William Chamberlayne (1619–79) were resurrected in Saintsbury's *Minor Poets of the Caroline Period* (see n. 2 above); the *Poems* of Thomas Traherne (1636–74) were not discovered in manuscript until 1897 and were first published in 1903.

dismisses as negligible; there remain only Cowley and Cleveland, and these two, with Donne, are the poets from whose work he draws all the illustrations for his famous essay.[8] And remember that he attaches a higher absolute value to the work of Cowley than to the work of Donne. Dryden, in his "Preface to *Sylvae*", refers to Cowley with what seems to us unmeasured praises; and in his references to Donne, seems more impressed by the *Satires*, than by any other portion of that poet's work.[9]

It will be seen, accordingly, that the invention and use of the term "metaphysical poetry" spring from what for us is hardly better than an accident. To this race of authors, Dryden and Johnson, neither fully qualified to judge, conceded profundity of thought and learning; and thought and learning, dressed in outlandish and difficult imagery, seemed to Johnson metaphysical. His description is perfectly just, and his criticism both legitimate and felicitous, when measured by the sort of passage which he quotes; but on the whole his use of our term is rather libellous of metaphysics, than illuminating of his authors. And these qualities which seemed to Johnson to make Donne and Cowley metaphysical, are themselves attributes which we must call into question: we shall scrutinise sceptically both the profundity of their thought, and the *quality* of their learning.

At this point we inevitably say to ourselves: let us then make a fresh start.

8 – In his *Life of Cowley*, Johnson stated that the 'kind of writing' characteristic of the metaphysical poets was 'borrowed' from Giambattista Marino (1569–1625), the foremost poet of the *seicentisti*, and 'recommended by the example' of Donne and Jonson. His list of their 'immediate successors' includes those 'of whom any remembrance can be said to remain', some of whom he considers to be but marginal associates: 'Denham and Waller sought another way to fame, by improving the harmony of our numbers. Milton tried the metaphysic style only in his lines upon Hobson the carrier . . . Suckling neither improved versification, nor abounded in conceits. The fashionable style remained chiefly with Cowley; Suckling could not reach it, and Milton disdained it'.

9 – In his 'Preface to *Sylvae*' (1685), Dryden acknowledges 'our admired Cowley' as a great authority on wit and applauds 'the happy genius of Mr Cowley' for having introduced Pindaric verse to his age, 'a noble sort of poetry so happily restored by one man, and so grossly copied by almost all the rest. A musical ear, and a great genius, if another Mr Cowley could arise in another age, may bring it to perfection'.

Though Dryden admired Donne's wit, he was only slightly less critical of the satires than of the poetry. In 'Of Dramatic Poesy' (1668), he compared the satires of Cleveland to those of Donne to argue 'that the one gives us deep thoughts in common language, though rough cadence; the other gives us common thoughts in abstruse words'. He described Donne in 'To the Earl of Abingdon' (1692) as 'the greatest wit, though not the best poet of our nation', but in the following year he dismissed both the poet and the satirist in 'A Discourse Concerning the Original and Progress of Satire': 'Would not Donne's satires, which abound with so much wit, appear more charming if he had taken care of his words, and of his numbers? But he followed

It is possible that the designation may be a complete misnomer. Let us then begin with those poets whom we can agree to be *echt metaphysisch*, disengage the essential metaphysical quality from their work, and apply it in the form of a definition to Donne and his fellows. They may prove to be more or less metaphysical, or not at all; in the latter event we will find a new name for them. You can make the term "metaphysical" equivalent to Mr. Santayana's term "philosophical" in his book *Three Philosophical Poets*.[10] This book, too little read, though one of the most brilliant of Mr. Santayana's works, consists of studies of Lucretius, Dante and Goethe. It is clear that for Mr. Santayana a philosophical poet is one with a scheme of the universe, who embodies that scheme in verse, and essays to realise his conception of man's part and place in the universe. This is not the place for a full consideration of Mr. Santayana's point of view or of his arguments. I will only say this much. If you identify "metaphysical" with "philosophical" and limit "philosophical" to those poets who have given expression to a system or some view of the universe, and man's place in it, which has some philosophical equivalent – as Epicurus, Aquinas, or, for Goethe, [the Faust legend,][11] which expresses half the philosophy of Europe from his own time

---

Horace so very close that of necessity he must fall with him. And I may safely say it of this present age, that if we are not so great wits as Donne, yet certainly we are better poets'.

10– TSE was familiar with the argument of the book even before it was published by Harvard University in 1910. George Santayana (1863–1952), Spanish-born American philosopher and Professor of Philosophy at Harvard University from 1899 to 1912, had instructed TSE in two courses: the introductory 'History of Modern Philosophy' in 1908 and the more advanced 'Ideals of Society, Religion, Art and Science in their Historical Development' in 1909. In his Preface of June 1910 Santayana states that the six lectures that comprise the book 'were based on a regular course which I had been giving for some time at Harvard College' (p. v). The book provided the foundation for TSE's writings on the relation of poetry, philosophy and belief, informing his early essays on 'Dante' (1920), 'Note sur Mallarmé et Poe' (1926), and *Dante* (1929), in the Preface to which he wrote, 'I owe something to Mr. Santayana's essay in *Three Philosophical Poets*' (p. 13).

11–Santayana characterizes and praises Goethe's treatment of the Faust legend as a 'philosophical journey', one that begins with Spinoza and explores a variety of liberating romantic philosophies: '*Faust* ends on the same philosophical level on which it began – the level of romanticism. The worth of life lies in pursuit, not in attainment; therefore, everything is worth pursuing, and nothing brings satisfaction – save this endless destiny itself' (p. 195). In 'Introduction to Goethe' (*Nation and Athenaeum*, 12 January 1929, p. 527), TSE was to state that 'Goethe is, as Mr. Santayana made clear . . . a philosophical poet. His philosophy, unfortunately, is that which the nineteenth century took up with, and it has therefore become too familiar to us in popular or degraded forms. Love, Nature, God, Man, Science, Progress: the post-Goethe versions of these terms are still current. But they are gradually being replaced; and as they are replaced, we shall be able to see Goethe more clearly and with more admiration'. When he subsequently discussed Dante, Lucretius and Goethe as philosophical poets in 'Shelley and Keats' (1933), TSE concluded that 'Of Goethe perhaps it is truer to say

to William James[12] – then the distinction is perfectly clear. Mr. Santayana's three will exhaust the list of metaphysical poets. But I think that the effect of Mr. Santayana's book is a little too clearly to *trancher les genres*. As a philosopher, he is more interested in poetical philosophy than in philosophical poetry. This stricture needs one qualification. I think that Mr. Santayana and myself have this common ground, that we do not mean by philosophical poetry that poetry which is given the sort of interpretation which is called "occult" – the term "occult", it must be remembered, includes a wide range of types from the *Sortes Virgilianae*[13] to certain interpretations of Shakespeare and Blake.[14] We have both, I imagine, a prejudice in favour of the clear and distinct; we mean a philosophy which is expressed, not one which is inexpressible.

I have no concern to attack any critic who finds in any poet an occult philosophy; nor to attack any poet who chooses to make his verse the

---

that he dabbled in both philosophy and poetry and made no great success of either' (*UPUC* 99/90–91), a statement that he was to quote and qualify in 'Goethe as the Sage' (1955) in praising Goethe as a poet who 'has wisdom of a greater range than other men' (*OPP* 220/257).

12 – William James (1842–1910) developed his primary philosophies in *Pragmatism* (1907) and in *Essays in Radical Empiricism* (1912). When TSE lectured on the relation between politics and metaphysics to the Harvard Philosophical Society in 1914 he stated that the flaw of Pragmatism was making man the measure of all things (Houghton), and when he subsequently reviewed James's *Human Immortality: Two Supposed Objections to the Doctrine* (1898), he observed that 'The sub-title of the lecture is characteristic of an attitude very frequent in James: the union of sceptical and destructive habits of mind with positive enthusiasm for freedom in philosophy and thought . . . He hated oppression in any form; the oppression of dogmatic theology was remote from him, who lived in the atmosphere of Unitarian Harvard; but the oppression of idealistic philosophy and the oppression of scientific materialism were very real to him'. TSE found the notes to the lecture 'more provocative than the lecture itself. They show that James was already struggling toward the philosophy barely outlined at his death, the "Radical Empiricism" which he considered more important than his Pragmatism' (*New Statesman*, 8 September 1917, p. 547). TSE was to write in 'Francis Herbert Bradley' (1927) that 'the great weakness of Pragmatism is that it ends by being of no *use* to anybody' (*SE* 454/403–4).

13 – Virgil's superstitious admirers, who believed in his occult powers, attempted to foretell the future by casting 'Virgilian lots'. TSE had come upon Johnson's suspicion in his *Life of Cowley* that Cowley may have been guilty of the practice in forecasting the successful negotiation of a Scotch treaty. As an editorial note in TSE's edition explains, 'Consulting the Virgilian Lots, Sortes Virgilianae, is a method of divination by the opening of Virgil, and applying to the circumstances of the peruser the first passage in either of the two pages that he accidentally fixes his eye on' (*LMEP* 4).

14 – In 1857 Delia Bacon startled the literary world with her *Philosophy of the Plays of Shakespeare Unfolded* (with a preface by Nathaniel Hawthorne, who got the book published), in which she sought to prove that Bacon and others in a secret literary sect produced the plays of 'Shakespeare' in order to direct a liberal political philosophy against the royal government. After the appearance of A. E. Waite's *The Real History of the Rosicrucians* (1887), a number of studies continued to link 'Shakespeare' to Bacon and occult societies, including W. F. C.

medium for conveying it; but its connexion with the poetry seems to me of no literary interest, whereas the connexion of the thought of Epicurus with the verse of Lucretius, or the thought of Aquinas with the verse of Dante, seems to me of very considerable literary importance. And I should agree with Mr. Santayana that Shakespeare is not a philosophical poet. But at this point I must offer, in distinction to Mr. Santayana's poets of complete systems, and on the other hand in distinction to the champions of the poetry of occult significance, a humble tentative account of the nature of philosophical poetry. It must be, *a priori*, an account which will include Dante and Lucretius, whom we take to be philosophical by immediate inspection and common consent. And it must be an account which will not include *all* good poetry, for that would be an absurdity. And it must proceed from the side of poetry, not from the side of philosophy. That is to say, we must restrict it to poetical work of the first intensity, work in which the thought is so to speak *fused* into poetry at a very high temperature.[15] Consequently we must leave out of account those works, even very fine works, such as Pope's 'Essay on Man', in which the blend is effected at a lower temperature, and those such as Blake's in which we are not certain that it takes place at all.[16]

It is a function of poetry both to fix and make more conscious and precise

---

Wigston in *Bacon, Shakespeare, and the Rosicrucians* (1888) and Mrs Henry Potts in *Francis Bacon and his Secret Society* (1891). TSE's sceptical characterization of such interpretations emerged in 'Seneca in Elizabethan Translation' (1927): 'In a comparison of Shakespeare with Dante, for instance, it is assumed that Dante leant upon a system of philosophy which he accepted whole, whereas Shakespeare . . . acquired some extra- or ultra-intellectual knowledge superior to a philosophy. This occult kind of information is sometimes called "spiritual knowledge" or "insight" ' (*SE* 96/80).

W. B. Yeats placed Blake firmly in the occult tradition in several critical editions and essays known to TSE, including the three-volume *Works of William Blake: Poetic, Symbolic, and Critical* (1893), the Introduction to *The Poems of William Blake* (1893) and the essays on Blake collected in *Ideas of Good and Evil* (1903).

15 – TSE had developed his chemical analogy of the 'transforming catalyst' for describing the creative process in 'Tradition and the Individual Talent' (1919), asserting that it is 'the intensity of the artistic process, the pressure, so to speak, under which the fusion takes place, that counts' (*SE* 19/8).

16 – TSE was to write in the Introduction to his edition of Ezra Pound's *Selected Poems* (1928): 'Indeed it might be said in our time that the man who cannot enjoy Pope as poetry probably understands no poetry' (p. xxi), and in 'The Mysticism of Blake' (1927): 'Blake is philosophically an autodidact amateur; theologically, a heretic . . . Blake was not one man in the Songs and another in the [Prophetical] Books: the genius and the inspiration are continuous. The Books are full of poetry, and fine poetry, too. But they show very sadly that genius and inspiration are not enough for a poet. He must have education, by which I do not mean erudition but a kind of mental and moral discipline. The great poet – even the greatest – knows his limitations and works within them' (*Nation and Athenaeum*, 17 September 1927, p. 779).

emotions and feelings in which most people participate in their own experience, and to draw within the orbit of feeling and sense what had existed only in thought. It creates a unity of feeling out of various parts: a unity of action, which is epic or dramatic; a union (the simplest form) of sound and sense, the pure lyric; and in various forms, the union of [things] hitherto unconnected in experience. You will see that Sappho's great ode, for instance, is a real advance, a development, in human consciousness; it sets down, within its verse, the unity of an experience which had previously only existed unconsciously; in recording the physical concomitants of an emotion it modifies the emotion.[17] When Catullus suddenly turns with the immense meditation:

> soles occidere et redire possunt
> sed nobis . . .

he is modifying an emotion by a thought and a thought by an emotion; integrating them into a new emotion, an emotion which with all its

17 – TSE alludes to Sappho's 'Ode to Anactoria' (c. 600 BC), the fragment preserved in Longinus' third-century treatise *On the Sublime*:

> Peer of gods he seemeth to me, the blissful
> Man who sits and gazes at thee before him,
> Close beside thee sits, and in silence hears thee
> Silvery speaking,
>
> Laughing Love's low laughter. Oh this, this only
> Stirs the troubled heart in my breast to tremble,
> For should I but see thee a little moment,
> Straight is my voice hushed;
>
> Yea, my tongue is broken, and through and through me
> 'Neath the flesh, impalpable fire runs tingling;
> Nothing see mine eyes, and a noise of roaring
> Waves in my ears sounds;
>
> Sweat runs down in rivers, a tremor seizes
> All my limbs and paler than grass in autumn,
> Caught by pains of menacing death, I falter,
> Lost in the love trance.
>
> (Trans. J. A. Symonds, 1883)

'Do you not marvel', Longinus asks, 'how she seeks to make her mind, body, ears, tongue, eyes, and complexion, as if they were scattered elements strange to her, join together in the same moment of experience?' *On Great Writing (On the Sublime)*, trans. G. M. A. Grube (New York: Liberal Arts Press, 1957), p. 18. TSE was to write in 'What Dante Means to Me' (1950): 'There are those who remain in one's mind as having set the standard for a particular poetic virtue . . . Sappho for having fixed a particular emotion in the right and the minimum number of words, once and for all' (*TCC* 127).

variations of subsequent poets, has been experienced, doubtless, by many generations of lovers.[18] Not that I suggest that the history of human emotion has been a steady accumulation, a progress onward and upward due to the united efforts of poets all pulling together. Not at all. Many feelings have to be abandoned, many are mislaid, many are corrupted, some seem to have disappeared, like the lost Atlantis, forever. What is left behind, the empty shell of a vanished unity of feeling, is usually called Literature.

Well! it can hardly be doubted that in any period all the poets have a [feeling] more or less in common – not from any co-operative zeal, but like the two characters in *The Hunting of the Snark*, who purely

> from necessity, not from good will,
> Marched along shoulder to shoulder.[19]

In our time, when there are more social circles than there were circles in Dante's *Inferno*, when there are more philosophies, complete, incomplete, and inchoate, than there were builders at Babel, more theories, more tastes, when physical communication between nations is almost perfect, and intellectual communication almost extinct, it is more difficult, certainly, to find a common denominator; but it can be found; for as genius tends towards unity, so mediocrity tends toward uniformity. But it is obvious that

---

18 – The second-line misquotation is queried in the margin in Herbert Read's hand, 'nobis cum semel?' TSE attempts to recall lines from Catullus's 'Carmina v' ('Vivamus, mea Lesbia, atque amemus'):

> soles occidere et redire possunt:
> nobis, cum semel occidit brevis lux,
> nox est perpetua una dormienda.

> Suns can set and rise again:
> we, when once our brief light has set,
> must sleep one never-ending night.
> (Trans. G. P. Goold, *Catullus*, p. 37)

He had correctly quoted the second and third lines in 'Andrew Marvell' (1921), where in a comparative discussion of lines from Horace, Marvell and Catullus he states that 'a whole civilization resides in these lines . . . The verse of Marvell has not the grand reverberation of Catullus's Latin' (*SE* 295/254).

19 – Misquoted from Lewis Carroll's *The Hunting of the Snark* (1876). In 'Fit the Fifth – The Beaver's Lesson' (lines 19–20), the Butcher and the Beaver become frightened during their determinedly separate sallies into a desolate valley in quest of the Snark:

> Till (merely from nervousness, not from good-will)
> They marched along shoulder to shoulder.

in certain periods the revolution of the sphere of thought will so to speak throw off ideas which will fall within the attraction of poetry, and which the operation of poetry will transmute into the immediacy of feeling. It is these moments of history when human sensibility is momentarily *enlarged in certain directions* to be defined, that I propose to call the metaphysical periods. Obviously, this statement needs a good deal of elucidation.

There are three principal forms in which thought can invest itself and become poetry. One is when a thought, which may be and most often is a commonplace ("rien de plus beau que les lieux communs" said Baudelaire)[20] is expressed in poetic form though in the language of thought. When Shakespeare says

> Man must abide
> His going hence, even as his coming hither;
> Ripeness is all,[21]

it illustrates this type. Such gnomic utterances occur very frequently in drama, where they gain a great deal of their force from the position which they occupy and the light which they cast on the dramatic action: the Greek choruses are full of them. The second type is the discursive exposition of an argument, such as we find in the "Essay on Man", and at its highest, in the passages in the *Purgatorio* expounding the Thomist–Aristotelian theory of the origin and development of the soul.[22] Immense technical skill is necessary to make such discourse fly, and great emotional intensity is necessary to make it soar. And the third type is that which occurs when an

---

20–Baudelaire made the entry in his posthumously published *Journaux Intimes*, in section LXXVI (*Notes précieuses*) of 'Mon Coeur Mis a Nu': 'Sois toujours poète, même en prose. Grand style (rien de plus beau que le lieu commun)'; *Oeuvres Posthumes et Correspondence Inédites* (Paris, 1887), p. 121. TSE held the phrase as a critical touchstone as late as 1952, when he discussed Gray's 'Elegy in a Country Churchyard' as 'a good example of a beautiful poem which is nearly all platitude. Such poems are untranslatable: they can only be paraphrased by another poet of genius who can clothe the same international platitudes in the beauties of his own language. *"Rien n'est plus beau que le lieu commun"* [sic] says Baudelaire somewhere. From Homer to our own day, poetry has depended upon it' ('Scylla and Charybdis', *Agenda*, 23 [1985], p. 11).

21–The misquotation from *King Lear*, v. ii. 9–11, is corrected, except for the punctuation, in black ink by an unidentified hand:

> Men must endure
> Their going hence, even as their coming hither.
> Ripeness is all.

22–Canto XVIII, lines 49–54, when Virgil discourses on love and free will, and Canto XXV, lines 34–66, when Statius, Virgil's Christian counterpart, discourses on generation.

idea, or what is only ordinarily apprehensible as an intellectual statement, is translated in sensible form; so that the world of sense is actually enlarged. An illustration. One of the capital ideas of Donne, the one which is perhaps his peculiar gift to humanity, is that of the union, the fusion and identification of *souls* in sexual love. To state it, to deposit it gnomically or to analyse it is nothing; to express it, to evoke it, is everything. It is hardly a thought at all; it differs radically from the two types mentioned a moment ago: but how many centuries of intellectual labour were necessary, how much dogma, how much speculation, how many systems had to be elaborated, shattered and taken up into other systems, before such an idea was possible! The soul itself had to be constructed first: and since the soul has disappeared we have many other things, the analysis of Stendhal,[23] the madness of Dostoevski,[24] but not this. Even Browning, who might have been a more philosophical poet had he been more of a philosopher, gives us only

> Infinite passion, and the pain
> Of finite hearts that yearn.[25]

It becomes clear after a little inspection that this type of thought, the *Word made Flesh*, so to speak, is more restricted in the times and places of its avatar than is immediately evident. It is *one form* of an enlargement of

23 – TSE probably alludes to *De l'Amour* (1822), one of Stendhal's early works, a copy of which he had in his library, in which the author conducts a psychological analysis of one of his own love affairs. In 'A Foreign Mind' (*Athenaeum*, 4 July 1919, p. 553), where a discussion of W. B. Yeats leads to a comparison of Joyce and Stendhal, he had declared that 'Mr. Joyce's mind is subtle, erudite, even massive; but it is not like Stendhal's, an instrument continually tempering and purifying emotion'.

24 – TSE's interest in the 'madness' of Dostoevski [or Dostoevsky] preceded the composition of 'The Love Song of J. Alfred Prufrock' (1910–11), which was influenced by his reading of *Crime and Punishment*, *The Idiot* and *The Brothers Karamazov* in French translation, and he had since described the reality of Dostoevsky's exploration of extreme psychological states in 'Beyle and Balzac' (*Athenaeum*, 30 May 1919, p. 392): 'If you examine some of Dostoevsky's most successful, most imaginative "flights," you find them to be projections, continuations of the actual, the observed . . . Dostoevsky's point of departure is always a human brain in a human environment, and the "aura" is simply the continuation of the quotidian experience of the brain into seldom explored extremities of torture. Because most people are too unconscious of their own suffering to suffer much, this continuation appears fantastic'.

25 – The concluding lines of 'Two in the Campagna', in which Browning's persona expresses his intense frustration that in spite of closest companionship he cannot submerge his being in that of his lover, that finite hearts cannot obtain the infinite passion beheld in beloved objects. The poems appeared in *Men and Women* (1855), which TSE had assigned to his Extension classes in 1916–17 (*RES* I, 170; II, 293).

immediate experience which, in one form or another, is a general function of poetry.[26] Examples might be multiplied. There are those which I gave, from Sappho and Catullus. When Helen looks out from Troy, and thinks she sees[27] her brothers in the host, and Homer tells us that they were already dead, we partake at the same time of her feelings and of those of an omniscient witness, and the two form one.[28] But the characteristic of the type of poetry I am trying to define is that it elevates sense for a moment to regions ordinarily attainable only by abstract thought, or on the other hand clothes the abstract, for a moment, with all the painful delight of flesh. To call it mystical is facile, and I hasten to discountenance the use of this word; for there are many kinds of qualities of mysticism, and I wish to emphasise the intellectual quality of this operation of poetry. With the more intellectual forms of mysticism, the *beatitudo*, or the experience of Theresa or John of the Cross, it may come in contact, as we shall see; but as this is a specific variation, and the generic character is not mystical at all, I prefer to keep the word mysticism out of the way.

Such poetry, though it may find a partial gospel in the *Banquet* of Plato (a work which influenced Donne indirectly through neo-platonism)[29] finds no

26 – TSE draws here and elsewhere in the lectures upon F. H. Bradley's doctrine of 'immediate experience', a non-relational moment of knowing and feeling in which subject and object are one. In the first chapter of his dissertation on Bradley, 'On our Knowledge of Immediate Experience', TSE defines that moment of unity, which falls apart of itself into the intellection of subjects and objects, as the starting point of knowledge: 'although we cannot know immediate experience directly as an object, we can yet arrive at it by inference, and even conclude that it is the starting point of our knowing, since it is only in immediate experience that knowledge and its object are one' (*KEPB* 19).
27 – Herbert Read has underlined 'thinks she sees' with a pencilled note in the top margin: 'She says expressly that she cannot see them, & discovers why they are not to be seen!'
28 – In the *Iliad*, Book III, Helen says that though she can see all the rest of the Achaians,

> Two princes of the people yet I nowhere can behold,
> Castor, the skilful knight on horse, and Pollux, uncontroll'd,
> For all stand-fights, and force of hand; both at a burthen bred;
> My natural brothers.
>
> (lines 256–9)

She imagines them elsewhere, but Homer intervenes with the dramatic irony of the scene:

> Nor so; for holy Tellus' womb inclos'd those worthy men
> In Sparta, their beloved soil.
>
> (lines 262–3; trans. George Chapman)

29 – Plato's dramatic dialogue, the *Banquet*, or *Symposium*, is set at a drinking-feast in the house of Agathon, where Aristodemus, Phaedrus, Pausanias, Aristophanes, Socrates, Alcibiades and Eryximachus honour the god of Love by making after-dinner speeches in definition of love.

place in the ancient world. To account for its absence would require a summary of the history of thought from classical antiquity to the thirteenth century; and as I think that the assertion will in the course of these lectures gradually reveal itself to you as true, I shall make no direct attempt to explain why it is true. The first distinguished exemplar of this type of poetry was of course Dante. If you recall my tentative division of the three types of philosophical poetry, you will see at once that Dante is the great exemplar not only for the type which forms the theme of these lectures, but of *every* type. I quoted from *King Lear*:

> Man must abide
> His going hence, even as his coming hither . . .[30]

alongside of which may be set the familiar

> Nessun maggior dolore
> Che di ricordar del tempo felice
> Nella miseria . . . . .[31]

Of the expository type I have already instanced Dante's account of the soul in the *Purgatorio*:

> Uscio di Dio. . . . .
> L'anima semplicetta, che sa nulle. . . . .[32]

30—See n. 21 above. The lines have again been corrected by the same unidentified hand:

> Men must endure
> Their going hence, even as their coming hither . . .

31—*The Inferno*, v, 121–3. When Dante discovers Francesca of Rimini with her lover Paolo in the Second Circle of Hell, he asks her how she came to know the 'dubbiosi desire', and she replies:

> Nessun maggior dolore,
> che ricordarsi del tempo felice
> nella miseria . . .

> There is no greater pain than
> to recall a happy time in wretchedness . . .
> (*TC* I, 54–5)

32—Misquoted from the *Purgatorio*, xvi, lines 85, 88. In the midst of his discourse on the Freedom of the Will, and on the Soul, Marco Lombardo says to Dante:

> Esce di mano a lui . . .
> l'anima semplicetta, che sa nulla . . .

> From the hands of Him . . . the simple soul, that knows
> nothing . . . (trans. TSE, *SE* 260/220).

TSE later adapted the passage for the first line of 'Animula' (1929): ' "Issues from the hand of

The third type is found throughout the *Vita Nuova* (to which I shall return) in one form, and in various places in the *Divine Comedy* in other forms. In the last canto of the *Paradiso*:

> La forma universal' di questo nodo
> Credi ch'io vidi, perchè più di largo
> Dicendo questo, mi sentii ch'io godo.
>
> Un punto solo m'è maggior letargo
> Che venticinque secoli all'impresa
> Che fe Nettuno ammirar l'ombra d'Argo.[33]

I shall ask you to remark, here and later, how Dante always finds the sensuous equivalent, the physical embodiment, for the realisation of the most tenuous and refined intensity (I say "tenuous intensity" not without forethought) of experience: it is as if his body were capable of maintaining life and consciousness – not only maintaining but indeed increasing it, for the last cantos of his poem are the most passionate – at a higher altitude and in a more rarified atmosphere than those of other men.

In turning from Dante (of course I must recur to him later) I do not wish to leave you under the impression that this gift of what I am going to call metaphysical poetry is his only or his supreme gift. I do not choose to assign precedence among his qualities. He had, as I said, *all* the possible qualities which could adorn a philosophical poet. And it is not, I imagine, any of these

---

God, the simple soul" '. He quoted the passage at length in 'Dante' (1929), because it and another 'are of the sort that a reader might be inclined to skip, thinking that they are only for scholars, not for readers of poetry, or thinking that it is necessary to have studied the philosophy underlying them. It is not necessary to have traced the descent of this theory of the soul from Aristotle's *De Anima* in order to appreciate it as poetry . . . It is the philosophy of that world of poetry which we have entered' (*SE* 261/221–2).

33 – The *Paradiso*, XXXIII, lines 91–6 (*TC* III, 404); minor mistranscriptions; lines 92–93, read 'Credo . . . mi sento ch'io godo'. TSE had quoted the first stanza in 'Dante' (1920) in arguing that 'a disgust like Dante's . . . is completed and explained only by the last canto of the *Paradiso*' (*SW* 168–9). When he returned to the stanzas in 'Dante' (1929), he freely adapted the Temple Classics translation and commented upon them: '*The universal form of this complex I think I saw, because, as I say this, more largely I feel myself rejoice. One single moment to me is more lethargy than twenty-five centuries upon the enterprise which made Neptune wonder at the shadow of Argo (passing over him).* One can feel only awe at the power of the master who could thus at every moment realize the inapprehensible in visual images. And I do not know anywhere in poetry more authentic sign of greatness than the power of association which could in the last line, when the poet is speaking of the Divine vision, yet introduce the Argo passing over the head of wondering Neptune . . . It is the real right thing, the power of establishing relations between beauty of the most diverse sorts; it is the utmost power of the poet' (*SE* 267–8/228).

three – the gift of magnificent sentences, the gift of exposition, or the gift of incarnation – which chiefly arrests the mind of Mr. Santayana, but rather that architectonic ability, that power of organisation and structure, in which Dante excelled every poet who has ever written.

But Dante was not the only poet of his time. And the poetic power which I am attempting to define is precisely the one which is shared most fully by his contemporaries. His group all had this power, in various degrees, of fusing sense with thought: and in the smaller works of smaller men it is perhaps more clearly perceived than in the complete and immense structure of the master. I propose, therefore, in the course of my future lectures, to draw parallels and comparisons between Donne and his group on the one hand and Guido Guinizelli, Guido Cavalcanti, Cino da Pistoia on the other.[34] In the general parallel I pretend no discovery: indeed, I wonder only that every critic of Donne has not drawn the comparison. It was left for an Italian critic, Signor Mario Praz, in a book which appeared only last year, *Secentismo e Marinismo in Inghilterra*, to confer a poem of Donne's with one of Guinizelli's, and to point to the general resemblance; but I shall draw from the resemblance some general inferences for which I shall not hold Signor Praz responsible.[35]

We then ask whether these two periods – the *trecento* in Italy and the Seventeenth Century in England, are the only periods in which this type of poetry is to be found. Certainly not. It is found, in various degrees of adulteration, indefinitely after Dante. There are traces before Donne and

---

34 – Members of Dante's 'group' include Guido Guinizelli (c. 1230–76), whose doctrine of Love Dante praises in the *Vita Nuova* (xx) and whom he recognizes as his literary father in the *Purgatorio* (xxvii); Guido Cavalcanti (c. 1255–1300), to whom Dante dedicates the *Vita Nuova* as 'the first among my friends'; and Cino da Pistoia (1270–1337), who wrote numerous sonnets to his friend Dante. Guinizelli's sonnets and *canzone*, Dante's sonnets to Cavalcanti and Cino, and theirs to him, were translated by Dante Gabriel Rossetti in *The Early Italian Poets* (1861), one of TSE's texts for the Clark Lectures.

35 – Praz compares Donne's 'The Extasie' to Guinizelli's famous *canzone*, 'Al cor gentil ripara sempre Amore' ('Of the Gentle Heart'), pp. 28–9. TSE's laudatory review of the book in *TLS* (17 December 1925, p. 878) led to his lifelong friendship with Mario Praz (1896–1982), Italian critic and translator of TSE's poems who was then Senior Lecturer in Italian at Liverpool University. 'My first acquaintance with the work of Mario Praz', he later wrote, 'came when . . . the *Times Literary Supplement* sent me for review his *Secentismo e Marinismo in Inghilterra*. I immediately recognised these essays – and especially his masterly study of Crashaw – as among the best that I had ever read in that field. His knowledge of the poetry of that period in four languages – English, Italian, Spanish and Latin – was encyclopaedic, and, fortified by his own judgment and good taste, makes that book essential reading for any student of the English "metaphysical poets" ' (*Friendship's Garland: Essays Presented to Mario Praz On His Seventieth Birthday*, ed. Vittorio Gabrieli, 1 [Roma, 1966], p. 3).

after. But I propose to cut my periods off more sharply for my purpose than one would be justified in doing were one composing a continuous history. I wish to show the type in its most typical form. And there is this consideration: that the study of derivation and influence is apt to mislead us. It is more often the form that passes on than the spirit. I shall therefore treat the period of Dante as one manifestation and the period of Donne as another. And I find a third period, not so clear, much more complex, but representing what seem to me distinctly "metaphysical" manifestations. Its parent is Baudelaire, it existed in France between 1870–1890, and the important poets for my purpose are Jules Laforgue, Arthur Rimbaud and Tristan Corbière.[36] And this period also I shall employ to aid in the survey of the seventeenth century.

It is important, in an undertaking of this kind, that we should scrutinise narrowly our method at every possible moment; that we should keep reminding ourselves of our aim; that we should keep testing our tools, knowing what to expect of each, not too much or too little; that we should ask ourselves at every moment whether we are using the right tools, neither too many nor too few. It will be obvious that my aim is not solely to arrive at a *definition* of metaphysical poetry. One must always be as exact and clear as one can – as clear as one's subject matter permits. And when one's subject matter is literature, clarity beyond a certain point becomes falsification.

36–Charles Baudelaire (1821–67), predecessor of the French Symbolist poets, published his *Les Fleurs du mal* in 1857, and his prose poems appeared posthumously in *Le Spleen de Paris* (1869). His abiding influence on TSE's poetry and prose first manifests itself in the 'Unreal City' and *'hypocrite lecteur!'* of *The Waste Land* (*CPP* 62–3/39); Jules Laforgue (1860–87), credited with inventing *vers libre*, had a strong influence on the early poetry of TSE, who was to write in the Introduction to Pound's *Selected Poems* (1928): 'My own verse is, so far as I can judge, nearer to the original meaning of *vers libre* than is any of the other types: at least, the form in which I began to write, in 1908 or 1909, was directly drawn from the study of Laforgue together with the later Elizabethan drama; and I do not know anyone else who started from exactly that point' (p. x); Arthur Rimbaud (1854–91) gave up writing at the age of nineteen or twenty after composing the prose poems that make up *Les Illuminations* (1886). In 'The Borderline of Prose' (1917), TSE had suggested that the prose poetry of the 1890s 'was probably based upon the work of a man much greater than any poet then living – and that is Arthur Rimbaud. Few people in England have heard of the *Illuminations* . . . They are short prose pieces, as obscure as *Kubla Khan* or *Christabel* and of a similar inspiration' (*New Statesman*, 19 May 1917, p. 158); Tristan Corbière (1845–75), who took much of his poetic material from the sailors and sea-coasts of his native Brittany, is known for his one volume, *Les Amours jaunes* (1873). TSE was to write in 'To Criticize the Critic' (1961): 'It is true that I owed, and have always acknowledged, an equally great debt to certain French poets of the late nineteenth century, about whom I have never written. I have written about Baudelaire, but nothing about Jules Laforgue, to whom I owe more than to any one poet in any language, or about Tristan Corbière, to whom I owe something also' (*TCC* 22). TSE's early poem, 'Tristan Corbière', is in the Berg Collection.

This is a very important restriction on the activity of literary criticism. When a subject matter is in its nature vague, clarity should consist, not in making it so clear as to be unrecognisable, but in recognising the vagueness, where it begins and ends and the causes of its necessity, and in checking analysis and division at the prudent point. In literature, one can distinguish, but one cannot dissect. For, as I said at the beginning, on the one hand you have the definition, on the other hand you have a mass of material, actual written poetry, and you must not hope to make the two quite fit. In dealing with a school or group of poetry, you are dealing with resemblances which are neither purely natural and unconscious, nor purely conscious and deliberate. You are dealing not only with what men thought and felt, but with what they thought they thought and felt; and your appeal, in the last resort, must be to your own feeling as well as your own thought. On the one hand, I make a tentative definition. But in making this definition, I have had to rely on my own immediate experience of poetry: obviously, I felt a resemblance between the affects of Donne, Guido and Laforgue before I formed any theory.

And on the other hand, I confess in advance that *any* definition of metaphysical poetry will be only a partial success, and this is in the nature of the subject matter. This will be evident from my choice of poets to represent the metaphysicals: Donne, Crashaw and Cowley – I have chosen these three deliberately in order to strain my definition to the utmost. Donne will take the leading place in *any* classification of metaphysical poets; Donne is a fixed point. Donne is as near typical as any one of them could be: on the other hand he is too individual to be a type. Now no theory which will be completely true to Donne will be true of any of the others. And one reason is this. If you define a school of poetry by the spirit, you will probably find either that your definition is so large as to include more than that school, [and] therefore will be useless, or that it is so narrow as to exclude almost everyone but the master. For the school is not wholly united by the spirit, and the more members you include the more tenuous becomes the spirit informing them all. The school is united as much by the letter – by the commonplaces they employ, the common vocabulary, the common locutions. In our study we shall have to investigate this common language of the seventeenth century: the use of hyperbole, of allusion, of conceit. But if we sought for our definition, our principle of unity, *merely* in the language and metrics, we should arrive merely at a catalogue or table of resemblances, which would never bring us anywhere near a definition, which must seek the *causes* of these resemblances, and their results. The causes of resemblance between contemporaries must be of three kinds: the common heritage of culture at the same time, common exposure to the same influences at the time, and their influence upon each other, both of personality and thought and of technique. And it must be remembered that the letter, as well as the spirit, giveth life. That Cowley, for instance, by aping the style and adopting the subjects of Donne, comes to resemble him somewhat in spirit as well as form – though no one was less gifted to this end by nature. And yet Cowley, I shall admit in advance, does not satisfy my definition of metaphysical poetry. He fails to make the Word Flesh, though he often makes it Bones.

And the best that I can hope for my definition, then, is that it will throw a sudden ray of light upon what I consider the most valuable aspect of metaphysical poetry. But I shall proceed to use the term "metaphysical poetry" in two senses: as the subject of my definition – because we must assume that every term is susceptible of definition – and as the collective title of the group of poets in question, and whom I shall take for convenience and also because I give the selection my full assent, to be those poets represented in Professor Grierson's admirable and almost impeccable anthology.[37]

There is one point, relatively unimportant, but which I must expound in passing, because it is sure to occur to your minds, and, if I ignore it, it is sure to stick there and take a more important place than it deserves; and that is this: why retain the title "metaphysical"? why not say "the lyric poets of the seventeenth century", or even the "psychological" poets? Well! there are very good reasons, which I hope to develop in subsequent lectures, why we should not say "psychological" poets – good reasons, that is, while we make use of my definition (which, as I have explained, is one partly imposed by force upon them); but in short, I intend to maintain exactly that the poets of the *trecento* in Italy were *not* psychological poets, and a term which would explicitly exclude the Italians would rob me of one of my points of triangulation. And the reason for calling the seventeenth century still "metaphysical", is that the term is consecrated by use. "Philosophical" is accordingly a more pretentious term than "metaphysical", which, as employed in literary criticism of the last two hundred and fifty years, has a connotation of "fantastic", "elaborated", which should not be suppressed.

Some years ago I had a correspondence with Mr. Saintsbury, in *The*

37–*Metaphysical Lyrics and Poems of the Seventeenth Century: Donne to Butler* (Oxford: Clarendon Press, 1921). See n. 2 above.

Times and privately, concerning the application of this term.[38] Mr. Saintsbury not only accepted the term, but wished to give it, by what seems to me almost a *jeu de mots*, a further and more exact significance based on its etymology. Metaphysics was, of course, originally only that work of Aristotle's which came after the *Physics*. But the metaphysical is, for Mr. Saintsbury, that which comes after the natural (I am not sure that Aristotle would not wish to qualify this statement): the metaphysical poets are those who seek something beyond or after nature – refinements of thought and emotion – ergo they are metaphysical. This definition of metaphysical poets as those who have and are chiefly interested in "second thoughts", in Mr. Saintsbury's phrase, is ingenious, and worth considering. But it seems to me to have the usual difficulty of applying to other poetry which we should not call metaphysical, and, still worse, of applying to the second rate still better than it does to the best. I have chosen a definition which is admittedly not comprehensive, but which I think will tend to ignore the inferior rather than the finer work. But Mr. Saintsbury's phrase should be kept in mind, because it implies an artificiality, perhaps a deliberate exploitation of the senses, which we shall have to examine.

We must, of course, devote the greater part of our time to Donne. I propose first to examine briefly the kind and extent of erudition possessed by Donne, with a view to deciding to what extent they determined the cast of his mind and in what way they find a place in his poetry. This part of our study will be largely a comment and criticism of the conclusions arrived at by Miss Ramsay, in her book *Les idées médiévales chez Donne*, and

38–Writing in response to TSE's review of Grierson's anthology, Professor Saintsbury suggested that one 'might very easily shift the last word from the title of a book about nature to its literal sense of "natural things," and so use "metaphysics" as equivalent to "second thoughts," things that come *after* the natural first; and, once more, this definition would, I think, fit all the poetry commonly called "metaphysical" . . . while "philosophical," though of course not seldom suitable enough, sometimes has no relevance whatever' (*TLS*, 27 October 1921, p. 698). TSE replied on 3 November: 'Mr. Saintsbury appears to believe that these poets represent not merely a generation, but a particular theory of poetry. The "second thoughts" to which he alludes are, I think . . . frequent in the work of many other poets besides, of other times and other languages' (p. 716; *L1* 483). On 10 November Saintsbury wrote that there was 'no *real* contradiction' between them: 'I fully agree with him that, in the great examples he quotes, and perhaps in all similar things, there is "second thought." I might even go so far as to say . . . that all true poetry must be in a way second thought, though much second thought is not in any way poetry. What I was endeavouring to point out was that, *in this period*, the quest of the second thought became direct, deliberate, a business almost itself a *first* thought' (p. 734). TSE's letters to Saintsbury are lost; Saintsbury's surviving letters to TSE (Houghton) contain no mention of the controversy.

making use of Miss Ramsay's profound researches.[39] It is important that we form an opinion concerning the proportion of [the] mediaeval and the Renaissance elements in his composition. From this we pass on to the analysis of Donne's theory of the emotions, of human and divine ecstasy, comparing it, in order still more closely to determine Donne's place between the old world and the new, with that of the Italian poets on the one hand, and with that of such a modern poet as Baudelaire on the other. And finally, we proceed to his mode of expression, his indebtedness and his resemblances to Elizabethan poets, his use of verse forms, and his use of conceits and images. In considering Donne, we must consider all the erotic verse of the time, and attempt to find the common principle, if any. In considering Crashaw, in his turn, we shall be examing the religious verse of his contemporaries – chiefly Herbert, Vaughan, Traherne – and shall attempt to find the common principle of that. In proceeding from Donne to Crashaw, we move from the general to the particular, in that we are concerned with a much more restricted intellect; yet Crashaw is much more typical of the general taste of Europe in that age, and especially of its religious or devotional mentality. A study of Crashaw must therefore be a study of the religion of the first half of the seventeenth century. In Cowley we reach the fringes of the metaphysical poetry; and I have elected to give him so much attention, because it was Cowley who represented this age to the next; and who, by a kind of fusion with Denham, Waller and others, effects a transition, less violent than we are often led to believe by the history books, to the Augustan Age. And at the end I propose again to treat the period as a whole, draw again the general comparisons with the *trecento* and the French poets of the nineteenth century whom I have mentioned, and extract therefrom the conclusions.

For two opposite reasons, I wish to recommend to those who think they have the fortitude to follow these lectures to the end, the constant use of Professor Grierson's anthology *Metaphysical Lyrics and Poems of the Seventeenth Century from Donne to Butler*. One reason is that our enquiry will often take us into discussions of philosophy and theology where poetry is easily forgotten, and I would not like you to forget that the matter in hand is not philosophy or theology but poetry, and not Poetry as an abstraction but particular poems which are living things capable of and intended to give

39–Mary Paton Ramsay, *Les Doctrines médiévales chez Donne, le poète métaphysicien de l'Angleterre (1573–1631)* (London: Oxford Univ. Press, 1917). The second edition had appeared in 1924.

enjoyment. The other reason is that this excellent collection contains practically all the poems of the period which we need, and you will find it a convenience whenever we are occupied with a detailed examination of a text.

Among other books

Praz: *Secentismo e Marinismo in Inghilterra.*[40]

Donne's Sermons: do not recommend L.P.S. preface[41]

Dryden's Essay on "The Proper Wit of Poetry".[42]

Johnson's Lives of Cowley, Denham, Milton, Waller & Dryden.[43]

Cowley's *Essays.*[44]

Gourmont: *Dante, Béatrice et la poésie amoureuse.*[45]

40–(Firenze: Società An. Editrice 'La Voce', 1925). Part of the study of Crashaw in the volume was translated by Praz and included in his *The Flaming Heart* (New York: Doubleday, 1958).

41–When TSE reviewed Logan Pearsall Smith's edition of *Donne's Sermons* (Oxford: Clarendon Press, 1919), he stated that 'we cannot appreciate the significance, the solitariness of this personal expression in Donne's sermons unless we compare him with one or two of the great preachers of his time, the great preachers whose sermons were fine prose. The absence of such comparison is the single important defect of Mr. Pearsall Smith's introduction' (*Athenaeum*, 28 November 1919, p. 1252). He was to reiterate the criticism in 'The Prose of the Preacher' (*Listener*, 3 July 1929, pp. 22–3), where he clarified the needed comparisons: 'Donne was by no means either the first or the last of the great English preachers; I believe that his contemporary, Bishop Andrewes, is greater, and Jeremy Taylor certainly must take equal rank. But Donne is undoubtedly the most readable. Hugh Latimer, Bishop of Worcester, was a great preacher and a great prose writer long before Donne' (p. 22).

42–TSE owned the Everyman Library edition of Dryden's *Dramatic Essays*, with an introduction by William Henry Hudson (London: J. M. Dent, 1912), which he purchased in April 1920. In this edition (pp. 189–96), the editor freely gives the title 'The Proper Wit of Poetry' to Dryden's 'An Account of the Ensuing Poem', prefixed to his historical poem, *Annus Mirabilis, the Year of Wonders, 1666* (1667). The imposed title comes from the third paragraph of the essay, which TSE has marked in his copy: '*Wit written* is that which is well defined, the happy result of thought or product of imagination. But to proceed from wit, in the general notion of it, to the proper wit of an Heroic or Historical Poem, I judge it chiefly to consist in the delightful imagining of persons, actions, passions, or things' (p. 192).

43–TSE owned the one-volume edition of Johnson's *Lives of the Most Eminent English Poets* in the Chandos Classics series, New Edition (London: Frederick Warne [1872]), which includes the lives of the five poets listed. He later inscribed the volume to Valerie Eliot: 'This copy I bought second-hand many years ago, I know not where, and with this copy I first became acquainted with Johnson's Lives'.

44–TSE used A. R. Waller's edition of *Abraham Cowley: Essays, Plays and Sundry Verses* (Cambridge: Cambridge Univ. Press, 1906), borrowed from the London Library.

45–Remy de Gourmont, *Dante, Béatrice et la poésie amoureuse* (Paris: Société du Mercure de France, 1908). TSE had referred Herbert Read to this work in his annotations on the outline (Victoria) of Read's article, 'The Nature of Metaphysical Poetry', which appeared in the *Criterion* in April 1923.

Rossetti: *Early Italian Poets*.[46]
Hobbes & Descartes.[47]
Hooker: *Ecclesiastical Polity*.[48]
Truc: *Les mystiques españols*.[49]

46–Though TSE had earlier assigned 'A few translations of Italian Sonnets in Rossetti's *Early Italian Poets*' to his 1918 tutorial class in Elizabethan Literature (*RES* II, 300), there is no edition in his library.

47–TSE's copy of Thomas Hobbes' *Leviathan* (1651) was published in the New Universal Library series (London: George Routledge & Sons [1907]). It is inscribed with his name and dated February 1914. For citing the works of René Descartes, TSE used *Oeuvres choisies de Descartes* (Paris: Garnier, 1865).

48–TSE owned the three-volume, leather-bound edition of Richard Hooker's *Works*, arranged by the Revd John Keble, second edition (Oxford: The University Press, 1841), but he also owned a copy (Houghton) of vol. II (Book V) of the Everyman edition (1907) of *The Laws of Ecclesiastical Polity* (1593–7; 1661), to which he referred in a later essay on 'The Genesis of Philosophic Prose: Bacon and Hooker' (*Listener*, 26 June 1929, p. 907).

49–Gonzague Truc's edition of *Les Mystiques espanols: Sainte Terese – Saint Jean de la Croix* (Paris: La renaissance du Livre [1921]). TSE used several of Truc's books and editions in preparing his lectures and had written to Herbert Read on 11 December 1925: 'Truc has a new book *Notre temps* (*Renaissance du livre*) I have not seen it, but I think rather well of him' (*L2*).

LECTURE II

{Donne and the Middle Ages}

I propose in this lecture to discuss the studies of Donne and their influence upon his mind and his poetry. For this purpose I shall employ chiefly the work of Miss Mary Ramsay before mentioned. Miss Ramsay conducted her investigation into Donne's reading with the thoroughness only possible to a candidate for a doctor's degree; there is not a single reference or allusion which she has not made indefatigable attempts to track down; and her book will, I expect, remain the standard work on the subject for many generations to come. Miss Ramsay draws certain conclusions regarding Donne's cast of mind; happily, her documentation is so complete that it provides itself the means for us to qualify some of these conclusions.

Miss Ramsay's thesis, as stated in her foreword, is this: that Donne possessed a "very complete" philosophical system and a profound mysticism and that his conception of the universe, and his philosophical technique, are essentially mediaeval. It is these assertions which I propose to examine.[1]

There is no question that Donne's natural inclination of mind bore him toward theological and legal studies. The tendency toward the law, more pronounced than a reader of Miss Ramsay's book might suppose, is of some

---

1 – In his review of Praz's book (see p. 58, n. 35) TSE had already stated his position regarding Miss Ramsay's thesis: 'What Signor Praz performs with greater care, in his study of Donne, is a correction of some of the excesses of that scholarly and standard book, "Les Doctrines médiévales chez Donne" by Miss Mary Ramsay. Miss Ramsay is inclined to class all philosophy earlier than 1500 as equally medieval, and to see in Donne, because his reading was chiefly in medieval lore and because of his apparent indifference to classical Roman literature, a man of medieval mind . . . But we think that Signor Praz's view is nearer to accuracy: that Donne was medieval in his education and in his taste, but Renaissance in mind and in sensibility. We should go even further than that, and say that the very indiscriminate variety of Donne's reading is evidence of his modernity. A man who quotes Aquinas so little, and who appears directly influenced by pseudo-Dyonisius, who turns to account indifferently doctrines Christian or heretical, Jewish or Arabic, would have been out of his place in the thirteenth century' (p. 878).

significance. Donne's reading in civil and canon law was so extensive that at one moment there was a question whether he should not look in this direction for a career: though we are also to infer, from Walton's *Life*, that his studies in law were pursued for many years without any such practical aim. In any case, they indicate some bias toward the more public and disputatious, rather than the more private and speculative attitude toward philosophy. Donne's reading, in law, in theology, in medicine, and in everything which at that time could be subsumed under the genus of philosophy, was immense. Even during his youthful period of dissipation – and we may suspect that Donne, like many other men, was not above the vanity of magnifying his adolescent debaucheries in retrospect – Walton tells us that he always reserved the hours from four until ten in the morning for study – leaving us to believe that after ten o'clock he was ready for the solicitations of whatever prospect of pleasure presented itself.[2] When we inspect the dreary index of his reading which Miss Ramsay most usefully gives us, we recoil.[3] No man of Donne's ability and attainments ever seems to have read more positive rubbish. But the lists themselves are interesting reading, and provide a pertinent comment on Miss Ramsay's thesis. For we remark at once, how large a part of this reading is in authors contemporary, or nearly so. True, as a thorough theologian, he was familiar with the fathers of the church, and with the most important of the mediaeval philosophers; but so, as Miss Ramsay herself says, was Hooker, and Miss Ramsay does not go so far as to say that Hooker's conception of the universe was mediaeval.[4]

2 – 'Nor was his age only so industrious, but in the most unsettled days of his youth, his bed was not able to detain him beyond the hour of four in the morning; and it was no common business that drew him out of his chamber till past ten; all which time was employed in study; though he took great liberty after it' (*The Complete Angler & the Lives*, pp. 225–6).

3 – In five appendices (pp. 271–97) Ramsay lists the authors cited by Donne in *Biathanatos* (1646), *Pseudo-Martyr* (1610), *Ignatius his Conclave* (1611), *Sermons* (1634–60) and *Essays in Divinity* (1651). TSE was to record the extent of his recoil to Donne's reading in 'Shakespeare and the Stoicism of Seneca' (1927): 'Miss Ramsay, in her learned and exhaustive study of Donne's sources, came to the conclusion that he was a "mediaeval thinker"; I could not find either any "mediaevalism" or any thinking, but only a vast jumble of incoherent erudition on which he drew for purely poetic effects' (*SE* 139/118–9).

4 – TSE later pencilled a note in the bottom margin: 'Though I believe that Hooker's philosophy was much more "mediaeval" than Donne's; but I shall deal with this elsewhere'. He was to clarify the note in 'Donne in our Time': 'That Donne was well read in scholastic philosophy is undoubted; but there is no reason to suppose that he was any better read than Hooker, or that he was so deeply influenced by mediaeval thought as Hooker' (*A Garland for John Donne*, p. 7). While his Lectures were in progress, TSE wrote to Herbert Read on 27 February 1926 about a proposal, later abandoned, to bring out a series of monographs on major critics: 'Renan and Taine are big subjects and I do not know who is competent or would care to tackle either of them. I should rather like to deal with Hooker myself if he were included' (*L2*).

Donne must have read Aquinas with care,[5] he quotes Bonaventura,[6] and Augustine of course influenced him very strongly.[7] But he was equally at home with later theologians, both Roman and Protestant. Walton tells us that when Donne, at the age of nineteen, betook himself seriously to the study of theology, for the purpose of resolving his hesitation between the Roman and the Reformed Church, he plunged into the study of Bellarmine,[8] so thoroughly that a year later he was able to show the Dean of Gloucester – that dean whose name Walton cannot remember[9] – all of Cardinal Bellarmine's works annotated by his own hand. Now this Bellarmine, for whom I cannot speak, but who enjoyed a very great reputation, was no mediaeval philosopher, but a contemporary some thirty years older than Donne, and still living when Donne studied his works. But Donne made himself in time equally familiar [with] the works of all the other contemporaries who distinguished themselves in theology, and of a great many whose distinction is now unintelligible, if it ever existed. He knew the works of Luther, of Calvin, of Melanchthon, of Peter Martyr, among Protestant writers;[10] of

5 – The influence on Donne of the Dominican philosopher and theologian St Thomas Aquinas (c. 1225–74), author of the *Summa Theologica* (printed 1485), is most apparent in the early prose works, but Donne also quotes him frequently in *Sermons*.

6 – Donne quotes and refers to the Franciscan theologian, St Bonaventura (Giovanni di Fidanza, 1221–74), in *Biathanatos* and in *Sermons* (*Ser* VII, 308; IX, 128).

7 – Donne quotes St Augustine (354–430) more than any of the Fathers in his *Sermons* and other prose works, drawing on a wide range of Augustine's thought from *Confessions*, *De Civitate Dei*, *De Doctrina Christiana* and other writings (see *Ser* X, 376–86).

8 – 'Being to undertake this search, he believed the Cardinal Bellarmine to be the best defender of the Roman cause, and therefore betook himself to the examination of his reasons' (*The Complete Angler & the Lives*, p. 191). Father Robert Bellarmine (1542–1621; canonized 1930), an Italian Jesuit and professor of theology at Louvain and Rome, was the author of *Disputations on the Controversies of the Christian Faith* (1586–93). A major figure in Catholic reform, Bellarmine was made Cardinal by Pope Clement VIII in 1598.

9 – Dr Anthony Rudd (1549–1615), a graduate and Fellow of Trinity College, Cambridge, was the Dean of Gloucester from 1584 to 1594.

10 – Donne quotes from and refers to the works of Martin Luther (1483–1546), leader of the German Reformation, in *Pseudo-Martyr*, in *Essays in Divinity* and in *Sermons*; John Calvin (1509–64), the French Protestant theologian and reformer, is frequently quoted and praised in *Sermons* as an expositor and interpreter of Scripture, and in *Biathanatos* (New York: Facsimile Text Society, 1930) Donne links him with Augustine 'for sharpe insight, and conclusive judgement, in exposition of places of Scripture' (p. 98); Philip Melanchthon (1497–1560), the German scholar and reformer whom Donne calls 'a man of more learning and temperance than perchance have met in any one, in our perverse and froward times') (*Ser* VII, 206), is frequently cited in the *Sermons* for his *Loci communes rerum theologicarum* (1521); Peter Martyr Vermigli (1500–62), an Italian convert to Protestantism and one of the most erudite of the Calvinist reformers, published his commentaries and tracts under the title *Locorum communium theologicorum tomi III* (1580–83), which Donne cites in *Biathanatos*, in *Essays in Divinity* and in *Sermons*.

Cajetan, Valdez and Fra Victoria among the more philosophical of Roman commentators:[11] the controversial literature of the Jesuits was at his finger-tips; finally, he was acquainted with many of those writers of the later Renaissance whose orthodoxy, from either a Roman or a Protestant standpoint, is rather doubtful, such as Nicholas of Cusa[12] and the host of students who exploited the Kabbalah, the hermetic writings and other compilations of the same sort. In the Kabbalah Donne was always inter-ested. It was the learned equivalent of the cross-word puzzle. In this connection it is not without significance to refer to Donne's ancestry. His great-grandmother was a sister of Sir Thomas More.[13] More wrote a biography of Pico della Mirandola, which was much admired by Donne.[14] Here is one influence already in the family: that of a man who is often taken as typical of the Renaissance, and who was certainly one of the most successful advertisers of neo-platonism and occultism of his age. More admired Pico, and was also influenced by Colet, who translated that recension of neo-platonic philosophy known as Dionysius the Areopagite.[15]

---

11 – Cajetan (Thommaso de Vio Gaetani, 1469–1534), head of the Dominican order and a leader of the neo-Thomist school of philosophers, worked against Luther in Germany and wrote biblical commentaries to which Donne refers in *Sermons* and *Essays in Divinity*; TSE appears to have confused the Spanish mystic and reformer, Juan de Valdes (Valdesso, c. 1500–41), whom Donne does not cite, with Donne's contemporary, Jacobus Valdesius (Diego de Valdes), whose *De dignitate regum regnorumque Hispaniae* (1602), is cited in *Pseudo-Martyr* and in a letter of 1603 to Robert Cotton (Gosse I, 123–5); Fra Victoria (1480–1546), Dominican leader of the neo-Thomist school, author of *Relectiones xii theologicae* (1557) and *Summa Sacramentorum Ecclesiae* (1561), is cited in *Biathanatos*.

12 – The German humanist Nicolaus de Cusa ('Cusanus', 1401–64), a neo-Platonist and Cardinal of the Roman Church, demanded reforms, attacked the supremacy of the papacy, and advocated the transcendence of reason and scepticism by mystical contemplation and intuitive knowledge. He is referred to as Cusanus in *Pseudo-Martyr* and in *Essays in Divinity*, where Donne expresses further interest in the cabalistic speculations of the Italian humanist Pico della Mirandola ('Picus', 1463–94); his follower, the German humanist Johann Reuchlin (1455–1522), author of *De Arte Cabbalistica* (1517); and F. Zorgi ('Francis George'), author of *De Harmonia Mundi totius cantica* (1525), a medley of neo-Platonic and cabalistic doctrines.

13 – Elizabeth Rastell (1482–1538), sister of Sir Thomas More (1478–1535).

14 – In 1504–5 More translated the Latin text (Bologna, 1496) of Pico della Mirandola's biography, written by Pico's nephew, and published it in 1510 as *The lyfe of Johan Picus Erle of Myrandula with dyvers epystles and other werkes of ye said Johan Picus*. Donne alludes parenthetically to the biography in *Essays in Divinity* (Oxford: Clarendon Press, 1952): '(happier in no one thing in this life, then in the Author which writ it to us)' (p. 13).

15 – John Colet (1467–1519), the English humanist, Oxford reformer, and Dean of St Paul's (1504–19), translated into Latin *Two Treatises on the Hierarchies of Dionysius*, first translated into English by J. H. Lupton (London: Bell Daldy, 1869). The author of the *Celestial Hierarchies* is actually Dionysius the Pseudo-Areopagite, known as Pseudo-Dionysius, a sixth-century Syrian writer who used neo-Platonism to interpret theology. He is often confused with,

The great-grandfather of Donne, More's brother-in-law, was active in theological controversy, which led to his conversion to Protestantism.[16] The grandfather of Donne was John Heywood, the author of the Interludes;[17] his uncle, whom he must have known, was Jasper Heywood, the author of the first translation of three of the plays of Seneca, who subsequently became a Jesuit.[18] In literary criticism heredity is not to be overlooked, and the ancestral dispositions behind Donne seem pretty clear. A remarkable family, and one which certainly kept up with the times: the influences that breathed on Donne's nursery do not seem to have been very mediaeval.

What Donne's reading does show is a pronounced taste, a passion, for theology of the more controversial and legal type – theology, in fact as it was practised in his day; and we think that King James was absolutely right when he forced Donne to take orders.[19] What Miss Ramsay does not show, or attempt to show, is that his reading was any more mediaeval than that of any other theologian of his time. What she makes abundantly clear is the

---

and his works were once attributed to, Dionysius the Areopagite, a first-century Athenian Christian converted by St Paul (Acts, 17:34).

16–John Rastell (1475–1536), a wealthy printer, lawyer, and dramatist, was drawn into religious controversy in 1530 with the publication of his *A Newe Boke of Purgatory*, a defence of Catholic doctrine, but he was answered so persuasively by a young Protestant, John Frith, that he converted to Protestantism.

17–John Heywood (1497–1578), court musician and steward, was the author of epigrams, songs, poems and at least six 'enterludes', or dramatic farces, including *The Play of Love* (1533), *The Play of the Weather* (1533), and *John, Tib, and Sir John* (1533). He married John Rastell's granddaughter, Elizabeth Rastell, and their daughter, Elizabeth Heywood (1540–1632) married John Donne (d. 1576), father of the poet.

18–Jasper Heywood (1535–98) was Lord of Misrule at Lincoln's Inn when he translated Seneca's *Troas* (1559) and Fellow at All Souls College when he translated *Thyestes* (1560) and *Hercules Furens* (1561). He then withdrew to Rome, became a Jesuit in 1562, and returned to England in 1581 as Papal Legate when Donne was eight years old. TSE was soon to introduce the Tudor Translations edition (1927) of Thomas Newton's *Seneca his Tenne Tragedies* (1581), which included Heywood's three translations. In the Introduction, reprinted as 'Seneca in Elizabethan Translation', TSE asserts that 'The first and best of the translators was Jasper Heywood' (*SE* 97/81).

19–James I, convinced that Donne had a divine calling, determined that he should have a church preferment or none at all, but Donne steadfastly resisted the calling for five or six years until 1612, when he announced his intention of taking holy orders. TSE was to write in 'Lancelot Andrewes' (1926) that 'it would be a great mistake to remember only that Donne was called to the priesthood by King James against his will, and that he accepted a benefice because he had no other way of making a living. Donne had a genuine taste both for theology and for religious emotion; but he belonged to that class of persons, of which there are always one or two examples in the modern world, who seek refuge in religion from the tumults of a strong emotional temperament which can find no complete satisfaction elsewhere' (*SE* 352/309).

partiality, as well as the immensity, of his reading. He had presumably been instructed in the Latin classics, if not in the Greek, by his tutors, but he makes little use of them. One allusion makes us believe that he had read the *Divine Comedy*, or had the opportunity of doing so;[20] but he was certainly very little affected by it. That he should have been indifferent to the poetry of his own age in England – in spite of his acquaintence with Jonson, who most nobly praises *him*[21] is more excusable: poets and prose writers too are sometimes very ignorant of the work of their contemporaries – sometimes, I make no doubt, by a self-protective instinct. But this point is of great importance: Donne was a theologian by profession, a poet only by avocation. When we understand this, I think that his mind will appear to us much less mediaeval than at first sight.

For some of the characteristics and tastes which seem to us to specify the Renaissance, do so because we are familiar with the works of poets and humanists rather than professional men. For instance, Donne seems to us less modern than Roger Ascham, who lived in an earlier generation. Ascham was indifferent to the thought of the Middle Ages, and was one of the first to develop the modern, or rehabilitate the ancient, standards of criticism of Latin literature – a stout partisan of Cicero.[22] But our ideas, vague as they

20–Edmund Gosse had pointed out (Gosse I, 41) that Donne made one of 'the very rare Elizabethan references' to Dante in his Fourth Satire: 'At home in wholesome solitarinesse / My precious soule began, the wretchednesse / Of suiters at court to mourne, and a trance / Like his, who dreamt he saw hell, did advance / It selfe on mee, Such men as he saw there, / I saw at court, and worse, and more' (Grierson I, 164).

21–In *Conversations with William Drummond of Hawthornden* (1619), Jonson, mixing praise and criticism, said to Drummond that 'he esteemeth John Done the first poet in the World in some things', but the most noble praise appeared earlier in *Epigrams* (1612?), 'XXIII. – To John Donne':

> Donne, the delight of Phoebus and each Muse,
> Who, to thy one, all other brains refuse;
> Whose every work, of thy most early wit,
> Came forth example, and remains so, yet:
> Longer a knowing than most wits do live,
> And which no' affection praise enough can give!
> To it, thy language, letters, arts, best life,
> Which might with half mankind maintain a strife;
> All which I meant to praise, and yet I would;
> But leave, because I cannot as I should!

22–The English humanist Roger Ascham (1515–68), a classical scholar and Ciceronian Latinist, became Latin Secretary to Queen Mary and wrote *The Scholemaster* (1570), 'a plain and perfite way of teachyng children to understand, write, and speake in Latin tong'. Through a bequest from his aunt in 1919, TSE owned the four-volume edition (many pages unopened) of *The Whole Works of Roger Ascham*, with a Life of the Author by the Revd Dr Giles (London:

are, of the Elizabethan mind, are derived mainly from the work of the humanising poets – Wyatt, Surrey, Spenser, with the derivations from French and Italian literature, Fulke Greville and the Senecals[23] – or from the work of the dramatists. Marlowe, Chapman and Jonson were classical scholars.[24] The dramatists were occupied with a new form; their occupation made them somewhat a special social group; they assimilated those influences which could be most easily turned to account; their communications were sometimes unedifying. Donne, even in his frequentation of "The Mermaid", can hardly more than have touched the fringe of this society.[25]

Nevertheless, it is remarkable that a man of Donne's mental curiosity should appear so little affected by some of the most potent influences of Tudor times. Three great influences of the dramatic age – Montaigne,

---

John Russell Smith, 1864/5). In 'The Sources of Chapman' (1927), TSE was to assert that 'We are apt to overlook the fact . . . that Ascham and [Sir John] Cheke, in England, have hardly any peers until the eighteenth century; and, particularly, that the Renaissance cannot be said to have understood Greek philosophy as well as the "Middle Ages" understood it. The last point has never been sufficiently insisted upon' (*TLS*, 10 February 1927, p. 88).

23 – Fulke Greville, Baron Brooke (1554–1628), was one of the Senecal dramatists that included Samuel Daniel (c. 1562–1619) and Sir William Alexander, Earl of Stirling (c. 1567–1640). TSE was to refer to them as 'those fastidious spirits, the Senecals, who tried to observe his [Seneca's] dramatic laws' (*SE* 99/83).

24 – Marlowe published verse translations of the first book of Lucan's *Pharsalia* and of Ovid's *Amores*, which TSE had praised for the 'strength and energy' of the translation (*SW* 36), and which he was to compare to other translations in 'Turbervile's Ovid' (*TLS*, 17 January 1929, p. 40): 'No one has translated Ovid better than Marlowe, who could not be called either rustic and pedestrian or pedantic'; Chapman translated Hesiod's *Georgics*, and TSE had recommended his translations of Homer's *Iliad* and *Odyssey* to his Extension class in 1918 (*RES* 11, 302). Jonson translated Horace's *Ars Poetica, Vitae Rusticae Laudes* and two odes, an epigram of Martial and a fragment of Petronius Arbiter.

25 – As Thomas Coryate confirmed in a facetious letter from India of 8 November 1615 to 'the High Seneschal' of his distant friends in London, Donne was one of the 'Right Generous, Jovial and Mercurial Sireniachs' who gathered at the Mermaid Tavern in Bread Street from about 1612 to 1615. Gosse stated that the letter 'is the principal, and indeed the only, authority existing for the statement that Donne attended the meetings at the Mermaid' (Gosse II, 86); however, nineteenth-century critics had fostered an improbable tradition, given credence in Gifford's *Works of Jonson* (1875), that Marlowe, Shakespeare, Beaumont, Fletcher, Jonson and other Elizabethan–Jacobean dramatists had been members of this thriving 'Mermaid Club' and that Shakespeare and Jonson had engaged in their 'wit-combats' there. Though this tradition was freely expanded by the popular 'Mermaid Series' of English dramatists (1887–96, 1903–09) and persisted in twentieth-century accounts, more recent studies have shown that the only dramatists whom Donne met at the Mermaid were Jonson, and possibly Fletcher, the attributive author of a verse-letter to Jonson c. 1613: 'What things have we seen, / Donne at the Mermaid!'

Machiavelli and Seneca – hardly reach him.[26] Seneca, it is true, he quotes, but it is the conventional "moral Seneca",[27] the prose Seneca, not the dramatist. But this also is accounted for by the speciality of his interests. It is not only the men and the profession, however, but the time. One reason why Donne appears so much more mediaeval than let us say Ben Jonson is that he belongs to a later age. For the early seventeenth century seems to us in some ways more remote than the sixteenth. It is not so: a step had been omitted, and a step which when taken brought the seventeenth century nearer to our own time. Not until the seventeenth century did many important works of the sixteenth century bear their fruit. But the century which was to [be] more perhaps than any other the century of theological politics was announced by the ascent of a Scottish theologian to the English throne, and this Scottish theologian made Donne his private chaplain.[28]

It is necessary to insist upon the unique character of this century which, just because it experienced the acute crisis of the transition from the old to the new Europe (to the Europe, we might say, of 1914), is the most difficult of all centuries to understand. Every man was a theologian at least to the extent that he lived in a world where questions of theology had become

26 – Increasingly preoccupied with the nature of their influence, TSE was to write in 'Seneca in Elizabethan Translation': 'How the influence of Seneca is related, in the Elizabethan mind, with . . . those of Montaigne and Machiavelli, I do not know; and I think it is a subject still to be investigated' (*SE* 95–6/79). He had been intrigued with the elusive influence of Montaigne since his essay on 'Hamlet' (1919), in which he wants to know 'whether, and when, and after or at the same time as what personal experience, [Shakespeare] read Montaigne, II. xii., *Apologie de Raimond Sebond*' (*SE* 146/126), and he had recently written in 'Shakespeare and Montaigne' (*TLS*, 24 December 1925, p. 895) that *Hamlet, Measure for Measure* and *Troilus and Cressida* 'must, we feel, owe something to Montaigne. But what and how much we shall never know'. In his review (*Athenaeum*, 10 October 1919, p. 1014) of J. Roger Charbonnel's *La pensée italienne au XVI me siècle* and *L'éthique de Giordano Bruno*, TSE had declared that 'almost the only name of permanent and general importance in the books is that of Machiavelli', and he was soon to declare in 'Niccolo Machiavelli' (1927) that the 'impersonality and innocence of Machiavelli is so rare that it may well be the clue to both his perpetual influence over men and the perpetual distortion which he suffers in the minds of men less pure than himself' (*FLA* 52/50).

27 – TSE alludes to the *Inferno*, IV, 141, where in the First Circle of Hell Dante encounters 'Seneca morale' ('Seneca the moralist'; *TC* I, 45). In his *Sermons* Donne frequently quotes phrases from the philosophical treatises of Seneca, often referring to him as the 'Morall man' (*Ser* III, 281) and as 'the Patriarch, and Oracle of Morall men' (*Ser* III, 406), but at one point he is careful to qualify his use of the Roman moralist in a Christian context: 'to think that we can . . . come to be good men out of *Plutarch* or *Seneca*, without a Church and Sacraments, to pursue the truth it selfe by any other way then he [Christ] hath laid open to us, this is pride, and the pride of the Angels' (*Ser* IX, 379).

28 – Shortly after Donne's ordination in January 1615, King James made him his chaplain and commanded him to preach before the court.

[74]

identified with politics, international and domestic. In international affairs, Protestantism had arrived at the point where it was no longer an affair of a few scattered heretical schisms, but had become identified with the rise of powerful nationalisms. England, having been a weak and almost bankrupt nation with a hostile nation on its northern frontier, had become powerful, prosperous and united Britain, in which the Roman element was becoming more and more negligible, and the activity of Protestant schismatics more and more important. Lutheranism had detached Scandinavia and northern Germany from southern Europe, and was making the slow preparations for another world power. Calvinism from Geneva supplied a constant source of dissension in France.²⁹ And it was in this world in which theological interests were becoming more and more identified with political interests, that the campaign of the Jesuits, prepared in the previous century and reinforced by the exaltation of Spanish mysticism, spent the greatest force.

That Jesuitism is a phenomenon typically of the Renaissance is a fact upon which I insist. It represents a very important point of disagreement between Mr. Middleton Murry and myself. Mr. Murry holds the opinion that Jesuitism is identical with Christianity, and that Christianity – Roman Christianity – is identical with classicism; therefore, Jesuitism is identical with classicism, and it is on these grounds that he has advised me to take a spiritual director.³⁰ I cannot help thinking that a little study of the history,

29–In 1536 the French religious reformer Guillaume Farel (1489–1565) persuaded Calvin to devote himself to the work of the Reformation in Geneva, where they instituted the most thoroughgoing reform of church practices. They were both expelled from Geneva in 1538 for the strictness of their measures, but they were welcomed back in 1541 and set about the task of organizing a government based on the subordination of the state to the Church.

30–John Middleton Murry (1889–1957), the former editor of the *Athenaeum* who had sought to make TSE his assistant editor in 1919, was then editor of the *Adelphi*. TSE felt free to allude to their public controversy on the nature of Classicism and Romanticism, begun in the pages of the *Adelphi* and the *Criterion* in 1923, because Murry had preceded him as Clark Lecturer in 1925 (see pp. 6–7). As Murry had not discussed the relation of Jesuitism and Classicism in print, TSE refers to personal conversation on the matter, but in 'The "Classical" Revival', published in the February and March issues of the *Adelphi* after TSE's lectures were in progress, Murry describes him as an 'unregenerate and incomplete romantic' and suggests a chasmic division between his classical principles and his romantic sensibility in *The Waste Land*, 'which expresses a self-torturing and utter nihilism'. 'To order such an experience on classical principles', Murry continues, 'is almost beyond human powers. It might conceivably be done, by an act of violence, by joining the Catholic Church' (*Adelphi*, February 1926, pp. 592–3).

In his review of Murry's *The Life of Jesus* (1927), TSE was to turn the table on Murry, portraying the non-Jesuit romanticist as the unregenerate and incomplete classicist: 'Mr. Murry has great gifts; gifts which would have led him, as a member of the Society of Jesus, to eminence, power and peace of mind . . . Mr. Murry is, doctrinally, inclined to Unitarianism,

constitution and practices of the Society of Jesus would show him that it has nothing to do with classicism, but is on the contrary, what I, if not he, would call Romantic, and excessively Romantic. The fact that the Society of Jesus is of Spanish origin is an indication that it is outside of the Graeco-Roman classical tradition. There is plenty of evidence that its founder St. Ignatius was a romantic, a reader of romances, an admirer of Amadis of Gaul, a sort of Don Quixote.[31] There is some evidence, too, that he drew his inspiration, and the constitution of his order, which differs radically from every other Christian order, not from Christian, but from Mohammedan examples. Its principles are non-Aristotelian, and are surprisingly like those of certain Moslem orders flourishing in Spain in Ignatius' time. I refer to an interesting and rare work, Herrmann Müller: *Les Origines de la société de Jésus.*[32] That the Spanish mystics of the sixteenth century were also romantics, that they and St. Ignatius have a certain affinity with Martin Luther and Rousseau, I hope to indicate at various points.

Now the very intensity of the theological battle in this time was itself a force of destruction to religion itself. This is not immediately evident, nor its bearing upon our subject. But it is my purpose to show that Donne was, as a theologian, very much of his time, and that this time was anything but mediaeval: and second, to lay bare the general aspect of the *catabolic* tendency, the tendency toward dissolution, which I find in Donne's poetry. Let us therefore consider the spirit which characterises, which had to characterise, the theological controversies of the time, contrasted with those of the twelfth and thirteenth centuries. Our prejudice about mediaeval philosophy, I think, is this: we conceive of the philosophers as merely playing a game which had a great many strict rules. They were not allowed to question the truth of innumerable dogmas: their thought was crushed by

---

and, emotionally, inclined to Jesuit Catholicism of the seventeenth century' (*Criterion*, May 1927, pp. 258–9).

31–Ignatius of Loyola (1491–1556; canonized 1622), Spanish founder of the Society of Jesus in 1540 and author of *Spiritual Exercises* (1548), confirms in his autobiography, dictated to Father Louis Gonzalez in 1555, that in his worldly youth and early martial manhood he read chivalric romances exclusively, particularly *Amadis de Gaula*, a fourteenth-century romance first published in 1508. Depicting the knightly exploits of Amadis, who is motivated by courtly love to combat the evils of his time, the work was immensely popular in France and Spain prior to the appearance of Miguel de Cervantes' *Don Quixote* (1605–15).

32–In *Les Origines de la Compagnie de Jésus: Ignace et Lainez* (Paris: Librarie Fischbacher, 1898), Herrmann Müller explores in detail the similarities of the six steps of a Jesuit novitiate's spiritual progress to specific Mohammedan practices. 'Ces latitudes', he writes, 'qui n'existent dans aucun autre ordre monastique, se retrouvent au contraire dans la pratique musulmane' (p. 101).

authority; and accordingly they spent their time in dividing hairs and determining the specific gravity of angels – much as a man, having to pass an hour in a country railway station without anything to read, might cast up the figures on the timetable. The belief in the triviality of their occupations, and in the restrictions to their liberty of thought, should be dissipated even by a cursory reading of a little primer, *La Philosophie au moyen âge*, by M. Etienne Gilson, who has done so much to make possible our understanding of this philosophy. I shall not attempt a précis of this book;[33] I shall merely call attention to two positive advantages enjoyed by this philosophy. The philosophers, unlike modern philosophers, held certain beliefs in common; it was therefore possible for them to some extent to understand each other – a feat impossible to our contemporaries. Second, the Church could and did afford them very great liberty. For the Church was one; it was not occupied with polemic or defence against other churches. The systems of the philosophers were hardly of a nature to inflame whole races to heresy. For they were philosophical systems; their inventors were concerned with the discovery of truth, of such truth as was accessible to them; they were men interested in ideas for their own sake. And [in] whatever degree of truth or error this philosophy issued, I think there is no question that the only hope of finding truth is to seek for it regardless of practical consequences.

Compare this situation of the thirteenth-century philosopher and theologian, in the freedom of their universities, unhampered, unhurried, unconcerned with wars and dynasties, with that of the Roman Church and of the Reformed Churches at the time of the Counter-Reformation. It is illustrated by the Society of Jesus. Nothing could be more different from the Orders of the Middle Ages. I speak with neither approval, disrespect nor bias, but purely as a detached critic. The Society of Jesus was formed for the purpose of combating heresy. It was military, not meditative or charitable, in its primary purpose. And admirably did it do its work. But though it produced accomplished men of letters, erudite and subtle commentators,

---

33 – TSE was to provide a précis of the book later in the year in 'Medieval Philosophy', his review (*TLS*, 16 December 1926, p. 929) of the second volume of Maurice de Wulf's *History of Medieval Philosophy*, which he discusses in relation to the critical works of Professor Gilson (1884–1978). He writes that de Wulf's book 'is a history, not an "introduction." The introduction to medieval philosophy already exists: it is Etienne Gilson's "La Philosophie au Moyen Âge," two tiny volumes in a popular collection of Payot [1922]'. Gilson's 'more brilliant' work, TSE explains, 'consists in detailed exposition of the ideas of the principal philosophers of the thirteen centuries' and challenges 'the assumption that modern philosophy begins with a complete break from the Middle Ages, with a wholly new examination of the world'.

though it had perhaps on the whole better brains, and far better organisation than did Protestantism, and though it counted among its numbers pious and devoted men, it produced no great philosopher, no advance in pure thought. Neither, for that matter, did the Protestant Churches. They were all too absorbed in controversy to have time for speculation. Politics cannot wait. It is in such an age that the legal mind, rather than the theoretical mind, flourishes in theology; such a mind, in fact, as that of Donne.

Theology which is bent on political controversy, theology at bay, extinguishes the light of pure ideas, the Greek disinterestednesss of mind, which the Middle Ages had revived; but it does not extinguish religious sentiment. On the contrary, the religious fervour of the sixteenth and seventeenth centuries burns with a fierce heat which is in itself alarming, as being a rapid combustion in acceleration of nature. And human curiosity, diverted in one direction, turns to another. Religion and theology, abandoning the pursuit of metaphysical truth, develop in the seventeenth century in the direction of psychology; an alteration which Signor Praz has well noted.[34]

We are now able to form a larger generalisation than that which I gave you concerning the position [of] theological philosophy then and in the thirteenth century. Men had lived for centuries under a church which was the incorporated *sensus communis* of Europe. When Europe was broken up by the several great national religions, Rome ceased to be the detached and Olympian arbiter of ideas, and became merely one combatant on the field. It no longer controlled the thought of northern Europe, it had no longer the same control over its own. It is possible – I hazard the suggestion without sufficient knowledge – that the experiences of St. Theresa and her fellow mystics in Spain would in an earlier and less dangerous period have been subjected to closer scrutiny, and been less quickly accepted by the Church. The schismatic Churches, of course, were in no better position: they also were forced to accept ideas for their immediate polemic value. But expediency was not the only new criterion; a more powerful one still was to arise, and make itself felt in philosophy outside of the Church and in literature: the success of ideas was to come to depend more and more upon the suffrage of a larger and larger semi-literate public. Success meant what pleased or

---

34—In his review of Praz's book (see p. 58, n. 35) TSE had pointed out Praz's extraordinary awareness 'of the world of difference between the religion of the seventeenth century and that of the thirteenth. It is the difference between psychology and metaphysics. Here Signor Praz is able to supply what has been a conspicuous defect of English criticism of Donne: a comparison between Donne and the metaphysical poets of the age of Dante. This is a point upon which he touches lightly, and which we wish he might examine in greater detail'.

impressed the greatest number of persons at any moment. We are already in full democracy.

I must plead pardon for these tedious generalities, which will not I hope appear so tedious when we come to make particular application of them. I now return to the point which I had introduced before this digression: the diversion of human inquiry from ontology to psychology. Not only a diversion of inquiry; it is rather as if, at certain times, the constitution of the human mind altered to adapt itself to the reception of new categories of truth, and new elements of thought. Often it has been remarked, the state of mind appropriate to a particular science comes into existence before the science itself. Diderot in this sense "anticipated" Darwin: Dostoevski, it is often said, though the evidence is less satisfactory, anticipated Freud; the fancies of Leonardo, the labours of the alchemists, were vague anticipations.[35] But in Donne we are concerned with a connection closer and less interrupted; though I cannot tell you in detail how it came about. But

35 – The French encyclopedist and philosopher Denis Diderot (1713–84) wrote *Pensées sur l'interprétation de la nature* (1753), an influential treatise on scientific method; the naturalist Charles Darwin (1809–82) published his revolutionary theories of evolution and natural selection in *On the Origin of Species* (1859). In 'Le roman anglais contemporain' (*Nouvelle Revue Française*, May 1927, pp. 670–71), TSE was to comment directly upon the literary gap between Dostoevsky and Freud: 'Il appartiendrait à un esprit mieux entraîné et plus spécialisé que le mien de dégager l'influence de la psycho-analyse sur la littérature et la vie depuis environ trente ans ... Il faudrait la distinguer de l'influence de Dostoïevsky; ou plutôt il faudrait reconstruire hypothétiquement ce que l'influence de Dostoïevsky aurait pu être si l'un des aspects de son oeuvre n'avait été extraordinairement accusé par la coïncidence de sa vogue en Europe occidentale avec l'ascension de Freud. Tout ce que je désire affirmer, c'est que presque tous les romans contemporains que je connais sont, soit directement inspirés par une étude de psycho-analyse, soit influencés par l'atmosphère qu'a créé la psycho-analyse, soit animés par le désir d'échapper à la psycho-analyse; et que, dans chaque cas, le résultat est une perte de sérieux et de profondeur, et la perte en tout cas de cette profondeur, que James a toujours cherchée, s'il ne l'a pas toujours atteinte' (pp. 670–71).

Among the scientific descriptions in Leonardo's notebooks, Freud discovered Leonardo's infantile vulture fantasy, which became the basis for his psychoanalytic study of Leonardo's work in *Leonardo da Vinci: A Psychosexual Study of an Infantile Reminiscence* (1910; Eng. trans. A. A. Brill; New York: Moffat, Yard, 1916): 'it seems as if the key to all his attainments and failures was hidden in the childhood phantasy of the vulture' (p. 129). In 'A Romantic Patrician' TSE had compared Leonardo to the soldier-statesman-critic George Wyndham as a 'many-sided' man: 'George Wyndham was not a man on the scale of Leonardo, and his writings give a very different effect from Leonardo's notebooks. Leonardo turned to art or science, and each was what it was and not another thing. But Leonardo was Leonardo: he had no father to speak of, he was hardly a citizen, and he had no stake in the community. He lived in no fairyland, but his mind went out and became a part of things' (*Athenaeum*, 2 May 1919, p. 266).

certainly Donne is in a sense a psychologist. You find it in his verse compared to earlier verse, in his sermons compared to earlier sermons. I am not here concerned with how the change came about, step by step; that would be a very interesting but long and exact study. But dissolution so frequently begins within, that I think that the Jesuits had a great deal to do with it: their fine distinctions and discussions of conduct and casuistry tend in the direction of a certain self-consciousness which had not been conspicuous in the world before. I am here more concerned with defining clearly the difference in point of view, a true Copernican revolution which occurred centuries before Kant was born,[36] a difference which marks the real abyss between the classic scholastic philosophy and all philosophy since. It was impressed upon the world by Descartes, like his own figure, and by his own figure, when he compared the impression of "ideas" on the mind to the impression of the seal on the wax; and when he clearly stated that what we know is not the world of objects, but our own ideas of these objects.[37] The revolution was immense. Instead of ideas as meanings, as references to an outside world, you have suddenly a new world coming into existence, inside your own mind and therefore by the usual implication inside your own head. Mankind suddenly retires inside its several skulls, until you hear Nietzsche – pretty well tormented in *his* cranial lodging –

36—TSE alludes to Kant's description of his approach to the intuition of objects as being analogous to a Copernican revolution, in the Preface to the second edition of *Critique of Pure Reason* (1787). At Harvard in 1912–13 TSE took Philosophy 15, The Kantian Philosophy, for which he wrote three reports on Kant (1724–1804) – 'on the Kantian Categories', 'on the Relation of Kant's Criticism to Agnosticism', and 'on the Ethics of Kant's Critique of Practical Reason' (King's). In his Introduction to Charlotte Eliot's *Savonarola* (1926), TSE wrote that 'Even Kant, devoting a lifetime to the pursuit of categories, fixed only those which he believed, rightly or wrongly, to be permanent, and overlooked or neglected the fact that these are only the more stable of a vast system of categories in perpetual change' (p. viii).

37—Descartes employs the extended trope of fresh wax to explore the relation of mind and body or object in 'Meditation II' ('Of the Nature of the Human Mind') in his *Meditations Concerning Primary Existence* (1641). Though he does not there employ the image of the seal that TSE associates with the wax, in 'Meditation III' ('Of God: that He exists') he develops the idea that God places ideas in the mind like the workman's mark, or seal: 'And one certainly ought not to find it strange that God, in creating me, placed this idea within me to be like the mark of the workman imprinted on his work; and it is likewise not essential that the mark shall be something different from the work itself' (*The Philosophical Works of Descartes*, I, trans. Elizabeth S. Haldane and G. R. T. Ross [Cambridge: Cambridge Univ. Press, 1967], p. 170). Descartes' belief that we know not objects but our ideas of those objects is explicitly argued in 'Meditation VI', quoted below (see n. 41). TSE had taken a course on the philosophy of Descartes, Spinoza and Leibniz at Harvard in the spring of 1912.

declaring that "nothing is inside, nothing is outside".[38] And the most brilliant of contemporary critics of criticism, Mr. I. A. Richards, declaring (after Kant and Descartes) that love is a spontaneous emotion bearing no relation to the object of affection.[39]

Descartes:[40] 6th. Meditation (Garnier p. 128):[41]

Je conçois donc [for dis-je], aisément que l'imagination se peut faire de cette sorte, s'il est vrai qu'il y ait des corps; et parce que je ne puis rencontrer aucune autre voie pour expliquer comment elle se fait, je conjecture de là probablement qu'il y en a: mais ce n'est que probablement; et quoique j'examine soigneusement toutes choses, je ne trouve pas néanmoins que, de cette idée distincte de la nature corporelle que j'ai en mon imagination, je puisse tirer aucun argument qui conclue avec nécessité l'existence de quelque corps.

This extraordinary crude and stupid piece of reasoning is the sort of thing which gave rise to the whole of the pseudo-science of epistemology which has haunted the nightmares of the last three hundred years.

38 – TSE had encountered Nietzsche's statement ('Nichts ist aussen, nichts ist innen, denn was aussen ist, ist innen') in Hermann Hesse's Blick ins Chaos (1920), a copy of which he bought and inscribed (King's) in Switzerland in 1921, and from which he quoted in the Notes to The Waste Land (CPP 79/54). Hesse employed the quotation as the motto for the first essay in the volume, 'Die Brüder Karamasoff oder der Untergang Europas' ('The Brothers Karamazov, or the Decline of Europe'), which TSE told Hesse he would have published in translation in the Criterion had it been shorter (L1 510).

39 – TSE refers to a recent article by his friend and intellectual antagonist, the critic and psychologist Ivor Armstrong Richards (1893–1979), then lecturer in English and Moral Sciences at Cambridge and a member of the audience for the Clark Lectures. In 'A Background for Contemporary Poetry' (Criterion, July 1925, p. 521), Richards had praised TSE for having effected 'a complete severance between his poetry and all beliefs' in The Waste Land, a poem which to Richards exhibits a disease of the modern sensibility. The blame for this disease, he argues, 'lies with man's habit of expecting the objects of his emotions to be also their justification. We expect the things we love or hate to be in themselves love-worthy or hate-worthy . . . The justification, or the reverse, of any attitude lies, not in the object, but in itself, in its serviceableness to the whole personality. Upon its place in the whole system of attitudes, which is the personality, all its worth depends'.

40 – TSE evidently made an ad lib transition to the following quotation from Descartes to illustrate his statements above. In 'Donne in our Time' (1931), he prefaced the same quotation: 'The kind of religious faith expressed in Donne's religious writings is wholly consistent with the employment in his poetry of the many scraps of various philosophies which appear there. His attitude towards philosophic notions in his poetry may be put by saying that he was more interested in ideas themselves as objects than in the truth of ideas. In an odd way, he almost anticipates the philosopher of the coming age, Descartes, as in his sixth Meditation' (A Garland for John Donne, ed. Theodore Spencer [Cambridge: Harvard Univ. Press, 1931], p. 11).

41 – TSE quotes from Oeuvres choisies de Descartes (see p. 65, n. 47), p. 128. The quotation is from the third paragraph of 'Meditation VI' ('Of the Existence of Material Things, and of the

I. A. Richards: *The Principles of Literary Criticism*. I have been unable to find again the passage alluded to.[42] But I will quote another specimen from this book: page 264: (in describing a view which Mr. Richards opposes in this place and which is similar to the Dantesque view):

Love not grounded upon knowledge would be described as worthless. We ought not to admire what is not beautiful and if our mistress be not really beautiful when impartially considered we ought, so the doctrine runs, to admire her, if at all, for other reasons. The chief points of interest about such views are the confusions which make them plausible. Beauty as an external [*for* internal] quality of things is usually involved, as well as Good the unanalysable Idea. Both are special twists given to some of our impulses[43] by habits deriving ultimately from desires. They linger in our minds because to think of a thing as Good or Beautiful gives more *immediate* emotional satisfaction than to *refer* to it as satisfying our impulses in one special fashion or another.

Far from me to throw myself into a battle of psychology for which I am not trained. I would only ask whether this is really a "confusion" on the part of the Italians, as Mr. Richards believes, or merely a different and alien point of view. I am not concerned which is *right*. I am only concerned to know whether the difference here between Guido Cavalcanti and Mr. Richards is not fundamentally a difference between what the late T. E. Hulme – the most *fertile* mind of my generation, and one of the glories of this University – would call the *Categories* of the thirteenth century and the Categories of the nineteenth century – a different mode of thought.[44] The difference

---

real distinction between the Soul and Body of Man'): 'I easily understand, I say, that the imagination could be thus constituted if it is true that body exists; and because I can discover no other convenient mode of explaining it, I conjecture with probability that body does exist; but this is only with probability, and although I examine all things with care, I nevertheless do not find that from this distinct idea of corporeal nature, which I have in my imagination, I can derive any argument from which there will necessarily be deduced the existence of the body' (*The Philosophical Works of Descartes*, I, pp. 186–7).

42 – TSE was under the mistaken impression that Richards' assertion in 'A Background for Contemporary Poetry' (see n. 39 above) was to be found in *Principles of Literary Criticism* (London: Kegan, Paul, Trubner, 1924). The passage below, as TSE indicates, is quoted from p. 264.

43 – TSE later pencilled a line from 'impulses' to the bottom margin for a holograph notation: 'Impulses are special twists given to our potentialities by Beauty, Ugliness etc.'

44 – TSE plays with the irony of the fact that Thomas Ernest Hulme (1883–1917), the Imagist poet and philosophical critic killed in the War, had been sent down from St John's College, Cambridge, in 1904 for indulging in a brawl (though he had been readmitted briefly in 1912 upon the recommendation of Henri Bergson). TSE had discussed Hulme's poetry and prose in

between what I call *ontologism* and *psychologism* – which is perhaps a different [form] of the old difference between realism and nominalism.

Now Donne is not consciously of this way of thinking. In the exact sense Donne had no philosophy at all, but exactly by having no philosophy he prepared himself within for the new state of mind. Miss Ramsay judges by what he read and the terms (scholastic) which he uses, and concludes that his mind was mediaeval. I judge him (apart from the large proportion of his reading which is not mediaeval at all) by the way in which he read, and judge him to be exactly of his own moment of time. What is clear is that Donne read a great deal without order or valuation, and that he thought in a spasmodic and fragmentary way when he thought at all. Tradition has really little weight with him; he wishes to read everything, and is willing to take something from everywhere, and is not too nice about coherence. A notion of Maimonides or Averroes[45] could exist in the mind of Donne along

---

his essays, reviews and Extension lectures from 1916 to 1919, and when Hulme's first collection of prose appeared posthumously as *Speculations* (London: Kegan Paul, 1924) TSE described him as the harbinger of a new classicism, 'as the forerunner of a new attitude of mind, which should be the twentieth-century mind, if the twentieth century is to have a mind of its own. Hulme is classical, reactionary, and revolutionary; he is the antipodes of the eclectic, tolerant, and democratic mind of the end of the last century' (*Criterion*, April 1924, p. 231). In *Speculations* Hulme distinguishes two abstract categories which respectively form the basis of Classicism and Romanticism: 'the Religious attitude', which holds a belief in absolute values and in the dogma of Original Sin, and 'the Humanist attitude', which holds the belief 'that life is the source and measure of all values, and that man is fundamentally good' (p. 47). TSE was to quote Hulme on these categories at the conclusion of 'Second Thoughts about Humanism' (1929): ' "I hold the religious conception of ultimate values to be right, the humanist wrong. From the nature of things, these categories are not inevitable, like the categories of time and space, but are *equally objective* . . . What is important, is what nobody seems to realize – the dogmas like that of Original Sin, which are the closest expression of the categories of the religious attitude. That man is in no sense perfect, but a wretched creature, who can yet apprehend perfection. It is not, then, that I put up with the dogma for the sake of the sentiment, but that I may possibly swallow the sentiment for the sake of the dogma" ' (*SE* 490–91/438).
45 – The Jewish rabbi and Hebrew scholar Maimonides (1135–1204) was influential in his attempt to combine the philosophy of Aristotle with the biblical texts of Hebrew theology. TSE evidently alludes to one of Donne's several citations in the *Sermons*: 'There is *defatigatio in intellectualibus*, says the saddest and soundest of the Hebrew Rabbins, the soule may be tired, as well as the body, and the understanding dazeled, as well as the eye' (IX, 5, 117–20). Donne's direct allusion to the Muslim philosopher Averroes (1126–98), known for his commentaries on Aristotle and Plato's *Republic*, appears in his letter of 1612 to Sir Henry Goodyer: 'It is not perfectly true which a very subtle, yet very deep wit, Averroes, says, that all mankind hath but one soul, which informs and rules us all, as one intelligence doth the firmament and all the stars in it; as though a particular body were too little an organ for a soul to play upon' (Gosse II, 8). TSE had himself considered the influence of Maimonides and Averroes on Leibniz in 'The Development of Leibniz's Monadism' (*The Monist*, October 1916).

[83]

with the same notion as assimilated by Aquinas. And the notions of the pseudo-Dionysius[46] are revived sometimes *tel quel*, as they are in the thought of the fifteenth-century Eckhardt.[47] The distinction may be made a very fine one. Miss Ramsay might say that Donne's mind is of the Middle Ages, though his feelings are of the Renaissance. I should say that where the feelings are, there will the mind be also; and that you cannot think with Aquinas unless you can feel with him. It is in the direction of his attention and interest, the direction in which Donne made his real observations, that I seek for his mind; in the examination of his own sensations and ideas and emotions.

I shall have occasion later, in connection with Crashaw, to refer to the Spanish mystics. And in my lecture of next week I shall call your attention to a mysticism of the twelfth century which is different from that of the Spaniards and different from that of the Germans, and which is in the direct classical, Aristotelian tradition, and which is the mysticism of Dante. There are several mysticisms. But it may be as well to make clear that to me the Spanish mystics of the sixteenth century – St. Theresa, St. John of the Cross, Luis of Granada, St. Philip Neri (to whom the church at Arundel is dedicated)[48] and St. Ignatius, are as much psychologists as Descartes, and Donne, and as much romanticists as Rousseau.

46 – In his *Sermons* Donne frequently quotes from and summons the authority of Pseudo-Dionysius (see n. 15 above), whom he variously names *Areopagitica, Dionyse, Denys* and *Dyonisius*, as when he states that the testament of *Areopagita*, 'who expresses it with equall elegancy and vehemency', might be added to testimonies on the invisibility of the Trinity: '*Dei nec sententia est, nec ratio, nec opinio, nec sensus, nec phantasia*: If we bring the very Nature and Essence of God into question, we can give no judgment upon it, (*non sententia*) we can make no probable discourse of it, (*non ratio*) we can frame no likely opinion, or conjecture in it, (*non opinio*) we cannot prepare our selves with any thing which hath fallen under our senses, (*non sensus*) nor with any thing which we can bring studiously, or which can fall casually into our fancy, or imagination, (*non phantasia*.)' (*Ser* VII, 343).
47 – The German Dominican philosopher and mystic Johannes Eckhardt ('Meister Eckhart', c. 1260–c. 1328) frequently cites Pseudo-Dionysius in his sermons as one of his favourite authorities.
48 – TSE was to write of the Spanish mystics in 'Thinking in Verse' (see p. 23, n. 36): 'The greatest were St. Theresa, and St. John of the Cross, both Carmelites. I think that St. John was the greater, or rather that his writings are very much more important than St. Theresa's; but probably Theresa had the greater influence' (p. 443). Luis de Granada (1504–88) was best known as a devotional writer and author of numerous mystical treatises, but St Philip Neri (1515–95), founder of the Congregation of the Oratorians in Rome in 1575, was an Italian priest and mystic. There is a pencilled note in the top margin in Herbert Read's hand, with a line drawn to St Philip Neri: 'also Brompton Oratory'. The Oratory of St Philip Neri was established in England in 1848 by John Henry Newman, in Birmingham; in 1849 F. W. Faber founded the Oratory in London, in King William Street, before it moved to Brompton in 1854.

And certainly there was here an immense unexplored field, which the following centuries were to exploit, but which Donne was one of the first to devote himself to. From one point of view, to turn the attention to the mind in this way is to create, for the objects alter by being observed. To contemplate an idea, because it is my idea, to observe its emotional infusion, to play with it, instead of using it as a plain and simple meaning, brings often curious and beautiful things to light, though it lends itself, this petting and teasing of one's mental offspring, to extremities of torturing of language, [as] we shall see. But it is not, as with the Elizabethans at their worst excesses (*mobled queen*),[49] the vocabulary that is the object of torment – it is the idea itself. Let us take the first poem in Professor Grierson's collection.

> I wonder by my troth, what thou, and I
> Did, till we loved? were we not wean'd till then?
> But sucked on country pleasures, childishly?
> Or snorted we in the seven sleepers' den?
> T'was so: But this, all pleasures fancies be.
> If ever any beauty I did see,
> Which I desir'd, and got, t'was but a dream of thee.[50]

This is an example, in Donne's lighter, though still not frivolous mood, of what I have called teasing the idea. Observe that the choice and arrangement of *words* is simple and chaste and extremely felicitous. There is a startling directness (as often at the beginning of Donne's poems) about the idea, which must have occurred to many lovers, of the abrupt break and alteration of life which such a crisis can make. These *trouvailles* in themselves are enough to set Donne apart from some of his imitators: Cowley never found anything so good. The point is, however, that Donne, instead of pursuing the meaning of the idea, letting it flow into the usual

---

The Church of St Philip Neri, Arundel, was commissioned by the Duke of Norfolk in 1868. Built at the top of Parson's Hill in late French Gothic style, it was dedicated to St Philip Neri and opened in July 1873. Praz was to ask doubtfully in his letter of 31 January 1927: 'Are you right in including S. Philip Neri among the Spanish mystics?' (*L2*). The erroneous association may have come from TSE's reading of Donne's *Ignatius His Conclave*, in which Ignatius treats his old friend Neri with contempt; Neri is the final adversary Ignatius must confront in a satire in which Donne identifies the Jesuits generally with Spanish policy.

49 – *Hamlet*, II.ii.524–7, the play within the play (mobled: muffled):

> *First Player* 'But who, oh, who had seen the mobled Queen –'
> *Hamlet* 'The mobled Queen'?
> *Polonius* That's good, 'mobled Queen' is good.

50 – 'The Good-morrow', lines 1–7 (*MLPSC* 1); partly modernized.

sequence of thought, *arrests* it, in order to extract every possible ounce of the emotion suspended in it. To such ideas of Donne's, therefore, there is a certain opacity of feeling; they are not simple significances and directions. In thus arresting the idea Donne often succeeds in bringing to light curious aspects and connections which would not otherwise be visible; he infuses, as it were, the dose of bismuth which makes the position of the intestine apparent on the X-ray screen.

Perhaps a parallel will make this point clearer; from another poet of the same century. When Phaedra recalls, at the sight of Hippolytus, the memory of his father in the time when she first knew him, she bursts into the famous passage

> Que faisiez-vous alors? Pourquoi, sans Hippolyte
> Des héros de la Grèce assembla-t-il l'élite? etc.[51]

Here is a similar thought used in a similar way: Donne's question, What was our life before we loved? and the question of Racine's heroine, Why were you not there, why were you not of proper age, at my proper time for loving you? They are, if you like, rhetorical questions: for Donne does not stay to know the answer; and to Phaedra's question there was indeed no answer. But each question has an intense emotional value; Phaedra's indeed has the very highest tragic value, it is charged with all the content of impossibility and frustration. The violence of the passion, the torrent of the alexandrines are such that we do not at first realise that Phaedra is being right metaphysical; that she is pursuing the fancy in order to squeeze every drop of agony for herself out of it. But Racine was indeed a psychologist, [a] far

---

51–In Racine's *Phèdre* (1677), Phaedra, passionately in love with Hippolytus, suddenly questions him after describing her previous love for her husband, King Theseus, father of Hippolytus by Antiope, Queen of the Amazons. TSE's 'etc.' at the end of the line indicates that he may also have quoted Phaedra's second question (ii.v.645–8), which he then paraphrases in the text:

> Que faisiez-vous alors? Pourquoi, sans Hippolyte,
> Des héros de la Grèce assembla-t-il l'élite?
> Pourquoi, trop jeune encor, ne pûtes-vous alors
> Entrer dans le vaisseau qui le mit sur nos bords?

> What were you doing then? Why without you
> Did he assemble all the flowers of Greece?
> Why could you not, too young, alas, have fared
> Forth with the ship that brought him to our shores?
> (Trans. John Cairncross, *Masterpieces of the Drama*, p. 352)

greater one than Donne; he is almost unique in his ability to give such thoughts the maximum of *both* poetic and dramatic value. For in fact they do not easily lend themselves to dramatic action.[52] It is very different from the operation of Sophocles when he crushed his Oedipus beneath the frightful repetition and variation of every aspect of his crime, in that great speech of his;[53] for that is a straightforward development of every implication of the direct meaning.

It is not so much in the thought, as in the development of the thought, that Donne's metaphysical peculiarity resides. Let us take similar ideas of violent contrast that are developed differently. There is a passage in the *Odyssey* which has been used by someone, I think Matthew Arnold,[54] as an illustration of sublimity; I should like to use it for another purpose. It is when Ulysses, on his visit to Hell, meets the shade of Elpenor, who, you remember, had fallen overboard and been drowned some time before.[55] The meeting is totally a surprise.

52 – In 'Marivaux' (1919) TSE had asserted that 'In the French theatre Racine is the first and the greatest anatomist of the heart . . . in Phèdre the analysis of love brings us close to Marivaux. Such analysis, as in the 'Que faisiez-vous alors?' of Phèdre . . . is marginal comedy' (*Arts and Letters*, Spring 1919, p. 84).

53 – TSE alludes to Oedipus's self-punishment speech after having plucked out his eyes in guilt over parricide and incest in *King Oedipus* (lines 1369–1415). The speech, spoken to the Leader of the Chorus, concludes:

> Hide me immediately away from men!
> Kill me outright, or fling me far to sea,
> Where never ye may look upon me more.
> Come, lend your hand unto my misery!
> Comply, and fear not, for my load of woe
> Is incommunicable to all but me.

[From the World's Classics edition of *Sophocles: The Seven Plays in English Verse* (1906), translated by Lewis Campbell (p. 125), two of whose editions of Sophocles were in TSE's library].

54 – The passage from the end of Book XI of the *Odyssey* does not appear in Arnold's works as TSE conjectures, and the apparently confused allusion (see following note) is untraced as an example of the sublime in another author.

55 – The phrase 'overboard and been drowned' has been underlined in pencil, with a right-margin note in Herbert Read's hand, 'Wrong death!' At the end of Book X, the drunken Elpenor toppled to his death from the roof of Circe's palace, whereupon his soul went down to Hades. Odysseus then encounters the shade of Elpenor in Book XI, The Book of the Dead (lines 52–80). TSE seems to confuse Elpenor with Palinurus, who in the *Aeneid* is lulled to sleep and pushed overboard by Phorbas. Palinurus woke and swam for four days, only to be murdered by natives when he reached shore, and Aeneas met his shade when he visited the Underworld. TSE was to write to Paul Elmer More (Princeton) on 2 June 1930: 'I have always *enjoyed* Virgil far more than Homer. Is not that shocking? Indeed, I feel very much more at ease in the company of Latin writers than of Greek – in verse'.

Elpenor! hast thou come faster on foot than we in our black ships?[56]

This question, like those of Donne and Phaedra, is a sort of *Annahme*; it implies something entertained but not precisely believed.[57] Donne, or a supersubtle heroine of one of Racine's tragedies, would have rung every change on this notion. Not so Homer; he deals with it literally, and passes on, for he is interested in the outside world, not in the world of floating ideas.[58] Another parallel, not quite so close, is found in the *Purgatorio*. The shade of Statius suddenly realises that the personage with whom he had been speaking is no less than Virgil; and the one transported falls at the feet of the other. Virgil withdraws from the embrace and says only

> Frate –
> Non far: chè tu sei ombra ed ombra vedi.

The other accepts the admonition with the words

> la quantite
> Puote veder dell'amor che a te mi scalda,
> Quando dismento nostra vanitate
> Trattando l'ombre come cosa salda.[59]

56–TSE quotes from no published translation, evidently citing the line from memory or translating from the Greek text of his signed but unmarked copy (King's) of *The Odyssey of Homer*, ed. John B. Owen (New York: American Book Company, 1859).

57–TSE takes the meaning of this term, the assumption or entertainment of ideas, from Alexis Meinong's study in object-theory, *Uber Annahmen* (1900, 1910), which he employed in his dissertation (misremembered in his Harvard class report of 1935 as 'Meinong's Gegen-standstheorie considered in Relation to Bradley's Theory of Knowledge'): 'There is a simple object which is real in the same way in which an hallucination is real, but this object is only part of the object of the assumption. The chief advantage which this theory pretends to offer over Meinong's is its greater consistency with Bradley's views on floating ideas. The *Annahme*, as I understand it, is such a floating idea. If reality is all of a piece, as the epistemologist believes, then the imaginary must be cut off and floating "like Mahomet's coffin" between earth and sky' (*KEPB* 126). He had also used the term in his Introduction to Paul Valéry's *Le Serpent* (London: R. Cobden-Sanderson, 1924): 'A poet who is also a metaphysician, and unites the two activities, is conceivable as an unicorn or a wyvern is conceivable: he is possible like some of Meinong's *Annahmen*; but such a poet would be a monster' (p. 13).

58–In his dissertation TSE refers frequently to Bradley's essay, 'Floating Ideas and the Imaginary' (1906), in which Bradley develops his general doctrine of the relation of the real and the ideal (see previous note).

59–In the *Purgatorio* (XXI, 131–2) Virgil says to the shade of the Roman poet Statius (c. AD 50–96), author of the *Silvae*, the *Thebaid* and the *Achilleid*, as Statius stoops to embrace his feet:

> 'Frate,
> non far, chè tu se' ombra, ed ombra vedi.'

The idea, you observe, received rather more development than Homer's; but only in the direction of the external reality which it intends; it is not a fancy, and it is not detached from the external facts.

My intention in this lecture was to present adequate reasons for treating Donne as wholly a man of his own time, and in doing so to define generally his time in its points of contrast with the Middle Ages. I believe that Jesuitism is one of the most significant phenomena of Donne's time, for the purpose of definition: and I tried to show that in Jesuitism the centre of philosophical interest is deflected from what it was for the Middle Ages, and that this marks an important alteration of human attitudes. Donne through-out his life was in contact with Jesuitism; directly in his early family life, later by his studies, and not least by his battle with the Jesuits. For you can hardly fight anyone for very long without employing his weapons and using his methods; and to fight a man with ideas means adapting your ideas to his mind. Conflict is contact. The air which Donne breathed was infused with Jesuitism. I have so far tried only to establish that Donne in his writings illustrates one form of the psychologism which arose with Jesuitism – I do not say solely in Jesuit form, or through the medium of Jesuitism.[60]

'Brother, do not so, for thou art a shade and a shade
thou seest.'

Statius, rising, replies (133–6):

> 'Or puoi la quantitate
> comprender dell' amor ch' a te mi scalda,
> quando dismento nostra vanitate,

> trattando l'ombre come cosa salda.'

> 'Now canst thou comprehend the measure of the love which
> warms me toward thee, when I forget our nothingness,
> and treat shades as a solid thing.'
> TC II, 266–7

The misquoted phrase, 'Puote veder', occurs only once in the *Commedia* (*Paradiso* XXVIII, 50): 'si puote / veder le volte tanto più divine' ('we may see the circlings more divine'). TSE correctly quoted Statius' reply to Virgil when he used it as the epigraph for *Ara Vos Prec* (1919) but consistently misquoted it ('Puote veder') when he made it the dedication passage for Jean Verdenal (1889–1915) in *Poems 1909–1925* and *Collected Poems 1909–1935*, corrected in subsequent editions.

60–In 'Lancelot Andrewes', published in September 1926, TSE was to observe that 'Donne many times betrays the consequences of early Jesuit influence and of his later studies in Jesuit literature; in his cunning knowledge of the weaknesses of the human heart, his understanding of human sin, his skill in coaxing and persuading the attention of the variable human mind to

My first lecture intended to form a definition, or less strictly to present a view of metaphysical poetry, starting from that of Donne's age and looking for *felt* resemblances elsewhere, which could include all the kinds of poetry which I myself feel to be metaphysical. In this second lecture I intended to arrive at a definition or view of Donne's peculiar type of metaphysical poetry, and to do this I had to place him in history. We shall have to see how far the connection of Donne's contemporaries can be based on identity under this definition, how far (as I warned you we must be prepared sometimes to find it) the resemblance is verbal or exterior, and how far we must go in framing variant but related definitions. I think we shall find that this general law of the supersession of ontology by psychology holds good everywhere, to the degree in which the various poets are distinct enough to merit definition at all. But before considering some of Donne's contemporaries, when we shall investigate their common tricks in the use of language, I wish next time to contrast the school of Donne with the school of Dante in the particular, but important and illuminating respect of their expressed or implied theories of the nature of human and of divine love.

There is one reservation to be made, in considering the argument of the preceding lecture. In treating Donne's psychological attitude toward ideas and emotions I have not meant to suggest that he was the direct ancestor, or even the collateral ancestor, of later poets. You must not ask me to apply my remarks on Donne *tel quel* to Browning:[61] and I should prefer you not to ask me, not yet at any rate, where is the psychological element in Collins' "Ode to Evening".[62] I do not say that this new attitude accounts for everything, as

---

Divine objects, and in a kind of smiling tolerance among his menaces of damnation' (SE 352/309).

61 – In 'Donne in our Time' (see n. 40 above), TSE was to remark that Browning's 'knowledge of the particular human heart is adulterated by an optimism which has proved offensive to our time, though a later age may succeed in ignoring it' (p. 15).

62 – In his famous 'Ode to Evening' (1746, 1748), William Collins (1721–59) declares himself to be 'musing slow' as he addresses Evening in a quiet, unhistrionic, classically restrained manner, but TSE may be alluding ironically to the fact that after Collins became insane there was a critical tendency to search for psychological signs of madness in his odes. In 'The Metaphysical Poets' TSE had stated that 'the best verse of Collins . . . satisfies some of our fastidious demands better than that of Donne or Marvell or King. But while the language became more refined, the feeling became more crude' (SE 288/247), and in 'Andrew Marvell' (1921) he stated more strongly that by the time we come to Gray and Collins, 'the sophistication remains only in the language, and has disappeared from the feeling. Gray and Collins were masters, but they had lost that hold on human values, that firm grasp of human experience, which is a formidable achievement of the Elizabethan and Jacobean poets' (SE 297/256).

I should by no means say that Aquinas accounts for everything in the thirteenth century. But it is surely one of the differences between the new world and the old; and in its various mutations it either accounts for or is related to the causes which account for, a great many of the phenomena even of our own time. The work of Marcel Proust, for instance, could hardly have appeared without it. But we must always be on guard to avoid confusing resemblances with influences. And even influences, we must remember, occur very frequently through misunderstanding; and some writers have exercised a great influence on account of the facility with which they can be misinterpreted. There is some resemblance between the fruit which St. Augustine stole from an orchard in his boyhood, and the cherries which Rousseau flung at Mademoiselle de Graffenried:[63] and these in turn bear some likeness to the forbidden fruit which Mr. Frank Harris has, I am told, recently preserved for posterity in a limited edition, privately printed.[64] But we are not to hold St. Augustine responsible for Mr. Harris.

On the other hand I insist on a general line of descent from the seventeenth century to the nineteenth. It would be traced partly in a history

---

63 – St Augustine describes his theft in the *Confessions*, Book II, chapter 4, confessing that he stole not out of need, 'but only to enjoy the theft itself and the sin':

> There was a pear-tree near our vineyard, loaded with fruit that was attractive neither to look at nor to taste. Late one night a band of ruffians, myself included, went off to shake down the fruit and carry it away, for we had continued our games out of doors until well after dark, as was our pernicious habit. We took away an enormous quantity of pears, not to eat them ourselves, but simply to throw them to the pigs. Perhaps we ate some of them, but our real pleasure consisted in doing something that was forbidden.
>
> (Trans. R. S. Pine-Coffin, Harmondsworth: Penguin Classics, 1981, p. 47).

Rousseau describes the sensuous scene in Book Four of his *Confessions*, though he drops the cherries not on Mademoiselle de Graffenried but on her companion, Mademoiselle Galley, whom he describes as being 'a year younger than her friend, and even prettier'. After dinner the three friends go into the orchard to pick cherries for their dessert:

> I climbed a tree and threw them down bunches; and they returned me the stones up through the branches. Once Mlle Galley presented such a mark with her apron held out and her head back, and I aimed so well, that I dropped a bunch into her bosom. How we laughed! 'Why are not my lips cherries?' I said to myself. 'How gladly would I throw them there, for both of them, if they were!'
>
> (Trans. J. M. Cohen, Harmondsworth: Penguin Classics, 1973, p. 135).

TSE lectured on Rousseau and placed the *Confessions* on the reading list of his 1916 Extension lectures on 'Modern French Literature' (*RES* I, 167).

64 – Frank Harris (1856–1931), Welsh novelist, journalist, biographer and pornographer, had published two volumes of his four-volume *My Life and Loves* (Paris: privately printed, 1922–7), in which he traces his sexual awakening and early sexual encounters.

of ideas, in which Locke would play the leading part;[65] and partly in a History of Sensibility. Crashaw, as we shall see, was immensely affected by St. Theresa: Crashaw influenced Pope in a poem in which already are the germs of eighteenth-century sentiment – the "Heloise to Abelard".[66] There was sentimentality before Rousseau, and sentiment reached the nineteenth century through other media as well as through Rousseau. In much English prose, even the finest, of the nineteenth century, I find more than a trace of intellectual psychologism, and just the faintest, undefinable perfume of femininity. I find it in Newman and Francis Bradley as well as in Ruskin and Pater. Or it is as if such prose had been written in a low fever; there is a slight temperature to it.[67]Would it be excessive to attempt to trace the influence of St. Theresa to Mr. Lytton Strachey?[68] I think not. But the point of these remarks is to remind you how useful a stimulant such speculation may be if it is carried on under the control of the *sensus communis*.

65 – In his review of James Gibson's *Locke's Theory of Knowledge* (1916), TSE was to concur with the author that in Locke 'the genesis of ideas is only a subordinate problem' (*New Statesman*, 13 July 1918, p. 297), and he was later to write in 'The Tradition and Practice of Poetry' (1936): 'The philosophy of Locke was not very angelic food, but it served the eighteenth century better than nothing at all' (*T. S. Eliot*, ed. James Olney [Oxford: Clarendon Press, 1988], p. 19).

66 – In Pope's 'Eloisa to Abelard' (1717), Eloisa, writing in a convent of her great love and sympathy for Abelard, from whom she had been separated after bearing his child, contrasts her distracted state to that of the 'blameless' brides of Christ, borrowing directly from Crashaw's 'Description of a Religious House' to characterize their untroubled religious life: ' "Obedient slumbers that can wake and weep" ' (line 212).

67 – TSE had earlier characterized the prose of these authors in 'Contemporary English Prose' (*Vanity Fair* [New York], July 1923, p. 51), where, in examining the negative effect of Carlyle on English prose, he found Ruskin 'often exaggerated and perverse; even Cardinal Newman, the possessor of the finest prose style of the nineteenth century, is limited to the autumnal coloring of his peculiar personal emotion'. After the 'orgy' of Carlyle, TSE continued, 'there is usually some exaggeration, some peculiar emotional limitation, as it were a slightly feverish temperature, and of no other writer is this more true than of Walter Pater . . . even in the magnificent austerity of Mr. Bradley's dry and boney prose one recognizes here and there a feverish flush, which is wholly alien to the tradition of Hobbes, Berkeley and Locke.'

68 – The biographer and critic Lytton Strachey (1880–1932) had been TSE's friend since 1919, though TSE was often critical of his point of view, as when Strachey's 'romantic mind' was the subject of TSE's discussion of his *Queen Victoria* (1921): 'he deals. . . with his personages, not in a spirit of "detachment," but by attaching himself to them, *tout entier à sa proie attaché*. He has his favourites, and these are chosen by his emotion rather than design, by his feeling for what can be made of them with his great ability to turn the commonplace into something immense and grotesque . . . Mr. Strachey is a part of history rather than a critic of it; he has invented new sensations from history, as Bergson has invented new sensations from metaphysics' (*Dial*, August 1921, pp. 216–17).

LECTURE III[1]

{Donne and the *Trecento*}

The channels through which the Italian poetry of the *trecento* derives from the Provençal is too well known for me to have any need to review it. I am no Provençal scholar, and anything that I could say would be obtained from translations or from credible authorities. The only point of which I have any need to remind you is the alteration of point of view which takes place, between the Provençal school and the group of Dante, in the matter of love.[2] The distinction is briefly put by Remy de Gourmont in an interesting if not wholly satisfactory little book entitled *Dante, Béatrice et la poésie amoureuse*.[3] Speaking of Provençal society, he says:

1 – A shortened version of this lecture was translated into French by Jean de Menasce and published as 'Deux Attitudes Mystiques: Dante et Donne' in *Le Roseau d'or*, Paris, 14 (1927), pp. 149–73; the translation, which TSE approved, is included as Appendix 1, pp. 309–318.

2 – TSE, who earlier mistitled *Ara Vus [for Vos] Prec* (1919) from the Provençal of *Purgatorio* XXVI, was to write in 'Dante' (1929): 'As for the Provençal poets, I have not the knowledge to read them at first hand. That mysterious people had a religion of their own which was thoroughly and painfully extinguished by the Inquisition; so that we hardly know more about them than about the Sumerians. I suspect that the difference between this unknown, and possibly maligned, Albigensianism and Catholicism has some correspondence with the difference between the poetry of the Provençal school and the Tuscan. The system of Dante's organization of sensibility – the contrast between higher and lower carnal love, the transition from Beatrice living to Beatrice dead, rising to the Cult of the Virgin, seems to me to be his own' (*SE* 275/235).

3 – TSE first read the novelist and critic Remy de Gourmont (1858–1915) in Paris in 1910–11. In writing the essays that comprise *The Sacred Wood* (1920), where he quotes from *Le Problème du Style* (1902) and *Lettres à l'Amazone* (1914), TSE refers to Gourmont as 'the critical consciousness of a generation' (*SW* 44), as 'the great critic' (*SW* 139), and says that 'Of all modern critics, perhaps Remy de Gourmont had most of the general intelligence of Aristotle' (*SW* 13). The falling away from Gourmont came with his subsequent reading of *Dante, Béatrice et la Poésie amoureuse*, subtitled 'Essai sur L'Idéal Féminin en Italie à la Fin du XIIIe Siècle' (see p. 64, n. 45). As TSE was to write in the Preface to the second edition of *The Sacred Wood* (1928), in the first edition he 'was much stimulated and much helped by the critical

Pour aimer, il fallait être marié et aimer en dehors du mariage. Pas plus qu'entre époux, entre jeunes gens libres l'amour n'était admis. Afin d'avoir droit aux hommages des chevaliers, il faut que la jeune fille se marie. Ce que nous laissent constamment entrevoir les poètes provençaux, c'est une dame noble, belle, puissante, entourée d'une cour de jeunes chevaliers, parmi lesquels il lui était permis, sinon dûment ordonné, d'en distinguer un et de se l'attacher. Le lien formé, ils se devaient mutuellement amour sous peine de déchéance; rien ne pouvait les séparer que, momentanément, la mort. C'était la fidélité dans l'adultère.

La dame provençale n'est nullement "angélisée". On ne la craint pas, on la désire.

La nouvelle école florentine . . . devait modifier profondément la conception de l'amour, et par conséquent les moeurs. L'amour des poètes devient pur, presque impersonnel; son objet n'est plus une femme, mais la beauté, la fémininité personifiée dans une créature idéale. Aucune idée de mariage ni de possession ne les hante. . . . L'amour a tous les caractères d'un culte, dont le sonnet et la canzone sont les hymnes.

C'est une date dans l'histoire de l'évolution des sentiments humains; c'est un pas vers la vérité et un progrès social immense.

I quote this admirable summary to emphasise the vast difference.[4]

---

writings of Remy de Gourmont. I acknowledge that influence, and am grateful for it; and I by no means disown it by having passed on to another problem not touched upon in this book: that of the relation of poetry to the spiritual and social life of its time and of other times' (*SW* viii).

4 – *Translation*: For love, one had to be married and love outside of marriage. No more than between husband and wife, love between free young people was not permitted. In order to have the right to receive homage from knights, the young woman had to be married. What the provençal poets constantly help us to catch a glimpse of is a noble lady, beautiful, powerful, surrounded by a court of young knights, among whom she was permitted, if not strictly commanded, to select one and to attach herself to him. The link established, they devoted themselves to each other under pain of forfeiture [of lover's rights]; nothing could separate them except, temporarily, death. It was fidelity within adultery. [p. 29]

The provençal lady is in no way 'angelic'. One does not fear her, one desires her. [p. 30]

The new Florentine school would profoundly modify this conception of love, and consequently, the mores. The poets' love becomes pure, almost impersonal; its object is no longer a woman but beauty, femininity personified in an ideal creature. No idea of marriage or of possession haunts them . . . Love has all the characteristics of a cult, of which the sonnet and canzone are the hymns. [p. 31]

It is a date in the history of the evolution of human feelings; it is a step towards the truth and an immense social progress. [p. 32]

The Dantesque attitude toward women should not be qualified as "chivalrous", or buried under the common obscuration of the term "mediaeval". The Provençal attitude is perhaps the more "chivalrous"; it pertains to a society aristocratic and worldly rather than scholarly, devoted to the art of music, a beautiful little enclave of paganism – though an enclave which comprehended a large part of modern France. Aesthetes of love and war, they had the satisfaction, denied to most aesthetes, of living out their aestheticism in a social existence. Between this society and that of Dante I do not wish to insinuate any judgment; though of course the latter produced the greater poetry. Indeed, the three attitudes towards love – of the Provençal, of the Italian, of the English seventeenth century – represent differences in the human spirit too wide for judgment; they belong to those differences which are reincarnated in different human beings every day, placing insuperable barriers between some of every handful of us. I judge them only, as a literary critic, by their literary fruits.

There are, as I tried to say in the first lecture, essentially two ways in which poetry can add to human experience. One is by perceiving and recording accurately the world – of both sense and feeling – as given at any moment; the other by extending the frontiers of this world. The first is the first in the order of generation – you find it in Homer; and I do not say that it is necessarily second in the order of value. A new and wider and loftier world, such as that into which Dante will introduce you, must be built upon a solid foundation of the old tangible world; it will not descend like Jacob's ladder. Among the poets who have thus extended reality – and I will admit that they are those who interest me the most – I place Dante first absolutely, and Baudelaire first in recent times.[5] Among those who have defined reality as it is, for various reasons I find it impossible to assign rank: I should certainly include Homer – yes, the Homer of the *Odyssey* also – Catullus, Chaucer. But, again as always in literary criticism, one must distinguish, but one cannot dissect. Any poet, almost, may be seen under the opposite aspect; every poet may exhibit something of both. Some may be called mixed; some may be called muddled. For there is a difference between fusion and confusion.

5 – As TSE was to write in 'Donne in our Time' (see p. 81, n. 40), 'We must assume, if we are to talk about poetry at all, that there is some absolute poetic hierarchy; we keep at the back of our minds the reminder of some end of the world, some final Judgment Day, on which the poets will be assembled in their ranks and orders. In the long run, there is an ultimate greater and less. But at any particular time, and we exist only in particular moments of time, good taste consists, not in attaining to the vision of Judgment Day . . . but in approximating to some analysis of the absolute and the relative in our own appreciation' (p. 5).

I have introduced this parenthesis in order to forestall the prejudice, in dealing with the metaphysical poetry of Dante and his age, that all this stuff – the *Vita Nuova* or the sonnets and *canzoni* and *ballate* of the two Guidos – is fantasy and foolery. Not many persons, perhaps, will admit that this is what they think, but so many have read of Paolo and Francesca, and read it wrong,[6] and so few have read the *Paradiso* and read it right, that this must be the attitude of a very large number. And I wish to insist that this poetry is not the quaint fashion of a primitive age, pre-Raphaelite, given to visions and Benozzo Gozzoli processions up to heaven,[7] but the product of men who felt and thought both clearly and beyond the ordinary frontiers of

6 – TSE alludes to Dante's encounter with Francesca of Rimini and her lover Paolo in the Second Circle, which contains the souls of carnal sinners (*Inferno*, V, 73–142). When Dante hears their painful story, he faints and collapses as if dead. In 'Dante' (1920), TSE had charged Walter Savage Landor with having misunderstood the passage 'by failing to perceive its relations: "In the midst of her punishment, Francesca, when she comes to the tenderest part of her story, tells it with complacency and delight." This is surely a false simplification. To have lost all recollected delight would have been, for Francesca, either loss of humanity or relief from damnation. The ecstasy, with the present thrill at the remembrance of it, is a part of the torture. Francesca is neither stupefied nor reformed; she is merely damned; and it is a part of damnation to experience desires that we can no longer gratify' (*SW* 165–6). TSE was to include J. M. Murry and Tennyson among the misreaders of the passage in 'Mr. Middleton Murry's Synthesis', where he argues that Francesca's line, 'There is no greater pain than to recall a happy time in wretchedness' (see p. 56, n. 31), is not, as Murry holds, a 'truth' but 'a dramatic statement; Francesca believed it, but there is no conclusive evidence that Dante believed it; it . . . fits in with the whole passage to show how far Francesca is from a state of grace. As an universal statement, it is simply *not* true' (*Criterion*, October 1927, p. 342). TSE was to return to this crucial passage yet again in 'Two Studies in Dante' (1928): 'Most of the romantic delight in the love of Paolo and Francesca, from Musset on, has been founded on a misconception. Now it is essential to the understanding of the Inferno to understand that all of these damned are damned *voluntarily*; they prefer damnation because they prefer to remain in their several states of mind rather than make any motion of discipline or surrender' (*TLS*, 11 October 1928, p. 732). 'When we come to fit the episode into its place in the whole *Comedy*', he wrote in 'Dante' (1929), 'and see how this punishment is related to all other punishments and to purgations and rewards, we can appreciate better the subtle psychology of the simple line of Francesca:

se fosse amico il re dell' universo

if the King of the Universe were our friend . . .' (*SE* 246/207).
7 – An allusion to *Il Viaggio dei Magi* (1459–61), the masterpiece of Benozzo Gozzoli (1420–97), in the Medici–Riccardi chapel in Florence. The fresco portrays a cavalcade of pilgrims on a winding, mountainous road to Bethlehem, set against a legendary background of fantastic landscapes and strange animals. TSE may have seen the work during his Italian tour of 1911, but he had already registered his impression of Gozzoli in his fine arts course on 'Renaissance Painters', where he wrote in his report on 'Fra Angelico in San Marco' that the *Adoration of the Magi* was 'a fairly good composition, although perhaps too suggestive of a pageant, such as Benozzo Gozzoli might have done' (King's).

mind. These were men of highly trained intellects, who also had their feet very firmly on the ground – a rather muddy ground of politics, amours and gang fighting. In short, they represent a civilisation in some respects superior to our own, and superior to that of the world of Donne. Their syntax and choice of words affirm their superiority. You cannot live on a high plane and indulge yourself in verbiage.

I have mentioned a small book by Remy de Gourmont. In recommending it I would add one caution. Gourmont's purpose is to prove that the Beatrice of Dante is practically a pure fabrication – if indeed the very name Beatrice was not chosen solely because [of] its meaning. Against any who assert that the *Vita Nuova* is a literal chronicle of an early passion, his claim is abundantly vindicated, though for any reader of intelligence such vindication should be superfluous. Gourmont exposes the arbitrary and symbolical chronology, and makes successful appeal to the similarity of Dante's visions to those of other vision literature such as the *Shepherd of Hermas*.[8] But Gourmont must always be taken with reservation. A brilliant literary critic, he was no philosopher; and being no philosopher, he was filled with all sorts of philosophical prejudices – about sex, for instance – after all, he lived in the time of Walter Pater.[9] When we read the book in question, we may receive the impression that the *Vita Nuova* is a dry and lifeless allegory. (The very word "allegory" is enough to condemn anything, to many people!) No such thing. The *Vita Nuova* is to my thinking a record of actual experiences reshaped into a particular form.[10] This is indemonstrable. It is a

8 – The *Shepherd of Hermas*, a second-century apocalyptic work written in Greek by Hermas, a manumitted Christian slave, describes visions and revelations granted to him by an angel in shepherd's dress. Divided into five Visions, twelve Mandates and ten Similitudes, or Parables, the work exhorts the reader to repent of post-baptismal sins. In 'Two Studies in Dante' (see n. 6 above), TSE was to state that 'To compare the "Vita Nuova" with any of its prototypes in vision literature or allegory – as "The Shepherd of Hermas" – is to become aware of a vast difference: with Dante there is always a foundation of personal human feeling, which, however, cannot be isolated from his philosophical and religious emotions'.

9 – TSE associates Remy de Gourmont and Walter Pater as sexual theorists of the Victorian age, however antithetical their orientation. He alludes to Pater's Platonic or homoerotic view of sexual love in *Plato and Platonism* (1893), a view that was sufficiently implicit in the 'Conclusion' to *The Renaissance* (1873) to lead to the chapter's exclusion from the second edition (1877), and to Gourmont's biologically-based view in *Physique de l'amour: essay sur l'instinct sexuel* (1903), translated by Ezra Pound as *The Natural Philosophy of Love* (1922), a post-Darwinian work which attempts to strip the moral and sentimental trappings from the instinctive reproductive mechanism of love. This thesis is dramatised in *Un Coeur virginal* (1907) and other novels.

10 – TSE was to re-cast his reservations about Gourmont's study in 'Dante' (1929), where he criticizes Gourmont for being 'misled by his prejudices into the pedantic attitude' and for thinking 'that if an author like Dante follows closely a form of vision that has a long history, it

kind of experience possible to a particular mental type, which persons of this type will always recognise. The emotions and sentiments, for instance, which Dante records as experienced at the age of nine, are not at all incredible; they are possible at an even earlier age, though I do not assert that a young person of nine would be able to formulate them consciously in those words.[11] I do not reject the part of allegory. Allegory itself may be only a mode of expression of a mind passionately eager to find order and significance in the world – though it may find order or set order in ways which we have come to neglect.

The causes by which took place so profound a change of mind as that between the Provençal and the *trecento* as illustrated by the *Vita Nuova* – so profound and apparently so sudden – are obscure; and most historians seem to content themselves with marking the change without accounting for it. I venture therefore timidly as well as tentatively to suggest that the poets of the *trecento* were (and the Provençals were not) in the direct current of European thought then flowing. We have, I believe, evidence of a high state of education among the choicer Provençal nobility; higher probably than in any part of Europe at that time; and a nobility which reads Ovid and Virgil is worthy of notice at any time. But apparently their reading was primarily classical – as much of the Latin classics as was then accessible. It seems a

---

proves that the story is mere allegory (in the modern sense) or fake. I find a much greater difference in sensibility between the *Vita Nuova* and the *Shepherd of Hermas* than Gourmont did. It is not at all the simple difference between the genuine and the fraud; it is a difference in mind between the humble author of early Christian times and the poet of the thirteenth century, perhaps as great as that between the latter and ourselves. The similarities might prove that a certain *habit* in dream imagery can persist throughout many changes of civilization. Gourmont would say that Dante borrowed; but that is imputing our own mind to the thirteenth century. I merely suggest that possibly Dante, in his place and time, was following something more essential than merely a "literary" tradition' (*SE* 274/234).

11 – TSE was to elaborate this position in 'Dante' (1929), where he argues that 'the type of sexual experience which Dante describes as occurring to him at the age of nine years is by no means impossible or unique. My only doubt (in which I found myself confirmed by a distinguished psychologist), is whether it could have taken place so *late* in life as the age of nine years. The psychologist agreed with me that it is more likely to occur at about five or six years of age. It is possible that Dante developed rather late, and it is also possible that he altered the dates to employ some other significance of the number nine. But to me it appears obvious that the *Vita Nuova* could only have been written around a personal experience' (*SE* 273/233). TSE had confided the anonymous psychologist's point of view to his translator, Jean de Menasce, and seized the opportunity to add a personal note at this point: 'Je pense même, avec le psychologue I. A. Richards, que cet ordre d'expérience est plus repandu à l'âge de quatre ou cinq ans'. See Appendix 1, p. 311, n. 1.

curious little Latin renaissance in the twelfth century. But the current of living thought was then flowing through the Church; and possibly certain heresies flourishing in Provence may have tended to isolate this part of France from the rest of Europe. The generation of Dante was nourished on *mediaeval* Latin culture. And no one who has read even a little of the Latin of the twelfth and thirteenth centuries can doubt that the delight in ideas, the dialectical subtlety, the intensity with which ideas were felt, and the clarity and precision of the expression, came partly from this source.

There is a type of religious mysticism which found expression in the twelfth century, and which is taken up into the system of Aquinas. Its origin is in the *Metaphysics* of Aristotle 1072b and elsewhere, and in the *Nichomachaean Ethics*, and it is the opposite of Bergsonism.[12] You know how the Absolute of Bergson is arrived at: by a turning back on the path of thought, by divesting one's mind of the apparatus of distinction and analysis, by plunging into the flow of immediate experience.[13] For the twelfth century, the divine vision or enjoyment of God could only be attained by a process in which the analytic intellect took part; it was through and by and beyond discursive thought that man could arrive at beatitude. This was the form of mysticism consummated in Dante's time. It is very different from the mysticism of Ignatius, Theresa and St. John of the Cross, who were romantics, and from that of Eckhardt, who was a heretic. In its own way it was perfect. But the human mind, when it comes to a terminus, hastens to look up the next train for almost anywhere. In the fourteenth century

12–In 1072b of the *Metaphysics*, Aristotle delineates the nature of the final cause and end of movement in the universe: 'The final cause, then, produces motion as being loved, but all other things move by being moved' (*Works of Aristotle*, VIII, ed. W. D. Ross (Oxford: Clarendon Press, 1928, p. 1072a). In 'Dante (1920) TSE was interested in the emotional expression of this transmitted philosophy, writing that in Dante's attempt 'to state a vision' in cantos XVI and XVII of the *Purgatorio* there 'occur passages of pure exposition of philosophy, the philosophy of Aristotle strained through the schools' (*SW* 169–70). Before the essay was revised for *The Sacred Wood*, TSE originally wrote: 'Several passages of the "Purgatorio" are the emotional extract of the "Nicomachean Ethics" filtered through the Schools . . . The range, the relation, and the *balance* of emotions are what distinguish the "Divine Comedy" from all other poems' (*Athenaeum*, 2 April 1920, p. 442). TSE was to give his own emotional expression of the philosophy in 'Burnt Norton': 'Love is itself unmoving, / Only the cause and end of movement, / Timeless, and undesiring' (*CPP* 175/122).

13–At Harvard in 1910–11 TSE drafted a paper on Bergson's theory of duration, 'which promised to abolish the "timeless" + eternal', but TSE had determined even then that 'whatever conclusion we come to, we cannot rest at the durée réelle. It is simply not final' (Houghton).

Meister Eckhardt and his followers – appropriately, in Germany – reasserted the God of the Abyss; the God, in short, of Mr. D. H. Lawrence.[14]

I wish to linger a little over this twelfth-century mysticism, not because we are interested in mysticism, but because we cannot get away from it. There is always some type of mysticism about, whether that of Mr. Russell, or Mr. Lawrence, or Mr. Murry; the number of types is limited, and it is possible and useful to be able to distinguish them.[15] It will help us, presently, in contrasting the *Vita Nuova* with "The Extasie" of Donne.

14 – See p. 84, n. 47. TSE alludes to Eckhart's doctrine of the Unknowable, the *wüste Gottheit*, or 'wilderness of Godhead', which TSE's teacher Josiah Royce lucidly characterized in his essay on Eckhart in *Studies of Good and Evil* (1898): 'Well, this mysticism consists in saying that all the knowledge of even a divine Self is rooted in the impenetrable mystery of existence, the nature, the inmost essence, of its own Selfhood. Whoever still obstinately and with divine love of the highest seeks to know this, must first lay aside the very conditions of knowledge, and pass into the still wilderness, where there is no longer either subject or object. But to do this is to reach the light above the light – is to touch the Absolute, and so to be in unity, and at peace, in the wilderness where no one is at home but the Godhead, and where even that is nothing determinate, and is yet the fountain of all things and determinations' (p. 283).

Eckhart's chief followers were Johannes Tauler (c. 1300–61) and Heinrich Suso (c. 1300–66), Dominican preachers who established a popular mystical movement to spread Eckhart's teachings. TSE had studied Suso's *Life of Henry Suso, by Himself*, translated by T. F. Knox (London, 1913) at Harvard, and was to write in 'Mystic and Politician as Poet' (1930; see p. 23, n. 36): 'One of the frequent characteristics of Christian mysticism has been a use of various imageries of light and darkness, sometimes indeed of a light which is at the same time darkness; such imagery is used by . . . Meister Eckhart and the German mystics' (p. 590).

15 – TSE frequently and antagonistically linked the theological views of this trio of 'romantic' contemporaries, and in his review of Russell's *Why I Am Not a Christian* (1927) he was to characterize their positions less obliquely: 'As we become used to Atheism, we recognize that Atheism is often merely a variety of Christianity. There is . . . the Tin Chapel Atheism of Mr. D. H. Lawrence. And there is the decidedly Low Church Atheism of Mr. Russell. For one only ceases to be a Christian by being something else definite – a Buddhist, a Mohammedan, a Brahmin . . . Mr. Russell is essentially a low Churchman, and only by caprice can call himself an Atheist. And there is the genuine Heretic – a very rare bird – such as Mr. Middleton Murry. But Mr. Murry is a theologian; we can take his Heresy seriously, as we cannot take Mr. Russell's Atheism. Just as Mr. Russell's Radicalism in politics is merely a variety of Whiggery, so his Non-Christianity is merely a variety of Low Church sentiment. That is why his pamphlet is a curious, and a pathetic, document' (*Criterion*, August 1927, p. 179).

TSE was to distinguish between modern and ancient types of mysticism in 'Religion Without Humanism' (1930): 'There is much chatter about mysticism: for the modern world the word means some spattering indulgence of emotion, instead of the most terrible concentration and askesis. But it takes perhaps a lifetime merely to realise that men like the forest sages, and the desert sages, and finally the Victorines and John of the Cross and (in his fashion) Ignatius really *mean what they say*. Only those have the right to talk of discipline who have looked into the Abyss' (*Humanism and America*, ed. Norman Foerster [New York: Farrar and Rhinehart, 1930], p. 110).

The most interesting example of a twelfth-century mystic that I know, and an example which should throw considerable light upon Dante, is Richard of St. Victor. Richard was, like the greater philosopher Hugh of St. Victor, a Scotchman who became prior of the Victorine monastery, the Riccardo of [the] *Paradiso*, Canto [x]:[16]

"Che a considerar fu più che vero".
"Who in contemplation was more than man".[17]

His works occupy the greater part of one volume in Migne's *Patrologia* – no small space;[18] they do not appear to be very well known, and I cannot myself profess acquaintance with any but a small part of them. But the most important, for our purpose, is the *De Gratia Contemplationis*, called the *Benjamin Major*.[19] This is a treatise on the operations and stages of the

16 – The typist left a blank space for the canto number to be inserted; TSE later entered 'xii' in black ink, subsequently corrected in pencil.

17 – Richard of St Victor (d. 1173), a philosopher and teacher born in Scotland, entered the Paris Abbey of St Victor in the early 1150s and became prior in 1162. He was preceded at the Abbey by Hugh of St Victor (c. 1096–1141), who was born in the Saxon diocese of Halberstadt in central Germany. A scriptural scholar, Augustinian philosopher and Master of the Abbey, Hugh established in his writings and teachings the Victorine contemplative tradition of which Richard was heir and chief exponent in the second half of the twelfth century. Richard, read and admired by Aquinas, Bonaventura and Dante, appears in the *Paradiso* (x, 130–32) with Isidore of Sevile (c. 560–636) and the Venerable Bede (c. 673–735):

> Vedi oltre fiammeggiar l'ardente spiro
> d'Isidoro, di Beda e di Riccardo
> che a considerar fu più che viro.

> See flaming next the glowing breath of Isidore,
> of Bede, and of Richard, who, in contemplating,
> was more than man.
> (*TC* III, 124–6)

18 – The French cleric and editor Jacques Paul Migne (1800–75) included Richard's writings in his monumental edition, the *Patrologia Cursus Completus* in 221 volumes (Paris, 1844–64). The text of Richard's work occupies 1379 of 1654 columns in volume 196 (1855). TSE had written to Richard Aldington (Texas) on 11 December 1921: 'By the way, should a Migne not be beyond our joint purses, I would be glad to split one with you, if we can agree as to who should possess which volumes, lending the others reciprocally. What I want chiefly is xii and xiii century philosophy, and Erigena; Prudentius and Tertullian and the fathers I should be content to borrow!' There are no volumes of Migne's edition in TSE's library.

19 – TSE later crossed out 'Major' and inserted 'Minor' in his own hand, with a second-thought notation in the bottom margin: 'But the B. Major also'. He had it right in the first instance: *De Gratia Contemplationis*, ('Of the Grace of Contemplation') was known by ancient scholars as the *Benjamin Major*, as Migne indicates, and in modern times as *The Mystical Ark*. TSE confuses this work with Richard's *De Praeparatione Animi ad Contemplationem* ('Of the Preparation of the Soul for Contemplation'), called the *Benjamin Minor*, more recently *The Twelve Patriarchs*. Following TSE's emendation, Jean de Menasce

mind in proceeding toward the beatific vision. You will observe some resemblance – no doubt wholly coincidental – to the classifications of some Indian mystical systems.[20] You will also observe that it is wholly impersonal – as impersonal as a handbook of hygiene – and contains no biographical element whatever; nothing that could be called emotional or sensational. In which it differs from the works of the Spanish mystics of the sixteenth century. And finally you may agree with me that it is written in a clear, simple and economical style – if, that is, you admit a style of Latin which is neither Cicero, Tacitus nor Petronius.[21] I will quote a passage from the part of the work named in which he is endeavouring to distinguish between *cogitation, meditation* and *contemplation* – the three stages of mental progress. Perhaps I should apologise first for my somewhat Italianated pronunciation of Latin.

Cogitatio per devia quaeque lento pede, sine respectu perventionis, passim huc illucque vagatur. Meditatio per ardua saepe et aspera ad directionis finem cum magna animi industria nititur. Contemplatio libero volatu quocunque eam fert impetus mira agilitate circumfertur. Cogitatio serpit, meditatio incedit et ut multum currit. Contemplatio autem omnia circumvolat, et cum voluerit se in summis librat. Cogitatio est sine labore et fructu. In meditatione est labor cum fructu. Contemplatio permanet sine labore cum fructu. In cogitatione evagatio, in meditatione investigatio, in contemplatione *admiratio*. Ex imaginatione cogitatio, lex ratione meditatio, ex intelligentia contemplatio. Ecce tria ista, imaginatio, ratio, intelligentia. Intelligentia

translated: 'La plus interessante pour nous est son *De Gratia Contemplationis*, qu'on désigne sous le nom de *Benjamin Mineur*' (p. 312).

20 – TSE had studied Sanskrit and Indian Philosophy with Professors Charles Rockwell Lanman and J. H. Woods at Harvard in 1911–12, and later wrote in his review of Sri Ananda Acharya's *Brahmadarsanam, or Intuition of the Absolute* (1917): 'There is . . . as certainly a History of Indian philosophy as of European; a history which can be traced in the dualistic Sankhya, for instance, from the cryptic early couplets through the commentary of Patanjali to the extraordinarily ingenious and elaborate thought of Vachaspati Misra and Vijnana Bhikshu. There is, moreover, extremely subtle and patient psychology in the later writers; and it should be the task of the interpreter to make this psychology plausible, to exhibit it as something more than an arbitrary and fatiguing system of classifications' (*International Journal of Ethics*, April 1918, p. 445).

21 – TSE had made an incidental remark about the modern taste for Latin prose styles in 'Euripides and Professor Murray' (1920): 'we do not believe that a good English prose style can be modelled upon Cicero, or Tacitus . . . and we think more highly of Petronius than our grandfathers did' (*SW* 76–7). TSE had chosen the epigraphs for *The Sacred Wood* and *The Waste Land* from Petronius' *Satyricon*, which he had studied as an undergraduate at Harvard.

obtinet supremum locum, imaginatio infimum, ratio medium. Omnia quae subjacent sensui inferiori, necesse est ea etiam subjacere sensui superiori. Unde constat quia cuncta quae comprehenduntur ab imaginatione, ea etiam aliaque multa quae supra jam sunt comprehendi a ratione. Similiter ea quae imaginatio vel ratio comprehendunt, sub intelligentia cadunt, et ea etiam quae illæ comprehendere non possunt. Vide ergo contemplarionis radius, quam late se expandat, qui omnia lustrat.[22]

Repetitious and monotonous it may seem. But on examination you find that every phrase makes what went before it a little more intelligible; there is not a word wasted. Furthermore Richard is very sparing of tropes and figures: there is only the main allegory running through the treatise, the comparison of the stages of the mind to the parts of the ark of the covenant – an allegory [which] causes no confusion. It is prose which seems to me to satisfy the primary demands of writing, that is, to write what you think in the words in which you think it, adding no embellishment; to avoid metaphors and figures of speech, and to keep your emotions out of it. (For if an emotion has enough force, it will make its way through in spite of everything: if it has not, it is much better away).

I should remark also that the method and the goal seem to me essentially the same as with Aquinas and Dante: the divine contemplation, and the development and subsumption of emotion and feeling through intellect into

22 – TSE quotes (his emphasis; minor mistranscriptions corrected) from Migne's edition (vol. 196) of *De Gratia Contemplationis*, Book I, Chapter III ('Concerning the particular nature of contemplation and in what it differs from meditation and thinking'), columns 66–7. *Translation*: By means of inconstant and slow feet, thinking wanders here and there in all directions without any regard for arriving. Meditation presses forward with great activity of soul, often through arduous and rough places, to the end of the way it is going. Contemplation, in free flight, circles around with marvelous quickness wherever impulse moves it. Thinking crawls; meditation marches and often runs; contemplation flies around everywhere and when it wishes suspends itself in the heights. Thinking is without labor and fruit; in meditation there is labor with fruit; contemplation continues without labor but with fruit. In thinking there is wandering; in meditation, investigation; in contemplation, wonder. Thinking is from imagination; meditation, from reason; contemplation, from understanding. Behold, these three: imagination, reason, understanding. Understanding occupies the highest place; imagination, the lowest; reason, the middle. Everything that is subject to the lower sense is also necessarily subject to the higher sense. Thus, it is evident that all things that are grasped by the imagination, as well as many other things that are above it, are grasped by reason. Similarly, those things which imagination and reason grasp, as well as things which they are not able to grasp, are perceived by the understanding. Thus, see how widely a ray of contemplation that illuminates everything expands itself. (Trans. Grover A. Zinn, *Richard of St Victor*, pp. 155–6).

the vision of God. Thus St. Thomas: "it results evidently that it is only in the divine vision that intelligent beings can find the true felicity" (Gilson: *St. Thomas*; in *Les Moralistes Chrétiens*).[23]

In passing, I wish to draw as sharply as possible the difference between this mysticism of Richard of St. Victor, which is the mysticism also of St. Thomas Aquinas and of Dante, and the mysticism of the Spaniards, which as we shall see later, is the mysticism of Crashaw and the Society of Jesus. The Aristotelian–Victorine–Dantesque mysticism is ontological; the Spanish mysticism is psychological. The first is what I call classical, the second romantic.

Incidentally, I think that if Mr. Middleton Murry would study carefully the works of St. John of the Cross, he would see that the parallel he draws between St. John and myself is quite illusory; for what St. John means by the "dark night" and what Mr. Murry means by my "dark night" are entirely different things.[24]

When Mr. George Santayana says that the mystic is the true epicurean,[25] he is saying what is true of the Spanish mystic rather than and in distinction to any other. It is no accident, in this connexion, that the town of Avila near Madrid has two glories: that of having given birth to St. Theresa and that of having given birth to Mr. George Santayana of Cambridge, Massachusetts. And of the Spanish mystic, we can easily prove Mr. Santayana right. For does not St. John of the Cross say (Truc, p. 145):

> Toutes les délices et toutes les douceurs des créatures ne sont que des peines et des amertumes très grandes, lorsqu'on les compare avec les

23 – TSE translates from Etienne Gilson's *Saint Thomas D'Aquin* in the series of texts and commentaries entitled 'Les Moralistes Chrétiens' (Paris: Librairie Victor Lecoffre, 1925): 'Il résulte donc évidemment de là que c'est par la vision divine seule que des êtres intelligents peuvent trouver la vraie félicité . . .' (p. 63).

24 – In 'The "Classical" Revival' (see p. 75, n. 30), Murry had compared the nihilistic voice of *The Waste Land* to the voice of St John of the Cross: 'Once its armour of incomprehensibility is penetrated the poem is found to be a cry of grinding and empty desolation. Nothing could conceivably be more remote from the complacent scepticism of the cynical Augustans. This is a voice from the Dark Night of the Soul of a St. John of the Cross – the barren and dry land where no water is' (p. 592).

25 – Santayana frequently discussed Epicurean detachment but had not made such an explicit statement in his published work; TSE may have heard him say it in class. He probably alludes, however, to a passage in *The Sense of Beauty* (1896): 'The simultaneous view of many things, innumerable attractions felt together, produce equilibrium and indifference, as effectually as the exclusion of all. If we may call the liberation of the self by the consciousness of evil in the world, the Stoic sublime, we may assert that there is also an Epicurean sublime, which consists in liberation by equipoise. Any wide survey is sublime in that fashion. Each detail may be beautiful' (Cambridge, MA: MIT Press, 1988, p. 150).

délices et les douceurs de Dieu. Celui-là donc ne mérite que des tourments, qui s'abandonne aux plaisirs du monde.[26]

And look at the *Spiritual Exercises* of Ignatius Loyola (based, according to M. Herrmann Müller, on Mohammedan patterns)[27]:

p. 96.......

[Contemplate – (1) Your apartment faintly lighted by the last rays of day, or the feeble light of a lamp; your bed which you will never leave except to be laid in your coffin; all the objects which surround you and seem to say, You leave us for ever! (2) The persons who will surround you: your servants, sad and silent; a weeping family, bidding you a last adieu; the minister of religion, praying near you and suggesting pious affections to you. (3) Yourself stretched on a bed of pain, losing by degrees your senses and the free use of your faculties, struggling violently against death, which comes to tear your soul from the body and drag it before the tribunal of God. (4) At your side the devils, who redouble their efforts, to destroy you; your good angel, who assists you for the last time with his holy inspirations.][28]

26 – TSE cites Gonzague Truc's edition of *Les Mystiques espagñols: Sainte Terese – Saint Jean de la Croix* (see p. 65, n. 49). The quotation is from *The Ascent of Mount Carmel*, Book I, Chapter IV, section 8: 'All the sweetness and all the pleasures which all the things of this world furnish to the will are, in comparison with the sweetness and pleasure which is God, supreme pain, torment, and bitterness. He, therefore, who shall set his heart upon them is, in the eyes of God, worthy of pain, torment, and bitterness, and can never attain to those delights with which the divine union abounds.' Trans. David Lewis (London: Thomas Baker, 1906), pp. 20–21. 27 – See Müller, p. 76, n. 32.
28 – TSE read from a separate unidentified text, which was not subsequently incorporated into the fair copy of the lecture, except to indicate that the passage appeared on 'p. 96. . . . . . .'. He evidently read from the 'Second Exercise on Death' in *Manresa: Or the Spiritual Exercises of St Ignatius, for General Use* (London: Burns and Oates, 1881), p. 96, as quoted above, an interpretation of Ignatius not included in standard texts of the *Spiritual Exercises*. TSE later wrote in the bottom margin: 'Father Yealey S.J. has notified me that the passage I quoted is probably not by Ignatius, but added much later. I had used it because of the remarkable similarity of imagery to that of Donne'. Francis Joseph Yealey (1888–1977), an American Jesuit from the St Stanislaw Seminary in Florissant, Missouri, was pursuing a doctoral degree at Christ's College, Cambridge, and attended the Clark Lectures. Yealey wrote to TSE on 13 March 1926 to point out that his quotation of 'a certain meditation on death' does not occur in the authentic Latin version of the *Spiritual Exercises*, explaining that it must have been added by a spiritual director who published his development of the text without explaining its relation to St. Ignatius: 'I think you will find St. Ignatius' own thought as austere and straightforward in its way as that of Richard of St. Victor. May I add that I did not think your comparision especially happy? Richard's treatise on contemplation is analytical and discursive. The Exercises, besides dealing primarily with the different though related business of asceticism, are not a treatise at all but a series of fairly obvious working-principles whose virtue is supposed to

Is this not a spiritual haschisch, a drugging of the emotions, rather than, as with Richard of St. Victor, an intellectual preparation for spiritual contemplation?

In the next lecture I shall revert to the relation of Donne's mental food to *his* style. I will only observe at the moment that such prose as that of Richard of St. Victor seems to me an admirable influence for the formation of style either in prose or verse. For the writing of *English* prose or verse, I should include it with Aristotle, *The Drapier's Letters, The Principles of Logic*, and the first volume of the *Principia Mathematica*.[29] In any case, I am not (please note) concerned with the question of any actual influence of Richard on Dante: though Dante certainly knew and appreciated his work. See [Dante's] *Epistola* to Can Grande, [which] refers to *De Contemplatione*.[30] I

---

lie partly in their arrangement and partly in being assimilated in the most intimate and practical manner possible by personal effort' (MS VE). Yealey supplied TSE with a copy of *The Text of the Spiritual Exercises*, 4th edition revised, trans. John Morris and others, from the original Spanish (London: Burns, Oates & Washbourne, 1923).

29–In 'The Possibility of a Poetic Drama' (1920) TSE had observed that 'Certain works of philosophy can be called works of art', including 'much of Aristotle' and 'Mr. Bradley's *Principles of Logic*' (*SW* 66). He had used the first edition (1883) of Bradley's 'classic' text, which exalts the idealist theory of knowledge at the expense of empirical logic, in his doctoral dissertation, and in his obituary of Bradley he wrote in the *Criterion* (October 1924, p. 2): 'Few will ever take the pains to study the consummate art of Bradley's style, the finest philosophic style in our language, in which acute intellect and passionate feeling preserve a classic balance . . . But upon these few, both living and unborn, his writings perform that mysterious and complete operation which transmutes not one department of thought only, but the whole intellectual and emotional tone of their being'.

In 'Charles Whibley' (1931) TSE was to write of Jonathan Swift's *The Drapier's Letters* (1724), a protest against the circulation of debased coinage in Ireland: 'Those persons who are drawn by the powerful attraction of Jonathan Swift read and re-read with enchanted delight *The Drapier's Letters*; and these letters . . . are such an important item now in English letters, so essential to anyone who would be well read in the literature of England, that we ignore the accident by which we still read them. If Swift had never written *Gulliver's Travels* . . . what would be the place of *The Drapier's Letters* now?' (*SE* 493–4/440).

TSE read the first volume of the *Principia Mathematica* (1910) of Bertrand Russell and Alfred North Whitehead in January 1910. He would later describe this classic of mathematical logic as a work 'of inestimable value to culture' (*Criterion*, April 1924, p. 233), and after the three volumes (1910–13) were re-issued (1925–7) he was to assert that secondary school students in England should 'come to understand how much the work of logicians has done to make of English a language in which it is possible to think clearly and exactly on any subject. The *Principia Mathematica* are perhaps a greater contribution to our language than they are to mathematics' (*Criterion*, October 1927, p. 291).

30–In *Epistola* X (c. 1318), addressed to the Veronan leader of the Ghibellines, Can Grande della Scala (1290–1329), to whom he dedicates the *Paradiso*, Dante explains that when he is met with carping incredulity about the reality of visions that cannot be related, he appeals first to scriptural authority: 'And if all this suffices not the carpers, let them read Richard of St Victor in his book *De Contemplatione* . . . and they will cease to carp' (*The Latin Works of*

cite the former only as a specimen of the sort of thinking and writing which went to the formation of Dante's mind and Dante's style.

In the passage from Remy de Gourmont quoted, it was observed that the love of the *trecentisti* was free from any notion of possession; and though this statement is much too absolute, it is generally true that the *trecentisti* are more concerned with the contemplation of the beloved object than with the feelings and sensations of union. What they record are the feelings and sensations of the one who contemplates the beloved.

> Chi è questa che vien, ch'ogni uom la mira,
> Che fa tremar di claritate l'aere?

(or, *che fe de clarità l'aer tremare*) says Cavalcanti in his best known sonnet: "who makes the air all tremulous with light" translates Rossetti;[31] and observe furthermore that this line is no mere compliment or flattering figure of speech, but an exact statement of the visual impression made by the beloved upon the lover – upon one type of lover at all events – which doubtless has its physiological explanation. And this is very significant. In the best of the erotic verse of Dante, Guinizelli, Cavalcanti and Cino you will find nothing of the merely courtly or eulogistic, no descriptions of the object, no attempt to express the emotions and sensations for their own sake, but solely an attempt to suggest the beauty and dignity of the object

---

Dante [London: J. M. Dent, Temple Classics Edition, 1924], trans. Philip H. Wicksteed, p. 360).

31 – TSE misquotes Cavalcanti's 'Sonetto VII', giving each variant of the second line but slightly misquoting in parentheses the line preferred by Ezra Pound, 'Che fa di clarità l'aer tremare!' See *The Sonnets and Ballate of Guido Cavalcante*, trans. Ezra Pound (Boston: Small, Maynard, 1912), p. 14. This is Sonnet IV, 'A Rapture concerning his lady', in Rossetti's *The Early Italian Poets* (p. 255):

> Who is she coming, whom all gaze upon,
>   Who makes the air all tremulous with light,
> And at whose side is Love himself? that none
>   Dare speak, but each man's sighs are infinite.
> Ah me! how she looks round from left to right,
> Let Love discourse: I may not speak thereon.
> Lady she seems of such high benison
>   As makes all others graceless in men's sight.
> The honour which is hers cannot be said;
>   To whom are subject all things virtuous,
>   While all things beauteous own her deity.
> Ne'er was the mind of man so nobly led,
>   Nor yet was such redemption granted us
>   That we should ever know her perfectly.

contemplated by stating the effect of that beauty and dignity upon the lover in contemplation. We shall see that this attitude differs still more from that of Donne and Lord Herbert of Cherbury than it does from that of the Provençaux.[32]

The difference is not one which can be illustrated by the material biographies of the poets in question. It may even be said that Donne is almost as much a poet of successful matrimony as Coventry Patmore, whereas the life of Dante was in this respect anything but successful or regular.[33] Nevertheless, the inner life of Dante was not only more extensive, but had heights of feeling unknown to the later poet.

Let us examine "The Extasie" of Donne and the "Ode" of Lord Herbert.

> Where, like a pillow on a bed,
> A pregnant bank swelled up, to rest
> The violet's reclining head,
> Sat we two, one another's best.[34]

32—Edward, Lord Herbert of Cherbury was best known for his 'An Ode upon a Question moved, whether Love should continue for ever?', a poem that had its origins in Donne's 'The Extasie'.

33—When Donne secretly married seventeen-year-old Anne More (1584–1617) in December 1601, in violation of Common and Canon Law, he had to plead with her choleric father Sir George More in prison and in court for months until the marriage was confirmed in April 1602, an event likely celebrated by Donne in 'The Canonization'. Before she died in childbirth, having borne him twelve children, Donne may have embodied the increasing richness of their wedded love in 'Loves Growth'.

In 1847 the poet and critic Coventry Patmore (1823–96) married Emily Augusta Andrews (1824–62), and in 1854 he published the first part of a long, four-part poem, *The Angel in the House*, designed to be the apotheosis of married love ('The Betrothal', 1854; 'The Espousals', 1856; 'Faithful for Ever', 1860; 'The Victories of Love', 1862). Tennyson, Browning, Ruskin and Carlyle lavished sincere praise upon the poem, which became a popular and commercial success, but Patmore's biographer was to judge the poem with a more critical eye, reflective of TSE's sardonic comparison with Donne: 'The obvious and unanswerable criticism is that the poet's professed subject of married life is only approached in the least successful parts of the poem, and hardly grappled with even there. The reason is plain: its domesticities were found incapable of poetic treatment' (*DNB*, First Supplement, vol. III [1901], p. 250).

Dante married Gemma Donati (d. 1343?) sometime between 1291, the year after the death of Beatrice, and 1298. She bore him four children. Boccaccio's speculative but widely accepted characterization of their allegedly unhappy married life in his *Vita di Dante* was based on evidence that the marriage had been arranged by Dante's relations to console him for the loss of Beatrice, that Gemma was a 'suspicious being' who attempted to domesticate Dante's imagination, that Dante never directly addressed her in his works, and that she never joined him again after his twenty-year exile from Florence.

34—*MLPSC* 16, lines 1–4; these and the following lines from the poem (5–20, 41–4, 49–52, 65–76) are partly modernized, with minor mistranscriptions.

Thus one of the finest poems of Donne, which is absolutely a very beautiful poem indeed, begins with one of the most hideous mixed figures of speech in the language. To compare a bank to a pillow (it is surely superfluous to add "on a bed" since a pillow may be presumed to have much the same shape wherever it be disposed) does neither dignify nor elucidate; but the simile comes into sharp collision with a metaphor – the bank is pregnant. Having already learned that the bank was shaped like a pillow, we do not require to be told that it was pregnant, unless an earthquake was preparing, which was not the case. I pass over the question of the beauty of obstetrical metaphors in general: they were in the taste of the epoch, which is not ours. The pregnant bank swells, which is just what it should not do, for the whole scene that follows is represented as static; otherwise it would not be an "ecstasy" at all. We then learn why the bank swelled up; it did this in order to provide a pillow for the drooping head of the violet. But for this accommodating behaviour of the bank to be justified, the violet would have to be imagined as growing, not on the bank, but beside it; and if the bank swelled only sufficiently to support the head of the violet, it was hardly of great enough size to deserve the name of bank. Finally, it is a violation of the order of nature to ask us to conceive of the violet as antecedent to the bank – unless we affirm that the final cause of banks is the support of violets' heads.[35]

Here are four lines wasted to let us know that the lovers sat on a bank.

> Our hands were firmly cemented
> With a fast balme, which thence did spring,
> Our eye-beams twisted, and did thred
> Our eyes, upon one double string.

In this quatrain you observe that over-emphasis, that strain to impress more than to state, which is the curse of seventeenth-century verse not in England alone, but throughout Europe. The first two lines are permissible, because it is possible to conceive of lovers as having a sensation *as if* their hands were materially attached – it may be said, that is, to be the statement of a feeling. But as for the threading of the eyes like buttons on a double thread, one thread proceeding from each eye to the other, it not only fails to render the

---

35 – In his letter to TSE of 31 January 1927, Praz remarked of this discussion: 'Of course the image of the bed and the pillow is preposterous, and the languor of the violet seems conventional, but Freud, perhaps, might find the poet's mood on that occasion mirrored even in an apparently superfluous detail like that one: it is a nuptial simile in a nuptial poem, and in so far it has its *raison d'être*' (L2).

sense of losing oneself in an ecstasy of gazing into the eyes of a loved person, it actually aggravates the difficulty of finding out what it is all about.

> So to entergraft our hands, as yet
> Was all the meanes to make us one,
> And pictures in our eyes to get
> Was all our propagation.

The blemish of this quatrain is first, that the figure of the hands as cemented is not left to itself, but is rubbed over by the more complicated image of grafting. Second, the "begetting" of "pictures" is a figure which violates nature. And third, the poet cannot keep his mind on the ecstasy, but must needs be comparing the state already with physical union in the ordinary sense.

> As 'twixt two equall Armies, Fate
> Suspends uncertain victorie,
> Our soules, (which to advance their state,
> Were gone out,) hung 'twixt her and me.

The meaning of this attractive figure, beyond the impression of trepidation and suspense which it certainly conveys, is not clear. I do not suppose the poet to imply a preparation for battle between the male and the female, or even battle between soul and body, yet one interpretation or the other seems inevitable. The former seems affirmed by the next quatrain.

> And whil'st our soules negotiate there,
> Wee like sepulchrall statues lay;
> All day, the same our postures were,
> And wee said nothing, all the day.

This stanza has always seemed to me particularly felicitous. Nothing could be more happy than the use of the word "negotiate", or the image of the effigies on a tomb, "sepulchrall statues"; while the "All day" beginning the third line, echoed by "all the day" at the end of the fourth, is a real *trouvaille* or euphony which goes to make one of the most perfect quatrains in this form that I have ever met.[36] And the *almost* affected simplicity of "And wee

---

36 – TSE had echoed Donne's phrase, 'all the day', in the third quatrain of 'Burbank with a Baedeker: Bleistein with a Cigar' (1919):

> The horses, under the axletree
> Beat up the dawn from Istria
> With even feet. Her shuttered barge
> Burned on the water all the day.

said nothing" – so characteristic of Donne, is perfection. The next several quatrains exhibit that playing upon an idea, arresting it and turning it about for examination, to which I called your attention in the preceding lecture as highly peculiar to Donne and his school. They lead up, however, to the introduction of a new and important idea.

> When love, with one another so
> Interinanimates two soules,
> That abler soule, which thence doth flow,
> Defects of lonelinesse controules.

Donne is often very well advised in his introductions of weighty Latin words, more or less philosophic, between several simple Saxon words. The idea of this quatrain is perhaps the cornerstone of the whole structure – an idea perhaps suggested to him by the *Banquet* of Plato – the isolation of soul from soul, its craving for the rare moments of semblance of fusion with another.[37] And this is something for which there seems no place in the amatory [verse] of the early Italian poetry. Indeed, I doubt whether, from a strictly orthodox Christian point of view – though I am not qualified to express an opinion – any more than from the point of view of a mystes of Eleusis – this union of human soul with human soul is intelligible. But has it not been the theme of much of the literature of love of the last 300 years?

This idea, strange itself and possibly heretical from the point of view of the thirteenth century, is the natural prelude to the theme of the remainder of the poem.

> But O alas, so long, so farre
> Our bodies, why doe wee forbeare?
> They are ours, though they are not wee, Wee are
> The intelligences, they the sphere.

37 – TSE alludes to Aristophanes' speech on love, in which he recounts how the gods divided the natures of what were originally three sexes – man, woman, and the androgynous sex common to both – and describes how ancient is the desire of lovers to make one of two and heal their divided natures: 'These are they who devote their whole lives to each other, with a vain and inexpressible longing to obtain from each other something they know not what; for it is not merely the sensual delights of their intercourse for the sake of which they dedicate themselves to each other with such serious affection; but the soul of each manifestly thirsts for, from the other, something which there are no words to describe, and divines that which it seeks, and traces obscurely the footsteps of its obscure desires' (*The Banquet of Plato*, trans. Percy Bysshe Shelley [Boston & New York: Riverside Press, 1908], pp. 58–9).

A stanza which illustrates very well that difficult habit of elision which, as Mr. Saintsbury remarks in one of his prefaces, becomes so intolerable in the poetry of this period.[38]

> So must pure lovers soules descend
I do not see why | To affection, and to faculties,
Mr. Grierson elides | Which sense may reach and apprehend,
here (T'affections) | Else a great Prince in prison lies.
when he has not done | To 'our bodies turne wee then, that so
so above.[39] | Weake men on love reveal'd may looke;
> Loves mysteries in soules doe grow,
> But yet the body is his booke.
> And if some lover, such as wee,
> Have heard this dialogue of one,
> Let him still marke us, he shall see
> Small change, when we're to bodies gone.

Here is posited, as clearly as may be, a distinction, a disjunction, between soul and body of which I think you will find no expression whatever in the *trecento*, and for which I do not think you will find much authority in Aquinas. Let us note first what Aquinas would say to the suggestion that two souls of separate bodies could form one. Combating a suggestion of St. Augustine by a reference to the *De Anima*,[40] he concludes:

38 – In his 'General Introduction' to the first volume of the *Minor Poets of the Caroline Period* (1905), Saintsbury deplores the 'slipshod' contractions that made their way into seventeenth-century poetry, exclaiming that the 'worst instances possess an offensiveness which is independent and intrinsic, and which is perhaps the greatest drawback to the enjoyment of this poetry . . . It was to get back the ten syllables into the heroic line, the eight into the "short" line (as Butler calls it) and no more, that these abominable Procrustean tortures were committed' (p. x).

39 – *MLPSC* 18, line 66: *read* 'T'affections, and to faculties,'.

40 – In question 76, 'Of the Union of Body and Soul', Article 2, 'Whether the Intellectual Principle is Multiplied According to the Number of Bodies?', Objection 6, Aquinas quotes St Augustine in *De Quantitate Animae*, xxxii, speaking on the grandeur of the soul: 'Further, Augustine says: *If I were to say that there are many human souls, I should laugh at myself*. But the soul seems to be one chiefly on account of the intellect. Therefore there is one intellect of all men'. Aquinas then counters Augustine with a citation from Aristotle, not from *De Anima* but from *Physics*, II, 3 (195b25–8): '*On the contrary*, The Philosopher says . . . that the relation of universal causes to universals is like the relation of particular causes to individuals. But it is impossible that a soul, one in species, should belong to animals of different species. Therefore it is impossible that one individual intellectual soul should belong to several individuals' (*Summa Theologica*, I, trans. Fathers of the English Dominican Province [1911; Christian Classics, 1981], p. 373). TSE was to express his familiarity with the Dominican translation in the *Criterion* (October 1927, p. 340).

Cum impossibile sit plurium numero differentium esse unam formam, sicut impossibile est quod eorum sit unum *esse*; oportet principium intellectivum multiplicari secundum multiplicationem corporum (Truc, p. 143–144).[41]

Concerning the difference between the body and the soul, he says:

anima distat a corpore plurimum, si utriusque conditiones seorsim considerentur; unde si utrumque ipsorum separatim *esse* haberet, oporteret quod multa media intervenirent. Sed in quantum anima est forma corporis, non habet *esse* seorsim ab *esse* corporis, sed per suum *esse* corpori unitur immediate. Sic enim et quaelibet forma, si consideretur ut actus; habet magnam distantiam a materia, quae est ens in potentia tantum.[42]

The effort of Aquinas is obviously to reconcile the theological necessities of the soul with the Aristotelian view; but even were there no effort of reconciliation to be made, he would in no case accept anything like the virtual *duplication* of the human animal effected in the poem of Donne, into two beings, one called the soul and the other called the body, whose only essential difference is that one is admirable and the other slightly shameful. However, we are only concerned with what Aquinas thinks because of what the *trecentisti* write. And I repeat that you will find no hint of such dichotomy there. The only difference there is between higher and lower, more and less worthy loves; in the distinguishing and experiencing of which differences it must be said that Dante and his friends were consummately

41 – TSE quotes from the corresponding Latin and French texts of Question 76, Article 2, in Gonzague Truc's edition of *La Pensée de Saint Thomas D'Aquin* (Paris: Payot, 1924). Truc takes both texts directly from F. Lachat's edition of *Somme Théologique*, III (Paris: Louis Vives, Libraire-Editeur, 1880), p. 150. *Translation*: 'Because it is impossible that there is one form for a number of diverse things, just as it is impossible that what belongs to each of them be one thing, it is necessary that the intellective principle be multiplied according to the number of bodies'.
42 – TSE quotes the final paragraph of Question 76, Article 7 ('Whether the Soul is United to the Animal Body by Means of a Body'), in Truc, pp. 185–6, as taken from Lachat, p. 175. *Translation*: 'The soul is indeed very distant from the body, if we consider the condition of each separately: so that if each had a separate existence, many means of connection would have to intervene. But inasmuch as the soul is the form of the body, it has not an existence apart from the existence of the body, but by its own existence is united to the body immediately. This is the case with every form which, if considered as an act, is very distant from matter, which is a being only in potentiality' (*Summa Theologica*, I, p. 381).

expert. There is no imagined struggle of soul and body, only the one struggle toward perfection.[43]

The separation of soul and body in this way is a modern conception; the only ancient parallel that occurs to me is the attitude of Plotinus toward the body as quoted by Porphyry;[44] and in the form employed by Donne represents a far cruder state of philosophical speculation than that of Aquinas. The apparent "glorification of the body" appreciated by many admirers of Donne is really a puritanical attitude. And the conception of the ecstasy of union between two souls is not only philosophically crude but emotionally limiting. The expression of love as contemplation of the beloved object is not only more Aristotelian, it is also more Platonic, for it is the contemplation of absolute beauty and goodness partially revealed through a limited though delightful human object. What is there for Donne? This union in ecstasy is complete, is final; and two human beings, needing nothing beyond each other, rest on their emotion of enjoyment. But emotion cannot rest; desire must expand, or it will shrink. Donne, the modern man, is imprisoned in the embrace of his own feelings. There is little suggestion of adoration, of worship. And an attitude like that of Donne leads naturally to one of two things: to the Tennysonian happy marriage – not very different from Donne's own – which is one sort of bankruptcy;[45] or to the collapse of

43 – Praz cautioned TSE about this passage in his letter of 31 January 1927: 'A little inaccuracy of interpretation, which remains unnoticed when slurred over in the course of a lecture, may wreck the whole work, when insisted upon and magnified in a book. I am not sure, for instance, about what you are saying in your III lect. . . . on the trecentisti having no idea of a dichotomy between soul and body. I have not gone very far into the question myself: but, before coming to any conclusion concerning Dante, for inst., I would examine carefully all the passages of his works bearing on the subject – a task rendered very easy to us by the admirable index *raisonné* appended to the Testo critico of Dante's Works, Bemporad 1921. I daresay you are familiar with it' (*L2*).

44 – Porphyry of Tyre (AD 233–304), friend, follower and editor of Plotinus (AD 205–70), opens his *Life of Plotinus* (303): 'Plotinus, the philosopher our contemporary, seemed ashamed of being in the body'. In his annotated, bookplate copy (King's) of *Plotini Enneades*, edited by Ricardus Volkmann in two volumes (Lipsiae, 1883), TSE notes of the fourth Ennead: 'He looks at soul 1st as possessed of faculties wh. refer to sensible world (Aristotle) 2 as rising above the world to union with God . . . Plotinus is a two substance man as against Aristotle's reduction of the soul to functions of the body'.

45 – TSE alludes sardonically to the marriage song that serves as the epilogue to *In Memoriam* (1850), Tennyson's elegy for Arthur Hallam. Written for the poet's sister, Cecilia, and Edmund Lushington, who were married in 1842, the epithalamium celebrates the 'happy hour, and happier hours' that await them, with the implication that marriage takes the couple closer to a paradisal state, that procreation establishes 'a closer link / Betwixt us and the crowning race / Of those that, eye to eye, shall look / On knowledge; under whose command / Is Earth and Earth's, and in their hand / Is Nature like an open book; / No longer half-akin to brute' (lines

the hero of Huysmans' *En Route*: "Mon dieu, que c'est donc bête!"[46] It leads in fact to most of modern literature; for whether you seek the Absolute in marriage, adultery or debauchery, it is all one – you are seeking in the wrong place. *Donna è laggiù.*[47]

This vain effort to find the permanent by fixing the transient is repeated magnificently in the "Ode" of Herbert of Cherbury. Sometimes this ode has seemed to me finer than Donne's "Extasie"; but that has been when it has taken me by surprise; on sober reflection I find more meat, more solidity, as well as greater technical beauty and more unpardonable defects, in the poem of Donne. It is the same cry:

> O you, wherein, they say, Souls rest,
> Till they descend pure heavenly fires,
> Shall lustful and corrupt desires
> With your immortal seed be blest?
>
> And shall our Love, so far beyond
> That low and dying appetite,
> And which so chaste desires unite,
> Not hold in an eternal bond?
>
> . . . .

128–33). In 'The Metaphysical Poets' TSE had criticized Tennyson's portrayal of the happy marriage and 'the perpetuation of love by offspring' in a passage from 'The Two Voices' (*SE* 287/246).

46 – Durtal, the Satan-drawn, faith-seeking protagonist of four novels by Joris-Karl Huysmans (1848–1907), makes this exclamation not in *En Route* (1895) but in *Là-bas* (1891), Chapter XIII, when Madame Chantelouve comes to him for an adulterous rendezvous. While she awaits him, Durtal mutters to himself: 'Decidedly she was in the right when she refused. It will be grotesque and abominable. I did wrong to insist; but no, it is her fault after all, she wished to go to this length, for else why did she come? And then, what silliness so to check one's ardour by delays! she is really clumsy; a moment ago, when I held her in my arms and craved so passionately to possess her, it might have borne some fruit, but now! And then, what do I look like? a newly wed husband waiting, a nincompoop! My God, how stupid the business is!' (Trans. Alfred Allinson, *Down There*, p. 233). In 'Baudelaire in our Time' (1927) TSE was to allude to this pivotal passage again in reference to Huysmans' third novel, *La Cathédrale* (1898): 'Huysmans . . . might have been much more in sympathy with the real spirit of the thirteenth century if he had thought less about it . . . he is much more "mediaeval" (and much more human) when he describes the visit of Madam Chantelouve to Durtal than when he talks about his Cathedral' (*FLA* 92–3/97–8).

47 – TSE reverses a characteristic vision of the *trecentisti* – *Donna è lassù* ('Lady up there') – to suggest its characteristic deflation by modern writers, *Donna è laggiù* ('Lady down there'), as Huysmans had done in *Là-bas* ('Down there').

And if every imperfect mind
Make love the end of knowledge here,
How perfect will our love be, where
All imperfection is refined?[48]

And against this I will set a passage from the *Vita Nuova*.

There came a day when certain ladies [. . .] were met together for the
pleasure of gentle company . . . One of them, who before had been
talking with another, addressed me by my name, saying, "To what end
lovest thou this lady, seeing that thou canst not support her presence?
Now tell us this thing, that we may know it: for certainly the end of
such a love must be worthy of knowledge" . . . Whereupon, I said thus
unto them: "Ladies, the end and aim of my love was but the salutation
of that lady of whom I conceive that we are speaking: wherein alone I
found that beatitude which is the goal of desire. And now that it hath
pleased her to deny me this, Love, my master, of his great goodness,
hath placed all my beatitude there where my hope will not fail me".
Then those ladies began to talk closely together; and as I have seen
snow fall among the rain, so was their talk mingled with sighs. But after
a little, that lady who had been the first to address me, addressed me
again in these words: "We pray thee that thou wilt tell us wherein
abideth this thy beatitude". And answering, I said but this [*for* thus]
much: "In those words that do praise my lady."[49]

The experience which forms the material of the *Vita Nuova* is the material
of adolescence; but it is handled by a mature man with a philosophy which
assigned a place to such experience. Later, we shall have occasion to
examine another poetry of adolescence, also, in our sense metaphysical –
that of Jules Laforgue. But the philosophy of Laforgue, such as it was, was
not one which could organise such experience, which remains, for him, the
effusion of adolescent sentiment; and he remains, for us, imprisoned within
his adolescence, with a philosophy which should have been mature. Neither
did Donne have a philosophy to deal with such experience; but he passed
through it, if he had it, to an early middle age. So Laforgue died appropri-
ately at twenty-seven; so Donne is perpetually, in his erotic life, forty or
thereabouts; but Dante is ageless. For Laforgue to have passed into a larger

48–*MLPSC* 30–31, lines 65–72, 117–20; minor mistranscriptions.
49–*La Vita Nuova*, XVIII, as translated by Rossetti in *The Early Italian Poets*, pp. 194–5;
minor mistranscriptions. See first epigraph, p. 40.

life would have necessitated a violent struggle, too violent for so delicate a constitution. Donne, I think, did not really pass; I mean that his religious writings, his sermons and his devotional verse, always give me the impression of an incomplete concentration, of a direction of forces more by a strong will than by surrender and assent. While with Dante there is no interruption between the first line of the *Vita Nuova* and the last line of the *Paradiso*. There was no compulsion, and no waste.

I propose in my next lecture to deal with the peculiarities of language of Donne and his school, with the conceit, with the quality of wit, and the relation of their modes of expression to their intellectual background.

LECTURE IV

{The Conceit in Donne}

In the preceding lecture I endeavoured to persuade you that the systematic Latin philosophy of the twelfth and thirteenth centuries, combining with the Provençal influence, produced in the *trecento* that conception of love which is expressed in the *Vita Nuova*. And I tried to present the *Vita Nuova* itself under the aspect, so to speak, of a scientific monograph, the record of experiments upon sentiment; the record of the method of utilising, trans-forming instead of discarding, the emotions of adolescence; the record of a discovery analogous to those concerning the use of the waste products of coal-tar in industry.[1] The result of this discovery was a real extension of the area of emotion, and an attitude both more "spiritual" and more "worldly" than that of Donne or that of Tennyson or that of Laforgue. And I wished to indicate that the chaotic intellectual background of Donne issues in a compromise with the flesh, rather than an acceptance of the flesh, and in exactly a *contraction* of the field of experience. I pointed out the different types of mysticism operant on the minds of the two men; there is no reason that I can see for calling either of the two men a "mystic", or for talking

---

1 – Recent reports in *The Times* of progress in the distillation of coal-tar may have stimulated TSE's penchant for using chemical processes as metaphors for creative processes (see p. 50, n. 15). The industrial production of coal-tar, a heavy, black viscous liquid obtained by the carbonization of coal, was developed in Germany after 1881 and was at this time conducted on a large scale in England. Its many chemical distillates and residues, such as napthalene, quinolin and tar acids, were used as raw materials for the production of dyes, preservatives, solvents and munitions, including poison gas. The chemist Sir James Dewar (1842–1923) had never tired of rehearsing the national danger should Britain fall behind in research into the by-products of coal-tar: 'By all means let us hope that the coal-tar chemistry in all its ramifications of dyes, drugs, and munitions will be firmly established in this country, and that we shall no longer run the risk of having our industries arrested and our national will to survive thwarted because another country is suddenly able to cut off our supplies' (*The Times*, 11 September 1923, p. 8).

about the "mysticism" of either Donne or Dante, unless a capacity for feeling beyond the ordinary boundaries of experience is always mysticism; but you can use the term if you like.

I want now to show, if I can, how the acceptance of one orderly system of thought and feeling results, in Dante and his friends, in a simple, direct and even austere manner of speech, while the maintenance in suspension of a number of philosophies, attitudes and partial theories which are enjoyed rather than believed, results, in Donne and in some of our contemporaries, in an affected, tortuous, and often over-elaborate and ingenious manner of speech.

If you examine the figures of speech employed by Dante, or by Cavalcanti, or the best of those of the other men, you will find, I think, that the difference between their images and those of Donne lies in the focus of interest. The interest of Dante lies in the idea or the feeling to be conveyed; the image always makes this idea or feeling more intelligible. In Donne, the interest is dispersed; it may be in the ingenuity of conveying the idea by that particular image; or the image itself may be more difficult than the idea; or it may be in the *compulsion*, rather than in the *discovery*, of resemblances. Part of the pleasure may be in the natural incongruity which is actually overcome; part of the feeling is the "feel" of an idea, rather than the feeling of a person who lives by that idea. It is an harmony of dissonances. But before analysing the speech of Donne let me leave in your memory, for the sake of contrast, one image of Dante. He is attempting to express the sense of entering the first heaven, at the beginning of the *Paradiso*.

> Pareva a me che nube ne coprisse
> lucida, spessa, solida e polita,
> quasi adamante che lo sol ferisse.

> Per entro sè l'eterna margarita
> ne recepette, com'acqua recepe
> raggio di luce, permanendo unita.

"Meseemed a cloud enveloped us, shining, dense, firm and polished, like diamond smitten by the sun. Within itself the eternal pearl received us, as water doth receive a ray of light, though still itself uncleft".[2]

You observe the strict utility of these images. They are to convey a supersensuous experience; the adjectives are chosen as they might be in a

2—*Paradiso*, II, 31–6; trans. *TC* III, 17 (typed as prose).

scientific treatise, because they are the nearest possible to approximate what he is driving at. The image of the light passing through water is undecorated and is not, nor is intended to be, interesting apart from the experience which it makes more apprehensible. And this I think is characteristic of all of Dante's similes and metaphors: they have a rational necessity.

Now I must not draw my distinctions too tight. I am perfectly aware that between the image of absolute necessity, like that above, and the extreme conceit, there are infinite degrees; you could present many images, and especially from the Elizabethans, of which it is difficult to say whether they are serviceable or ornamental. Speaking of the Elizabethans, I think of a figure used in one of the Martin Marprelate tracts, which I can never forget; when the author, speaking of his adversary Bishop Cooper, says that he "Has a face like old wainscot, and would lie as fast as a dog would trot". As for the bishop's veracity, there is no doubt something to be said on both sides, but in my memory, that simile sticks to him like wax; he will never be free of it.[3] These are properly, rhetorical images; they emphasise rather than elucidate; and in strict reason, it is meaningless to compare rapidity of lying, even [by analogy], to rapidity of dog's trotting. And the image of old wainscot is a variable one: that is to say, it may have effect equally on various minds to which it suggests different things. To me it means an old, weatherbeaten, pitted as if worm-eaten, brown face; and in juxtaposition with the dogtrot, suggests great villainy. This variable margin of suggestion is what I call rhetorical effect. But it is quite different from the well-known

3 – Martin Marprelate was the pseudonym signed to a series of highly vituperative pamphlets (1588–9) against the prelacy of the Church of England by several Puritans who were bitter over Queen Elizabeth's failure to rid the Church of its Roman Catholic remnants. In 'The Epistle' the author attacks Thomas Cooper (1517?–1594), Bishop of Winchester, as the 'most wretched' of Popish bishops for preaching and defending the heresy 'that men might find fault, if they were disposed to quarrel, as well with the Scripture as with the Book of Common Prayer', and for proclaiming to Her Majesty that all is well in the Church: ' "Nay," says my Lord of Winchester, like a monstrous hypocrite – for he is a very dunce, not able to defend an argument, but, till he come to the pinch, he will cog and face it out, for his face is made of seasoned wainscot, and will lie as fast as a dog can trot – "I have said it. I do say it, and I have said it." And say I, you shall one day answer it, without repentance, for abusing the Church of God and her Majesty in this sort' (*The Marprelate Tracts 1588, 1589*, ed. William Pierce [London: James Clark, 1911], pp. 70–72). As early as 1919 TSE was writing that 'as no one reads Nashe, or Lancelot Andrewes, or Martin Marprelate, the impression is very strong that Elizabethan prose is very bad' (*Athenaeum*, 4 April 1919, p. 135). 'Who reads them now?' he was to ask in 1931, 'except a very small number of people, those who interest themselves in the religious squabbles of that epoch, and those who interest themselves in the prose styles of that epoch. They are not considered a part of the necessary education of the cultivated English-speaking person' (*SE* 494/441).

figure of Dante when he is trying to make you visualise exactly that dolorous twilight in which moved the form of Brunetto Latini – the famous image of the old tailor threading a needle:

> sì ver noi aguzzevan le ciglia,
> come vecchio sartor fa nella cruna

"they knitted their brows at us, like an old tailor threading a needle".[4] This image, whether one has ever seen an old tailor threading a needle or not, is exact and the same for everybody; and it does make you see how the people looked, better than if it had not been used at all. On the other hand, I admit that sometimes the suggestiveness of an image of Dante will, for me at any rate, exceed the exact meaning:

> Poi si rivolse, e parve di coloro
>   che coronno a Verona il drappo verde
>   per la campagna; e parve di costoro
> quegli che vince e non colui che perde.

"Then he (Brunetto Latini) turned back, and seemed like one of those who run for the green cloth at Verona through the open field; and of them seemed he who gains, not he who loses".[5] Of course the sports at Verona may be assumed to be better known to Dante's original audience than they are to us. But I know not why, the notion of this sinning and defeated soul running off "like a victor" is very poignant to me. But in any case, the figure itself is exact enough to help us to visualise the man running.

I know that it will occur to you to ask, as I criticise the conceit and the language of Donne, whether this is anything peculiar to the metaphysical

4 – *Inferno*, XV, 20–21: TSE departs from the Temple Classics translation here and in 'Dante' (1929): 'and sharpened their vision (knitted their brows) at us, like an old tailor peering at the eye of his needle' (*SE* 244/205). Dante's encounter with his friend Brunetto Latini (c. 1210–94), the Florentine Guelf and political leader, was to become the model for TSE's encounter with 'some dead master' in 'Little Gidding' (1942), where the 'knitted brows' of the troop of spirits that examine Dante and his guide become 'That pointed scrutiny with which we challenge / The first-met stranger in the waning dusk' (*CPP* 193/140).

5 – *Inferno*, XV, 121–4; trans. *TC* I, 165. In 'Tradition and the Individual Talent' (1919), TSE had written of this concluding quatrain: 'great poetry may be made without the direct use of any emotion whatever: composed out of feelings solely. Canto XV of the *Inferno* . . . is a working up of the emotion evident in the situation; but the effect, though single as that of any work of art, is obtained by considerable complexity of detail. The last quatrain gives an image, a feeling attaching to an image, which "came", which did not develop simply out of what precedes, but which was probably in suspension in the poet's mind until the proper combination arrived for it to add itself to' (*SE* 18–19/8).

poets of the seventeenth century – especially as it is part of my thesis that it is not peculiar to metaphysical poetry in general – or whether it is not merely the inheritance of the bombast of the Elizabethans. And if I were giving a longer course of lectures, or if in this course I were dealing only with the language of the metaphysical poets, it would be my duty to go into this question in some detail. All that I can say is this: you cannot establish such a definition that no figure of speech chosen before a certain date will not be conceited, and so that every figure of speech in the poetry after that date will be conceited. But in general, the excesses of the Elizabethans are verbal and declamatory, for the sake of the sound, or else, without any *arrière pensée*, for the pleasure of introducing some image of eye or ear which is beautiful or jolly in itself. And there are kinds of figures of speech, of which it would be tempting to multiply examples, which abound in Shakespeare and which would be impossible for Dante, which are of the highest rank. To take one which I have often quoted: from *Antony and Cleopatra* –

> She looks like sleep
> As she would catch another Antony
> In her strong toil of grace.[6]

You would not say that this had the same *rational* necessity as an image of Dante, but necessary it is, in some other way; and it is an image of which Dante never would have thought. It is an image absolutely woven into the fabric of the thought; and the whole of Cleopatra's disastrous power over men and empires and navies is evoked in it.[7]

6 – *Antony and Cleopatra*, v.ii.349–51 (line 349, *read* 'But she looks like sleep,'). TSE had quoted the last line in 'Studies in Contemporary Criticism' (*Egoist*, October 1918, p. 114) as a 'complicated metaphor' that 'adds to the strength of the language; it makes available some of that physical source of energy upon which the life of language depends'; again in 'Philip Massinger' (1920) as an example of 'fusing into a single phrase, two or more diverse impressions' (*SE* 209/185); and yet again in his review of Andrew Marvell's *Miscellaneous Poems* (*Nation and Athenaeum*, 29 September 1923, p. 809), to argue in a discussion of conceits that Shakespeare's passage 'is not a conceit. For instead of contrast we have fusion: a restoration of language to contact with things. Such words have the inevitability which makes them appropriate to be spoken by any character'.
7 – When TSE compared Dante's description of Brunetto with Shakespeare's description of Cleopatra in his review of Marvell's *Miscellaneous Poems* (see previous note), he observed that the former lines 'have a rational necessity as well as suggestiveness; they are, like the words of Shakespeare above, an *explication* of the meaning'. In 'Dante' (1929) TSE was to compare Shakespeare's description of Cleopatra directly to Dante's description of the meeting with Brunetto Latini: 'The image of Shakespeare's is much more complicated than Dante's, and more complicated than it looks . . . But whereas the simile of Dante is merely to make you see more clearly how the people looked, and is explanatory, the figure of Shakespeare is expansive rather than intensive; its purpose is to *add* to what you see . . . a reminder of that fascination of

I have said that you cannot define the conceit so that it shall never occur before a certain date; on the other hand I would point out that some of Donne's best lines – and some of those by which he is best known – are not conceited at all, are not of an age or a fashion but eternal. If you have the Grierson anthology by you, turn to 'The Funerall' on page 18 and to 'The Relique' on page 21. They are as well known as anything he wrote, and they are variations on the same theme.

> Who ever comes to shroud me, do not harm
> > Nor question much
> That subtile wreath of hair, which crowns my arm;
> The mystery, the signe you must not touch,
> > For 'tis my outward Soule,
> Viceroy to that, which then to heaven being gone,
> > Will leave this to controule;
> And keep those limbes, her provinces, from dissolution.[8]

This is typical of Donne's procedure. The first three lines are perfectly simple; the adjective "subtile" is exact, though its exactness be not to us immediately apparent in the literal sense of the word which has so suffered from the abuse of the kindred word "subtle"[9]; the only blemish is the very slightly distracting over-emphasis of the metaphorical verb "crown". But with line 5 he becomes wholly and characteristically conceited: you find yourself in a tangle of souls and deputy-souls, kings, viceroys and territories. And yet, though it is irrelevant, though it diminishes rather than develops the thought, though it represents an inward chaos and disjection, it is pleasing. In order to get the full flavour out of Donne, you must construe analytically and enjoy synthetically; you must hold the elements in suspension and contiguity in your mind, as he did himself. And you will observe that in his conceits he is equally serious as elsewhere. How the "wit" in these lines develops into "wit" as we know it, the development from juxtaposition to ironic contrast, is a problem we shall have to attack later; sufficient

---

Cleopatra which shaped her history and that of the world, and of that fascination being so strong that it prevails even in death. It is more elusive, and it is less possible to convey without close knowledge of the English language' (*SE* 244/205).

8–'The Funerall', lines 1–8 (*MLPSC* 18); partly modernized; minor mistranscriptions; line 8, *read* 'these limbs'.

9–In Donne's usage 'subtile' denotes the most delicate sense of 'thin', a literal meaning obscured by the accumulated connotations of 'subtle' and by the tendency of most modern editions to print the modernized spelling of the word.

at the moment to remark that when we speak of the wit of Donne, the wit of Dryden, the wit of Swift, and our own precious wit, we are not speaking of the same thing, and we are not speaking of different things, but of a gradual development and different stages of the same thing.

We turn then to "The Relique".

> When my grave is broke up againe
> Some second ghest to entertaine,
> (For graves have learn'd that woman-head
> To be to more than one a Bed)
> And he that digs it, spies
> A bracelet of bright haire about the bone,
> Will he not let us alone,
> And thinke that there a loving couple lies,
> Who thought that this device might be some way
> To make their soules, at the last busie day,
> Meet at this grave, and make a little stay?[10]

In this version we observe that the procedure is reversed. It begins with the conceit, and proceeds to the more simple and direct. In some ways this version has the better of it. To place the discovery of the token at the moment when the grave is broken open, instead of at the moment of shrouding the body of the late deceased, intensifies and makes more perdurable the passion, makes more vivid and significant the wreath about the arm, now bone. But the notion of the violation of the grave for "entertaining" a "second guest", and still more the analogy of the fickleness of graves with the fickleness of women, are of very doubtful value in this place. Still more, the reference to female wantonness, of doubtful taste in itself, is particularly out of place in a poem intended to celebrate an instance of reciprocal fidelity –

> Will he not let'us alone,
> And thinke that there a loving couple lies . . .

But the famous line

> A bracelet of bright haire about the bone

is an example of those things said by Donne which could not have been put equally well otherwise, or differently by a poet of any other school. The

---

10–*MLPSC* 21, lines 1–11; some line positions mistranscribed.

associations are perfect: those of "bracelet", the brightness of the hair, after years of dissolution, and the final emphasis of "bone", could not be improved upon.[11] And the close of the stanza is impeccable. Yet even here,

> Who thought that this device might be some way
> To make their soules, at the last busie day,
> Meet at this grave, and make a little stay?

is there not a slight distraction, a slight diversion, an over-development, after the ultimacy of the great line, in the suggestion of a conscious purpose in the symbol, a motive beyond the pure instinctive clinging to any contact or memory of contact?

In the next verse, Donne is in full cry after the *concetti*:

> If this fall in a time, or land,
> Where mis-devotion doth command,
> Then, he that digges us up, will bring
> Us, to the Bishop, and the King,
>   To make us Reliques; then
> Thou shalt be a Mary Magdalen, and I
>   A something else thereby;
> All women shall adore us, and some men;
> And since, at such time, miracles are sought,
> I would have that age by this paper taught
> What miracles wee harmelesse lovers wrought.[12]

Here, you see, Donne has lost his focus on the *meaning* of the notion of the bracelet on the bone; he is occupied with the possible consequences of the notion. And I think that it is safe to say that Donne's method is frequently to proceed from the greater to the less, from the central to the peripheral, from the passionate to the reflective. And in this he is honest to his own mind, and sympathetic to ours. For passion, unless it be of an astounding simplicity

---

11–TSE had first discussed this line in 'Reflections on Contemporary Poetry' (*Egoist*, September 1917, p. 118). In pointing to the imbalance of emotion and object in some poets, he asserts that in Donne 'the feeling and the material symbol preserve exactly their proper proportions. A poet of morbidly keen sensibilities but weak will might become absorbed in the hair to the exclusion of the original association which made it significant; a poet of imaginative or reflective power more than emotional power would endow the hair with ghostly or moralistic meaning. Donne sees the thing as it is'. In 'The Metaphysical Poets' he had quoted the line as an example of Donne's ability to secure the powerful effects of his verse by a characteristic 'telescoping of images and multiplied associations' (*SE* 283/242–3).
12–*MLPSC* 21, lines 12–22; some line positions mistranscribed.

and ingenuity, or unless it be sustained by a high philosophy which interprets it into something else, must always fade out. In Donne it fades into the play of suggested ideas; and Donne is the great ruler of that borderland of fading and change. It is only one more step in metaphysical poetry, to the conscious irony of conflict between feeling, and the intellectual interpretation which feeling wishes to give itself, and reason.

Signor Mario Praz, to whose book I have already referred, remarks shrewdly that (p. 102) "whilst in other singers the whole poem vibrates under the impulse of the first impetus, with Donne on the other hand the impulse is suddenly . . . broken by an anticlimax of ratiocination";[13] and I would suggest that one of the reasons why we find Donne so sympathetic is that we also, provided with no philosophy which can assign a serious and dignified place to the original impulse, take refuge in the anticlimax of ratiocination; only, with us, the contrast is more conscious and complete.

This ironical contrast is illustrated by another well known poem in the Grierson book, "The Blossome" (page 20), with the last two stanzas:

> Well then, stay here; but know,
> When thou hast stayd and done thy most;
> A naked thinking heart, that makes no show,
> Is to a woman, but a kinde of ghost;
> How shall she know my heart; or having none,
> Know thee for one?
> Practise may make her know some other part,
> But take my word, she doth not know a Heart.
>
> Meet me at London, then,
> Twenty dayes hence, and thou shalt see
> Mee fresher, and more fat, by being with men,
> Than if I had staid still with her and thee.
> For Gods sake, if you can, be you so too:
> I would give you
> There, to another friend, whom wee shall finde
> As glad to have my body, as my minde.[14]

13 – Translated from *Secentismo e marinismo in Inghilterra*, p. 102: 'Pero mentre negli altri cantori il resto della poesia vibra tutto sotto l'impulso di quell'impeto iniziale, non offrendovi contrasto o resistenza alcuna, ma piegandosi elasticamente sotto la spinta de quella nota di chiave, nel Donne invece l'impeto e subito smorzato, reciso da un anticlimax di natura raziocinativa . . .'

14 – Lines 25–40; partly modernized; minor mistranscriptions.

In these lines – and one would go to gaol for ten years if it would help to write as good lines as these! – there is a good deal of what is called cynicism – and cynicism of a very modern type. Substitute the *jeune fille* for the mature woman of Donne, and it might be Laforgue speaking,[15] or another. "Mummy, Possessed".[16] But cynicism is always the indication of a mental chaos, or at least a mental disjunction and lack of unity. In these lines of Donne there is a great deal of the modern *recherche de l'absolu*,[17] the disappointed romanticism, the vexation of resignation at finding the world other than one wanted it to be. The literature of disillusionment is the literature of immaturity. It is in this way that I have ventured to affirm that Dante is more a man of the world than is Donne. He knew what he could get, and he took it, without criticising the condition of its teeth.

But, to turn from restriction to praise, how wonderful, how impeccable, the diction and versification of Donne! And what a profound change he operated! In this respect, he is the child of Ben Jonson, the parent of Dryden, the ancestor of Pope, Goldsmith and Samuel Johnson[18] – as much or more, I think, than Waller, Denham or Oldham.[19] The change of style from

15 – TSE alludes to the '*jeune demoiselle*', the object of Laforgue's cynical day-dreaming about the ideal in the first 'Dimanches' of *Derniers Vers* (1886), and to '*Les Jeunes Filles*' who come to represent womankind as a whole in the second 'Dimanches', both of which are discussed in Lecture VIII.

16 – Slightly misquoted from the concluding line of Donne's 'Loves Alchymie': 'Sweetnesse and wit, they'are but *Mummy*, possest;' TSE's phrase 'or another' may be a self-reference to 'Whispers of Immortality': 'Donne, I suppose, was such another' (*CPP* 52/32).

17 – The phrase originates in Balzac's *La Recherche de l'Absolu* (1834), which appeared as part of his *Etudes Philosophiques* before it took its place in *La Comédie Humaine* in 1845. Balzac's protagonist, Balthazar Claes, an adept of Lavoisier, gradually becomes possessed by his relentless chemical search for the Absolute, or philosopher's stone. The tyranny of the quest had been described to him earlier by a Polish officer, who had tried unsuccessfully to relinquish his studies: 'My inmost soul is rapt in the contemplation of one fixed idea, engrossed by one all-absorbing thought – the Quest for the Absolute' (Saintsbury edition [London: Dent, 1895], p. 78). Ruined and broken in health by the tragic search, Claes perceives the Absolute in a sudden illumination at the very moment of his death.

18 – The Irish-born novelist Oliver Goldsmith (c. 1730–74) became a member of Samuel Johnson's circle and was best known as a poet for *The Deserted Village* (1770). In his 'Introductory Essay' to Johnson's *London: A Poem and the Vanity of Human Wishes* (London: Etchells & Macdonald, 1930), TSE was to compare the two poets: 'Goldsmith is more a poet of his time, with his melting sentiment just saved by the precision of his language' (p. 15).

19 – TSE had written to Richard Aldington on 6 November 1921, while awaiting Aldington's article on Waller's poems, 'When am I to see your notes on Waller? I shall be interested, because I made nothing of him, though I admire Denham and Oldham' (*L1* 486). He wrote again after reading the piece: 'I do think it is worth while discussing these questions of derivation, neglected in English criticism, but important for the "tradition". I should like to know,

Provençal to early Italian is the change from the lyrical to the philosophical; the change from Elizabethan to Jacobean is the change from lyrical to rhetorical. I am using the term "rhetorical" as exactly as I can, and, be it well noted, without any implication whatever of eulogy or defamation. It is different in kind, neither better nor worse. Some years ago, I wrote a short note on "rhetoric" which was included in my volume *The Sacred Wood*, which in the main I still approve. But it was written in a different context than this, and I was thinking chiefly of so-called "dramatic" rhetoric. But I said even then, that I could not admit any antithesis between the "rhetorical" and the "conversational".[20] Rhetoric may be merely a development of conversation: Cicero *talked* his discourses; the actors of the Elizabethan dramatists shouted them. Any literary mode is a development out of speech; sometimes it gets too far away from speech: in philosophy, Professor Husserl or Professor Cohen is a good deal farther away from speech, it seems to me, than Berkeley or Leibnitz or even Kant; Adam Smith is a good deal nearer to the conversational style than most of our modern economists.[21] I mean that the Elizabethan styles were closer to *song* – even in

---

however, why it should be Waller, rather than Denham, who seems to me just as smooth and gives a deal more pleasure, who should have had the influence. Can you tell?' (*L1* 488). The satirical poet John Oldham (1653–83) is best known for his *Satires upon the Jesuits* (1681). In 'John Marston' (1934) TSE was to argue that 'The Satire, when all is said and done, is a form which the Elizabethans endeavoured to naturalize with very slight success; it is not until Oldham that a satire appears, sufficiently natural to be something more than a literary exercise' (*SE* 223–4; not included in US edition; *TLS*, 26 July 1934, pp. 517–18).

20 – In ' "Rhetoric" and Poetic Drama' (originally 'Whether Rostand Had Something about Him', 1919), TSE had written: 'At the present time there is a manifest preference for the "conversational" in poetry – the style of "direct speech", opposed to the "oratorical" and the rhetorical; but if rhetoric is any convention of writing inappropriately applied, this conversational style can and does become a rhetoric – or what is supposed to be a conversational style, for it is often as remote from polite discourse as well could be. Much of the second and third rate in American *vers libre* is of this sort; and much of the second and third rate in English Wordsworthianism' (*SE* 38/26).

21 – TSE began reading the *Logische Untersuchungen* (1900–01) of Edmund Husserl (1859–1938), professor at Göttingen and Freiburg, in July 1914 at Marburg University, where he had gone to study philosophy. On 5 October he wrote to his Harvard professor, James Houghton Woods, 'I have been plugging away at Husserl, and find it terribly hard, but very interesting; and I like very much what I think I understand of it' (*L1* 60). Professor Hermann Cohen (1842–1918), leader of the neo-Kantian school at Marburg, was described by T. E. Hulme, who preceded TSE at Marburg, in *Speculations* (1924): 'I remember being completely overawed by the vocabulary and scientific method of the various philosophers of the Marburg School, and in particular by Herman Cohen's "Logik der reinen Erkenntniss." . . . It becomes possible to see a good deal of Cohen's work as the rigid, scientific expression of an attitude that is neither rigid nor scientific, but sometimes romantic, and always humanist'. The style of Adam Smith (1723–90), known for his monumental *Inquiry into the Nature and Causes of the Wealth of Nations*

their dramatic verse – than the styles of the seventeenth century. It is a variation of focus: the focus is shifted, even if ever so little, from sound, to sense; from the sound of the word to the sound of the sense of the word, if you like; the sense of the sound or the sound of the sense; to the consciousness of the meaning of the word and a pleasure in that sound having that meaning – no amount of subtlety can quite express the fine shades of transition. Analagous to the transition [is] the shift of focus from metaphysics to psychology; the word is not merely the noise, as in the lyric, not merely the meaning, as in philosophical poetry; the word is interesting for its own meaning, as well as for what the writer means to mean by it. In other words, the conceited style is really the origin of the style of those who, as Dryden and Dr. Johnson, were its chief censurers. Rhetoric tends toward the law courts, lyricism toward the musical instrument, the verse of Dante and Cavalcanti toward the Sorbonne; they all have the same relation to "conversation".

On one side the conceit is merely the development in poetry of an expository device known to preachers from the earliest times, the extended, detailed, interminable simile. The Buddha used it in the Fire Sermon and elsewhere;[22] even Richard of St. Victor uses something similar in his allegorical interpretations of the Scriptures;[23] and Donne, in his own sermons, employed it in almost the same form as that used by Bishop Latimer. See, in the Oxford Selections from the Sermons, the figure of the

---

(1776), is aptly described in Francis W. Hirst's study: 'a love of the concrete, a faculty for the picturesque, and withal a nervous force and vigour in argument quite peculiar to himself. It has been said that Smith hunted his subject with the inveteracy of a sportsman. With a wonderful knowledge of history, law, philosophy, and letters, he combined an intuitive insight into the motives of men and the unseen mechanism of society' (*Adam Smith* [London: Macmillan, 1904], p. 187). TSE had written to Herbert Read about the effects of jargon on the quality of prose in technical studies: 'Psychology is worse than anything, because it is a young science (if it be a science) and hardly born before jargonising was well advanced. There are Berkeley and Hume, of course. Economics is ruined by it, although Adam Smith could write well'(*L*2).

22–As in his notes to *The Waste Land* (*CPP* 79/53), TSE refers to Henry Clarke Warren's translation of the Buddha's Fire Sermon in *Buddhism in Translations* (Harvard Oriental Series, 1896), where fire is the extended simile (p. 352):

'All things, O priests, are on fire. And what, O priests, are all these things which are on fire?

'The eye, O priests, is on fire; forms are on fire; eye-consciousness is on fire; impressions received by the eye are on fire; and whatever sensation, pleasant, unpleasant, or indifferent, originates in dependence on impressions received by the eye, that also is on fire'.

23–See p. 103, where TSE observes that Richard of St Victor 'is very sparing of tropes and figures: there is only the main allegory running through the treatise, the comparison of the stages of the mind to the parts of the ark of the covenant'.

Ship.[24] In his verse, one of the most successful extended conceits is in that beautiful poem "A Valediction".[25]

> As virtuous men passe mildly away,
> And whisper to their soules, to goe,
> Whilst some of their sad friends doe say,
> The breath goes now, and some say, no:
>
> So let us melt, and make no noise,
> No teare-floods, nor sigh-tempests move,
> T'were prophanation of our joyes
> To tell the layetie our love.
>
> Moving of th'earth brings harmes and feares,
> Men reckon what it did and meant,
> But trepidation of the spheares,
> Though greater farre, is innocent.

Here there is no flaw, no criticism can be cast upon the verse; no one has ever handled this quatrain form better than Donne. The astronomical comparison gives some trouble; when grasped, it appears to be what I call a rhetorical figure, for its effect is emphasis and over-statement; it is to say, that so huge an event as this separation of lovers is like the immense but imperceptible movements of heavenly bodies.

> Dull sublunary lovers love
> (Whose soule is sense) cannot admit
> Absence, because it doth remove
> Those things which elemented it.

This verse illustrates again the exaggeration so characteristic of the seventeenth century and Marinism: these lovers are (in modern language) "cosmic", all other are "sublunary".

24—As in the sermons of the English preacher Bishop Hugh Latimer (1485–1555), who used the extended simile in 'Of the Card' (1529) and in 'The Plough' (1548). Donne employs the technique in Sermon 44, 'Mundas Mare', as published in Logan Pearsall Smith's edition of *Donne's Sermons* (pp. 72–4). Though Donne extends the simile of the ship briefly on p. 74, the sea is the primary simile of the sermon, as TSE confirms in a second reference to the passage in 'The Prose of the Preacher' (1929; see p. 64, n. 41): 'we can then proceed to study the ingenuity with which Donne, in a long passage, will employ one simile, and develop it in immense detail. . . . One specimen is found on p. 72 of Mr. Pearsall Smith's selection "The World is a Sea", in which he brings forth every possible interpretation of this metaphor' (p. 23).
25—'A Valediction: Forbidding Mourning' (*MLPSC* 14–15, lines 1–12; alternate line indentations not followed here or in lines 13–24 below, but followed in lines 25–36 below.

But we by a love, so much refin'd,
That our selves know not what it is,
Inter-assured of the mind,
Care lesse, eyes, lips, and hands to misse.

Our two soules therefore, which are one,
Though I must goe, endure not yet
A breach, but an expansion,
Like gold to ayery thinnesse beate.

Note how close the conceit may come to the compliment. Donne is not expounding or implying any theory of the soul in which he could be said to believe; it is never quite certain that he believes anything. The figure does not make intelligible an idea, for there is properly no idea until you have the figure; the figure creates the idea – if gold can be beaten out thin, why should not a soul? He is not, and is never, stating a philosophical theory in which he believes. When Guido Cavalcanti says

Amor, che nasce di simil piacere,
Dentro del cor si posa,
Formando di disio nova persona,
Ma fa la sua virtù 'n vizio cadere

he is more serious, because he believes it.[26] He is maintaining substantially the same theory as that of *Purgatorio* XVIII: "Then, even as fire moves upward by reason of its form, whose nature it is to ascend, there where it endures longest in its material; so the enamoured mind falls to desire, which is a spiritual movement, and never rests until the object of its love makes it rejoice".[27]

If they be two, they are two so
As stiffe twin compasses are two,

26–From *Ballata XII*, slightly misquoted: *read* 'de simil piacere, / Dentro dal cor si posa, / Formando di desio'; printed in *Pound's Cavalcanti*, ed. David Anderson (Princeton: Princeton University Press, 1983), p. 158; trans. Ezra Pound (p. 159):

Love that is born of loving like delight
Within my heart sojourneth
And fashions a new person from desire,
Yet toppleth down to vileness all his might.

27–In Canto XVIII, lines 28–33, Virgil defines for Dante the nature of Love (trans. *TC* II, 217).

Thy soule the fixt foot, makes no show
To move, but doth, if th'other doe.

And though it in the center sit,
Yet when the other far doth rome,
It leanes, and hearkens after it,
And growes erect, as that comes home.

Such wilt thou be to mee, who must
Like th'other foot, obliquely runne;
Thy firmnes makes my circle just,
And makes me end, where I begunne.

This figure has been greatly admired, and it must freely be admitted to be highly successful, intelligible, apt and striking. But there is always that that makes us feel that Donne is hovering on the edge of *vers de société* – that the idea has been developed to suit the image, that the image and not the idea is the important thing.

It may be thought that what I have said about Donne's use of conceits casts doubt upon his sincerity, and this I must hasten to deny. It implies only that Donne is not with the greatest, that he is not with Shakespeare, or Dante, or Guido, or Catullus. But of certain secondary modes he is an indisputable master; he is a mind of the *trecento* in disorder; capable of experiencing and setting down many super-sensuous feelings, only these feelings are of a mind in chaos, not of a mind in order. The immediate experience passes into thought; and this thought, far from attaining *belief*, is immediately the object of another feeling. If you like you may call the thought "insincere", because it does not reach belief; but his feeling of the thought is perfectly sincere. And this isolation of thought as an object of sense could hardly have been possible before the seventeenth century.

In my opinion, which may be heretical, he is most successful in some of his longer poems, and especially the two Anniversaries.[28] For where he has greater space, the rhetorical style shows to greater advantage.

Or as sometimes in a beheaded man,
Though at those two Red Seas, which freely ran,

28 – In this instance TSE alludes separately to 'The First Anniversarie' (1611) and 'The Second Anniversarie' (1612), though his habit, as in 'The Devotional Poets of the Seventeenth Century' (see p. 23, n. 36), was to describe the two poems that make up the former as the 'two Anniversaries': 'there is none so fine in my opinion, as one called "The Anatomy of the World," otherwise the two Anniversaries' (p. 552).

One from the trunk, another from the head,
His soul be sail'd to her eternal bed,
His eyes will twinkle, and his tongue will roll,
As though he beckoned and call'd back his soul;
He grasps his hands, and he pulls up his feet,
And seems to reach, and to step forth to meet
His soul; when all these motions which we saw,
Are but as ice, which crackles at a thaw,
Or as a lute, which in moist weather rings
Her knell alone, by cracking of her strings.[29]

Here, in the longer reach of thought, the curious image of the Red seas is properly submerged and gives no offence; and the couplet, crude enough from the standpoint of Dryden or Denham, but always, in Donne – as seldom in Hall or Marston – with a rugged melody of its own, suits, by its lack of form or limit, the errant and endless mental activity of the author.[30]

What has been said of the conceit of Donne will apply, externally at least, to the conceit of several other minor poets – the Italianate Crashaw excepted – who must be dealt with separately. The resemblances to Donne are strongest in the smallest poets. None can compete with Donne in power of thought, in power of sensualising thought; and they are apt to be excellent, in so far as they are not metaphysical. Two of the very finest of those poems which are closely patterned upon Donne, are the "Ode" of Lord Herbert previously mentioned, and "The Definition of Love" of Marvell (Grierson, page 77).

29–From *The Second Anniversarie* ('Of the Progresse of the Soule'), lines 9–20 (Grierson I, 251); partly modernized; minor mistranscriptions.

30–TSE was to clarify the historical context of this remark in 'The Minor Metaphysicals' (1930; see p. 23, n. 36): 'Neither the ten-syllable couplet nor the genre of satire was the invention of Dryden. In Elizabethan times, this combination has an honourable history, with the names of Hall and Marston, and of course, the satires of Donne. But it was then only a minor mode of verse . . . The first poet to accomplish anything in what may be called definitely the new style was an insignificant and rather ignominious figure, Sir John Denham' (pp. 641–2). In 'Sir John Denham' (1928), TSE was to write of Denham's poetry: 'Besides the famous "Cooper's Hill," there are but two or three poems . . . that can be read with any pleasure; and even these are only just above the line at which pleasure expires . . . In being reckoned as one of the inventors of the Augustan couplet Denham has received rather more and rather less than his due' (*TLS*, 5 July 1928, p. 501). The English bishop and theologian Joseph Hall (1574–1656) was a minor poet, best known for his books of verse satire in *Virgemidarium* (1597, 1598). The playwright John Marston (1575–1634) was best known as a poet for his coarse poetic satires in *The Scourge of Villainy* (1598). In his review of A. G. Barnes's *A Book of English Verse Satire* (*TLS*, 24 June 1926, p. 429), TSE suggested that 'a specimen of Marston might have been added, if only to show the superiority of both Donne and Hall'.

My Love is of a birth as rare
As 'tis for object strange and high;
It was begotten by Despair
Upon Impossibility.[31]

Of neither of these poems is it necessary to say anything more than is said of
Donne; but the latter should be read to understand how much less need be
said: compared to the twistings of the brain of Donne, this is mere parroting
of anagrams.[32] For Marvell, in spite of the fantastic Marlborough House
poem,[33] was not at his best really metaphysical at all – I refer to the
"Horation Ode", rightly excluded from the Grierson book.[34] The first
paragraph of "The Coy Mistress" is verbally conceited, but not metaphysi-
cal in spirit; for his brilliant *jeux d'esprit* have a very different inspiration
from the meditation of Donne. He is humourous and then serious, and in
Donne the humour and the seriousness are fused; and when Marvell
becomes suddenly quite serious, he is, to my mind, much more Latin in spirit
than any of his contemporaries.

But at my back I always hear
Time's winged chariot hurrying near,
And yonder all before us lie
Deserts of vast eternity.
Thy beauty shall no more be found;
Nor in thy marble vault shall sound

31 – Though TSE parenthetically cites *MLPSC* 77, he actually quotes from a different printing
of the stanza in Grierson's Introduction, *MLPSC* xxxv.

32 – In 'Mystic and Politician as Poet' (1930; see p. 23, n. 36), originally delivered as a BBC
broadcast, TSE was to ask his listeners to 'Look at the graceful ingenuity of "The Definition of
Love": if anything, it is too clever an imitation of Donne. Marvell, the moderate Puritan,
outrages the conceit as ruthlessly as does Crashaw' (p. 591).

33 – A slip for Marvell's 'Upon Appleton House', which TSE had briefly criticized for some of
its 'undesirable images' (*SE* 297/256) in 'Andrew Marvell' (1921), images further identified in
'Mystic and Politician as Poet' as those meant to compliment the owner, Lord Fairfax (lines
49–52), but which unhappily suggest 'that Lord Fairfax was a very fat man rather than a very
great man' (p. 591). Marlborough House, in Pall Mall near St James's Palace, was built by
Christopher Wren in 1710 for the Duchess of Marlborough (1660–1744). Richard Aldington
recounts a walk down Pall Mall with TSE in 1919: 'To my horror Eliot lifted his derby hat to
the sentry outside Marlborough House. You would have to be born British and serve in the
army to understand the complex violations of etiquette involved in this generous and well-
meant gesture. I wish I knew what the sentry thought' (*Life for Life's Sake* [London: Cassell,
1968], p. 202).

34 – TSE had stated in 'Andrew Marvell' that Ben Jonson 'never wrote anything purer than
Marvell's *Horation Ode*; this ode has that same quality of wit which was diffused over the
whole Elizabethan product and concentrated in the work of Jonson' (*SE* 301/260).

My echoing song; there worms shall try
Thy long-preserved virginity . . .[35]

Until we reach the worms which try "Thy long-preserved virginity" there is
nothing conceited about this his most famous passage; and there is little
strictly metaphysical in the whole poem.

On the other hand, there is one poem of Bishop King which seems to me
quite metaphysical, although not wholly conceited. I call it an original
contribution to metaphysical poetry because of fusion, not merely analogy,
of the image of the journey – an image held up for inspection as Donne
himself would hold it, until a new emotion appears also – with the progress
of the soul in time toward eternity.

But heark! My Pulse like a soft Drum
Beats my approach, tells Thee I come;
And slow howere my marches be,
I shall at last sit down by thee.[36]

In much lesser men we find the conceit employed and multiplied so rapidly
that the inspiration of Donne becomes completely lost among these spawn-
ing metaphors. What are we to say to this, of John Cleveland:[37]

Since 'tis my doom, Love's undershrieve,
Why this reprieve?
Why doth my she-advowson fly
Incumbency?

35 – Lines 21–8, slightly mistranscribed from TSE's copy of the Muses' Library edition of
Marvell's *Poems*, ed. G. A. Aitkin (London: George Routledge & Sons, [1904]), pp. 56–7;
lines 27–8, *read* 'then worms shall try / That long-preserved virginity'.
36 – 'The Exequy', lines 111–14 (*MLPSC* 206); minor mistranscriptions. The poem, the most
notable of King's elegies, was written on the death of his young wife. In his 1923 review of
Marvell's *Miscellaneous Poems* (see n. 6 above), where he describes King as 'greater than
Marvell', TSE quotes the first two lines as constituting a conceit: 'If the drum were left out it
would cease to be a conceit – but it would lose the valuable associations which the drum gives
it' (p. 809). In 'The Metaphysical Poets' he pointed to the lines as possessing 'that effect of
terror which is several times attained by one of Bishop King's admirers, Edgar Poe' (*SE* 284/
244), and in 'Prose and Verse' he described King's poem as 'great poetry', a poem in which 'a
human emotion is concentrated and fixed' (*Chapbook*, April 1921, p. 7). Pound discouraged
TSE from including his own poem, 'Exequy', in *The Waste Land* (see *WLF* 101).
37 – 'To Julia to expedite her Promise' (lines 1–9), as printed in Saintsbury's *Minor Poets of the
Caroline Period*, III (1921), p. 83. In his review of Marvell's *Miscellaneous Poems* (see n. 6
above), TSE had stated that 'we must understand that the conceits which seem to us to fail are
formed by exactly the same method as the conceits which seem to us to succeed. For that
understanding we must read the whole of Marvell. But we must not only read the whole of
Marvell; we must read Cleveland as well'.

Panting expectance makes us prove
The antics of benighted love,
And withered mates when wedlock joins,
They're Hymen's monkeys, which he ties by th' loins,
To play, alas! but at rebated foins.

A stanza which, I admit, I have never taken the trouble to understand. Or this, of Benlowes:[38]

Who steals from Time, Time steals from his the prey:
Pastimes pass Time, pass Heav'n away:
Few, like the blessed thief, do steal Salvation's Day.

Fools rifle Time's rich lott'ry: who misspend
Life's peerless gem, alive descend;
And antedate with stings their never-ending end.

Cleveland is not very remunerative; Benlowes' verses, like those of Miss Gertrude Stein, can, for anyone whose taste has already been disciplined elsewhere, provide an extremely valuable exercise for unused parts of the mind.[39] But they both bring us to the question: how far can our definition of "metaphysical verse" be stretched?

38 – TSE quotes from Canto I, stanzas xxxvi–xxxvii of 'Theophilia', as printed in Saintsbury's *Minor Poets of the Caroline Period*, I (1905), p. 337.

39 – In 'The Minor Metaphysicals' (see p. 23, n. 36), TSE was to write sympathetically of Benlowes: 'Remember that almost everyone, even in his own day, despised his verses; one satirist asserted that someone had been made ill merely by wearing a hat lined with pages of Benlowes' poems . . . I confess myself to a mild partiality to this man's verse – which is perhaps more likely to do my reputation harm than to do Benlowes' good . . . I have spoken of Benlowes, not merely because of my fondness for this inglorious but by no means mute Browning; but in order to show how a versifier of much above the ordinary level, a man of original and ingenious fancy, better than half the poets who were well reviewed yesterday or will be well reviewed to-morrow, can bring a good idiom to such a point that a drastic reform of language is needed' (p. 641). On 10 March 1941 TSE was to write to Anne Ridler on the compositon of *East Coker*: 'My intention was to avoid a pastiche of George Herbert or Crashaw – it would be folly to try – and to do something in the style of Cleveland or Benlowes, only better' (*CFQ* 109).

Praz was to conclude his letter of 31 January 1927 with a comment on Gertrude Stein (1874–1946), who lived in Paris: 'Very amusing your remark about Miss Stein's verse: an extremely valuable exercise for unused parts of the mind. But is it not better to let those parts of the mind get entirely atrophied?' (*L*2). TSE was then to write in 'Charleston, Hey! Hey!': 'There is something precisely *ominous* about Miss Stein . . . Moreover, her work is not improving, it is not amusing, it is not interesting, it is not good for one's mind. But its rhythms have a peculiar hypnotic power not met with before. It has a kinship with the saxophone. If this is of the future, then the future is, as it very likely is, of the barbarians. But this is the future in which we ought not to be interested' (*Nation and Athenaeum*, 29 January 1927, p. 595).

I attempted to show the sensuous interest of Donne in his own thoughts as objects, and I attempted to show that this interest naturally led him to expression by conceits. A conceit is the extreme limit of the simile and metaphor which is used for its own sake, and not to make clearer an idea or more definite an emotion. But the conceit was not the sole offspring of the peculiar intellect of Donne. It was already prepared by the Elizabethans, although, owing to the difference of mind, the bombast of the sixteenth century and the conceit of the seventeenth century are two different phenomena. The conceit also appears in Italy; and in its Italian origins, analogous with the origins of baroque art, we shall presently examine it in the poetry of Crashaw. Not until we have examined this can we arrive at any conclusions which will enable us to distinguish the conceited clearly from the metaphysical, and to conclude how far the whole generation may be called metaphysical and how far merely conceited – how far that is, the common ground is on tricks of language rather than habits of thought. For you will have seen that it works both ways: that the metaphysical mind in poetry, with the background of the seventeenth century which I so briefly outlined in the second lecture, tends toward the conceit; and on the other hand common tricks of language tend to induce common habits of thought and feeling, and any poet who is conceited is likely to be more or less metaphysical. The influence of Donne runs out in three channels: the courtly poets of *vers de société*, such as Carew and Suckling, and moving toward Rochester and then Prior;[40] the fantastical poets, like Cleveland and Benlowes; and Cowley. We shall have to reascend these streams,[41] and again collate Donne, Marvell and King. But meanwhile we must investigate a wholly different inspiration, that of Crashaw, and connect it with Donne, if we can, through the other devotional poets. It is therefore to Crashaw, to St. Theresa, and to Marino that I shall turn next week.[42]

---

40 – John Wilmot, Earl of Rochester (1647–80), poet and courtier, was best known, aside from his amorous lyrics and scandalous reputation in the court of Charles II, for his satiric verses, notably *A Satire Against Mankind* (1675). The poet and diplomat Matthew Prior (1664–1721) was the author of light amatory verse and two long satiric poems, *Alma; or the Progress of the Soul* (1718) and *Solomon* (1718). In 'The Metaphysical Poets' TSE had observed that 'courtly' poetry 'expires . . . with the sentiment and witticism of Prior' (*SE* 282/241–2).

41 – TSE alludes to Henry James's technique of reascending the stream of thought behind his tales and novels in the Prefaces to the New York Edition of his works, particularly to the often-quoted phrase in the Preface to *The American* (New York: Charles Scribner's Sons, 1907): 'as I remount the stream of composition' (p. xii).

42 – After delivering this fourth lecture on 16 February, TSE decided in the interim to lecture on Donne's long poems on 23 February and to delay his lecture on Crashaw until 2 March.

{Donne's Longer Poems}

It has seemed to me desirable that in this lecture, before passing on to Crashaw and Cowley, I should consider the longer poems of Donne in their main groups: the *Satires*, the *Epistles*, the *Voyage*,[1] the *Anatomy of the World*, and the *Progress of the Soul*. The longer poems, and especially the *Satires*, contributed as much or more toward his original reputation as the short poems better known to most of us. It is not therefore unprofitable to determine how far the metaphysical, and how far the conceited, enter into these poems.

Enough has been said, I think, to suggest that "metaphysical poetry" in general, and "metaphysical poetry" of the seventeenth century in particular, has not one positive and unmoving centre upon which one can put the finger. If you concentrate upon the work of one man, you introduce elements which are not metaphysical at all and you exclude others equally metaphysical with those found in that man's work. We have seen that the conceit is, in England, due to various fusions of the influence of Donne with the influence from Italy, and perhaps more difficult influences to define also. By the dangerous method of comparing isolated figure of speech with figure, we can find certainly fullblown conceits in Donne, innumerable; and what look very much like conceits in the work of earlier and much more truly Elizabethan men. The *perfect* example of the conceit is not to be found. For when you go past Donne to slightly later men, you find that the conceit has developed under Italian influence, but also that it has lost something

1 – The earliest of Donne's epistles, or verse letters, 'The Storme' and 'The Calme', are here conflated as 'the *Voyage*' after the adventurous occasions of composition – Donne's presence on the storm-damaged 'Islands Voyage' expedition led by the Earl of Essex in search of the Spanish Fleet on its return from the West Indies in the summer of 1597, and on the subsequent expedition to encounter the Fleet in the Azores, where Donne's ship was seriously becalmed.

conceited which was personal to Donne. It is only by grasping the move-ment of the whole period, from Elizabeth to Cromwell, as an integrity, that one can form any conception of the conceit or of this type of metaphysical poetry. And as the frontiers are nowhere, even in the work of one man, clearly defined, we must be content to examine some poetry which is not, on the face of it, metaphysical.

Of the two groups of Donne's poems which I now propose to examine, that which includes the *Satires* and the *Epistles* is apparently the less metaphysical. However, the nature of satiric poetry is (or was) such that its exercise gave play to some of the faculties, which became completely developed in his metaphysical poetry. And by this I do not mean that Donne was a satirist in the modern sense, or that the irony and wit displayed in other of his poems is in the same sense of a satiric kind. For we must be quite clear on this point: that "satire" has two meanings – one is a *verse form* or *genre*, the other a mood or attitude. It is the fact that there are these two meanings, usually undistinguished, that tends to stultify the conscientious, comprehensive and intelligent book of Professor Hugh Walker on English Satire.[2] You can certainly trace the history of a form; it is perhaps possible to trace the history of a mood; it is almost impossible to trace the history of what is now one, now the other, and sometimes both. By the time you have admitted Chaucer, Thackeray, *both* Samuel Butlers, as well as Swift,[3] there

2 – TSE had favourably reviewed (*TLS*, 10 December 1925, p. 854) Hugh Walker's *English Satire and Satirists* (1925), granting that Walker had succeeded within the difficulties of his task: 'Literary history of this type has peculiar limitations. The history of any *genre* within the limits of one language is liable to be no more than a chronicle; for the reason that the really interesting and fruitful generalizations can hardly be drawn within such boundaries. General-izations will probably trespass beyond the limits of language – the development of satire, for instance, is a European, not a local affair – or outside the boundaries of the *genre* in question. And there is no more difficult subject to treat in such a scheme than the subject of satire. For it has not – as has the drama for instance – any definite technique. And the authors of satire have often occupied themselves with other literary activities as well; or like Chaucer, have not been primarily satirists at all'. Walker's study ranges from the pre-Chaucerian satirists of the twelfth century to Samuel Butler in the nineteenth century.

3 – After having taught several of Thackeray's satires to his Extension classes, TSE wrote to his cousin, Eleanor Hinckley, on 1 April 1918: 'Thackeray could do the *Yellowplush Papers* and the Steyne part of *Vanity Fair*, but he had a picture of himself as a kindly satirist. Not at all, he hadn't brains enough, nor courage enough to find out really what he could do well, which was high society sordidness, and do it' (*L1* 228). The satirist Samuel Butler (1612–80) is known for his *Hudibras* (1663–78), a burlesque of the Puritan followers of Cromwell and their Commonwealth. The other Samuel Butler (1835–1902), the prose satirist, wrote *Erewhon* (1872) and *The Way of All Flesh* (1903), both of which TSE taught to his Extension class in 1917 (*RES* II, 295). In his review of Hugh Walker's book (see previous note), TSE had written that 'Dr. Walker is not only sound but new' on Butler: 'his opinion marks a sane reaction

seems little reason for making your history of Satire anything but a general history of English Literature. As for Satire as a *genre* of verse, I confess that it would be very difficult to trace the history of that even, and mark the point of its disappearance, in English verse. Does it end with, let us say, Churchill, or does it include Crabbe?[4] And all we can do is to point to its origins, and define the nature of its origins – that is to say, the feeling or feelings which allied with poetic talent required this particular outlet, and measure the English practitioners by the degree of their divergences from the originals.

Now Skelton and Dunbar, and Langland, are "satiric" writers in the modern sense,[5] but they did not write "satires" or *saturae*. The satire, as a *form*, is of course derived from Persius and Juvenal, and it is only in relation to these authors, I think, especially Persius, that the satires of Donne are to be understood.[6] In Latin satire, as Conington well said, "the poet pours out desultory thoughts on contemporary subjects in his own person . . . familiar compositions in verse . . . relieved from the trammels which necessarily

---

against the exaggerated applause which followed complete neglect. "The Way of All Flesh" commits greater offences against *literary* taste than does the often reprehended "Voyage to the Houhynyms" '. TSE concluded that Swift 'rose as near to the highest as it [satire] ever has risen, or ever is likely to rise'.

4 – The poet and satirist Charles Churchill (1731–64), made severe attacks upon theatrical personalities in *The Rosciad* (1761), upon political figures in *The Prophecy of Famine* (1763), and upon William Hogarth in *An Epistle to William Hogarth* (1763). TSE had written of Hugh Walker's treatment of minor satirists: 'Of the small he raises many to their proper places. To Churchill he is just'. George Crabbe (1754–1832), whose sensibility had more affinity with the early nineteenth than with the eighteenth century, wrote early in his career *The Village* (1783), a realistic satire of the cult of rural simplicity and sentiment in pastoral literature. In his review of Barnes's anthology (see p. 134, n. 30), TSE observed that 'Crabbe, who is rightly represented in this collection, seems to belong only just within the confines of satire; his choice of country subjects makes him an anomaly'. TSE was later to write of Crabbe in 'What Is Minor Poetry?' (1944): 'I think that George Crabbe was a very good poet, but you do not go to him for magic: if you like realistic accounts of village life in Suffolk a hundred and twenty years ago, in verse so well written that it convinces you that the same thing could not be said in prose, you will like Crabbe' (*OPP* 49/47).

5 – The poet and clergyman John Skelton (c. 1460–1529) wrote poetic satires on ecclesiastics, notably on Cardinal Wolsey in 'Why Come Ye Nat to Courte, Collyn Clout', and other subjects; William Dunbar (c. 1460–1521), a Scots poet and clergyman, wrote satiric verse on court and town life, friars and women, notably 'The Twa Maryit Wemen and the Wedo'; William Langland (c. 1332–c. 1400) was the author of *Piers Plowman* (c. 1395), a satire of ecclesiastical corruption.

6 – In his review of Barnes's anthology (see p. 134, n. 30), TSE asserted that Barnes was right 'to date satire only from the period when English poets began consciously to emulate Persius and Juvenal. We are spared the selections from Langland, Skelton, and Dunbar, which would only confuse us, and which most anthology makers would have included'.

bind every dramatic production'.[7] It was, or was eminently supposed to be, by the early Latinising English satirists, a character of satiric verse to be even affectedly rough and unpolished, and they outdid Persius or Juvenal in roughness. Satire seems to have responded, with the late Elizabethan satirists, as well as with the Roman (Persius is said to have shown no enthusiasm for Seneca)[8] to a need for relief from the sublime – as did the Aristophanic farce among the Athenians. Latin poetry was not wholly of the sublime order; but on the whole its descriptions were limited, and its emotions purified and simplified, beyond those of daily life. Indignation (a vague term) is not a principle, but a by-product, of satire; it is the topicality of indignation which makes it appropriate to satire; it is an emotion which we undergo more frequently than love, and it merges very easily into the peevishness and irritability which we experience every day, and which also we can sometimes relieve by composing verses. I do not purpose to analyse the spirit of formal satire in detail; that would involve an examination almost line by line of several satirists; I only wish to indicate that the satiric spirit is not simple but complex, and that a number of qualities, and perhaps a number of defects, go [to] the formation of the satiric poet. One of the qualities is an active ratiocinative intellect, interested in a variety of subjects rather than co-ordinated to one intent; and another is a keen eye for common observation. Both of these Donne had.

Certainly the indignation in Donne's satire is wholly faked, and in conformity with tradition. Indignation was never the strong side of satire. If we suspect that of Persius and Juvenal, how can we put up with that of Marston, who lays it on with a trowel, and gives us nothing else?

> Grim-faced Reproof, sparkle with threatning eye!
> Bend thy sour brows in my tart poesy!
> Avaunt! ye curs, howl in some cloudy mist,
> Quake to behold a sharp-tongued satirist!

7 – TSE elides and slightly alters the sequence of the quotation from John Conington (1825–69), Professor of Latin at Oxford, as stated in his 'Lecture on the Life and Writings of Persius', delivered at Oxford on 24 January 1855 and printed as a commentary with his translation of *The Satires of A. Persius Flaccus*, ed. Henry Nettleship (Oxford: Clarendon Press, 1872): 'It is certainly not a little remarkable that the countrymen of Aristophanes and Menander should not have risen to the full conception of familiar compositions in verse in which the poet pours out desultory thoughts on contemporary subjects in his own person, relieved from the trammels which necessarily bind every dramatic production, however free and unbridled its spirit' (p. xxiv).

8 – TSE paraphrases Conington: 'At a later period Persius made the acquaintance of Seneca, but did not admire him' (pp. xvi–xvii).

he cries, in "The Scourge of Villainy" (1598);[9] and I am much mistaken if any cur, listening to this sharp-fanged satirist, would do anything but curl up and go to sleep. Marston under the shadow of Rome probably took himself seriously. But with Donne a very different note is heard.

> Away thou fondling motley humorist,
> Leave me, and in this standing wooden chest,
> Consorted with these few bookes, let me lye
> In prison, and here be coffined, when I dye;
> Here are God's conduits, great divines; and here
> Natures Secretary, the Philosopher;
> And jolly Statesmen, which teach how to tie
> The sinewes of a cities mystique bodie;
> Here gathering chroniclers, and by them stand
> Giddie fantastique poets of each land.[10]

While the *soul* of Juvenal may have entered into Ben Jonson (see the prologues to *The Poetaster* and *Catiline*)[11] and, if so, greatly advanced by the transmigration, the clothes of Persius are assumed by Donne.[12] Donne in his satires is the parent of Dryden, and Oldham. But let us look first at the overtones which Donne in the piece quoted, and in his satires generally, manages to convey. "This standing wooden chest, / Consorted with these few bookes, let me lye / In prison" – is that not truly Donne? It does not

---

9–From Satyre IX, 'Here's a Toy to mocke an Ape indeede', lines 1–4 (line 4, a slip: *read* 'sharp-fanged satirist!'). Though TSE modernizes the spelling, he keeps the points of exclamation in lines 1, 2 and 3 of the third edition (1599), as printed in Vol. III of *The Works of John Marston*, ed. J. O. Halliwell (London: John Russell Smith, 1856), p. 293, borrowed from the London Library.

10–'Satyre I' (1593), lines 1–10, minor mistranscriptions; line 5, a slip: *read* 'grave Divines', quoted correctly in the paragraph below (Grierson I, 145).

11–TSE refers to the prologues, replete with Juvenalian violence and intensity, of Sylla's Ghost in *Catiline His Conspiracy* (1611) and of Envy in *The Poetaster* (1601), both of which he had characterized in 'Ben Jonson' (1919): 'in lines of invective, Jonson makes Sylla's ghost, while the words are spoken, a living and terrible force . . . Turning then to the induction of *The Poetaster*, we find another success of the same kind – *Light, I salute thee, but with wounded nerves* . . . Men may not talk in that way, but the Spirit of Envy does, and in the words of Jonson Envy is a real and living person. It is not human life that informs Envy and Sylla's ghost, but it is energy of which human life is only another variety' (*SE* 150–51/130).

12–As Edmund Gosse writes in his *Life and Letters of John Donne* (1899), 'Donne and Hall would be drawn to Persius because, like him, they were young and bookish . . . they took him for a Heaven-sent stoic, who scourged the age and died at twenty-six . . . To resemble Persius, to reproduce his manner, was evidently the devout aim of Marston and Donne, Hall and Guilpin alike' (Gosse I, 34).

matter that Donne loved the Court as much as anybody; it does not matter [that] his hatred of courtiers, so far as it is sincere, is that of a man who spent a large part of his life, and wrote a great many of his letters, in courting courtiers. What matters is that in this loose and desultory form of Satire he found a type of poetry which could convey his random thoughts and reflections, exercise his gift for phrasing, his interest in the streets of London, his irritability and spleen. "Here are Gods conduits, grave Divines".

> Not though a Captaine do come in thy way,
> Bright parcell gilt, with forty dead men's pay . . . . . .
>
> At last his Love he in a window spies,
> And like light dew exhaled, he flings from me
> Violently ravished to his lechery.[13]

This in its fun, in its dexterity of phrase, suggests no one more than Dryden; though it is truest Donne.

Satire, though it professes blunt plain speech, and repudiates elegance and fine writing, yet lends itself to a crabbedness and ingeniosity of wit that portends the conceit. Persius, though he ridicules *Berecyntius Attis* and *costam longo subduximus Appennio* ("We have fetched off a rib from the long side of Appennius") (l.95),[14] utters sometimes phrases like

> *liquido cum plasmate guttur*
> *mobile collueris* . . . .

("after gargling your supple throat by a liquid process of tuning")[15] which seems to me, who am no Latin scholar, tortured and fantastic enough. So Donne

> Like a wedge in a blocke, wring to the barre,
> Bearing-like Asses; and more shamelesse farre,
> Than carted whores, lye, to the grave Judge; for
> Bastardy abounds not in Kings' titles, nor
> Symonie and Sodomy in Churchmens lives,
> As these things do in him. . . . .[16]

13 – 'Satyre I', lines 17–18, 106–8; partly modernized; minor mistranscriptions (Grierson I, 145, 149).
14 – Satire I, line 95; trans. Conington, *The Satires*, p. 27: *read* 'the long sides'.
15 – Satire I, lines 17–18; trans. Conington, *The Satires*, p. 13.
16 – Satyre II (1593), lines 71–6; minor mistranscriptions (Grierson I, 152).

verses which might well have shocked both the mind and the ear of Dryden – though they have to the ear, a kind of grating harmony which becomes in time very pleasing. They hardly bear out the assertion of Dryden concerning the heroic couplet, that the rhyme "bounds and circumscribes the fancy"![17]

The *Satires* are one step in the development of a metaphysic wit; the *Elegies* were more important. I agree with Professor Grierson that they are based on facts, rather than, as Sir Edmund Gosse accepts them, a literary transcription of a certain love-affair.[18] They are still more different from Ovid and Propertius[19] – whom Donne should have at this period admired, whether he did or not – than the *Satires* are from Persius and Juvenal. I agree with Grierson that the "depravity is in part a reflected depravity",[20] and I should add that the passion is in large part a reflected passion – I find in it far less intensity than either of the two Roman poets, Ovid and Propertius, who also belonged to a civilisation which, with all its limitations, was far more *mature* than Donne's. The young Propertius is far more mature, with a Latin maturity, far more experienced in disillusion and disgust, than the young Donne; he writes of experience that made and spoilt his life, Donne only, at most, of a passing adventure. The description, the epithet of Donne, is exact; the feeling artificial. His *Satires* have that same ferocity of language which would have made us wait in St. Paul's all night to hear a two hour sermon by him; and the ferocity is in the language rather than in the experience. The first is typical, and is one of the best.

17 – 'To Roger, Earl of Orrery', prefixed to *The Rival Ladies* (1664): 'But that benefit which I consider most in it, because I have not seldom found it, is, that it bounds and circumscribes the fancy' (*Dramatic Essays*, p. 187).

18 – In his Introduction to *The Poems of John Donne* (1912), Grierson asserts that 'Whether we can accept in its entirety the history of Donne's early amours which Mr. Gosse has gathered from the poems or not, there can be no doubt that actual experiences do lie behind these poems as behind Shakespeare's sonnets' (p. xli). Edmund Gosse had argued in his *Life and Letters of John Donne*, 1 (1899) that the *Songs and Sonnets* and the *Elegies* must be read together as 'the adventures of his body and soul' (p. 63), particularly as an accurate record of Donne's illicit passion for a beautiful married lady: 'His heart, hitherto whole and callous, was shattered into reflecting fragments like a mirror, was torn into rags like a garment. His passion completely overwhelmed him; for the first time, though he had loved so often, he felt the genuine tyranny of love' (p. 68).

19 – TSE alludes to Ovid's *Amores*, poems which depict the stages of his love affair with a certain Corinna, and to Propertius' *Cynthia Monobiblos*, primarily a depiction of his turbulent affair with Hostia, a courtesan whom he calls Cynthia.

20 – Grierson writes in his Introduction to *The Poems of John Donne*: 'And yet even in these more cynical and sensual poems a careful reader will soon detect a difference between Donne and Ovid. He will begin to suspect that the English poet is imitating the Roman, and that the depravity is in part a reflected depravity' (p. xl).

Fond woman, which woulds't have thy husband die,
And yet complain'st of his great jealousie;
If swoln with poison, he lay in his last bed,
His body with a sere-bark covered,
Drawing his breath, as thick and short, as can
The niblest crocheting Musician,
Ready with loathsome vomiting to spew
His soul out of one Hell, into a new,
Made deaf with his poor kindred's howling cries,
Begging with few feigned tears, great legacies,
Thou woulds't not weep, but jolly and frolicke be,
As a slave, which tomorrow should be free;
Yet weeps't thou, when thou seest him hungerly
Swallow his own death, heartsbane jealousie.
O give him many thanks, he is courteous,
That in suspecting kindly warneth us.
We must not, as we us'd, flout openly,
In scoffing ridles, his deformity;
Nor at his boord together being satt,
With words, nor touch, scarce looks adulterate.
Nor when he swolne, and pampered with great fare,
Sits downe, and snorts, cag'd in his basket chaire,
Must we usurp his own bed any more,
Nor kiss and play in his house, as before.
Now I see many dangers; for that is
His realme, his castle, and his diocesse.
But if, as envious men, who would revile
Their Prince, or coyne his gold, themselves exile
Into another countrie, and do it there,
Wee play'd in another house, what should we feare?
There we will scorne his household policies,
His seely plots, and pensionary spies,
As the inhabitants of Thames right side
Do Londons Major; or Germans, the Popes pride.[21]

---

21 – 'Elegie I, Jealosie', quoted in full; partly modernized; minor mistranscriptions (Grierson I, 79–80).

(The sequence of "household policies" by "pensionary spies" suggests the influence of Ben Jonson, and elsewhere Donne uses the phrase "household spies" entire).[22]

Here we get the voice of the preacher. Compare a sermon of Donne's on Hell with a Catholic sermon, take the sermon on Hell given *in extenso* in James Joyce's *Portrait of the Artist*,[23] and you will see that Donne is always transferring his attention from the idea to the figure, and from the figure to an idea suggested by the figure. In this elegy his wit is too lively to keep to the point; and indeed the peculiar fascination of Donne's verse resides in this curious trick of vagrant thought; or it is as if his theme picked up every possible felicity of image and oddity of thought in its neighbourhood, and became as unrecognisable as the sea-god Glaucus.[24] In the famous ivth Elegy,[25] for example, we are distracted from the emotion of parting to the vigorous image of the creature he shall be on his return from the seas:

> Here take my Picture; though I bid farewell,
> Thine, in my heart, where my soule dwels, shall dwell.
> Tis like me now, but I dead, 'twill be more
> When wee are shadowes both, than 'twas before.
> When weather-beaten I come backe; my hand,
> Perhaps with rude oars torne, or sunbeames tanned,
> My face and brest of haircloth, and my head
> With cares rash sodaine stormes, being o'erspread,
> My body a sack of bones, broken within,
> And powders blew staines scatter'd on my skin.

The image of the powder-blue-stained skin is admirable, but what remains of the idea of parting? Even the notion of the meaning of the picture

22 – TSE alludes to Jonson's description of the beneficent 'household' in 'To Penshurst' and to the seducer's confidence that he and Celia can 'delude the eyes / Of a few poor household spies' in 'Come, My Celia' (*Volpone*, iii, vii). Donne used the latter phrase in 'Elegie xii', line 41: 'And those so ambush'd round with household spies' (Grierson i, 101).

23 – Father Arnall gives the Jesuit Sermon on Hell at the annual retreat in Chapter iii of *A Portrait of the Artist as a Young Man* (1916). James R. Thrane has established that Joyce used the text of Giovanni Pietro Pinamonti, SJ, *Hell Opened to Christians, to Caution them from Entering into it*, as his main source for the sermons (*Modern Philology*, February 1960, pp. 177–98).

24 – In Ovid's *Metamorphoses* (xiii, 920 ff.) Glaucus, fisherman of Anthedon in Boeotia, is changed into a sea-god after eating a divine herb sown by Saturn. TSE frequently quoted and translated Dante's use of Glaucus' transformation in the *Paradiso*, i, 67–8: '*Gazing on her, so I became within, as did Glaucus, on tasting of the grass which made him sea-fellow of the other gods*' (*SE* 265/225).

25 – A slip for the vth Elegy, 'His Picture', lines 1–10, partly modernized (Grierson i, 86–7).

is overlaid; even the image of the sailor himself breaks into its component details. But note that with Donne the emotion, the feeling, does not simply stop at one point, and verbiage begin; rather, it is never verbiage because there is always *some* emotion or feeling present. We watch a strange kaleidescope of feeling; with suggested images, suggested conceits, the feeling is always melting, changing, into another feeling; we get a kind of unity in flux, which is Donne. There is no *structure* of thought, but every thought is felt, every image has a peculiar feel to it.

There is only one important trick, but a very important trick it is, of Donne's shorter poems which is not illustrated in most of the longer; it is perhaps one which makes the shorter poems so much more read, and leave so much deeper impression, than the longer. It is the trick, to which I have alluded in a previous lecture,[26] of first stating a simple and startling idea of direct and easily apprehensible emotional value, and *then* proceeding to all the variations and changes —

> I wonder by my troth, what thou, and I
> Did till we lov'd? . . . . .[27]
>
> Twice or thrice had I loved thee . . . . .[28]
>
> I long to talke with some old lover's ghost . . . .[29]

But all the others are there, including the metrical beauties which Donne discovers everywhere; and I cannot think *The Anatomy of the World* inferior to anything he ever wrote. "The Storm" and "The Calm", so admired by Ben Jonson,[30] illustrate his gift of observation and at the same time the excess of image which both attracts and distracts the eye. In the IInd Elegy,[31] we saw how he used, to realise the situation of the jealous husband, certain *obsessing* ideas; he conceives the husband on his death-

---

26 – See pp. 124–5.
27 – 'The Good-morrow', lines 1–2 (*read* 'Did, till we lov'd?').
28 – 'Aire and Angels', line 1.
29 – 'Loves Deitie', line 1 (*read* 'lovers ghost').
30 – Jonson's admiration for Donne's 'The Bracelet' (Elegy XI) and 'The Calme' is recorded in *Conversations with William Drummond of Hawthornden* (1619): 'his verses of the Lost Chaine, he heth by Hert & that passage of the calme, that dust and feathers doe not stirr, all was so quiet. affirmeth Done to have written all his best pieces err he was 25 years old' (*Ben Jonson*, vol. 1, ed. C. H. Herford and Percy Simpson [Oxford: Clarendon Press, 1925], p. 135); a 1934 inventory (Bodleian) of TSE's library listed three volumes of this edition in his library.
31 – A slip for 'Elegie I, Jealosie', quoted above.

bed; the associations are unexceptionable, yet they seem to conjure up the "friends of the friends" as Henry James might say,[32] the associations of the associations. An image in "The Storm" illustrates this curious disposition more clearly;

> Some coffin'd in their cabbins lye, equally
> Griev'd that they are not dead, and yet must die;
> And as sin-burdened soules from graves [will] creep,
> At the last day, some forth their cabbins peepe,
> And tremblingly aske what newes, and doe heare so,
> Like jealous husbands, what they would not know.[33]

The associations here are just, and witty. Yet how singular this preoccupation with coffins, the day of judgment, sin, and even, perhaps, with jealous husbands! But to investigate these recesses of Donne's mind is not my *métier*: I wish only to indicate how often we feel that there is something else, some preoccupation, in Donne's mind, besides what he is talking about; his attention is not only often dispersed and volatile; perhaps it is so because it is really distracted. But this bewildering obscurity is part of the attraction of Donne's mind, and is perhaps what gives the peculiar emotional colour to his every idea, and causes the variety and dispersion of his intellectual curiosity.

Donne, is, in a way, part Jesuit and part Calvinist; I venture the suggestion that a profound examination of the doctrines of both sects, and an attempt to entertain both guests on equal terms, might, if it did not kill the experimentor, throw some light on Donne's mind. None of his poems is more difficult, more unpleasant, more disturbing, more satisfactory, or contains more startling lines, than the apparently unfinished *Progress of the Soul*.[34] I simply confess myself incapable of understanding this rebus: and no critic that I have perused has given me the slightest help. It is, for me, a

32 – An allusion to James's story, 'The Friends of the Friends', which originally appeared as 'The Way It Came' (1896) before it was re-titled and published in vol. 17 of *The Novels and Tales of Henry James* (New York Edition), 1907–9. TSE was to write about James to Herbert Read on 18 January 1927, revealing that he liked 'some of his poorer stuff better than his best; in his poorer stuff something bigger appears without his knowing it – e.g. I like specially "The Altar of the Dead" and "The Friends of the Friends"' (*L2*).

33 – 'The Storme', lines 45–50; partly modernized (Grierson I, 176).

34 – Donne's unfinished satire, dated 16 August 1601 and originally titled 'Metempsychosis', is not to be confused with the later 'Of the Progress of the Soul: The Second Anniversary' (1612). Though unfinished, at 520 lines it is Donne's longest poem.

voyage into strange seas of feeling,[35] but the feeling I get from it is one I cannot define, and cannot connect with the explicit meaning. I am quite unable to catch the drift of this history of the metamorphosis of the soul which inhabits at one moment or another an apple, a fish, a whale and a monkey. The wildly conceited vision of the whale which

> spouted rivers up, as if he meant
> To joyne our seas, with seas above the firmament,[36]

suggests that Donne probably saw whales on his voyages, but to me it suggests nothing more. Nor am I able to interpret the stanza which is sometimes supposed to refer to Queen Elizabeth:

> For the great soule which here amongst us now
> Doth dwell, and moves that hand, tongue, and brow,
> Which, as the Moone the sea, moves us: to heare
> Whose story, with long patience you will long;
> (For tis the crowne, and last straine of my song)
> This soule to whom Luther, and Mahomet were
> Prisons of flesh; this soule which oft did teare,
> And mend the wracks of th'empire, and late Rome,
> And liv'd when every great change did come,
> And first in Paradise a low, but fatal roome.

I cannot for the life of me see how every line of this stanza can refer to the Queen.[37] But the tendency of the poem is plain: it is a tendency toward intellectual anarchy, from the second line, which I believe springs from the doctrine of some unorthodox scholastic –

> Fate, which God made, but doth controule. . . .

to the last lines –

---

35 – A mock-allusion to the most famous of the later additions to Wordsworth's *The Prelude* (1850), where he describes the 'silent face' of Newton's statue in the antechapel of Trinity College, Cambridge, as 'The marble index of a mind forever / Voyaging through strange seas of thought alone' (Book III, 62–3).

36 – Stanza xxxii, lines 319–20, partly modernized (Grierson I, 308).

37 – Stanza vii, lines 61–70, minor mistranscriptions; line 70, read 'Had first in Paradise, a low, but fatall roome' (Grierson I, 297). TSE disagrees with Grierson's commentary on the stanza: 'it is evident from the poem that in his first intention Queen Elizabeth herself was to be the soul's last host. It is impossible to attach any other meaning to the seventh stanza' (Grierson II, 219).

There's nothing simply good, nor ill alone,
Of every quality comparison,
The only measure is, and judge, opinion.[38]

I can only offer it to any deep psychologist who may be interested.

But we can turn with confidence to *The Anatomy of the World*, for its obscurity is not of the same disturbing kind, and its beauty is much more assured. From one point of view, it is merely a couple of insincere funerary poems on the daughter (whom he had never seen) of a rich man whose favour he wished to cultivate.[39] But I think that insincerity is the last sin of which one would accuse Donne: that is the advantage of being sincerely interested in something else than what you are talking about. It is a meditation upon death. But what a meditation! It has no philosophy, no structure or unity, no "central idea", no real beginning or end; but it is the most metaphysical of all Donne's metaphysical poems.

If the poem is nominally the celebration of the virtues of Drury's dead daughter, and actually a meditation upon death, is it not, in a sense, a poem of double meaning? By this I do not mean merely an allegory or a puzzle, I mean a category to which certain poetry, which may appear at first sight to be metaphysical, but really is not, belongs. A great exemplar of this type, whom I choose because he may, being a contemporary of Donne, be thought to be himself metaphysical, is Chapman in his tragedies. I have always been impressed, and once discussed in a paper, by the sense of a "double world" in the tragedies of Chapman, and which made me compare him to Dostoevski.[40] Here and there the actors in his drama appear as if following

38—Stanza i, line 2; Stanza lii, lines 518–20, partly modernized (Grierson I, 295, 316).

39—When Elizabeth Drury, the fourteen-year-old daughter of Sir Robert Drury (1575–1615), died suddenly in December 1610, Donne, who said he 'never saw the Gentlewoman', was prompted to write 'A Funerall Elegie' for the grieving parents. Sir Robert, a wealthy landowner who had been no more than a slight acquaintance, befriended Donne, who was desperately unsuccessful in seeking employment abroad, and invited him to the Continent as his well-remunerated secretary. Before their departure late in 1611, Donne wrote an extended complement to the first poem, 'An Anatomy of the World', and the two were published together as *An Anatomy of the World* (1611), reprinted as *The First Anniversarie. An Anatomie of the World* (1612).

40—TSE gave his lecture on Chapman before the Cam Literary Club at Cambridge University on 8 November 1924. The next day I. A. Richards wrote to Dorothea Pilley: 'In the evening I heard Eliot's paper. Stuff about Chapman. Not very definite but we had a good deal of discussion on general topics and he seems to have some sound views (mine I mean)' (*Selected Letters*, p. 31). On 12 November TSE wrote to Virginia Woolf that after all the labour it had not proved worthy of publication (*L2*), and on 30 November he wrote to Ottoline Morrell, pleased that she liked some poems that he had sent: 'They are part of a larger sequence which I am doing — I laid down the principles of it in a paper I read at Cambridge, on Chapman,

another train of thought, listening to other voices, feeling with other senses; and acting out another scene than that visible upon the stage. Hence they appear irrational and incoherent in the same way as the characters of Dostoevski. In *The Revenge of Bussy D'Ambois*, for example, there runs the curious theme of reconciliation, quite inconsistent with the motives and intentions of the personages, but never ludicrous, because it seems to belong to another plane of reality from which these persons are exiles. Even in the splendid final outburst of the dying hero of the previous play –

> Fly, my soul,
> To where the evening, in the Iberian vales,
> Bears on her swarthy shoulders Hecate
> Crowned with a grove of oaks; fly, where men feel
> The cunning axletree, and those that suffer
> Beneath the chariot of the snowy Bear,
> And tell them all that D'Ambois now is hasting
> To the eternal dwellers. . . .

it seems as if he, or Chapman through him, is conversing with an immaterial audience.[41] This *doubleness* is not only found in Chapman; it appears for

---

Dostoevski & Dante – and which is a sort of *av*ocation to a much more revolutionary thing I am working on' (*L2*). He planned to revise and publish the essay in the *Criterion*, where he announced to his readers that due to illness the editor had been 'unable to prepare his essay on "A Neglected Aspect of George Chapman" for this number' (April 1925, p. 341). The essay is lost, but TSE may have given a summary of it in a recent review, 'Wanley and Chapman' (*TLS*, 31 December 1925, p. 907): 'In Chapman we have a dramatist by accident, who was a poet and a man of thought as well as a scholar. Ideas, and the "sensibility" of thought, meant more to Chapman than to any of his contemporary dramatists; he was much more an "intellectual" than Ben Jonson, and in his way far more a mystic than any. He is a precursor of the metaphysicals. Chapman himself is mixed; his classical stoicism is crossed with a strain – perhaps out of Marsilio Ficino and similar writers – of otherworldliness; resulting, here and there in his tragedies, in a sense of double significance which gives him here and there a curious resemblance to Dostoevsky'. TSE did not return to the manuscript, writing regretfully in the preface to a new edition (1955) of *Elizabethan Essays* (1934) 'that I did not, during that period of my life at which these essays were written, have occasion to write about the work of that very great poet and dramatist, George Chapman. It is too late now: to attempt to repair such a gap, after many years' neglect, would be almost as futile as to attempt to remove the blemishes . . . in one's early poems' (p. x).
41—The dying Bussy speaks these misquoted lines (v. iv. 101–7) in *Bussy D'Ambois* (c. 1604), which preceded *The Revenge of Bussy D'Ambois* (c. 1610). TSE's thin-paper edition (1904) of W. L. Phelp's Mermaid edition of *George Chapman* (1895) misprints 'cunning axletree' for 'burning axletree' (p. 216):

> Fly, where the evening from th'Iberian vales,
> Takes on her swarthy shoulders Hecate,

instance in a more obvious form in Browning's *Childe Roland to the Dark Tower Came*. It is as different from the allegory as it is from the daydream, the *Kubla Khan* of Coleridge.[42] As different in principle: in practise it is sometimes very difficult to place a particular poem. In so baffling a poet as Gérard de Nerval, about whom I have never yet been able to make up my mind,[43] there are passages obviously of the daydream type –

> Dans la nuit du tombeau, toi qui m'as consolé,
> Rends-moi le Pausilippe et la mer d'Italie!

or

—

> Crown'd with a grove of oaks: fly where men feel
> The cunning axletree: and those that suffer
> Beneath the chariot of the snowy Bear:
> And tell them all that D'Ambois now is hasting
> To the eternal dwellers; . . .

TSE first misquoted this passage in 'Reflections on Contemporary Poetry' (1919), where he points to Chapman's borrowing from Seneca's *Hercules Furens* as an example of '*saturation* which sometimes combusts spontaneously into originality*' (Egoist*, July 1919, p. 39), and in that year he adapted a line from the passage for 'Gerontion' – 'whirled / Beyond the circuit of the shuddering Bear' (*CPP* 39/23). In 'Seneca in Elizabethan Translation' (1927) he was to observe how Seneca's lines 'must have lain long in the memory of Chapman before they came out in *Bussy d'Ambois*' (*SE* 74/59), and again in the Conclusion to *The Use of Poetry* (1933) he was to discuss 'the probability that this imagery had some personal saturation value, so to speak, for Seneca; another for Chapman, and another for myself . . . I suggest that what gives it such intensity as it has in each case is its saturation . . . with feelings too obscure for the authors even to know quite what they were' (*UPUC* 147–8/140–41). And finally, in 'Thinking in Verse', he was to describe Chapman's passage as 'a complicated harmony of feeling . . . with a complex richness unknown to Seneca' (*Listener*, 12 March 1930, p. 442).

42 – In Browning's poem (1855), which some critics find evoked in Part v of *The Waste Land*, his hero, on a weary, interminable quest, is directed by an aged cripple towards the dark Tower, where his abiding sense of otherworldliness is intensified in a vision 'Of all the lost adventurers my peers, / . . . yet each of old / Lost, lost!' (lines 194–8). TSE was to discuss Coleridge's *Kubla Khan* ('Or, A Vision in a Dream. A Fragment.',1797) in the context of Chapman's 'saturation' in previous images, evoking his own image from *The Waste Land*: 'The faith in mystical inspiration is responsible for the exaggerated repute of *Kubla Khan*. The imagery of that fragment, certainly, whatever its origins in Coleridge's reading, sank to the depths of Coleridge's feeling, was saturated, transformed there – "those are pearls that were his eyes" – and brought up into daylight again. But it is not *used*: the poem has not been written' (*UPUC* 146/139).

43 – Gérard de Nerval (1808–55), a poet of dreams and extreme experience, the author of short tales (*Sylvie*, 1853) and a narrative of madness (*Le Rêve et la Vie*, 1855), was eventually overcome by a madness that culminated in his suicide. In his review of Peter Quennell's *Baudelaire and the Symbolists* (1930), TSE was to write: 'Although *literary* criticism compels us to consider Villiers and Gérard de Nerval when we consider the whole movement after Baudelaire, we must remember that Villiers and Gérard . . . are distractions from the main issue' (*Criterion*, January 1930, p. 358).

J'ai rêvé dans la grotte où nage la sirène,
Mon front est rouge encore du baiser de la reine. . . .[44].

as well as the line so admired by Arthur Symons –

Crains, dans le mur aveugle, un regard qui t'épie!

which seems to me consciously of the double-world type.[45] But the meta-physical, as illustrated by *The Anatomy of the World*, is different from either the allegorical, the narcotic, or the otherworld. It gives the emotional equivalent of thought, a rarified, but perfectly definite world. Only, whereas with Dante and his circle, the feelings are organised according to an organized view of the universe, so that there is given the feeling-equivalent for every detail in the system and *also* for the consummation of the system –

La forma universal' di questo nodo
credo ch'io vidi, perchè più di largo,
dicendo questo, sentii ch'io godo.

Un punto solo m'è maggior letargo
Che venticinque secoli all 'impresa
Che fe Nettuno ammirar l'ombra d'Argo.

and *also* for the system as a whole.[46] On the other hand, with Donne – and it is placing Donne very high to compare him to the circle of Dante – the

44 – TSE quotes from Nerval's sonnet, '*El Desdichado*', lines 5–6 ('You who consoled me, in the night of the tomb, give me back Posilipo and the Italian sea'), but reverses the order of lines 10–11 ('My brow is still red from the queen's kiss; I have dreamed in the cave where the siren swims . . .' (*PBFV* 381–2). The latter lines of the sonnet had informed the concluding lines of TSE's 'The Love Song of J. Alfred Prufrock' ('We have lingered in the chambers of the sea / By sea-girls wreathed with seaweed red and brown'), and the second line of the sonnet, '*Le Prince d'Aquitaine à la tour abolie*', had been quoted in the concluding passage (line 430/429) of *The Waste Land* (*CPP* 75/50).

45 – The poet and critic Arthur Symons (1865–1945) quoted line 9 from Nerval's 'Vers Dorées' ('Gilded Verses') in *The Symbolist Movement in Literature* (1899), which TSE first read when the second edition appeared in 1908: 'The sun, as he mentions, never appears in dreams; but, with the approach of night, is not every one a little readier to believe in the mystery lurking behind the world?

Crains, dans le mur aveugle, un regard qui t'épie!

he writes in one of his great sonnets; and that fear of the invisible watchfulness of nature was never absent from him' (revised edition [New York: Dutton, 1919], pp. 77–8). *Translation*: 'Fear then, in the blind wall, the prying glance'; trans. Geoffrey Wagner, *Selected Writings of Gérard De Nerval*, p. 255.

46 – *Paradiso*, XXXIII, 91–6; minor mistranscriptions; line 93, *read* 'dicendo questo, mi sento ch'io godo'; see p. 57, n. 33.

peculiarity is the absence of order, the fraction of *thought* into innumerable *thoughts*. Donne is a poet, a true poet, perhaps even a very great poet, of chaos. And this fraction of thought into thoughts means that the only thing that holds his poems, or any one poem, together, is what we call unsatisfactorily the personality of Donne. In this, he is a modern poet. Personality is not only an unsatisfactory term; what we mean or seem to mean or think we mean by it is an unsatisfactory thing.

We must, I think, take *The Anatomy of the World* in this way in order to understand and appreciate. It is a meditation of thoughts floating about separately, floating ideas turned in upon themselves. And, as I think I said in a previous lecture,[47] this introversion has curious consequences; this spectacle of thought in dissolution produces colours and iridescences never apparent in a living and organic system. Let us take a passage, almost at random, from the *First Anniversary*.

> Some moneths she hath [beene] dead (but being dead,
> Measures of times are all determined)
> But long she 'ath been away, long, long, yet none
> Offers to tell us who it is that's gone.[48]

In a parenthesis you have to swallow the idea of the indeterminability of time in the future state, and then pass on at once to the difficult idea, startlingly expressed, of the namelessness of the soul, of its distinction from the breathing composite of soul and body which we knew, and consequently of the deep abyss between two kinds of life that isolates the living from the dead. The feeling is as it were shocked into existence by the suddenness of this; and having evoked it, Donne passes on again. He seems determined to exhaust every possibility of thought and of feeling that can be associated with the death of a young woman. Presently we find him at this point –

> Let no man say, the world itself being dead,
> 'Tis labour lost to have discovered
> The world's infirmities, since there is none
> Alive to study this dissection;
> For there's a kind of world remaining still,
> Though she, which did inanimate and fill

47–See pp. 88–9.
48–'An Anatomy of the World', lines 39–42; minor mistranscriptions (Grierson I, 232).

> The world, be gone, yet in this last long night
> Her Ghost doth walke. . . . .[49]

In these seven and a half lines we have already had two thoughts, two transitions, the beginning of a third thought. To follow these Anniversaries to the end, tasting the full flavour of every idea, is a task requiring you see not a little application and fortitude.

These are two points of detail to which I would draw your attention. A passage often quoted, and justly admired, is the following –

> One whose clear body was so pure and thinne,
> Because it need disguise no thought within.
> 'Twas but a through-light scarfe, her mind to inroule;
> Or exhalation breathed out from her soule.[50]

Of this beautiful passage, I would only ask you to read the whole poem, and ask, whether this is the view of the relation of body and soul taken everywhere throughout the poem? I think not: it seems to me inconsistent with my own interpretation of a passage quoted above, with its sharp distinction between soul and body –

> yet none
> Offers to tell us who it is, that's gone.[51]

The question, and similar questions, as you will have seen, are capital: for it is the question, raised already, whether Donne is attending to the *meaning* of an idea or to its *existence* (the latter being the *Pensée* of Descartes).[52]

The other point will have greater interest for us when we come next week

---

49 – Lines 63–70; partly modernized; minor mistranscriptions (Grierson I, 233).
50 – 'A Funerall Elegie', lines 59–62; partly modernized; minor mistranscriptions (Grierson I, 247).
51 – 'An Anatomy of the World', lines 41–2; minor mistranscription (Grierson I, 232).
52 – TSE appears to confuse the '*Pensée*' of Pascal for the '*Méditation*' of Descartes, possibly thinking of Pascal's criticism of Descartes' distinction between meaning and existence, a criticism which TSE was to quote in 'The *Pensées* of Pascal' (1931), where he argues that Pascal 'succeeds where Descartes fails' and that 'in a few phrases about Descartes . . . Pascal laid his finger on the place of weakness. *Je ne puis pardonner à Descartes; il aurait bien voulu, dans toute sa philosophie, se pouvoir passer de Dieu; mais il n'a pu s'empêcher de lui faire donner une chiquenaude, pour mettre le monde en mouvement; après cela, il n'a plus que faire de Dieu*' (*SE* 415/367); translated in the edition for which TSE's essay served as the 'Introduction': 'I cannot forgive Descartes. In all his philosophy he would have been quite willing to dispense with God. But he had to make Him give a fillip to set the world in motion; beyond this, he has no further need of God' (*Pascal's Pensées*, trans. W. F. Trotter [New York: E. P. Dutton & Co., 1931], p. 23).

to consider the work of Crashaw. It is in the Funeral Elegy to the *First Anniversary* (line 80 in the Grierson edition, page 248):

> For though she could not, nor could chuse to dye,
> She 'ath yeelded to too long an ecstasie.[53]

Which shows pretty clearly the influence of the *Life* of St. Theresa[54] and perhaps of other Spanish saints (it was St. Philip Neri, I think, he to whom is dedicated the church at Arundel, who became so habitually ecstatic that he was obliged to pray that he might receive the divine influx less frequently).[55] The *Second Anniversary* is, if anything, more crowded with beauties than the first; it was, as we shall see, characteristic of Crashaw's and of the Italian and the Spanish and even the Dutch poetry of the baroque period to be crowded with beauties; but nowhere, I think, do they occur in greater profusion than in these two poems of Donne. And nowhere did he rise to greater heights of verbal and metrical beauty; everything that we find in his lyrics, everything that we find in his sermons, is here. Compare, for instance, the funeral sermon in which recurs so persistently the word "DEAD", as a musical bar by itself. The passage is given in Mr. Pearsall Smith's selections.[56] Compare it with the recurrence in variation in the *First Anniversary* of

53 – 'A Funerall Elegie', lines 81–2; *read* 'extasie' (Grierson 1, 248).
54 – Though Donne does not refer directly to Saint Theresa, there are several analogous passages in their works, as Mary Ramsay had observed in *Les Doctrines médiévales chez Donne* (p. 235); and though the first English translation of her *Life* did not appear until 1611, after the composition of Donne's poem in 1610, he probably could have read her work in Spanish.
55 – See p. 84, n. 48. TSE probably read Donne's account of this anecdote in 'A Sermon Preached at Paul's Cross' (1616): 'This is that Pureness in the *Romane Church*, by which the founder of the last Order amongst them, *Philip Nerius*, had not only utterly emptied his heart of the world, but had fill'd it too full of God; for, so (say they) he was fain to cry sometimes, *Recede a me Domine*, O Lord go farther from me, and let me have a less portion of thee' (*Ser* I, 186; recounted (1626), *Ser* VII, 334). The tenth of the twelve panels representing stages of St Philip Neri's life in the Chapel of St Philip, Arundel, which TSE evidently visited, depicts him rapt in ecstasy while offering Mass.
56 – 'Death of James I' (*Donne's Sermons*, pp. 57–8; *Ser* VI, 290): 'When you shall find that hand that had signed to one of you a *Patent* for *Title*, to another for *Pension*, to another for *Pardon*, to another for *Dispensation, Dead*: That hand that settled Possessions by his *Seale*, in the *Keeper*, and rectified *Honours* by the *sword*, in his *Marshall*, and distributed relief to the *Poore*, in his *Almoner*, and *Health* to the *Diseased*, by his *immediate Touch*, Dead: That Hand that ballanced his *own three Kingdomes* so equally, as that none of them complained of one another, nor of him, and carried the *Keyes* of all the Christian world, and locked up, and let out *Armies* in their due season, Dead; how poore, how faint, how pale, how momentany, how transitory, how empty, how frivolous, how Dead things, must you necessarily thinke *Titles*,

Shee, shee is dead; she's dead: when thou know'st this,
Thou know'st how lame a cripple this world is. . . . .

Shee, shee is dead; she's dead: when thou know'st this,
Thou know'st how ugly a monster this world is. . . . .

Shee, shee is dead; she's dead: when thou know'st this,
Thou know'st how wan a Ghost this our world is. . . .

Shee, shee is dead; she's dead: when thou know'st this,
Thou know'st how drie a Cinder this world is. . . . . .[57]

A precisian might object that if the world is a cripple it cannot be also a cinder. That is a detail: my main point is that this deliberate over-stimulation, *exploitation* of the *nerves* – for such it is – has in it, to me, something unscrupulous. It is the work of a man of profound and subtle intellect, for whom thought has lost its primary value which it should always have; a voluptuary of thought, as St. Theresa and St. John of the Cross were voluptuaries of religion, recklessly playing his part – for every man's part is a small part – in the destruction of a civilisation.

At this point we terminate our direct connexion with Donne. I have tried to fix the nature of metaphysical poetry as illustrated in Donne; but, as I warned you, we may find the centre of gravity of metaphysicality at a different point with Crashaw, whom we shall consider next week, and at a different point still with Cowley, whom we shall consider the week after. When we have taken up these three in turn, and made the necessary comparison with Dante and with the school of Baudelaire, we shall, I think, have made as complete an examination as possible.

I have, in all probability, made this lecture difficult by keeping your attention upon two points at once: the nature of metaphysical poetry in general involves both the *resemblances* and the *differences* between Donne and Dante. The differences involve a certain theory of the disintegration of the intellect in modern Europe. Therefore I would remind you that I am here concerned primarily with poetry, not with modern Europe and its progress or decline; but that if and when I speak of "disintegration", "decay", or "decline", I am unconcerned with the emotional or moral co-efficient of

and *Possessions*, and *Favours*, and all, when you see that Hand, which was the *hand of Destinie*, of *Christian Destinie*, of the *Almighty God*, lie dead?'
57–'An Anatomy of the World', lines 237–8, 325–6, 369–70, 427–8; partly modernized; minor mistranscriptions (Grierson I, 238, 241–2, 244).

these terms. The "disintegration" of which I speak may be evitable or inevitable, good or bad; to draw its optimistic or pessimistic conclusions is an occupation for prophets and makers of almanacks, of whom I am not one.

LECTURE VI

{Crashaw}

I feel some sense of shame at having arranged matters so that, after devoting four lectures solely to Donne, I must condense what I have to say about Crashaw into one. But I would remind you, in extenuation, that what I have undertaken is not a series of lectures on metaphysical poets, but an attempt to deal with three poets as different examples of metaphysical poetry, and of the metaphysical poetry of that age in particular. Donne's mind is typical of his age, but his poetry is not altogether typical of the poetry of his age; and it was with him a much greater difficulty than with the others, to distinguish that which is peculiar to him from that which is general of the period. I have insisted that Donne is not in any way mediaeval; but he is not a pure type; for he represents the transition from the sixteenth to the seventeenth century; Crashaw represents the more serious aspect of the *Caroline* mind; and owing to the influences which he absorbed, and the life which he lived, is also more representative of the mind of Europe. But I shall attempt in this lecture – not to enter upon a discussion of his mind and the world in which he lived – for that would distract us from our purpose, and I intend to consider this more fully in written studies – and indeed a book of the length, scope and importance of Sainte-Beuve's *Port-Royal* might be written on this subject[1] – but merely to indicate his most important differences from Donne.

1 – This is TSE's first mention of his intention to write *The School of Donne*, and of his initial conception of the model and scope of the study. He had written of Praz's book (see p. 58, n. 35) that it 'suggests that there is ample material, for some patient Sainte-Beuve, for an extensive "Port-Royal" of English literature', and later in 1926 he was to declare that it 'has become more and more manifest of late that the seventeenth century is a period of capital importance and that there are a number of companion works to Sainte Beuve's "Port Royal" to be written' (*TLS*, 11 November 1926, p. 789). TSE had studied the writings of Charles Augustin Sainte-Beuve (1804–69) under Irving Babbitt at Harvard, and he had in his library the seven-volume

Donne was born in 1573; Crashaw in 1612.[2] The difference of nearly forty years is important. By the time that Crashaw was old enough to pick and choose for himself, the currents which had been gathering head in Italy, Spain and France were strong enough to unite with the already-great prestige of Donne in England in forming his generation. Subtract from Donne the powerful intellect, substitute a feminine for a strongly masculine nature, posit a devotional temperament rather than a theological mind, and add the influence of Italian and Spanish literature, take note of the changes in the political and ecclesiastical situation in England, and you have Crashaw. Crashaw was a man of learning, and a man of some intellect; but he was primarily a devotional, a fervent, temperament; a Roman Catholic, he would have had more in common with Cardinal Newman[3] than with Thomas Aquinas. The current of feeling that starts with Newman, and passes through Arnold, Ruskin, and Pater to Francis Thompson, Lionel Johnson, Aubrey Beardsley, and even in a degraded and popularised form to Oscar Wilde, had not quite dwindled away.[4] It would be a matter of too much difficulty, and an enterprise of too great extent for my present purpose, to show how sensibility and intellect have been divided against each other since the seventeenth century; I assume this part of my thesis; I

---

edition of *Port-Royal* (1869–71), a study of the seventeenth-century controversy between the Jansenist religious society of Port-Royal and the Society of Jesus. He would write of the conflict that 'the best account, from the point of view of a critic of genius who took no side, who was neither Jansenist nor Jesuit, Christian nor infidel, is that in the great book of Sainte-Beuve, *Port Royal*' (*SE* 406/358). He was soon to reveal his affinity for Sainte-Beuve in 'Experiment in Criticism' (1929), where he argues that modern criticism begins with his work: 'he was a man of restless curiosity about life, society, civilization, and all the problems which the study of history arouses . . . He is a typical modern critic in that he found himself obliged to brood over the larger and darker problems which, in the modern world, lie behind the specific problems of literature' (*Bookman*, November 1929, p. 229).

2 – At this time it was customary to give Donne's birthdate as 1573 (as in *DNB*), but it has since been established that he was born between 24 January and 19 June 1572. The precise date of Crashaw's birth, usually given as 1613, is still unknown, but it was towards the end of 1612 or early in 1613. TSE was to give Donne's date as 'about 1573' and Crashaw's date as 1613 in 'The Devotional Poets of the Seventeenth Century' (p. 553; see p. 23, n. 36).

3 – John Henry Newman (1801–90), an ordained Anglican priest and leader of the Oxford Movement, was received into the Catholic Church in 1845, ordained a priest the following year, and made a cardinal in 1879. He published the history of his changing religious positions in *Apologia Pro Vita Sua* (1864). Crashaw, whose ordination records were destroyed, took a curacy in the Anglican Church in 1639 and was received into the Catholic Church in 1645.

4 – TSE was to explore this current of feeling in 'Arnold and Pater' (1930), where his specific aim 'is to indicate a direction from Arnold, through Pater, to the 'nineties, with, of course, the solitary figure of Newman in the background' (*SE* 431/382).

only point out that this, like the problem of soul and body discussed in the third lecture, is another dichotomy not found in the *trecento*; and that Crashaw is one of those who are on the side of feeling rather than thought.

There are a few main points to remember about Crashaw. He was born into an atmosphere of religious devotion. He lost his mother, and even his step-mother, very early;[5] it is possible that unsatisfied filial cravings are partly responsible for his adoration of St. Theresa. (Incidentally, it is possible that St. Theresa herself suffered from somewhat the same trouble; we remark that in her vision of paradise, the first persons she identified were her father and mother).[6] His father had a library stocked at least with the Latin verse of the epoch, and this Latin verse was largely Jesuit in origin.[7] For the Jesuits, as I observed in an early lecture,[8] had originated a vast campaign of propaganda among persons of culture. On the one hand they did not fail to encourage among their order those members who showed a talent for philosophical speculation or for controversy, but on the other, they realised that an appeal to the sensibility is, for making converts, worth all your philosophy, and many of the order were actually engaged in composing verses which are by no means without literary merit. I suppose that, taking it in bulk, it would compare more than favourably with the same number of tons of printed verse of today in the vernacular. Jesuitism

---

5 – Crashaw's mother, Helen, daughter of John Routh, died in his infancy; his stepmother, Elizabeth Skinner, who was eulogized for her affection to him, died in childbirth in 1620 when he was seven years old.

6 – The vision is described in Chapter XXXVIII, para. 1 of *The Life of St. Teresa of Jesus*, 2nd ed, trans. David Lewis (London: St Anselm's Society, 1888): 'I remained there but a few moments thus, when I was rapt in spirit with such violence that I could make no resistance whatever. It seemed to me that I was taken up to heaven; and the first persons I saw there were my father and my mother. I saw other things also; but the time was no longer than that in which the *Ave Maria* might be said, and I was amazed at it, looking on it all as too great a grace for me' (p. 324).

7 – William Crashaw (1572–1626), a rigorous Puritan clergyman educated at Cambridge, had gathered a large library of 500 manuscripts – including Virgil, Statius, Ovid, Gower, Hugh and Richard of St Victor – and 3000 printed books – many of them accumulated as a polemical collector-inquisitor of Catholic, specifically Jesuit, literature. Motivated by a desire to denounce the Pope and expose Jesuit heresies, he published such anti-Catholic pamphlets as *The Jesuites Gospel* (1610); determined to link his Puritan faith with the uncorrupted Church Fathers, he published his own English versions of orthodox Latin poems in *A Manuall for True Catholickes. A Handful, or rather a Heartfull of Holy Meditations and Prayers* (1611). Though he sold a large portion of the library to St John's College, Cambridge, in 1615, enough remained for his poet son to have been introduced ironically to Catholic authors and the Catholic spirit.

8 – See p. 77.

came to Donne through the intellect, and in his mind and memory it had to compete with Calvinism, Lutheranism, and everything else. It entered Crashaw's mind through poetry, by the sensibility and emotions, and it found practically nothing in his mind to struggle against.

It is very little wonder that Crashaw found the poetry of Italy, already strongly affected by Jesuit taste, very much to his liking; it is no wonder that before he joined the Church of Rome he found the church of Archbishop Laud the most sympathetic, of Laud who took his stand for the liturgy and "the beauty of holiness".[9] And going up to Cambridge, and finding congenial company as a don of one of the colleges which most stoutly stood by Laud and King Charles, a college which was later to suffer most severely for its loyalty;[10] and, the motherless young man, falling under the influence of the remarkable Mary Collett, and the cloistral society of Little Gidding near Huntingdon:[11] could his life have followed any other course, could it

9—William Laud (1573–1645), Archbishop of Canterbury and leader of the High Anglican, or Laudian party, was a vigorous opponent of Puritan influences in the Church of England, particularly against demands for liturgical changes. In his 'The Answer . . . to the Speech of the Lord Say and Seal, Touching the Liturgy' (*Works*, VI [Oxford: John Henry Parker, 1857], p. 107), Laud argues that in Psalm CX of *The Booke of Common Prayer* 'the people are said "to offer their freewill offerings with an holy worship," or "in the beauties of holiness:" and though, perhaps, his Lordship will not allow of this translation, yet so far he may as to see the use of the phrase. And "in the beauties of holiness," (which keeps close to the original,) will please him less; since a barn with them is as good as a church.' Later in this year TSE was to make his own appeal against the destruction of City Churches, not 'in the name of Christopher Wren and his school', but 'in the name of Laud and the *beauty of holiness*' (*Criterion*, October 1926, p. 629). When Herbert Read wrote to TSE on 29 May 1948 about the meaning of the phrase, using it in his *Coleridge as Critic* (1949) to mean 'a mode of living – something almost behaviouristic, ritualistic', TSE replied on 7 June that 'my interpretation is the same as yours, and I tend to think of it rather as collective; that is as referring to life in the congregation or community rather than as an isolated perfection. I have an impression that the phrase was favoured by Archbishop Laud and it may be some recollection of that which suggested ritualistic to you' (Victoria).

10—In 1635 Crashaw was elected to a Fellowship at Peterhouse, the Cambridge stronghold of Laudian High-Churchmanship, and in a poem of that year ('On a Treatise of Charity') he was to denounce those who identified the Pope with Antichrist and those who attacked the papacy as 'a point of Faith'. In December 1643, following the outbreak of the Civil War, the chapel at Peterhouse was desecrated, its religious ornaments, statues and paintings destroyed by the Parliamentary Commissioners, who forced the Fellows to take the Solemn League and Covenant. Crashaw refused the oath, was expelled, left England and joined the Roman Church.

11—Mary Collett (1601–80) was the eldest daughter of John Collett, whose large family made up the greatest part of the small devotional community established in 1626 by his brother-in-law, Nicholas Ferrar (1592–1637). When Crashaw began to visit Little Gidding in 1632 at the age of nineteen, the skilful and versatile Mary, who had resolved to lead a life of celibacy and spiritual devotion, had become 'The Mother' of the community, and she was to become, in

have ended otherwise than it did? He was buried in Italy, after finding the bread of exile very salt, and the stairs of the Vatican very steep, and the "gente" indeed "malvagia e scempia".[12] He was a born convert. He was Marius the Epicurean.[13]

I have to show how the influence of St. Theresa coalesced with that of Giambattista Marino, how this Spanish-Italian influence combined with that of Donne, and how the result differs from the work of Donne. Incidentally, to show how the conceit of Crashaw differs from that of Donne.

It is not quite clear how much Spanish Crashaw knew. It is reported that he picked it up, with Italian, by solitary study. It is more probable that he knew Italian well than that he knew Spanish well; and he may have read the *Life* of St. Theresa (Mother Theresa as she was then called) in an English translation of 1612.[14] Theresa's autobiography is almost essential to any understanding of Crashaw. It is not only a very interesting book, but a really great book; it is great because of the real beauty of character, and the transparent honesty and scrupulousness and piety of the writer. When, for instance, she tells how the Lord took her crucifix from her, and returned it adorned with pearls, she adds conscientiously that no one was ever able to see the pearls except herself.[15] (Seventeenth-century poetry is much like a

—

effect, the spiritual mother of Crashaw. He alluded to her in his poems and described her in a letter as 'the gentlest, kindest, most tender-hearted and liberal-handed soul I think this day alive'. TSE was himself to visit Little Gidding in 1936 and in 1942 to write the last of his *Four Quartets*, 'Little Gidding', a place 'Where prayer has been valid' (*CPP* 192/139).

12 – TSE alludes to Cacciaguida's words to Dante (*Paradiso*, XVII, 58–60), after he tells him that he must sever himself from Florence ('Thou shalt make trial of how salt doth taste another's bread, and how hard the path to descend and mount upon another's stair'), but TSE misquotes 'gente' for 'compagnia' in line 62 ('la compagnia malvagia e scempia'), where Cacciaguida begins to describe the 'vicious and ill company' which shall weigh down Dante's shoulders (*TC* III, 212–13). When Crashaw, an attendant to Cardinal Palotta in Rome, complained to him of the wickedness of those in his service, the Italian followers so turned upon Crashaw that the Cardinal had to dismiss him to save his life. In April 1649 he was appointed sub-canon of the church of Our Lady of Loreto, and he was buried in Loreto after his death in August of that year.

13 – Walter Pater's only novel, *Marius the Epicurean* (1885), is set in second-century Rome and traces Marius' successive encounters with Paganism, Epicureanism, Stoicism and finally Christianity. In 'Arnold and Pater' (1930) TSE was to become highly critical of the 'incoherent' novel and to complain that Marius 'merely *drifts* towards the Christian Church, if he can be said to have any motion at all; nor does he or his author seem to have any realization of the chasm to be leapt between the meditations of Aurelius and the Gospel. To the end, Marius remains only a half-awakened soul' (*SE* 441–2/392).

14 – i.e. 1611; see p. 157, n. 54.

15 – TSE recalls the vision described in Chapter XXIX, para. 8 of the *Life*, where the returned crucifix is not adorned with pearls but made of supernatural stones: 'On one occasion, when I was holding in my hand the cross of my rosary, He took it from me into His own hand. He

crucifix ornamented with pearls, except that we are able with some trouble to perceive the pearls). But what I wish to emphasise is that the tendency of St. Theresa is to *substitute* divine love for human love, and for the former to take on the characteristics of the latter. Into the psychological implications I do not care to go; they have already been discussed by Brenier de Montmorand and somewhat by Henri Delacroix;[16] they are irrelevant to my thesis; and it would be necessary to defend the memory of a great saint against calumny or degradation. I only point out the literary consequences of this substitution. In contrast, Dante and his contemporaries were quite aware that human love and divine love were different, and that one could not be *substituted* for the other without distortion of the human nature. Their effort was to enlarge the boundary of human love so as to make it a stage in the progress toward the divine. Dante's words before Beatrice appears to him in the *Paradiso*[17] leave no doubt that his feeling toward Beatrice in heaven, an exalted feeling toward an exalted being, differs in kind from his feeling on the revelation of the godhead. The fire runs through his body –

Cognosco i segni dell antica fiamma

he says.[18] But of the poetry of the *seicento* Signor Praz says truly that "the general tendency of the epoch was to make the divine passions a true mirror

---

returned it; but it was then four large stones incomparably more precious than diamonds; for nothing can be compared with what is supernatural. Diamonds seem counterfeits and imperfect when compared with these precious stones. The five wounds were delineated on them with most admirable art. He said to me, that for the future that cross would appear so to me always; and so it did. I never saw the wood of which it was made, but only the precious stones. They were seen, however, by no one else, – only by myself' (*The Life of St Teresa*, p. 231).

16–In his two chapters on St Theresa in *Etudes D'Histoire et du Psychologie du Mysticisme* (Paris, 1908), Henri Delacroix traces the succession of mystical states in St Theresa's writings and provides a psychological analysis based on the material. As a Harvard student TSE had read and taken notes (Houghton) on the volume.

In *Psychologie des Mystiques Catholiques Orthodoxes* (Paris, 1920), Antoine Brenier de Montmorand draws upon specific theories (James-Lange, Krafft-Ebing, Nordau, Leuba, Myers, James, Delacroix) in his study of the psychological and pathological nature of St Theresa's mystical sensibility.

17–A slip for the *Purgatorio*. TSE was to correct the oversight when revising this paragraph for the Turnbull Lectures (see p. 276).

18–*Purgatorio*, xxx, 48: *read* 'conosco'. When Beatrice appears before him, Dante turns to Virgil to say that nearly all of his blood trembles: 'I recognise the tokens of the ancient flame' (*TC* II, 380–81).

of the human passions" (p. 148).[19] It has been, I think – it is for me, at all events – one of the reasons for the general inferiority, or let us say less positively, of the general unsatisfactoriness, of the devotional verse of the last three hundred years, this *substitution* of the divine passion by the human. Instead of being presented with a new passion, we find only the old one with a new, and slightly unreal object. The emotion is the same emotion watered down. I used to think that my inability to feel devotional verse – such as that of Christina Rossetti, who is a diluted Theresa[20] – was due to the weakness of my own flesh and spirit; but that was before I had read the *Paradiso*, or any of the Latin hymns from Prudentius to Aquinas.[21]

If my criticism of the way in which St. Theresa and Crashaw sought religious ecstasy is just, it is applicable to nearly all religious verse since their times. These two are the finest, the most passionate examples of the type. It is, I think, the same thing in George Herbert, allowing for the fact that Herbert was a man of far less intensity altogether, that he was not celibate, that he was a member of the Church of England instead of the Church of Rome, that he walked slightly to the left of the *via media*,[22] that he was quite

19 – Translated from *Secentismo e marinismo in Inghilterra*, p. 148: 'La general tendenza dell' epoca e di rendere le passioni divine uno specchio fedele delle passioni umane'.

20 – TSE was to make a sharper comparison between Christina Rossetti (1830–94), the devout Anglican poet whom he had presented as a poet of religious faith in his 'Course of Lectures on Victorian Literature' (*RES* II, 293), and George Herbert: 'Of all devotional poets, certainly of all Anglican poets, George Herbert seems nearest in feeling to Christina Rossetti . . . But a certain resemblance of temperament immediately suggests profound differences. Christina's religious verse suffers, when we read much of it together, from a monotony due to a narrower range of emotion and an inferior intellectual gift' ('George Herbert', *Spectator*, 12 March 1932, p. 361).

21 – Prudentius, the fourth-century convert who became known as the first poet of the Christian Church, was the author of the *Liber Cathemerinon*, 'Hymns for the day', in which he drew on Old and New Testament stories. TSE had written parenthetically to Richard Aldington on 17 November 1921, after criticizing H.D.'s poetry for a limp Hellenism and 'a neurotic carnality': '(I imagine you dislike equally the Prudentianism of myself and Mr. Joyce . . .)' (*L1* 488). St Thomas Aquinas' four hymns in celebration of the Eucharist, including the *Laude Sion Salvatorem*, were written for the Mass and Office of his 'Feast of Corpus Christi' (1264) and are classed among the greatest of Christian hymns.

22 – In 1559, a year after Elizabeth I took the throne, Parliament enacted legislation (the Supremacy Act and the Act of Uniformity) that effected the Elizabethan Settlement, or *via media*, which placed the English Church on broad middle ground between extreme Catholics on the right and extreme Protestants on the left. 'In its persistence in finding a mean between Papacy and Presbytery', TSE was to write in 'Lancelot Andrewes', 'the English Church under Elizabeth became something representative of the finest spirit of England of the time' (*SE* 342/300). Herbert, a devout Anglican and a moderate opponent of the Puritans and Calvinists, took orders in the Church of England, and the devotional poems in *The Temple* (1633) fairly represent the *via media* of the Church in his time. TSE, implicitly indicating his own relation to

a normal human being who partook his affections between his wife and his God. It is the same in most of the minor devotional verse, without Herbert's sometimes startling felicity of phrase. That there are exceptions I do not deny: an age is to be judged by the way the scale inclines. But the exceptions seem to me almost accidents. The famous line of Vaughan

> I saw Eternity the other night
> Like a great ring of light[23]

is an accidental echo of Dante's

> La forma universal' di questo nodo
> Credo ch'io vidi. . .
>
> Ciò ch'io dico è un semplice lume . . .[24]

It is a moment of contemplation, not enjoyment. But Vaughan is too much a poet of lines rather than poems, for our purpose.[25]

Donne might be called a voluptuary of thought; Crashaw could be called a voluptuary of religious emotion. He has a more ingenious wit, he has stronger feeling, than his Italian models; of all the poets of the age, he is the one who is the closest in sensibility to St. Theresa herself. Donne enters into

———

the *via media*, was to describe John Bramhall as 'a perfect example of the pursuit of the *via media*, and the *via media* is of all ways the most difficult to follow. It requires discipline and self-control, it requires both imagination and hold on reality' (*SE* 358/315–16).

23 – TSE misquotes the opening lines of Henry Vaughan's 'The World' (1650): 'I saw eternity the other night / Like a great ring of pure and endless light'. Vaughan, a Welsh country doctor who referred to himself as the Silurist (South Welshman) on the title-pages of his works, was much indebted to George Herbert for the devotional poems in his most significant volume, *Silex Scintillans* (1650). TSE had borrowed a line from Vaughan's 'The Night' ('Burn invisible and dim') for his 'Mr. Eliot's Sunday Morning Service' (*CPP* 54/34).

24 – Evidently for the purpose of analogy, TSE reverses the sequence of these lines from *Paradiso*, XXXIII, 90–92:

> che ciò ch'io dico è un semplice lume.
>
> La forma universal di questo nodo
> credo ch'io vidi . . .
>
> what I tell of is one simple flame.
>
> The universal form of this complex I think that
> I beheld . . .
>
> (*TC* III, 404–5)

See p. 57, n. 33, and p. 154, n. 46.

25 – TSE was to write at greater length on Vaughan in his review of Edmund Blunden's *On the Poems of Henry Vaughan* (*Dial*, September 1927, pp. 259–63), where he re-examines the observation that 'Vaughan is usually considered as the poet of occasional fine lines, and of no perfect poem' (p. 261).

his mind, the Italians [into] his language, but St. Theresa enters into and takes possession of his heart as she could not possess his more frigid Italian prototypes. The sensationalism which seems deliberate in Marino seems spontaneous in Crashaw. But as with Donne the thought is split up into thoughts, each inspected and tasted, so with Crashaw the emotion is split up into emotions; instead of one emotion informing the whole poem, you have emotion piled on emotion, as a man drinks when he is afraid of becoming sober. There is the same constant diversion and dispersion as in Donne; thought, which I have called *thoughts*, and which you see I shall shortly call *wit*, is called upon to stimulate, to over-stimulate feeling, lest it should flag.

Before proceeding to the more important poems of Crashaw, let us compare one verse of his paraphrase of the *Vexilla Regis* with the original hymn of Fortunatus.[26] This translating and adorning of hymns and psalms was a frequent pastime of the epoch.

> Vexilla regis prodeunt,
> Fulget crucis mysterium
> Quo carne carnis conditor
> Suspensus est patibulo . . .

This is not, I think, one of the finest hymns of the Church, and there is a suspicion of wit in the line "carne carnis conditor", but see what Crashaw makes of it:

> Look up, languishing Soul! Lo where the fair
> Badge of thy faith calls back thy care,
> And biddes thee ne're forget
> Thy life is one long debt
> Of love to Him, who on this painful Tree
> Paid back the flesh he took for thee.[27]

26 – Fortunatus (d. c. 600), was born in Italy and lived in Ravenna before he was driven to France by the Lombards. He became Bishop of Poitiers and composed the *Vexilla Regis* (c. 569) for the consecration of a church in Poitiers, though the hymn was later expanded by two stanzas and sung during Vespers at Passiontide. Crashaw's version, 'Vexilla Regis', first published in *Steps to the Temple* (1648), was expanded as 'Vexilla Regis, the Hymn of the Holy Crosse' in *Carmen Deo Nostro* (1652).

27 – 'Vexilla Regis, the Hymn of the Holy Crosse', lines 1–6. On 12 February 1926 TSE had asked the London Library to send him 'The best possible edition of Crashaw's Poems' (*L*2); he used A. R. Waller's Cambridge English Classics edition of Crashaw's *Poems* (1904), which he later described in his review (*Dial*, March 1928, p. 246) of L. C. Martin's edition of *The Poems English Latin and Greek of Richard Crashaw* (1927): 'It was a good edition for its time; but the text was neither well established nor complete; and for an ordinary reader it had the disadvantage that one sometimes had to hunt to find the poem one wanted' (*FLA* 117–18/129).

Observe the *ad hominem* exhortation to the "languishing soul" (in Crashaw's time souls readily languished and swooned, as Theresa literally did), the introduction of the distracting conceit of the debt and the repayment, the duty of "love" to the Creator, and the hortatory tone of a seventeenth-century sermon.

> Lo, how the streames of life, from that full nest
> Of loves, thy lord's too liberall breast,
> > Flow in an amorous flood
> > Of Water wedding Blood,
> With these he wash't thy stain, transferr'd thy smart,
> And took it home to his own heart.[28]

Observe the "nest of loves", the "amorous flood", the wedding of water and blood, the personal relationship of the Lord and the devotee. And observe the tendency to a *sequence* of emotions, each in a separate image, rather than to any *structure* of emotion. For it *is* the tendency of sensationalism to follow up one impression by another, rather than to build one into another; it leads us to William James's *Radical Empiricism*.[29]

This inclination to make a poem a string of pearls, a garden of beauties pressed together without design, is very marked in the continental Jesuit poetry of the period, and has been well discussed by Signor Praz, in a most interesting passage in which he shows the predilection of these versifiers for the Greek Anthology.[30] A poem was often no more than a string of little

28–Stanza ii, lines 7–12; minor mistranscriptions (*Poems*, p. 231).

29–See p. 49, n. 12. Building upon earlier empiricist philosophies that all knowledge is ultimately derived from disparate impressions of sensations and reflections, James asserted in his *Essays in Radical Empiricism* (1912) that knowledge derives from the conjunctive relations of 'pure experience', the name he gives to 'the instant field of the present', 'the immediate flux of life which furnishes the material to our late reflection with its conceptual categories'. TSE drew upon the work in his dissertation for a discussion of immediate experience and its object: 'At the beginning then consciousness and its object are one . . . We can say with James (*Radical Empiricism*, p. 23) "the instant field of the present is . . . only virtually or potentially either subject or object". Confining ourselves to this instant field (which we must remember is only an abstraction) we grant that no division can be found between an awareness and that of which it is aware' (*KEPB* 29).

30–See *Secentismo e marinismo in Inghilterra*, pp. 221–3, and 225–34, where Praz quotes from a number of Jesuit poets and directs the reader (p. 222n) to *Parnassus Societatis Iesu* (1654) for a comprehensive collection of Jesuit poetry in Latin. In the version of his study translated in *The Flaming Heart*, Praz explains that the Jesuit poets 'cultivated this art of the epigram with an ingenuity that had been well trained at the school of casuistry, equivocation, and sacred eloquence' (p. 209). *The Greek Anthology*, a collection of over 4000 pagan and Christian epigrams from 700 BC to AD 900, was compiled by several anthologers between the first and fourteenth centuries prior to the printing of the *Planudean Anthology* in 1494. TSE

poems or epigrams, each containing some striking figure of speech. Two poems of Crashaw, one very bad, one much better, and both, in the *seicento* manner, beautiful, illustrate this: I mean "The Tear" and "The Weeper".[31] The secretion of the lachrymal glands, I may observe, was a function which fascinated not only Crashaw, but his continental contemporaries; and to psychologists who might be interested in recurrent poetic symbols, I suggest the study of this seventeenth-century phenomenon.

Of the two poems, I prefer to examine "The Tear" in detail; for though it is less disconnected than the other, it is more grotesque and more hideous, and therefore if we can at the same time realise that it is also in its way *beautiful*, we shall accomplish something like a triumph of understanding, and shall have gone a long way toward comprehending the taste and temper of the seventeenth century. The tear in question is shining in the eye of the Virgin Mary (for I believe this poem to concern Her and not the Magdalen, who is the subject of the "Weeper"). The eight stanzas are eight several fancies concerning this tear.

> What bright soft thing is this
> Sweet Mary thy faire eyes expence?
>   A moist sparke it is,
> A watry Diamond; from whence
> The very terme I thinke was found,
> The water of a Diamond.

"Soft thing" is good, for a tear; but "moist spark" is better, an excellent pass of pate;[32] "the water of a diamond" is good wit.

> O 'tis not a teare,
> 'Tis a star about to drop
>   From thine eye its spheare,
> The Sun will stoop and take it up,

---

was familiar with W. R. Paton's five-volume edition in the Loeb Classical Library (1916) and with J. W. Mackail's selected edition (1906), which he was to criticize in his Introduction to Pound's *Selected Poems* (1928), stating that 'Mackail's selections from the Greek Anthology are admirable except for being selections: that is, they tend to suppress the element of wit, the element of the epigram, in the anthologists' (p. xix).

31–'The Teare' and 'Sainte Mary Magdalene or The Weeper' first appeared in *Steps to the Temple* (1646).

32–An allusion to Stephano's description of Trinculo's sally of wit in *The Tempest*, IV.i.243–5: 'Wit shall not go unrewarded while I am King of this country. "Steal by line and level" is an excellent pass of pate – there's another garment for't'.

> Proud will his Sister be to weare
> This thine eyes Jewell in her eare.

Next, "O 'tis a teare" we are told, and this is proved satisfactorily. So we proceed, if procession it be, to stanza 6;

> Faire drop, why quak'st thou so?
> Cause thou streight must lay thy head
> In the dust? O no,
> The dust shall never be thy bed;
> A pillow for thee will I bring,
> Stuft with down of Angels wing.[33]

This is going Donne one better. Donne, you remember, supplied a bank as pillow for the drooping head of a violet; but Crashaw supplies a pillow, stuffed with down, and down from moulting angels at that, a pillow for the *head* — of a tear. One cannot conceive the state of mind of a writer who could pen such monstrosities. The only way is to repeat the stanza to oneself until its odd beauty comes out, like a palimpsest — for, I repeat, it has beauty. And the effect, I believe, is not merely on the ear. There is, I am sure, not only some amount of intellectual labour performed in preparing such a freak as this imagery is, but there is a certain intellectual ingredient in the enjoyment. It is as if you destroyed the natural connections between sense and thought, and built up some quite arbitrary connection out of the fragments. Note the resemblances and differences between this type of poetry and that of Shelley and Swinburne. The resemblance between at least three poems of Crashaw — "The Tear", "The Weeper", and "The Supposed Mistress" (it is right that Crashaw's only poem of earthly love should be to a *supposed* mistress)[34] — and Shelley's "Skylark" is obvious and has been often noted. "The Skylark" is a succession of disconnected images, epigrams, of an iridescent and opulent beauty, which will not bear looking at too closely. Even the melody is reminiscent of Crashaw:

> The dew no more will weep
> The primroses pale cheek to deck;

33 — Stanzas 1, 2 and 6, partly modernized; minor mistranscriptions (*Poems*, pp. 71–2).
34 — 'Wishes. To his (supposed) Mistresse' appeared in *The Delights of the Muses* (1648). Crashaw, who never married, wrote in this same volume an epigram 'On Marriage': 'I Would be married, but I'de have no Wife, / I would be married to a single Life'.

The dew no more will sleep
Nuzzled in the lily's neck. . .[35]

or

Golden though he be,
Golden Tagus murmures tho;
Were his way by thee,
Content and quiet he would goe.
So much more rich would he esteem
Thy sylver, than his golden stream.[36]

What is the difference between these lines of Crashaw's "Weeper", and

Sound of vernal showers
On the twinkling grass,
Rain-awakened flowers –
All that ever was
Joyous and clear and fresh – thy music doth surpass.[37]

or

The world's great age begins anew,
The golden years return,

35 – 'The Weeper', stanza viii, lines 1–4, partly modernized; minor mistranscriptions (*Poems*, p. 260).
36 – 'The Weeper', stanza xiii; minor mistranscriptions. In 'The Devotional Poets of the Seventeenth Century' (1930; see p. 23, n. 36), TSE was to select these two stanzas again for comparison with Shelley's 'To a Skylark': 'If you read the whole poem ["The Weeper"] through, it must remind you of Shelley's "Skylark", in its melody, and apparently in its succession of images. But if you look at the "Skylark" you will see that Shelley's images are a straight succession of plain similes, with none of the delight in intellectual ingenuity . . . which, when combined with emotional intensity, gives the peculiar character of this poetry of the first half of the seventeenth century' (p. 553).
37 – Shelley, 'To a Skylark' (1820), lines 56–60, as printed in TSE's copy of *The Oxford Book of English Verse 1250–1900*, ed. Arthur Quiller Couch (Oxford: Clarendon Press, 1918), p. 704. In 'A Note on Richard Crashaw' (1927) TSE was to intensify his comparative discussion of Crashaw and Shelley: 'I have found that the more I studied the meaning of Crashaw's verse, and his peculiar use of image and conceit, the less resemblance the music of it seemed to have to Shelley's . . . Crashaw's images, even when entirely preposterous . . . give a kind of intellectual pleasure . . . There is brain work in it. But in "The Skylark" there is no brain work. For the first time perhaps in verse of such eminence, sound exists without sense' (*FLA* 122–3/135).

> The earth doth like a snake renew
> Its winter weeds outworn.[38]

or

> Violets that plead for pardon
> Or pine for fright[39]

or

> That noise is of Time,
> As his feathers are spread
> And his feet set to climb
> Through the boughs overhead,
> And my foliage rings round him and rustles, and branches
> are bent with his tread,[40]

I pass over the general differences due to two hundred years of thought and faith and doubt and invention; I would proceed from the more minute differences. The imagery of Donne, of Marvell, of Crashaw, of Marino is often perverse; it is always deliberate. Meanings are twisted, likenesses are forced, but always to produce a deliberate pleasure; it is a distinct sensation to try to imagine supporting the head of a tear on a pillow made of angels' down. But the imagery of Shelley and Swinburne is merely careless. They lack that wit of the seventeenth century, which is a deliberate method of stimulating the mind. The *trecento* had an exact statement of intellectual order; the *seicento* had an exact statement of intellectual disorder; Shelley

---

38—Shelley, *Hellas* (1822), from the Chorus, lines 1060–63, printed separately in *OBEV* 701; *read* 'Her winter weeds outworn'. TSE had quoted the lines correctly for his commentary in 'John Dryden' (1921): 'It is not so easy to see propriety in an image which divests a snake of "winter weeds"; and this is a sort of blemish which would have been noticed more quickly by a contemporary of Dryden than by a contemporary of Shelley' (*SE* 306/265).
39—Misquoted from Swinburne's 'Before the Mirror', lines 3–4, from *Poems and Ballads* (1865): 'Snowdrops that plead for pardon / And pine for fright'. TSE had employed the lines correctly in 'Swinburne as Poet' (1920), where he argued that Swinburne is less interested in objects than he is in words and in the 'vague associations of idea that the words give him'. In apt illustration, he compared Swinburne's snowdrops with Shakespeare's 'daffodils that come before the swallow dares. The snowdrop of Swinburne disappears, the daffodil of Shakespeare remains' (*SE* 326/284). Here the snowdrops are displaced in memory by the more substantial object of Donne's 'The Extasie', 'The violets reclining head' (see pp. 108–9). Swinburne's poem appears in TSE's review copy of *Selections from A. C. Swinburne*, p. 31.
40—Swinburne, 'Hertha', lines 116–20, from *Songs Before Sunrise* (1871), which TSE taught in his 1917 Extension Class (*RES* II, 294); in *Selections from A. C. Swinburne*, p. 122; mistranscription of line break in lines 119–20.

and Swinburne had a vague statement of intellectual disorder. When I assert that neither Shelley's nor Swinburne's verse will bear close examination, I do not imply that they were fools. Both were learned; Shelley had a sort of philosophy; even Swinburne must have thought more often than he gets credit for; his "Hertha", from which I quoted, bears signs of a hasty reading of Emerson.[41] But their minds were like clocks hurriedly put together by the hand of a child; there is no real *intimacy* between the thought and the feeling in their verse. Read *Epipsychidion* and you go off into a reverie;[42] read *The Anatomy of the World*, and your mind is continuously exercised. And this is perhaps a clue to the comparative crudity of the verbal music of Shelley and Swinburne. It is hardly too much to say that after the Caroline period, English versification, with the exception of one or two forms perfected during the eighteenth century, steadily deteriorates. Some of the verse of Tennyson shows immense technical skill, is better than anything of Shelley or Swinburne.[43] I cite Tennyson's consummate skill to show that it is not merely a question of the slipshod, or of a degeneration of the ear. It is something deeper than that. It is a further stage in the disintegration of the intellect, the further separation of sound, image and thought. The revivification of the technique of French

41 – In Swinburne's poem, Hertha, an ancient Teutonic earth-goddess, announces herself as the embodiment of the human over-soul:

> Out of me God and man;
> I am equal and Whole;
> God changes, and man, and the form of
> them bodily; I am the soul.
> (lines 3–5)

The poem is indebted in part to Emerson's transcendentalist philosophy, particularly as expressed in 'The Over-Soul' (1841, 1847), 'within which every man's particular being is contained and made one with all other . . . We live in succession, in division, in parts and particles. Meantime within man is the soul of the whole; the wise silence; the universal beauty, to which every part and particle is equally related; the eternal ONE.

42 – TSE was to examine further the relation of thought and feeling in *Epipsychidion* (1822) and other poems in 'Shelley and Keats' (1930): 'Shelley seems to have had to a high degree the unusual faculty of passionate apprehension of abstract ideas. Whether he was not sometimes confused about his own feelings, as we may be tempted to believe when confounded by the philosophy of *Epipsychidion*, is another matter' (*UPUC* 89–90/81).

43 – TSE was to focus on Tennyson's technical skill in 'In Memoriam' (1936), where he discusses specific poems and presents Tennyson as 'the master of Swinburne; and the versification of Swinburne, himself a classical scholar, is often crude and sometimes cheap in comparison with Tennyson's. Tennyson extended very widely the range of active metrical forms in English: in *Maud* alone the variety is prodigious' (*SE* 328/286).

verse in the nineteenth century came from Baudelaire, a man of distinctly metaphysical mind. The seventeenth century dissociated the intellect and dissociated the emotions; the dissociation of sound and sense in verse came later; the sort of reassociation that was effected, in English verse, was inorganic, and resulted in the crudity of versification of which I speak. Read Swinburne's "Hertha", or Arnold's "Scholar Gypsy" before you pass judgment on this theory.[44]

If my theory is right, then it is incorrect to accuse Marino or his chief contemporaries of vapidity. I am no authority on the Italian poetry of the sixteenth and seventeenth centuries; and it is anything but congenial to my taste; but I have arrived at finding a peculiar beauty in his poetry. Take a poem like his "La Maddalena ai piedi di Christo", a subject akin to those of Crashaw, and treated in the same way, in a series of disconnected conceits. There is everywhere a kind of exercise for the mind, which gives a beauty to the language and a firmness to the verse.

> Dalla testa e da'lumi
> e di chiome e di lagrime confonde,
> sparse in lucide stille e'n tepid'onde,
> costei, torrenti e fiumi,
> Oh ricchezza, oh tesoro!
> Due piogge: una d'argento e l'altra d'oro.

> In convito pomposo
> offerse Cleopatra al difo amante
> di perle in vasel d'oro
> cibo insieme e tesoro;
> ed or la tua fedel, caro amoroso,
> il questa ricca mensa, a le tue piante,

44—Arnold's 'The Scholar-Gipsy' appeared in *Poems* (1853); Glanville refers to it as the 'Scholar-Gypsy' in the passage which Arnold summarizes in his note to the poem. In 'Reflections on "Vers Libre" ' (1917) TSE had pointed to Arnold's versification in 'The Strayed Reveller' to show that 'the *vers librists* are by no means the first out of the cave' (*TCC* 188), and in 'Matthew Arnold' (1933) he was to observe more generally that 'Arnold's poetry has little technical interest' and that 'he was so conscious of what, for him, poetry was *for*, that he could not altogether see it for what it is. And I am not sure that he was highly sensitive to the musical qualities of verse. His own occasional bad lapses arouse the suspicion; and so far as I can recollect he never emphasises this virtue of poetic style, this fundamental, in his criticism' (*UPUC* 105, 118/97, 111).

mira, deh, mira come
offre in lagrime perle ed oro in chiome![45]

To a modern mind this ingenious reference to Cleopatra in a poem to St. Mary Magdalen (which is also decorated with the Vulgate text of the episode) might seem inappropriate, but not so to a seventeenth-century mind.[46] These Italian poets could write beautifully and in similar terms of Venus and the Virgin. Marino, like Crashaw, luxuriates in amorous fervour in his religious verse. Mary Magdalen *innamorò gli angeli e Dio* – made God and the angels fall in love with her; she was *amata amante* of Christ; it sounds very unlike the *primo amore* of Dante.[47] And gold, pearls, marble and alabaster abound in the most opulent baroque style.

I am not presenting Marino as a supersubtle Italian who led the simple

45–Stanzas six and seven (minor mistranscriptions: *read* 'in questa ricca mensa') of 'La Maddalena ai Piedi di Christo', number IX of twenty-one poems in 'Versi Morali e Sacre', in *Poesie Varie*, ed. Benedetto Croce, 1913, p. 371, borrowed from the London Library. *Translation:*

> From the head and from the eyes
> she mingles flowing hair and tears,
> scattered in glistening drops and in tepid waves.
> She, streams, and rivers,
> Oh richness, oh treasure!
> Two rainfalls: one of silver and the other of gold.

> At a sumptuous banquet
> Cleopatra offered her faithful lover
> some pearls in a golden vessel,
> food as well as treasure,
> And now your faithful one, dear lover,
> at this rich banquet, at your feet,
> look, ah, do look how
> with her tears offers pearls, with her hair, gold!

46–In 'Dante' (1929) TSE was to discuss Dante's 'power of association' in *Paradiso* XXXIII as being 'utterly different from that of Marino speaking in one breath of the beauty of the Magdalen and the opulence of Cleopatra (so that you are not quite sure what adjectives apply to which) (*SE* 268/228). The above stanzas are headed by a Latin extract from the Vulgate text of Luke 7:38, '*Lachrymis coepit rigare pedes eius et capillis capitis sui tergebat*' ('she began to wet his feet with her tears, and wiped them with the hair of her head', Revised Standard Version).
47–From Marino's 'Maddalena di Tiziano', lines 104, 8 (*Poesie Varie*, pp. 245, 242). The sensual overtones of Marino's portrait of Mary Magdalen as Christ's 'amata amante' ('beloved lover') are not characteristic of Dante's representations of human and divine love in the *Divine Comedy*, where 'primo Amore' ('primal Love') first appears over the Gates of Hell in the *Inferno*, III, 7, and subsequently in *Paradiso*, XXVI, 38, and XXXII, 142. TSE was to clarify the distinction in 'A Note On Richard Crashaw' (1928): 'Dante . . . always seems perfectly aware of every shade of both human and divine love; Beatrice is his means of transition between the two; and there is never any danger of his confounding the two loves' (*FLA* 125/137).

Englishman Crashaw astray; in extravagance of conceit, as well as in intensity of somewhat morbid feeling, the Englishman could give him a large handicap. There may be in Marino, but I have never come across it, some conceit as astounding as that of the pillow for the head of the tear. And Signor Praz, who gives many interesting examples of *concetti* from Marino, Guarini[48] and the Latin Jesuits, agrees that Crashaw is more baroque than the baroque, more *seicento* than the *seicentisti*.[49] Had he lived today he could only have dwelt in Florence or in Rome.

The two most remarkable poems of Crashaw are undoubtedly those to St. Theresa, "To the Name and Honour" and "To the Book and Picture" (it was in the humour of the time to write poems to pictures and statuary).

> Love, thou art absolute, sole Lord
> Of life and death.

A movement which is new and original in the history of octosyllabic rhythm.

> To prove the word
> We'll now appeal to none of all
> Those thy old soldiers, great and tall,
> Ripe men of martyrdom, that could reach down
> With strong arms their triumphant crown:
> Such as could with lusty breath
> Speak loud, unto the face of death,

---

48 – Giovanni Battista Guarini (1538–1612) is known for his pastoral tragicomedy, *Il Pastor Fido* (*The Faithful Shepherd*, c. 1591), which, with its elegant style, sentiment and sensuality, foreshadowed the arrival of baroque poetry in Italy. In a lengthy note (pp. 109–11n), Praz demonstrates the similarity of conceits in some of Donne's poems to those in Guarini's madrigals and sonnets, including the famous simile of the compasses in Donne's 'A Valediction: Forbidding Mourning', also found in one of Guarini's madrigals (xcvi).

49 – In his discussion of the baroque qualities in two of Crashaw's masterpieces, 'Bulla' and 'Musicks Duell', Praz declares (p. 269; trans. *The Flaming Heart*, p. 251): 'In these bold attempts at surpassing the limits and possibilities of his own art, Crashaw, better than any of the poets who were his contemporaries, achieves a result which may be said to have been the common aspiration of baroque art: that inextricable complexity of presentation, that one universal Art in which all the arts should blend and become an indistinguishable whole'. Impressed by Praz's assertion, TSE was to conclude his 'A Note on Richard Crashaw' (1927): 'Indeed Mr. Mario Praz ... puts Crashaw above Marino, Góngora, and everybody else, merely as the *representative* of the baroque spirit in literature' (*FLA* 125/137–8). 'The strange thing is', he was to write of Crashaw in 1930, 'that the finest baroque poetry should have been written by an Englishman in English, in a country outside the direct current' (*Listener*, 26 March 1930, p. 553).

Their great Lord's glorious name; to none
Of those whose spacious bosoms spread a throne
For love at large to fill. Spare blood and sweat:
We'll see Him take a private seat,
And make His mansion in the mild
And milky soul of a soft child.[50]

The rhythm is wholly Crashaw's own, in an age which handled this verse form better, and with greater variety, than it has ever been handled before or since; it is as different, technically, from the couplet of Marvell or King as it is from that of Swift – another master of this form in a later time. The language is simple and the vocabulary unaffected, far less "artificial" than that of Gray and Collins;[51] and it is not easy reading. You have to move slowly with it and ponder it out; you cannot race through it as you not only can, but must, race through Swinburne even at his best. But the most amazing passage is that from the "Book and Picture" which must have been written at another hour and at a greater intensity than the rest of the poem, and which is given by itself in *The Oxford Book of English Verse*.[52]

O thou undaunted daughter of desires!
By all thy dower of lights and fires;
By all the eagle in thee, all the dove;
By all thy lives and deaths of love;
By thy large draughts of intellectual day,
And by thy thirsts of love more large than they;
By all thy brim-filled bowls of fierce desire,
By thy last morning's draught of liquid fire;
By the full kingdom of that final kiss
That seized thy parting soul, and seal'd thee His;
By all the Heav'n thou has in Him

---

50 – 'A Hymn to the Name and Honour of the Admirable Saint Teresa' (1646, 1648), lines 1–14; minor mistranscription (*OBEV* 362).
51 – In 'The Metaphysical Poets' TSE had written that the '*structure* of the sentences' of the metaphysical poets 'is sometimes far from simple, but this is not a vice; it is a fidelity to thought and feeling. The effect, at its best, is far less artificial than that of an ode by Gray' (*SE* 285/245).
52 – The following lines (93–108) of 'Upon the Book and Picture of the Seraphical Saint Teresa' comprise the last sixteen of twenty-four new lines added to the poem after the first version was published in 1648; minor mistranscriptions (*OBEV* 367). TSE's copy of *The Oxford Book of English Verse* (see n. 37 above), was given to him by the students in his Southall Tutorial Literature class in 1918.

(Fair sister of the seraphim!)
By all of Him we have in thee;
Leave nothing of myself in me.
Let me so read thy life, that I
Unto all life of mine may die!

I should not like to quote anything more of Crashaw, or any kindred verse, after quoting this. A little acquaintance with the English and Italian verse of the period enables us to recognise several stock conceits, the lights and fires, lives and deaths and thirsts; but they are fused beyond analysis and perfected beyond criticism. This is the ultimate literary expression of the religious feeling of that strange period of sensual religious intensity.

We have now arrived at the point where we ought to be able to determine the difference between the conceit of Donne and the conceit of Crashaw, between the metaphysicality of Donne and the metaphysicality of Crashaw. In Donne, the conceit in its most characteristic form, as the lovers and the pair of compasses, is the extravagant development of a simile or a metaphor to emphasise an idea; the focus is transferred from the original idea to the pleasure in the exactness with which the simile or metaphor can be carried out in detail. The image is usually original and is usually or often drawn from the peculiar stores of learning that Donne possessed. Cleveland, for instance, in the verses which I quoted

Why doth my she-advowson fly
Incumbency?[53]

was directly under the influence of Donne. Such imagery, I dare say, would have seemed barbarous and pedantic to the Italians and Italianates, and also to Góngora,[54] whom I have not mentioned, because I do not know Spanish well enough to read such a difficult poet fluently, and because for English poetry the influence of Gongorism seems to me much less than that of

---

53 – 'To Julia to expedite her Promise'; see p. 136, n. 37.
54 – The Spanish poet and priest Luis de Góngora y Argote (1561–1627) developed an extravagantly conceited style under the influence of a young soldier-poet, Luis de Carillo y Sotomayor (1583–1610), who had himself been strongly influenced by Marino while serving in Italy. Góngora's verse remained unpublished until the year of his death, when it was published under the title of *Works in Verse of the Spanish Homer*. TSE was later to publish E. M. Wilson's translation of lines from Góngora's *Las Soledades* (1614) in the *Criterion* (July 1930, pp. 604–5).

Marinism.[55] With Crashaw, as with Marino, the imagery is limited and conventional, as the intellectual interests are much narrower. What is in Donne a kind of vagrancy of thought becomes in Crashaw almost a perversity of feeling. The conceit of Crashaw is briefer, the shocks and surprises more violent and more frequent, almost rhythmically regular. The intellectual effort is limited in its scope and is concentrated into a legerdemain, into epigram. Donne gives the impression of rambling because it pleases him spontaneously; Crashaw the impression of moving in a deliberate pattern. Crashaw is much more artificial, if the word "artificiality" be not misleading. With Donne the disintegration of thought produces the conceit, but the conceit springs from original thought; with Crashaw the disintegration of thought has, with the assistance of Italian models, become almost an aesthetic; Donne thought, whether he fabricated conceits or no; Crashaw thought in and for the conceit. And the conceit could be carried no further.

Crashaw was influenced by Donne as well as by the Italians; some of the other poets were also influenced by both. Marvell, for instance, in his more conceited verse, resorts to both. When he speaks of the fisherman who

like Antipodes in shoes
They shod their heads in their canoes,[56]

he is using a kind of conceit which Donne might have used, but would have used at greater length. Where Donne tends to expand, the others tend to contract. But when Marvell speaks of

55–Here TSE later made a holograph 'x' in black ink for a corresponding notation in the bottom margin: 'cf. Fitzmaurice Kelly: Spanish Literature'. James Fitzmaurice-Kelly (1858–1923), historian and critic of Spanish literature, observes in his *A History of Spanish Literature* (1898) that 'Gongorism derives directly from the Marinism propagated in Spain by Carillo, though it must be confessed that Marino's extravagances pale beside those of Gongora . . . Marino's conceits were, so to say, almost natural to him, while Gongora's are a pure effect of affectation . . . It took Spain a hundred years to rid her veins of the Gongoristic poison, and Gongorism has now become, in Spain itself, a synonym for all that is bad in literature' (New York & London: Appleton, 1918), pp. 285, 292. Grierson had earlier cited Fitzmaurice-Kelly's discussion in arguing that Gongora's influence on Donne 'is out of the question, for Gongora did not begin to cultivate the extravagant conceits of his later poetry till he came under the influence of Carillo's posthumous poems in 1611 . . . nor is there much resemblance between his high-flown Marinism and Donne's metaphysical subtleties' (Grierson II, 4).
56–From the final stanza of 'Upon Appleton House', lines 771–2, slightly misquoted from his copy of the Muses' Library edition of Marvell's *Poems* (see p. 135, n. 33), p. 35: read 'like Antipodes in shoes, / Have shod their heads in their canoes'. TSE had quoted these lines correctly in 'Andrew Marvell' (1921) as an example 'of images which are over-developed or distracting; which support nothing but their own misshapen bodies' (*SE* 297/256).

> Annihilating all that's made
> To a green thought in a green shade[57]

he is employing a conceit that passes the bounds of simile or metaphor, and becomes a wholly arbitrary yoking of the dissimilar; and when he says

> the brotherless Heliades
> Melt in such *amber* tears as these[58]

he is wholly in the aesthetic of Crashaw and the Italians.

This aesthetic is an addiction to the pursuit of "beauty" of a luxuriant sort, without intellectual scruple, but never without an enjoyment from the torturing of the intellect. But it is not on the grounds of his use of the conceit that I class Crashaw as a metaphysical poet. If that were so, I should have to admit Marino, Guarini, Góngora and the rest as metaphysical also. The conceit is apt for the expression of the metaphysicality of the seventeenth century, but concettism and metaphysicality are not identical. It is because Crashaw is definitely, and far more than George Herbert, or Traherne,[59] or Vaughan, one of those who have definitely brought a part of what belongs ordinarily to the sphere of thought within the sphere of feeling. That the result is far less a triumph for the human spirit than the work of the group of Dante, that the result is suspect in its nature and dangerous, that it is a *substitution* of human feelings rather than an extension of them, is another matter. In Dante, as I have said again and again, you get a system of thought and feeling; every part of the system felt and thought in its place, and the

---

57–'The Garden' (1681), lines 47–8, as printed in the Muses' Library edition, p. 100.
58–'The Nymph complaining for the Death of her Fawn', lines 99–100; TSE's emphasis; minor mistranscription (the Muses' Library edition, p. 52). In 'Andrew Marvell' (1921) TSE had quoted these lines in his comparison of Marvell's poem with William Morris's 'The Life and Death of Jason': 'These verses have the suggestiveness of true poetry . . . and we are inclined to infer that the suggestiveness is the aura around a bright clear centre . . . Marvell takes a slight affair, the feeling of a girl for her pet, and gives it a connexion with that inexhaustible and terrible nebula of emotion which surrounds all our exact and practical passions and mingles with them' (*SE* 300/259).
59–Though TSE stated toward the end of Lecture 1 (p. 63) that he would be examining the religious verse of Traherne 'chiefly' with that of Herbert and Vaughan, he did not in the end do so, but he was to summarize his view of Traherne's verse in 'Mystic and Politician as Poet' (see p. 23, n. 36): 'He is more mystic than poet; Vaughan just preserves the balance where Traherne upsets it. He has not the richness and variety of imagery which poetry needs . . . His chief inspiration is the same curious mystical experience of the world in childhood which had also touched Vaughan; he read deeply, but the rest of his life was a prolonged meditation over his experience . . . Traherne seems to me to remain a remarkable curiosity, an isolated specimen' (pp. 590–91).

whole system felt and thought; and you cannot say that it is primarily "intellectual" or primarily "emotional", for the thought and the emotion are reverse sides of the same thing. In Donne you get a sequence of thoughts which are felt; in Crashaw you might say, by slightly straining an antithesis, that you have a sequence of feelings which are thought. In neither do you find a perfect balance.

It remains now to study the last transformation before the poetry of metaphysic disappears: in a man who was mediocre in both thought and feeling, compared to either Donne or Crashaw; yet who in some respects had an individuality more marked than that of any of the minor poets whom we have not discussed, and who therefore makes an excellent specimen: Abraham Cowley.[60] And with Cowley this enigmatic seventeenth century of the first Charles fades into the modern intelligibility of Dryden, Swift, Pope, Gay and Bolingbroke,[61] whose mental and emotional structure, I imagine, was very much like our own.

---

60 – On 15 February 1926 TSE wrote to the London Library to request the following books for Lecture VII:

1. Abraham Cowley – Complete Poems.
2. Abraham Cowley – Letters
   both in the Oxford Editions if possible,
3. The best Life of Cowley (if any).
4. The Poems of Waller.
5. The Poems of Denham.
6. The Poems of Oldham. (L2)

61 – The poet and dramatist John Gay (1685–1732), a friend of Pope, is best known for *The Beggar's Opera* (1728) and two volumes of verse, *Fables* (1727, 1738). The *Collected Works* of Henry St John Bolingbroke, 1st Viscount (1678–1751), Tory politician, political philosopher, sometime poet and friend of Pope, were published in 1754. In 'Augustan Age Tories' (1928) TSE was to assert that F. J. C. Hearnshaw 'has done less than justice to the brilliance of Bolingbroke's literary style' but rightly exhibits Bolingbroke 'as a study of failure through lack of character . . . There is much of great value in his writings; but there is a fatal flaw in the substance of them' (*TLS*, 15 November 1928, p. 846). TSE later criticized his friend Charles Whibley for having 'somewhat overpraised the virtues, and too much extenuated the faults, of Bolingbroke as a statesman, because of the brilliance and vigour of Bolingbroke's style, and the great attraction of his personality' (*SE* 496/443).

LECTURE VII

{Cowley and the Transition}

Donne was born in 1573; Crashaw in 1612; Cowley in 1618. The difference of a literary generation between Donne and Crashaw is indicated by the years; but the years do not indicate the difference that there is between Crashaw and Cowley. Crashaw is Caroline of the first Charles; Cowley is Caroline of the Exile – for indeed he is antiquated in the Restoration.[1] I know of no figure at once so mediocre and so important as Cowley. For in much of his work he is the most faithful disciple and mimic of Donne; and on the other side he is the prototype of the man of letters of the late seventeenth and early eighteenth century. We have seen that Donne by his greatness, Crashaw by his catholicity of culture, become symbols of the origin of modern Europe; Cowley is a symbol of the change from seventeenth- to eighteenth-century England. With Cowley, all problems are reduced in size and artificially simplified. One illustration to begin with will show the difference of proportion. In the mind of Donne we find all the ideas of his time co-existent in their most abstract form; that is to say, we find in Donne the emotional co-efficients of the most general ideas. Some of these ideas are of contemporary science, some of contemporary theology; but they are all entertained on an equal footing; and this is typical of his time. In the mind of Cowley, many of these ideas no longer find entrance; what are left are

1 – TSE was to draw directly on passages in this chapter for two subsequent essays, 'The Minor Metaphysicals' (1930; see p. 23, n. 36), and 'A Note on Two Odes of Cowley', in *Seventeenth Century Studies Presented to Sir Herbert Grierson*, ed. John Purves (Oxford: Clarendon Press, 1938), pp. 235–42. In the former he was to re-cast and extend the preceding sentence to read, 'Cowley, as a biographical figure, is definitely a William-and-Mary or late Stuart museum piece rather than an early Caroline. The fervent spirituality of the early seventeenth century has gone; Cowley is a busy little enquiring mind of a rationalistic cast' (p. 641), and in the latter to read, 'He is neither Caroline nor Restoration: his state of mind would appear rather to be that of the Exile' (p. 235).

[185]

certainly more coherent and orderly, but are not *believed* by himself with the same intensity with which the ideas of Donne were *entertained* by himself. It is difficult to expound my meaning here, for the subject is really the subject for a book on The History of *Belief*. I suggest to psychologists that Belief alters from age to age, so that when a person asserts "I believe X." we must take into account the position in time of the author of the statement. The eighteenth century appears much more settled, orderly and positive and confident in some aspects than the seventeenth; but its belief is of a different, I think of an inferior quality to that of the thirteenth century. And mind you, I am not speaking of the *object* of belief, but of the believing itself.[2]

So Cowley, already Cowley, appears much more settled than Donne. It is that his mind, like the minds of greater men than he, Dryden, Pope, even the colossal Swift, the greatest writer of English prose, and the greatest man who has ever written great English prose – his mind was restricted. With all the psychological differences that I have tried to indicate, between himself and Dante, Donne was still able to find the emotional equivalent of highly abstract or generalised ideas. Dryden, or Pope, or Swift, or any later man, is only able to find the equivalent, when he does find it, by reducing the idea. In Donne the essence of modern science was co-existent, in an *entertained* form, with the essence of theological science. Cowley kept his theology and science separate by dwarfing them both. He was a man of scientific tastes, and he had known the great Hobbes,[3] and men of science in Paris probably,

2–This passage was addressed obliquely to the critic-psychologist I. A. Richards, who in the *Criterion* of July 1925 (see p. 81, n. 39), had stated that in *The Waste Land* TSE had effected 'a complete separation between his poetry and *all* beliefs'. This article, and subsequent conversations with Richards on the topic, were to provoke TSE's 'A Note on Poetry and Belief' (*Enemy*, January 1927, p. 16), in which he summarizes his theory: 'But I am convinced – even from the study of the history of poetry alone – and I think that the history of Christian dogma could be made to support the view – that belief itself has been in constant mutation (not always progress, from any point of view) from the beginning of civilisation. To limit ourselves to *Christian* belief, there is religious verse in the 13th century, in the 17th, and in the 19th centuries. It would be rash to say that the *belief* of Christina Rossetti was not as strong as that of Crashaw, or that of Crashaw as strong as that of Dante; and among the propositions believed by these persons there must be a number of dogmas, expressed in substantially the same words, believed heartily by all three; nevertheless they are all as different from each other as they are from myself. As for the poem of my own in question, I cannot for the life of me see the "complete separation" from all belief – or it is something no more complete than the separation of Christina Rossetti from Dante'.

3–Cowley met Hobbes in Paris in 1646, became a disciple and praised him lavishly for his eloquence, reason and wit in 'To Mr. Hobs' (1655). TSE was to criticize the philosophy of Hobbes severely in 'John Bramhall' (1927), where he describes Hobbes as 'one of those extraordinary little upstarts whom the chaotic motions of the Renaissance tossed into an eminence which they hardly deserved and have never lost . . . There was nothing particularly

and what was his science? Botany. He was an enthusiastic gardener.[4] He loved to formulate schemes for founding institutions for scientific research. He was almost as enthusiastic as Mr. H. G. Wells.[5] His scheme for the foundations of a college of science was almost practical enough to be laid before any philanthropic capitalist today; according to this scheme, income and expenditure are equal, and the latter allows for "Four Old Women" to make the beds of the professors.[6] And he was, so far as I know, the first person to suggest the foundation of colleges for the teaching of agriculture as a science.[7] Would that his advice had been taken!

I have not touched upon these matters to make pleasant anecdotes, but to lead to the appreciation of the vast difference between the lyrics of Donne and the *Mistress* of Cowley.[8] It shows, I think, the essential place of Donne

---

new about the determinism of Hobbes; but he gave to his determinism and theory of sense perception a new point and piquancy by applying it, so to speak, almost to topical questions; and by his metaphor of Leviathan he provided an ingenious framework on which there was some peg or other to hang every question of philosophy, psychology, government, and economics' (*SE* 355/312).

4–In 1663 Cowley left London to pursue his lifelong love of gardening, first at Barn Elms, an old estate in Surrey, followed by a move to a farm in Chertsey in 1665. Cowley opens his letter-poem, 'The Garden' (1667), with a declaration of his dedication: 'I Never had any other desire so strong, and so like to Covetousness as that one which I have had always, that I might be master at last of a small house and large garden, with very moderate conveniences joyned to them, and there dedicate the remainder of my life only to the culture of them and study of Nature' (*Abraham Cowley: Essays*, p. 420).

5–TSE was ever critical of the social, political and scientific writings of the novelist and historian H. G. Wells (1866–1946). In 'The Minor Metaphysicals' (see p. 23, n. 36) he was to change this sentence to read 'He had almost as many ideas as Mr. H. G. Wells' (p. 641), and in 'A Note on Two Odes of Cowley' (see n. 1 above) to read, 'The world of Cowley, indeed, is partly the world of Mr. H. G. Wells' (p. 580). In 'Thoughts After Lambeth' (1931) he was softly to generalize his critical view of Wells: 'I suspect that there is some taint of Original H. G. Wells about most of us in English-speaking countries; and that we enjoy drawing general conclusions from particular disciplines, using our accomplishment in one field as the justification for theorizing about the world in general' (*SE* 371/328).

6–In *A Proposition for the Advancement of Experimental Philosophy* (1661), Cowley proposed that a 'Philosophical Colledge' be situated within three miles of London and that the company received into it include 'Four old Women, to tend the Chambers, keep the House clean, and such like services' (*Abraham Cowley: Essays*, p. 248).

7–Cowley suggested such a discipline in 'Of Agriculture', included in his posthumous *Essays* (1668): 'But, Did ever any Father provide a Tutor for his Son to instruct him betimes in the Nature and Improvements of that Land which he intended to leave him? That is at least a superfluity, and this a Defect in our manner of Education; and therefore I could wish (but cannot in these times much hope to see it) that one Colledge in each University were erected, and appropriated to this study, as well as there are to Medecin, and the Civil Law' (*Abraham Cowley: Essays*, p. 404).

8–*The Mistress: or, Several Copies of Love-Verses* was first published in 1647, without Cowley's permission, while he was in France.

in an English tradition, the fact that this moderate and uninteresting man Cowley, who was himself to have so much influence, should have reverted to, and perpetuated, the influence of Donne. Especially considering his acquaintance with, and admiration for Crashaw, recognised in one of his finest poems.[9] Cowley is the link between Donne and Dryden. Let us see what of Donne is preserved in Cowley.

> This obligation to amorous ditties owes, I believe, its original to the fame of Petrarch, who, in an age rude and uncultivated, by his tuneful homage to his Laura, refined the manners of the lettered world, and filled Europe with love and poetry. But the basis of all excellence is truth; he that professes love ought to feel its power. Petrarch was a real lover, and Laura doubtless deserved his tenderness. Of Cowley, we are told by Barnes, who had means enough of information, that, whatever he may talk of his own inflammability, and the variety of characters by which his heart was divided, he in reality was in love but once, and then never had resolution to tell his passion.[10]

Without pausing to comment on the strange mixture of good sense, good phrasing, misinformation and cheap journalism (e.g. the word "tuneful") so characteristic of Dr. Johnson, we may observe that the heart of another is a dark forest, and whatever Cowley felt is a mystery, for there is no evidence any way. It is certain that *The Mistress* does not exhibit Cowley's passions, whatever they were, with any ingenuousness. I choose first a specimen which is not included in Professor Grierson's collection:[11]

> Now by my love, the greatest oath that is,
> None loves you half so well as I:
> I do not ask your love for this;
> But for Heaven's sake believe me, or I dye.

9 – Cowley and Crashaw had known each other since they were undergraduates at Cambridge. News of Crashaw's death in 1649 did not reach Cowley until 1651, when he began his elegy, 'On the Death of Mr. Crashaw', first published in *Miscellanies*, the first section of Cowley's *Poems* (1656); *MLPSC* 193–5.

10 – Johnson, *LMEP* 3; minor mistranscriptions.

11 – 'My Dyet', from *The Mistress*. TSE had written to Aldington on 3? October 1921: 'Would you like me to lend you my Cowley's Poems – apparently complete, four little volumes in an old edition of British poets?' (*L1* 474). This was *The Poetical Works of Abraham Cowley*, in four volumes, Bell's edition of the Poets of Great Britain from Chaucer to Churchill (Edinburgh, 1778). Though the edition was still in his library, he borrowed from the London Library A. R. Waller's edition of the *Poems* (Cambridge: Cambridge Univ. Press, 1905). 'My Dyet' appears on p. 89; partly modernized; minor mistranscriptions.

No servant e're but did deserve
His master should believe that he does serve;
And I'll ask no more wages, though I starve.

'Tis no luxurious diet this, and sure
    I shall not by't too lusty prove;
    Yet shall it willingly endure,
If't can but keep together life and love.
    Being your priso'ner and your slave,
I do not feasts and banquets look to have,
A little bread and water's all I crave.

On a sigh of pity I a year can live,
    One tear will keep me twenty at least,
    Fifty a gentle look will give;
An hundred years on one kind word I'll feast:
    A thousand more will added be,
If you an inclination have for me;
And all beyond is vast eternity.

One speculates whether Cowley had not read Marvell's "Coy Mistress", as well as Donne's "I wonder, by my troth. . . ."[12] and others. But observe the cleverness and the vapidity. There is no single line or image, even stanza, which might not have dignified a poem by Donne; he even imitates, as he does elsewhere, the direct and emphatic beginning; every detail is faithfully reproduced, but the *movement* is completely absent. In Donne you get always an emotional continuity, a movement from the central to the peripheral, from feeling to thought, to the feeling of that thought, and so on; and in Donne even the diversion, the descents have a significance of feeling which sophisticates and complicates, without destroying, the original impulse. In Donne there is an emotional requirement of the conceit; in Marino, in Crashaw, there is an emotion *in* the conceit; with Cowley there is an effort to reconstitute that curious amalgam of thought and feeling through the conceit. Cowley is an inferior Petrarch; that Petrarch whom Johnson treats with the respect only given to a subject one knows nothing about and does not wish to take the trouble of looking into. Original movements of mind created the forms; you cannot by simulating the forms revive the mind.

12—i.e. 'The Good-morrow'.

I will quote one more specimen of Cowley's erotic verse to emphasise the difference; from a poem in which he endeavours to revive "The Extasie" of Donne:[13]

> Indeed I must confess,
>   When soules mix 'tis an happiness;
> But not complete till bodies too combine,
> And closely as our minds together join;
> But half of heaven the souls in glory taste,
>   'Till by love in heaven at last,
>   Their bodies too are plac't.
>
> That souls do beauty know,
>   'Tis to the bodies help they owe;
> If when they know't, they strait abuse that trust,
> And shut the body from't, 'tis as unjust,
> As if I brought my dearest friend to see
>   My Mistress, and at th'instant he
>   Should steal her quite from me.

I have said that "The Extasie" of Donne compared to the *Vita Nuova* represents a decline of intellect and spirit; is there any need to point out the degradation from "The Extasie" to Cowley's "Platonic Love"?

You will perhaps think it unjust of me, when my opinion of Cowley is so low, to have singled him out at all, and only for contempt. But this is not by any means the whole story; and if Cowley was a poor metaphysical, as we shall see, he was excellent in other ways. No one could mimic Donne so well and so badly without a power of appreciation. One of our telescopes for viewing the metaphysic mind – to use a conceit like his own – is this man whose own wit was at the large eyepiece.[14] Cowley had considerable critical ability, and his criticism, as well as his skill in phrase and versification, is shown in his ode on "Wit". As far as it goes, this ode is better criticism of

---

13 – 'Platonick Love', stanzas 1 and 4 (*Poems*, pp. 75–6); partly modernized; minor mistranscriptions.

14 – An allusion to Cowley's telescope conceit in the second stanza of 'Ode: Of Wit' (1656):

> Some things do through our Judgment pass
>   As through a *Multiplying Glass*.
> And sometimes, if the *Object* be too far,
> We take a *Falling Meteor* for a *Star*.
>   (*Poems*, p. 17)

Donne than anything written by Dryden or Pope or Johnson, who were all too remote in spirit to understand him, though not too remote to be descended from him. I have already observed in the first lecture, that Wit is not the same thing for Johnson as it was for Dryden; it must now be added, that Wit was not the same thing for Dryden that it was for Cowley. I shall illustrate this assertion in the reverse of chronological order.

Johnson:
If, by a more noble and adequate conception, that be considered, as wit which is at once natural and new, that which, though not obvious, is, upon its first production, acknowledged to be just; if it be that which he that never found it, wonders how he missed; to wit of this kind the metaphysical poets have seldom risen. Their thoughts are often new, but seldom natural; they are not obvious, but neither are they just; and the reader, far from wondering that he missed them, wonders more frequently by what perverseness of industry they were ever found.[15]

You will remark that for Johnson there is nothing organic about Wit; Wit is still serious, is not closely associated with "humour"; but it is not a spirit animating the whole, but in the dignifying and embellishing [of] a theme. In the loosest of Donne's compositions there is a kind of continuity in change, so that there is an effect of the whole poem which is not the effect of any of its parts. In Johnson's greatest poem, "The Vanity of Human Wishes",[16] as in eighteenth-century poetry at its best, there is much greater *neatness* and *decorum*, but neatness and decorum do not make order – though they require cleanliness. In the "Vanity of Human Wishes" there are plenty of intellectual variations on a main moral reflection; as notions, they are sufficiently arranged and distinguished. But the emotion is on the whole monotonous; it is applied with very little modulation to a succession of topics; and monotony is the total effect. That is why two or three couplets of Johnson's poem, or of Goldsmith's, suffice to represent the poem in our

15–*LMEP* 9; first two commas added.
16–In his 'Introductory Essay' to *London: A Poem and the Vanity of Human Wishes* (1930; see p. 128, n. 18), TSE was to describe the two poems, first published in 1738 and 1749, as being 'among the greatest verse Satires of the English or any other language; and so far as comparison is justifiable, I do not think that Juvenal, his model, is any better. They are *purer* satire than anything of Dryden or Pope, nearer in spirit to the Latin. For the satirist is in theory a stern moralist castigating the vices of his time or place; and Johnson has a better claim to this seriousness than either Pope or Dryden' (p. 15).

memory, in spite of the exquisite variation of the verse.[17] He does not succeed in constituting that unity of feeling, out of elements perhaps the most disparate and remote, which is perhaps the highest unity of all.

Dryden had a greater power of cohering a diversity of feeling than Johnson, and a higher conception of Wit.

> The composition of all poems is, or ought to be, of wit; and wit in the poet, or *Wit writing* (if you will give me leave to use a school distinction), is no other than the faculty of imagination in the writer, which, like a nimble spaniel, beats over and ranges through the field of memory, till it springs the quarry it hunted after; or, without metaphor, which searches over all the memory for the species or ideas of those things which it deigns [*for* designs] to represent . . . . . The first happiness of the poet's imagination is properly invention, or finding of the thought; the second is fancy, or the variation, deriving, or mould-ing, of that thought, as the judgment represents it proper to the subject; the third is elocution, or the art of clothing and adorning that thought, so found and varied, in apt, significant, and sounding words: the quickness of the imagination is seen in the invention, the fertility in the fancy, and the accuracy in the expression.[18]

17 – TSE had slightly misquoted 'some of the best lines' of 'The Vanity of Human Wishes' in 'The Metaphysical Poets' (*SE* 283/243):

> His fate [*for* fall] was destined to a barren strand,
> A petty fortress, and a dubious hand;
> He left a [*for* the] name at which the world grew pale
> To point a moral, or adorn a tale. [lines 219–22]

And he was to begin and end his 'Introductory Essay' with an account of his discovery of the lines in 1900 and his present judgment of them: 'But if lines 189–220 of The Vanity of Human Wishes are not poetry, I do not know what is' (p. 17). TSE alludes further to Goldsmith's *The Deserted Village* (see p. 128, n. 18). In 'Johnson as Critic and Poet' (1944) he was to state that 'there is a poem, by a contemporary and friend of Johnson, which has a high degree of organization. I place *The Deserted Village* higher than any poem by Johnson or by Gray' (*OPP* 181/208).

18 – 'The Proper Wit of Poetry', p. 192 (see p. 64, n. 42). In 'Dryden the Critic, Defender of Sanity' (*Listener*, 29 April 1931, pp. 724–5), TSE was to quote the last half of this passage as 'testimony of the clarity of Dryden's expression, and the just sobriety of his theory', observing that 'it does not occur to Dryden to distinguish to the point of isolation the reasoning from the imaginative faculty; it would not have occurred to him that there was or should be anything irrational in poetic imagination . . . The distinction between the thought and the image, and the distinction between the thought and the clothing of it in elocution, is foreign to modern theory of poetry; but I think that these distinctions are safer than many that more recent writers have made; and the part of inspiration (or free association from the unconscious) and the part of conscious labour are justly kept in place' (p. 725).

You will not fail to have noticed how much more masculine is the analysis, how much more clear and philosophic the thought of Dryden than of Johnson. The fact is, in any case, that Wit is a word which has been gradually losing its extension. To Dryden it was tantamount to imagination. You may therefore think that its extension could be no greater; but there is a real contraction of the spirit even between Cowley and Dryden. Even Cowley defines Wit in contrast to what we should call cheapness; but it is probable that he is protecting Wit against those who would take cheapness for Wit, than against any who might identify Wit and cheapness. It must be admitted that in the same stanza Cowley appears to make the *blush* of the author the *fire* which should purge away the dross of obscenity: a figure which we should not allow to distract us from the excellence of his criticism.[19]

> Tell me, O tell, what kind of thing is Wit,
> Thou who master art of it.
> For the first matter loves variety less;
> Less women love't, either in love or dress;
> A thousand different shapes it bears
> Comely in thousand shapes appears.
> Yonder we saw it plain; and here 'tis now,
> Like spirits in a place, we know not how.
>
> . . . .
>
> 'Tis not to force some lifeless verses meet
> With their five gouty feet.
> All ev'ry where, like mans, must be the soul,
> And reason the inferior parts control. . . . .
>
> Yet 'tis not to adorn, and gild each part;
> That shows more cost, than art.

19 – TSE prefaces his quotation of selected passages from Cowley's 'Ode: of Wit' by reference to the specific characterization of Wit in stanza 6 (*Poems*, p. 18):

> 'Tis not when two like words make up one noise;
> Jests for *Dutch Men*, and *English Boys*.
> In which who find out *Wit*, the same may see
> In *An'grams* and *Acrostiques Poetrie*.
> Much less can that have any place
> At which a *Virgin* hides her face,
> Such *Dross* the *Fire* must purge away; 'tis just
> The *Author blush*, there where the *Reader* must.

Jewels at nose and lips but ill appear;
Rather than all things wit, let none be there. . . . .

'Tis not such lines as almost crack the stage
    When Bajazet begins to rage. . . . .

In a true piece of Wit all things must be,
    Yet all things there agree.
As in the ark, joyn'd without force or strife,
All creatures dwelt; all creatures that had life.
    Or as the primitive forms of all.

(If we compare great things with small)
Which without discord or confusion lie,
In that strange mirror of the deity.[20]

This is not only good poetry itself, Cowley at his best, but it is a better criticism of Donne than either Dryden or Johnson could have made. And yet it is a poem which as a poem Dryden or Johnson could have understood better than either could have understood Donne.[21]

    Cowley is indeed a small man; a pathetic little celibate epicurean, paraphrasing Horace on the virtues of a country life, and complaining that he can get no money from his tenants, and has his meadows eaten up every night by cattle put in by his neighbours.[22] And yet, though every one of the elements which made up his mind was shrunk, there is something of magnificence in the way they were put together, just as there was some pluck in the temper of this little college mouse who spied for the royal cause.[23]

20 – 'Ode: of Wit', stanzas 1 (line 4, *read* 'And reason the inferior powers control'), 4 (lines 1–4), 5 (lines 1–4), 7 (lines 1–2) and 8, of 9 stanzas (*Poems*, pp. 16–18); partly modernized; last three lines of stanza 8 separated from preceding lines.

21 – TSE was to re-cast the preceding sentence more felicitously in 'A Note on Two Odes of Cowley': 'This is not only good poetry, Cowley at his best, but it is better criticism of Donne than either Dryden or Johnson has made, while as a poem it was probably more congenial to either Dryden or Johnson than anything of Donne's' (p. 240).

22 – TSE alludes to 'A Paraphrase upon the 10th Epistle of the first Book of Horace' in 'Of Agriculture' (*Abraham Cowley: Essays*, pp. 416–18), and to Cowley's querulous letter of 21 May 1665 to Dr Thomas Sprat, his biographer, after arriving at Chertsey farm: 'This is my personal fortune here to begin with. And, besides, I can get no money from my tenants, and have my meadows eaten up every night by cattle put in by my neighbours'. TSE, who found this letter printed in Johnson's *Life of Cowley* (*LMEP* 8), had written to Richard Aldington in October 1921: 'I don't know Cowley's letters at all. I am sorry to say' (*L1* 474).

23 – TSE plays allusively upon the country mouse and the city mouse in Cowley's 'The Country Mouse. A Paraphrase upon Horace 2 book, Satyr. 6' (*Abraham Cowley: Essays*, pp. 414–16). As a Royalist fellow of Trinity College, Cambridge, Cowley was a keen observer of events prior to the outbreak of Civil War, and at St John's College, Oxford, he was intimate with Royalist

There was still a kind of comprehensiveness about his mind, though he be preserved rather because he happens to be the last of the metaphysicals and the first of the Augustans. He is Augustan in his puerile epicureanism, in which he provides an analogy to Saint-Evremond, and the French free-thinkers;[24] Augustan also in being a good churchman. A new poetry was arising:

> My eye descending from the hill, surveys
> Where Thames among the wanton vallies strays.
> Thames, the most loved of all the Ocean's sons
> By his old fire, to his embraces runs;
> Hasting to pay his tribute to the sea,
> Like mortal life to meet eternity.
> Though with those streams he no resemblance hold,
> Whose foam is amber, and whose gravel gold. . . .
> Oh could I flow like thee, and make thy stream
> My great example, as it is my theme!
> Though deep, yet clear; though gentle, yet not dull;
> Strong without rage, without o'erflowing full. . . . .

These lines of Denham, though here and there they might issue out of Sylvester, are in the new style.[25] It is rather through Dryden, in the "Alexander's Feast" and "St. Cecilia" that we trace the descent from

---

leaders until he followed the Queen to Paris in 1646, but he was not directly engaged as a spy for the Royalist cause until he returned from exile in 1656, whereupon he masked his position by taking an MD at Oxford.

24 – After the Restoration, Cowley fraternized in London with the fashionable French exile Charles de Marguetel de Saint Denis, Seigneur de Saint-Evremond (1614–1703), wit, epicurean, courtier, sceptic and littérateur who had earlier published a satire on the French Academy, *Comédie des académistes* (1643), and a satire on religious belief, *Conversation du maréchal d'Hocquincourt avec le père Canaye* (1658). TSE draws upon Richard Aldington's essay, 'Cowley and the French Epicureans' (*New Statesman*, 5 November 1921, pp. 133–4), where he discusses the influence on Cowley of the Epicurean philosopher Pierre Gassendi (1592–1655) and his followers, including Saint-Evremond. TSE had written to Aldington on the day the article appeared: 'The ignorance about the subject is so universal that the erudition will hardly be noticed. Gassendi, for example, is no more that a name to me, and I know *nothing* of T.[héophile] de Viau' (*L1* 485).

25 – 'Cooper's Hill' (1642, 1665), lines 159–66, 189–92; as printed in volume VII of *The Works of the English Poets*, ed. Alexander Chalmers (London: C. Whittingham, 1810), borrowed from the London Library; several mistranscriptions: *read* 'By his old sire', 'their gravel gold', 'make thy streams'. In 'Sir John Denham' (1928), his review of a new edition of the works (see p. 134, n. 30), TSE states that 'the poem set the model for a succession of didactic or meditative monologues suggested by the contemplation of natural scenery. In most of them, as in "Cooper's Hill," the importance of the view or scenery contemplated is slight; for Denham it

Donne;[26] Dryden in his early poems – as the "Astraea Redux"[27] – was a late conceited poet; and in the ode he and Cowley meet. I like to quote, both as an example of this link between Donne and Dryden, and because it illustrates Cowley's enthusiasm for the philosophy of *his* day – different from that of Donne's – Cowley's ode to *Mr. Hobs*.

> Vast bodies of philosophy
> I oft have seen, and read,
> But all are bodies dead,
> Or bodies by art fashioned:
> I never yet the living soul could see,
> But in thy books and tree.
> 'Tis only God can know
> Whether the fair Idea thou dost show
> Agree entirely with his own, or no.
> This I dare boldly tell,
> 'Tis so like truth 'twill serve our turn as well.
> Just as in nature thy proportions be,
> As full of concord their variety,
> As firm the parts upon their centre rest,
> And all so solid are that they at least
> As much as nature, emptiness detest.
>
> Long did the mighty Stagirite retain
> The universal intellectual reign,

————

is merely the starting point for a succession of common-place but well phrased reflections. What is remarkable in "Cooper's Hill" is the neatness of construction of these 358 lines. It is a succession of reflections and formal images, but none is pushed to excess or continued to monotony; they glide easily and naturally into each other; and each exists long enough to be distinct but not long enough to tire.'

Joshua Sylvester (1563–1618) was a minor Elizabethan poet whose versatile range as a writer of elegies, epistles, odes, hymns and occasional poems was obscured by his achievements as a translator, particularly of the French poet Du Bartas's *His Divine Weekes and Workes* (1605).

26–In 'John Dryden' (1930; see p. 23, n. 36) TSE was to assert that in Dryden's two odes, 'Alexander's Feast' (1697) and 'A Song for St Cecilia's Day' (1687), he 'has now arrived at both freedom and originality of rhythm, and at precision and dignity of language'. The latter poem, particularly, 'is very different from the lost music of Donne, who already seems a long way behind us, yet it comes from Cowley' (p. 688). In 'The Minor Metaphysicals' (1930; see p. 23, n. 36), TSE was to show that 'a man like Cowley imitates Donne consciously and anticipates Dryden unconsciously: compare his two odes mentioned ['Ode: Of Wit', 'Ode to Mr Hobbes'] with Dryden's "Alexander's Feast" or his "Ode on St. Cecilia's Day" ' (p. 641).

27–'Astrea Redux' (1660) celebrates the return of Charles II to his throne.

Saw his own country's short-liv'd leopard slain;
The stronger Roman Eagle did outfly,
Oftener renew his age, and saw that die.
Mecca itself, in spite of Mahumet possest,
And chased by a wild deluge from the east,
His monarchy new planted in the west.
But as in time each great imperial race
Degenerates, and gives some new one place:
      So did this noble empire waste,
      Sunk by degrees from glories past,
And in the schoolmen's hands it perisht quite at last.
      Then nought but words it grew,
      And those all barbarous too.
      It perisht, and it vanisht there,
The life and soul breathed out, became but empty air.[28]

In my last lecture I shall examine some nineteenth-century specimens of metaphysical poetry, in order that we may come as near as possible to a definition valid for all times up to the present. But we have already arrived at the point where we should reconsider the characteristics of the metaphysical poetry of the age of Donne. The metaphysical thought is partly prepared by the meditative verse of such poets as Davies and Fulke Greville (and therefore perhaps partly by the choruses of Seneca);[29] and the conceited

28 – The first two of six stanzas from Cowley's Pindaric ode, 'To Mr. Hobs' (Poems, p. 188), partly modernized; minor mistranscriptions (stanza 1, line 6, read 'But in thy books and thee'). The ode first appeared in The Mistress but was enlarged in 1655 for the second part of Poems (1656). TSE was to write of the poem in 'A Note on Two Odes of Cowley': 'In the age of Cowley the traditional form of belief was broken, and of this breach his ode To Mr. Hobbes is a monument. The romantic form of belief, belief in one's individual feelings, or in collective feeling, had not yet been evolved. There was, in Cowley's world, no object of belief capable of eliciting from him a response of the highest poetic intensity. There is therefore an adequacy in the ode to Hobbes, absent from The Mistress, which makes it satisfying' (p. 238).
29 – Sir John Davies (1569–1626) is known for his 'Orchestra, or A Poem of Dancing' (1594), and his philosophical poem, Nosce Teipsum ('Know Thyself', 1599), to which TSE alludes. Later in the year he was to describe it as 'a long discussion in verse of the nature of the soul and its relation to the body', as a poem written in 'the language and the tone of solitary meditation; [Davies] speaks like a man reasoning with himself in solitude, and he never raises his voice' (TLS, 9 December 1926, p. 906; OPP 133, 136/150, 154). TSE was to draw on both poems in the composition of Four Quartets.
    In 'Seneca in Elizabethan Translation' (1927), TSE was to record his appreciation for 'some magnificent passages, especially in the choruses' of Fulke Greville, but admits that 'they have much dullness also; and they do not imitate Seneca nearly so faithfully as either those of Alexander or those of Daniel' (SE 94/78).

THE VARIETIES OF METAPHYSICAL POETRY

style is partly anticipated by the bombastic styles of the Elizabethans and perhaps also by euphuism in Lyly and in Sidney.[30] Between 1580 and 1680 the Word – verb, substantive and adjective – undergoes a very great change, a change which may be apprehended by studying the language of Donne in contrast with the language of Marlowe, and then studying the language of Donne in contrast with the language of Dryden. It is remarkable how often, in the history of poetry, it is difficult to distinguish *reaction* from *tradition*. To us, the Romantic poets of the early nineteenth century seem merely to prolong with more excitement the language and sentiments of the latter half of the eighteenth; to themselves, they seemed in complete revolt. And further – to react against a style is to be influenced by it. Donne, with his interest in contemporary actualities, his accurate observation, his magazine of science and philosophy, his comparatively plain speech unembellished from Grecian mythology, is yet both a reformer and a continuator of the Elizabethan language. Dryden with his plain good sense, his reasonable mind, his clear distinctions and distaste for the far-fetched, is in revolt against Donne, whose influence on the other hand he continues.

The excesses of the ultimate descendants of Dryden were worse than the excesses of the immediate descendants of Donne. In the Caroline poetry in general there is a simplicity of language, a freshness and directness of phrase, more common than at any other time. It is the thought, not the language, which is tormented. The influence of Donne coalesced with the new influences from Italy to form a second type of metaphysical poetry, which is best and most completely illustrated by Crashaw. Crashaw had I think little

30–John Lyly (1554–1606), a popular writer for the Elizabethan court, was the author of *Euphues: the Anatomy of Wit* (1578), a sequel, *Euphues and His England* (1580), and several court comedies. TSE had lectured on 'The style of *Euphues* and of Lyly's plays' to his 1918 Extension class (*RES* 11, 299), and he had asked in ' "Rhetoric" and Poetic Drama' (1919), 'Is the style of Lyly, is Euphuism, rhetorical? In contrast to the elder syle of Ascham and Elyot which it assaults, it is a clear, flowing, orderly and relatively pure style, with a systematic if monotonous formula of antitheses and similes' (*SE* 37/25). In 'The Early Novel' (1929), however, he was to assert that Lyly's inventions 'did not represent any serious development in mind or sensibility' (*TLS*, 25 July 1929, p. 589), and in 'The Elizabethan Grub Street' (1929) he was to omit 'two novels which are not in the Grub Street class: the *Arcadia* of Sidney and the *Euphues* of Lyly. The latter is a very dull book; the former I believe to be absolutely the dullest novel in the language . . . and just because they are more studied and artificial and "literary", remain as curiosities of the literature of a period, rather than as documents of life' (*Listener*, 19 June 1929, p. 853). Sir Philip Sidney (1554–86) reacted against the vogue of euphuism in his heroic romance, *Arcadia* (1590), preferring a less artificial, more meandering style, and he criticized Lyly's over-elaborate use of similes in *A Defence of Poesie* (1595). In 'Apology for the Countess of Pembroke' (1932), TSE was again to describe the *Arcadia* as 'a monument of dulness' (*UPUC* 51/44).

direct influence upon style, for as you have witnessed, Cowley, through whom the metaphysical influence was propagated, reverted to Donne. Nevertheless, I believe that Crashaw, with his introduction of the Spanish Mood into English literature, brought something which became an element on the degraded sentiment and sensibility of the later eighteenth century.

We have therefore to consider the centre of gravity of metaphysical poetry to lie somewhere between Donne and Crashaw, but nearer the former than the latter. The remaining poets whom at the beginning I classified tentatively with these writers, fall either primarily under Crashaw or under Donne, with greater or lesser proportions of the other. I take Donne and Crashaw to be metaphysical by their types of mind, and therefore metaphysical in virtually everything they wrote. The others are metaphysical either at moments, or through acquiring certain mental habits of association of ideas, or are sometimes not metaphysical at all. The most mixed and baffling of this mixed type is Marvell; the purest and most elegant is George Herbert. The best example of that approximation to the metaphysical thought through the conceited style is that which I have quoted from Marvell –

> Annihilating all that's made
> To a green thought in a green shade[31]

a play with words which is a real play with thought. A compression which is conceited and metaphysical, and which shows the effect also of the immense compressions of meaning operated by Shakespeare, is the line of Herbert

> At length I heard a ragged noise and mirth[32]

where what was *heard* was the noise, qualified as *mirthful*, and as being the *kind of* mirthful noise produced by ragged people (thieves and murderers.) Another curious instance from Herbert is the

> churchbells beyond the stars heard; the soul's blood,
> The land of spices; something understood.[33]

31 – 'The Garden', lines 47–8; see p. 182, n. 57.
32 – 'Redemption', line 12, a sonnet from *The Temple* (1633). The line is marked in TSE's copy of the World's Classics edition of *The Poems of George Herbert* (Oxford, 1907), p. 35 (*read* 'ragged'). TSE was to quote the entire sonnet in *George Herbert* (1962) to show that 'Herbert is a master of the simple everyday word in the right place, and charges it with concentrated meaning . . . The phrase "ragged noise and mirth" gives us, in four words, the picture of the scene to which Herbert wishes to introduce us' (p. 28).
33 – 'Prayer I' (1633), lines 13–14. The lines are marked in TSE's copy of *The Poems of George Herbert* (p. 45), but TSE evidently quotes from memory as he modernizes the spelling and alters the punctuation. In 'The Devotional Poets of the Seventeenth Century' he was to quote the entire sonnet, 'because it suggests very strongly the influence of Donne', and to argue that

where the effect is not the *sum* of the effects of the four images; the direct meaning of the images in a very remarkable way cancel each other out; so that at the end an exact suggestion is obtained which is not even partially present in any of the images taken alone; an extension, and no vague one, beyond the bounds of thought.

Such instances might be multiplied indefinitely. What is constantly performed by these poets is the refinement and subdivision of a simple emotion by infusing it into a turn of thought of some difficulty, and this is often done by Carew; and less often the evocation of new feelings which appear as the equivalents of mental speculations. This latter, of course, is more than anyone's the property of Donne. Crashaw at his greatest yokes a simple passion, only of great intensity, to an unfamiliar object. The essential differences between Dante and Donne, and Dante and Crashaw, are, to sum up, these: that in Dante there is a system of thought to which is exactly equivalent a system of feeling, whilst with Donne there is only a kind of flow of thought to which is equivalent a flow of feeling; and that Dante alters or transforms his human feeling into divine feeling when applying it to divine objects, whilst Crashaw applies human feelings, though of intensity equal to any ever applied to human objects, almost unaltered to divine objects.

It is a postulate implicit in all metaphysical poetry that nothing is ineffable, that the most rarified feeling can be exact and exactly expressed. If you cease to be able to express feelings you cease to be able to have them, and sensibility is replaced by sentiment, in the end by the vague expression of the vague, and poetry degenerates into a diversity of noises. If the foregoing sentence has any meaning, it implies that Swinburne's *Triumph of Time* follows in a certain logical order of history, and in its due place, such a poem as Young's *Night Thoughts* or even Darwin's *Loves of the Plants*.[34]

---

the last two lines, quoted above, 'are so fine as to reflect a glory on what precedes . . . lines which have some of the magic of Keats's magic casements' (p. 553). In *George Herbert* he was to compare the poem to Donne's 'Batter my heart' and again to Keats's 'Ode to a Nightingale' (lines 69–70), describing the concluding lines as 'the kind of poetry which, like "magic casements, opening on the foam / Of perilous seas, in faery lands forlorn" may be called *magical*' (p. 18).

34 – In *The Triumph of Time* (1862) a lover whose mistress had rejected him for another seeks oblivion in sin, death and damnation. TSE had described the 'diffuseness' of the painful monologue in 'Swinburne as Poet' (1920): 'His diffuseness is one of his glories . . . You could not condense *The Triumph of Time*. You could only leave out. And this would destroy the poem; though no one stanza seems essential' (*SE* 324/282). The poet and dramatist Edward Young (1683–1765), achieved renown for his didactic poem of religious optimism, *The Complaint, or Night Thoughts on Life, Death, and Immortality* (1742–5, collected 1750), a series of nine long poems concerned with moral reflections on life, death, the immortality of

The poetry of the eighteenth century was given a direction by Dryden and subsequently by Pope, men who differed very much from each other, but who resemble each other in great force and great precision within narrow limits. I do not mean that Dryden was limited to the mock heroic or the burlesque; I once attempted in an essay to point out the considerable range of moods that Dryden could treat.[35] But *each one* of these moods, however *numerous* they may be, is limited; compare Dryden's Antony with Shakespeare's, and you see that poetry has lost much of its flexibility to the variations of life.[36] Instead of poetry, you get *genres* of poetry; in Milton you have the greatest writer who has ever existed of a limited *genre*. The poetry of Milton, the poetry of Dryden, the poetry of Pope, each so excellent in its kind, and so satisfying, was inevitably followed by an outburst of sentiment. This [has] of course a certain parallel in French literature, and the *Rêveries d'un promeneur solitaire*[37] provide a complete illustration of the outburst of sentiment, of the ineffable emotion; the degradation, from John of the Cross to Rousseau, is complete. But the approach of sentiment is already faintly apparent in Pope, and clearly

---

man and the promise of Christianity. TSE's 'Whispers of Immortality' (1917) had been tentatively and ironically titled 'Night Thoughts on Immorality' (Berg). Erasmus Darwin (1731–1802), poet, physician, scientist and grandfather of the naturalist, first published *The Loves of the Plants* in 1789. The poem versifies scientific details and humanizes the methods of fertilization in flowers with repeated descriptions of vegetable courtship.

35 – In 'John Dryden' (1921) TSE argued that from the wit in 'MacFlecknoe' to the elegy on Oldham, the 'capacity for assimilation, and the consequent extent of range, are conspicuous qualities of Dryden' (*SE* 312/271).

36 – TSE was to compare the plays and their passages at some length in 'Dryden the Dramatist' (*Listener*, 22 April 1931, p. 681): 'There is one great play [of Dryden's] in blank verse, "All for Love", and the difficulty about that is that Shakespeare's play on the same subject, "Antony and Cleopatra", is very much greater – though not necessarily a much finer play . . . I shall not venture here to investigate the nature of the dramatic in poetic drama, as distinguishable from the poetic in poetic drama; only to point out that the problem is much more of a tangle than it looks'.

37 – Rousseau's last work, *Rêveries d'un promeneur solitaire* (*Reveries of a Solitary Walker*, 1782), is comprised of ten essays or 'Walks' in which he explores and explains his feelings and sentiments solely for self-enlightenment. TSE had characterized the emotionally charged volume in his 1917 review of *Diderot's Early Philosophical Works*, where in recounting the cry of Diderot's blind man, that this mechanistic world has 'a merely transitory appearance of order', he remarks: 'This is not an unknown voice; but it is a voice which was beginning to be heard more loudly in the eighteenth century. It is heard from the *promeneur solitaire*; it is the voice of emotional scientific rationalism . . . Rousseau's accents were the more emotional, Diderot's the more scientific; but whoever wishes to understand how the nineteenth century sprang from the eighteenth, must read Diderot as well as Rousseau' (*New Statesman*, 17 March 1917, p. 573).

distinguishable in Gray and Collins and the inferior Shenstone;[38] rigidly
excluded by the satirists to Churchill and Johnson, it grows in strength in
the verse of the descriptive poets, Thomson[39] and Young to Wordsworth
and Coleridge (Chamonix),[40] in the last of whom it is allied with a kind of
philosophy from the German stream.[41] The maudlin provincialism of
Burns adds to it.[42] Now we have seen that in the best of the metaphysical
poetry there is exactness; the object of feeling is always definite. And this is
perhaps one of the healthier reasons why their poetry is popular today; by a
healthy reaction against vagueness. It is also one of the reasons why there is

38 – The poet and letter-writer William Shenstone (1714–63) was best known for *The School-mistress* (1742), which Samuel Johnson described as 'the most pleasing of Shenstone's performances . . . we are entertained at once with two imitations, of nature in the sentiments, of the original author in the style, and between them the mind is kept in perpetual employment. The general recommendation of Shenstone is easiness and simplicity; his general defect is want of comprehension and variety' (*LMEP* 466). In the 'Introductory Essay' for his edition of Samuel Johnson's poems, TSE was to describe Shenstone's eclogues as being 'consummately dull' (p. 14).

39 – James Thomson (1700–48), born and educated in Scotland, became the most popular nature poet of the eighteenth century with his often-reprinted descriptive sequence, *The Seasons* (1730; revised and expanded, 1744). 'The great defect of "The Seasons" ', wrote Johnson, 'is want of method; but for this I know not that there was any remedy . . . His diction is in the highest degree florid and luxuriant . . . It is too exhuberant, and sometimes may be charged with filling the ear more than the mind' (*LMEP* 448).

40 – TSE alludes to Coleridge's 'Hymn before Sun-Rise, in the Vale of Chamouni' (1802), descriptive of the valley of Chamouni [or Chamonix] and Mount Blanc in the Savoy Alps. 'Indeed', wrote Coleridge in a note that preceded the first publication of the poem, 'the whole vale, its every light, its every sound, must needs impress every mind not utterly callous with the thought – Who *would* be, who *could* be an Atheist in this valley of wonders! If any of the readers . . . have visited this vale in their journeys among the Alps, I am confident that they will not find the sentiments and feelings expressed, or attempted to be expressed, in the following poem, extravagant'. As TSE knew, Coleridge never saw Chamouni and never acknowledged that he was indebted for the germ of the poem to Frederika Brun, a German poetess. In his bookplate copy (Houghton) of *The Poetical Works of Samuel Taylor Coleridge*, ed. James Dykes Campbell (London: Macmillan, 1907), TSE made a pencil note to the poem (p. 165): 'From the German of Frederika Brun, but infinitely superior'.

41 – After the publication of *Lyrical Ballads* in September 1798, Coleridge travelled to Germany to study German language and literature. In February 1799 he matriculated at the University of Göttingen, where he read Kant, Schiller and the post-Kantian philosophers who were to strongly influence his aesthetics and philosophy. TSE was later to express his doubt 'that Coleridge learned so much from German philosophers, or earlier from Hartley, as he thought he did; what is best in his criticism seems to come from his own delicacy and subtlety of insight as he reflected upon his own experience of writing poetry' (*UPUC* 80/71).

42 – TSE was to come to the defence of the Scots poet Robert Burns (1759–96) in 'Matthew Arnold' (1933), where he suspects Arnold 'of helping to fix the wholly mistaken notion of Burns as a singular untutored English dialect poet, instead of as a decadent representative of a great alien tradition' (*UPUC* 106/98).

so little that I should call metaphysical in the nineteenth century: the age was still campaigning against the restrictions of the so-called age of reason. Before entering upon the question of metaphysical poetry in France in the nineteenth century, it is necessary to clear up any doubts that there may be. Metaphysical poetry involves the existence of a background of thought, of a definite system or fragments of definite systems. Behind Dante there was Aquinas, behind Donne the fragments of every philosophical system and every theological system up to his own time; and although the whole was chaos, the fragments were still sharp and identifiable. Behind Crashaw were the Spanish mystics and the Catholic Church of his day. Behind Cowley was chiefly Donne – it is mostly second hand; except that he did have toward Hobbes something of the feeling of a metaphysical poet toward a philosopher. One may say, was there not a philosophy behind Pope? Even if only the philosophy of Bolingbroke? I think that the answer is, that Pope did in places *use* a sort of philosophical system of discourse, but that this philosophy does not in any way direct, control, restrain or provide a definite object for his feelings. The words *classic* and *romantic* have been so widely employed that their contrast can easily be reduced to absurdity; for it follows from what I have been saying that the first "classic" poet (in the Augustan sense) – Pope – is also one of the first "romantic" poets in my context of the history of emotion or sensibility.

In the nineteenth century I cannot think of any English poet who was able so to *feel* a philosophical idea as to make it yield its emotional equivalent. There are meditative poets – Arnold or George Meredith, for instance.[43]

43 – In 'Matthew Arnold' (1933), one of the few occasions when he turned from the criticism to the poetry of Arnold, TSE was to characterize Arnold's meditative and narrative verse as 'academic poetry': '*Empedocles on Etna* is one of the finest academic poems ever written . . . I cannot but think of *Tristram and Iseult* and *The Forsaken Merman* as charades. *Sohrab and Rustum* is a fine piece, but less fine than *Gebir* . . . With all his fastidiousness and superciliousness and officiality, Arnold is more intimate with us than Browning, more intimate than Tennyson ever is except at moments, as in the passionate flights in *In Memoriam*' (*UPUC* 105/97–8).
In 1917 TSE gave an Extension lecture on 'Philosophy in Poetry – George Meredith' (*RES* II, 293), subsequently writing of Meredith in 'In Memory of Henry James' (*Egoist*, January 1918, pp. 1–2): 'In England ideas run wild and pasture on the emotions; instead of thinking with our feelings . . . we corrupt our feelings with ideas . . . George Meredith (the disciple of Carlyle) was fertile in ideas; his epigrams are a facile substitute for observation and inference' (p. 2). In his review of J. H. E. Crees's *George Meredith* (1918), TSE attacked Crees's discernment of a 'profound philosophy' in the poetry, asserting that 'most of Meredith's profundity is profound platitude' (*Egoist*, October 1918, p. 114). Meredith's 'Lucifer in Starlight', a poem from his first meditative volume, *Poems and Lyrics of the Joy of Earth* (1883), had provided TSE with the concluding line of 'Cousin Nancy' – 'The army of unalterable law' (*CPP* 30/18).

There are reflective poets, such as Browning.[44] There is Swinburne, whom Mr. Saintsbury calls "metaphysical", but who seems to me, and I hope will on consideration seem to you, at the opposite pole from metaphysicality or even Marinism.[45] Can you find in any of these that identity, that unity in difference

E fue due in uno ed uno in due[46]

or is there not everywhere that separation, with consequent waste, of thought and feeling of which I have spoken? I admit doubtful poems, perhaps doubtful cases; I am not sure that Francis Thompson does not sometimes, by an extraordinary *tour de force* in an exhausted idiom,

---

44 – TSE had placed Browning in this category in 'The Metaphysical Poets': 'The sentimental age began early in the eighteenth century and continued. The poets revolted against the ratiocinative, the descriptive; they thought and felt by fits, unbalanced; they reflected. In one or two passages of Shelley's *Triumph of Life*, in the second *Hyperion*, there are traces of a struggle toward unification of sensibility. But Keats and Shelley died, and Tennyson and Browning ruminated' (*SE* 288/248).

45 – In responding to TSE's 'The Metaphysical Poets' in *TLS* (see p. 62, n. 38), Professor Saintsbury quoted lines from the Chorus of Swinburne's *Atalanta in Calydon* (1865), 'Time, with a gift of tears; / Grief, with a glass that ran', and declared that 'it is certain that Mr. Swinburne, here and elsewhere, was "right metaphysical" in his method' (27 October 1921, p. 698). TSE replied (3 November 1921, p. 716; *L1* 483) that he could not believe 'that Swinburne thought twice, or even *once*' before he wrote the lines, and Saintsbury then admitted (10 November 1921, p. 734) that his 'Swinburnian illustration was perhaps capable of misconstruction. I hope I need hardly say that, if I rank Mr. Swinburne in the Metaphysical Israel, it is as of the tribe of Donne, not that of Cleveland'. TSE had earlier quoted the lines in 'Swinburne as Poet' (1920) to illustrate the separation of object and language in Swinburne's poetry (*SE* 326/284).

46 – TSE misquotes Dante's description (*Inferno*, XXVII, 125) of Bertrand de Born (1140–1215), the Provençal troubadour who is said to have instigated a quarrel between Henry II of England and his son Prince Henry. Decapitated in hell for the offence, Bertrand holds up his head by the hair like a lantern when Dante and Virgil encounter him in the ninth bolgia among the sowers of discord:

> Di se faceva a se stesso lucerna,
>> ed eran due in uno, ed uno in due;
>> com' esser puo, quei sa che si governa.

> Of itself it made for itself a lamp,
> and they were two in one, and one in two;
> how this can be, He knows who so ordains.
>   (*TC* III, 318–19)

In 'Dante' (1929) he named the episode 'among those which impress themselves most at the first reading' (*SE* 247/208).

approach his master Crashaw.[47] But one must also distinguish between the poets, like perhaps Francis Thompson and certainly Shelley, who had metaphysical gifts, and their actual accomplishment, which is of their age.

There remains I think only the doubtful case of Blake, which has not been placed.[48] Blake is I think in one aspect like Chapman, and rather like Mr. Yeats, in being a poet of juxtaposition of two worlds, rather than a metaphysical.[49]

> What are these golden builders doing
> In melancholy, ever-weeping Paddington?[50]

And a verse like

> My Spectre around me night and day
> Like a wild beast guards my way:

47 – The poet and Roman Catholic Francis Thompson (1859–1907) had been absorbed in and devoted to Crashaw's verse since childhood, had expressed his critical admiration in 'Richard Crashaw' (1889), and had drawn upon Crashaw's imagery and use of the ode in some of his most successful poems – 'Ode to the Setting Sun', 'Daisy', and 'From the Night of Forebeing'. TSE had lectured on Thompson as a 'poet of religious faith' and as a poet of the nineties in his 1917 Extension courses (RES II 293, 295), and in 1936 he had in his library a copy of Thompson's best-known poem, The Hound of Heaven (1893), which describes his futile flight from God.

48 – TSE first attempted to place Blake in the poetic tradition in 'The Naked Man' (1920), later titled 'William Blake', his review of Charles Gardner's William Blake the Man: 'What his genius required, and what it sadly lacked, was a framework of accepted and traditional ideas which would have prevented him from indulging in a philosophy of his own, and concentrated his attention upon the problems of the poet . . . The concentration resulting from a framework of mythology and theology and philosophy is one of the reasons why Dante is a classic, and Blake only a poet of genius' (SE 322/279–80).

49 – In contrast to his fascination with Chapman's 'double world' (see pp. 151–2), TSE had been highly critical of the otherworldliness of his contemporary, the poet and occultist William Butler Yeats (1865–1939), having reviewed his The Cutting of an Agate (1919) under the title 'A Foreign Mind': 'When we read it we are confirmed in the conviction . . . that its author, as much in his prose as in his verse, is not "of this world" – this world, of course, being our visible planet with whatever our theology or myth may conceive as below or above it' (Athenaeum, 4 July 1919, p. 552). He was to continue this criticism in After Strange Gods (1934), where he states that Yeats's supernatural world 'was the wrong supernatural world. It was not a world of spiritual significance, not a world of real Good and Evil, of holiness or sin, but a highly sophisticated lower mythology' (ASG 46/50). In 'Yeats' (1940), however, TSE was to set aside their differences 'in the field of doctrine' and praise him as a great poet, 'one of those few whose history is the history of their own time, who are a part of the consciousness of an age which cannot be understood without them' (OPP 262/308).

50 – Misquoted from Blake's Jerusalem (1804–20), Chapter 1, Plate 27, 'To the Jews' ('The fields from Islington to Marybone'), lines 25–6: read 'What are those Golden Builders doing / Near mournful ever-weeping Paddington'. TSE was to echo the first line in 'East Coker': 'What is the late November doing' (CPP 178/124).

> My Emanation far within
> Weeps incessantly for my sin.[51]

is not the emotional equivalent of thought, and it is to me – it is an heretical admission – uncertain whether it is poetry. When thought, such as that of Dante or Donne, is clearly expressible in another form, *then* it is not necessary to understand the thought to appreciate the poetry, for the poetry and the thought are quite distinct; and [when they are] one, it is sufficient that the author of the verse understand what he means. But here as so often with Blake, I feel that here is the thought itself; and that my enjoyment is not as with Dante a double enjoyment, but a confused enjoyment, the direct emotional enjoyment of an idea which I do not understand, and which if I understood, I should enjoy as an idea rather than as poetry. This is a difficult and debatable ground. For if, after absorbing a quantity of Dante and Guido and Donne and Crashaw, you take up Blake and feel that Blake's poetry *is* definitely metaphysical, either in my sense or in some other sense which you choose to give it, then, so far as you are concerned, my whole theory collapses. If you take the trouble to do this, I shall be interested to know what happens.

51–'My Spectre around me night and day', lines 1–4, from the Rossetti MS (c. 1800), as printed in *The Poetical Works of William Blake*, ed. John Sampson (Oxford: Oxford Univ. Press, 1913), p. 128; minor mistranscription. This edition was listed in an inventory of TSE's library in 1934 (Bodleian), since removed.

LECTURE VIII

{The Nineteenth Century: Summary and Comparison}

For several generations, we have been told by philosophers and half-philosophers, that if you cease to believe in Good and Evil, they do not exist. Good and Evil are concepts which have had their birth and their development, according to Westermarck and others – remember that Westermarck is a Scandinavian and therefore a Lutheran – and concepts which have or have had at best economic, genetic, or hygienic justifications.[1] We have not been so often told, what is equally true, that if we *do* believe in Good and Evil then they *do* exist. One generation doubted, one disbelieved, and the present generation has forgotten, that Good and Evil can be real. Most of the literature of England, and part of the literature of France, in the nineteenth century, is based on the doubt or disbelief in Good and Evil. I name at random Alfred de Musset, Charles Dickens, Thackeray and Thomas Hardy.[2] On the other hand a great part of French literature – and

1–Edward Alexander Westermarck (1862–1939), Finnish anthropologist and Professor of Sociology at the University of London from 1907 to 1930, had published *The Origin and Development of Moral Ideas* in 1908, a book that TSE first read in February 1915 at Oxford for an essay on 'Ethics' (Houghton). An advocate of 'ethical subjectivism', Westermarck holds to the emotional origin of all moral concepts and argues that objective or absolute notions of good and evil are illusory because the personal emotions on which they are based fall outside the category of truth.

2–TSE studied the pessimistic French poet and playwright Alfred de Musset (1810–57), author of *Confession d'un enfant du siècle* (1836), at Harvard in 1907–8; in the context of a later discussion of Good and Evil, TSE said of Dickens's novels, 'the religion is still of the good old torpid eighteenth century kind, dressed up with a profusion of holly and turkey, and supplemented by strong humanitarian zeal' (*ASG* 53–4/58); in 'Religion and Literature' (1935), he was to associate Thackeray with the first phase of authors who contributed to the secularization of the novel, who 'took the Faith, in its contemporary version, for granted, and omitted it from its picture of life' (*SE* 392/347); and he was to write of Hardy, in comparing his novels and tales to works by Sophocles, Joseph Conrad and Henry James, 'I do not object to horror . . . But there is horror in the real world; and in these works of Sophocles, Conrad and

[207]

this is why in my opinion the French literature of the nineteenth century is above the English literature of the same period – requires a background of Good and Evil, even if these abstractions do not appear on the front of the stage. I name Stendhal and Balzac.[3] Baudelaire was preoccupied with the problem.[4] As for moral detachment – George Eliot, the author of [*Amos Barton* –][5] could give points on *detachment* to Flaubert, who was in his way and in his time as much occupied with moral realities – contrasted with *social* realities – as was Dante himself.[6]

James we are in a world of Good and Evil. In *Barbara of the House of Grebe* we are introduced into a world of pure Evil. The tale would seem to have been written solely to provide a satisfaction for some morbid condition' (*ASG* 57–8/62).

3 – TSE had altered his view of Balzac since writing 'Beyle and Balzac' (1919; see p. 54, n. 24), where the 'atmosphere' of Balzac's world is thought to be less substantial than that of Stendhal and Flaubert: 'The exposure, the dissociation of human feeling is a great part of the superiority of Beyle and Flaubert to Balzac. Balzac, relying upon atmosphere, is capable of evading an issue . . . Beyle and Flaubert strip the world; and they were men of far more than the common intensity of feeling, of passion . . . they suggest unmistakably the awful separation between potential passion and any actualization possible in life. They indicate also the indestructible barriers between one human being and another. This is a "mysticism" not to be extracted from Balzac' (p. 393).

4 – In 'The Lesson of Baudelaire' (*Tyro*, Spring 1921, p. 4), TSE had written that 'All first-rate poetry is occupied with morality; this is the lesson of Baudelaire. More than any poet of his time Baudelaire was aware of what most mattered: the problem of good and evil. . . . Baudelaire, a deformed Dante . . . aimed, with more intellect *plus* intensity, and without much help from his predecessors, to arrive at a point of view toward good and evil'.

5 – A space in the typescript was left blank for the insertion of a title by George Eliot. TSE probably left the space to check the correct title of *The Sad Fortunes of the Reverend Amos Barton*, one of the novellas in *Scenes from Clerical Life* (1858). As early as 1916 he had written in a review of 'the seriousness which controls *Amos Barton* and not *The Mill on the Floss*' (*New Statesman*, 24 June 1916, p. 234), and though he had written to his mother on 6 February 1918 that he 'cannot endure George Eliot' (*L1* 219), on 4 March he wrote that he 'was surprised to enjoy her so much . . . I think my memory of pleasure is based chiefly on one story – *Amos Barton* – which struck me far and away ahead of the rest' (*L1* 221). On 1 April he wrote to his cousin that 'George Eliot had a great talent, and wrote one great story, *Amos Barton*, and went steadily down hill afterwards. Her best stunt was just this exact realism of country life, as good in its way as anything in Russian' (*L1* 227–8), and in the Introduction to *The Sacred Wood* (1920) he had, in a passage similar to the present context, asked 'How astonishing it would be, if a man like Arnold . . . had compared Thackeray with Flaubert, had analysed the work of Dickens, had shown his contemporaries exactly why the author of *Amos Barton* is a more *serious* writer than Dickens, and why the author of *La Chartreuse de Parme* is more serious than either?' (*SW* xiii).

6 – Flaubert dispassionately explored the moral realities of his characters in such characteristic works as *Madame Bovary* (1857), *L'Education sentimentale* (1869), *La Tentation de Saint-Antoine* (1874) and *Bouvard et Pécuchet* (1881). TSE had written in 'Andrew Marvell' that the 'firm grasp of human experience, which is a formidable achievement of the Elizabethan and Jacobean poets . . . leads toward, and is only completed by, the religious comprehension; it leads to the point of the *Ainsi tout leur a craqué dans la main* of Bouvard and Pécuchet' (*SE* 297/256). In his later discussion of religious comprehension in the novels of Jane Austen,

The rebirth of Good and Evil in the nineteenth century is often abortive and never led to a full growth. Its ancestry is mixed, but by an odd accident, Byron (I believe) had something to do with it.[7] With Byron, if you like, everything was pose, but the existence of a pose implies the possibility of a reality to which the pose pretends. One of the constant by-products of this revival of morality is Satanism; but even Satanism – the cultivation of Evil – in any of its curious forms, in part of Baudelaire, in Barbey d'Aurevilly, in Huysmans, in Wilde's *Pen, Pencil and Poison* – is a derivative or an imitation of spiritual life.[8] The present age, which is far better behaved and far less moral than the so-called "Nineties", is also far more Victorian.

Byron influenced Poe, and Poe – a writer almost completely unappreciated by Anglo-Saxon readers – is, with the exception of Hawthorne and Henry James, who are almost equally unappreciated, although admired – influenced Baudelaire.[9] I do not suggest that the influence of Poe is the only

---

Dickens and Thackeray, he remarked: 'These novelists were still observers: however superficial – in contrast, for instance, to Flaubert – we find their observations to be' (*ASG* 54/58).

7 – TSE was to delay his full estimate of Byron until 1937, when in the conclusion to 'Byron' he characterized the virtues of his vices: 'With his charlatanism, he has also an unusual frankness; with his pose, he is also a *poète contumace* in a solemn country; with his humbug and self-deception he has also a reckless raffish honesty; he is at once a vulgar patrician and a dignified toss-pot; with all his bogus diabolism and his vanity of pretending to disreputability, he is genuinely superstitious and disreputable. I am speaking of the qualities and defects visible in his work, and important in estimating his work: not of the private life, with which I am not concerned' (*OPP* 206/239).

8 – TSE was to assert in 'Baudelaire' (1930) that Baudelaire's Satanism 'amounts to a dim intuition of a part, but a very important part, of Christianity. Satanism itself, so far as not merely an affectation, was an attempt to get into Christianity by the back door' (*SE* 421/373). Jules-Amédée Barbey d'Aurevilly (1808–89), poet and novelist, explored a Catholicism steeped in eroticism, sadism, blasphemy and occultism in such works as *Un Prêtre Marié* (1865) and *Les Diaboliques* (1874). TSE was to write that Huysmans, who made his excursion into occultism and Satanism in *Là-bas*, 'only succeeds in making his diabolism interesting when he treats it externally, when he is merely describing a manifestation of his period (if such it was). His own interest in such matters is, like his interest in Christianity, a petty affair' (*SE* 426-7/378). In *Pen, Pencil and Poison* (1889), one of four essays in *Intentions* (1891), Wilde traces the aesthetic career and the casual attitude toward evil of Thomas Wainewright, an artist, writer and poisoner who, when reproached for one of his murders, replies with a shrug: 'Yes; it was a dreadful thing to do, but she had very thick ankles'. TSE had written earlier that 'I am much deceived if *Dorian Grey* [sic] be not perfect rubbish, and the best of Wilde be not in *Intentions*' (*Vanity Fair*, November 1923, p. 44).

9 – In 'From Poe to Valéry' (1948) TSE was to state that 'Poe has been regarded as a minor, or secondary, follower of the Romantic Movement: a successor to the so-called "Gothic" novelists in his fiction, and a follower of Byron and Shelley in his verse. This however is to place him in the English tradition; and there certainly he does not belong' (*TCC* 29). Baudelaire discovered the works of Edgar Allan Poe in 1847 and wrote biographical and critical prefaces for his translations of Poe's stories. TSE's early critical interest in Nathaniel Hawthorne and

considerable influence upon Baudelaire, or that other influences did not lead him to his moral view of the world. Baudelaire and D'Aurevilly begat Huysmans, the author of *En Route* (and begetter, upon Walter Pater, of Oscar Wilde);[10] Baudelaire and Théophile Gautier produced Mallarmé, who begat Valéry;[11] Baudelaire, I believe, plus certain other influences produced Laforgue and Corbière, who are responsible for Jean Cocteau and Blaise Cendrars;[12] and Baudelaire with other influences produced Rim-

———

Henry James was stirred by James's study (1879) of the 'deeper psychology' of Hawthorne's works, a study that informed his writing of 'In Memory of Henry James' (1918) and 'The Hawthorne Aspect [of Henry James]', in which he argued that the deeper psychology 'separates the two novelists at once from the English contemporaries of either. Neither Dickens nor Thackeray, certainly, had the smallest notion of the "deeper psychology"; George Eliot had a kind of heavy intellect for it (Tito) but all her genuine feeling went into the visual realism of *Amos Barton*' (*The Little Review*, August 1918, p. 50).

10 – In his 1930 review of Peter Quennell's *Baudelaire and the Symbolists* (see p. 153, n. 43), TSE was to describe Huysmans as 'a sort of Zola crossed capriciously with all that is least important about Baudelaire' (p. 358). Huysmans' notorious 'yellow book', *A Rebours* (1884), hailed by Arthur Symons as 'the breviary of the Decadence', and Pater's philosophy of aestheticism were among the strongest influences on Wilde's *The Picture of Dorian Gray* (1891).

11 – TSE was to compare Baudelaire with the poet and novelist Théophile Gautier (1811–72) in 'Baudelaire' (1930), arguing that in his minor verse forms Baudelaire 'never indeed equalled Théophile Gautier, to whom he significantly dedicated his poems: in the best of the slight verse of Gautier there is a satisfaction, a balance of inwards and form [sic], which we do not find in Baudelaire. He had a greater technical ability than Gautier, and yet the content of feeling is constantly bursting the receptacle' (*SE* 424/375). Stéphane Mallarmé (1842–98) was for a long time mentor and friend of Paul Valéry (1871–1945), who had in turn become a friend of TSE. In 'From Poe to Valéry', TSE was to state that the influence of Poe on the French tradition 'is the more impressive, because of the fact that Mallarmé, and Valéry in turn, did not merely derive from Poe through Baudelaire: each of them subjected himself to that influence directly, and has left convincing evidence of the value which he attached to the theory and practice of Poe himself' (*TCC* 28).

12 – Jean Cocteau (1889–1963), author, composer and film-maker, had just published his 'Scandales' in the January number of the *New Criterion*, and the English translation (*A Call to Order*) of his new collection of essays, *Le rappel à l'ordre* (1926), had been placed on the spring list at Faber & Gwyer. TSE probably wrote the blurb: 'Jean Cocteau is not only known as one of the most interesting of the younger poets and novelists in Paris, but still more widely as a leader in contemporary developments of painting, music, and the arts of the theatre. He is known by his *Poésies*, by two novels, *Le Grand Ecart* and *Thomas l'Imposteur*, and by the new conceptions of the drama which he realised by his remarkable adaptations of *Romeo and Juliet* and *Antigone* for the modern stage in Paris. To the British public he is probably best known as the collaborator with Diaghilev, Picasso, Stravinsky and Satie of the Russian Ballets, and by two other ballets, *Le Boeuf sur le Toit* and *Les Mariés de la Tour Eiffel*, which have been produced in London.' The Swiss poet and novelist Blaise Cendrars (Frédéric Sauser Hall, 1887–1961) had in 1918 published *Le Panama*, a surrealistic reverie of his mother's description to him as a child in Panama of letters received from her seven brothers in Galveston, Alaska and other distant places.

baud,[13] who produced the contemporary *surréalistes*. If there were world enough and time it would be my duty to show where the metaphysical element begins, how it is manifested, and where it ends, in this genealogy; Baudelaire is much more than a metaphysical poet, Cocteau or Breton[14] much less; I will merely pick out two intermediate figures: Laforgue and Corbière.[15] The foregoing is merely intended to state the theory that the *real* metaphysical poetry of the nineteenth and twentieth centuries springs from the belief in Good and Evil, and consists in a conscious and deliberate contrast *and* confusion of the moral and intellectual with the non-moral and unintellectual. In the post-metaphysical poetry of the nineteenth and twentieth centuries the contrast and confusion no longer exist, one of the terms has been suppressed, and you get *Le Panama, Les Mariés de la Tour Eiffel*,[16] and *Le Poisson soluble*.[17] Or you get the purely conceited, the stuffed bird of Paradise.[18]

13–See p. 59, n. 36.

14–André Breton (1896–1966), poet, novelist and automatic writer, was one of the founders of the Surrealist movement. In October 1924 Breton had published his *Manifeste du surréalisme*, which posits the existence of a '*surréalité*' in which the contradictory states of dream and reality may be resolved by a pure psychic automatism in the absence of rational control and moral or aesthetic preoccupation.

15–In his review of *Baudelaire and the Symbolists* (see p. 153, n. 43), TSE was starkly to simplify the Baudelairean genealogy: 'The only important successors of Baudelaire are Laforgue, Corbière and Mallarmé' (p. 358).

16–Cocteau's *Les Mariés de la Tour Eiffel* ('The Wedding on the Eiffel Tower') was first performed at the Théâtre des Champs-Elysées on 18 June 1921. He described the notorious production as a 'Spectacle','a sort of secret marriage between Ancient Greek Tragedy and a Christmas Pantomime'. The story takes place on the newly-built Eiffel Tower of the 1890s and satirizes a *petit-bourgeois* Wedding Party, which represents the clichés and banalities of daily life. The meaning of the plot was secondary to the show's function as a vehicle for theatrical amusement. As Cocteau wrote: 'Here, I renounce the mysterious, I illuminate everything, I underline everything. Sunday vacuity, human beastliness, ready-made expressions, dis-association of ideas from flesh and bone, ferocity of childhood, the miraculous poetry of everyday life: these are my play, so well understood by the young musicians who composed the score for it.'

17–Breton's *Poisson Soluble*, a series of thirty-two surrealistic prose poems depicting imaginary promenades in exotic landscapes, was appended to his *Manifeste du surréalisme* (Paris: Editions du Sagittaire, 1924) to exemplify automatic writing. Breton explained the title: 'L'esprit qui plonge dans le surréalisme revit avec exaltation la meilleure part de son enfance . . . Je suscite sur mes pas des monstres qui guettent . . . voici le "poisson soluble" qui m'effraye bien encore un peu. POISSON SOLUBLE, n'est-ce pas moi le poisson soluble, je suis né sous le signe des Poissons et l'homme est soluble dans sa pensée!' (pp. 36–7).

18–An allusion to the sentimental title poem of *The Bird of Paradise and Other Poems* (1914), by the Georgian poet William H. Davies (1871–1940), in which a prostitute describes the death of her friend, also a prostitute, who cries out in her delirium, 'Don't touch that bird of paradise, / Perched on the bed-post there!' In 'Reflections on Contemporary Poetry' (1917) TSE had discussed Davies's poetry as being in sharp contrast to that of Donne by deriving its

Jules Laforgue was a young man who died at the age of twenty-seven in the year 1877. He was "reader" to a German princess, and in Berlin picked up some of the language and a good deal of the philosophy, especially Kant, Schopenhauer and Hartmann, married an English girl (some of whose language he also acquired) became tuberculous and died in poverty. I believe the widow died soon after.[19] I think the first note about him in English was by Sir Edmund Gosse, but Mr. Arthur Symons wrote an attractive study in his book *The Symbolist Movement*.[20] His poetry, and even his prose, is immature, rough and sentimental. He was a young man of ardent feelings, of *no* cynicism, of active and abstract intellect, and with a singular gift for the emotions of metaphysics. He had an innate craving for order: that is, that every feeling should have its intellectual equivalent, its philosophical justification, and that every idea should have its emotional equivalent, its sentimental justification. The only world in which he could have satisfied himself, therefore, was a world such as Dante's. The disintegration of the intellect, in Laforgue, had reached a much more advanced stage than with Donne: for Laforgue, life was *consciously* divided into thought and feeling; but his feelings were such as required an intellectual completion, a *beatitude* and the philosophical systems which he embraced

---

emotion from the object, 'and such emotions must either be vague (as in Wordsworth) or, if more definite, pleasing' (*Egoist*, September 1917, p. 118).

19–Laforgue had been in Berlin for four years as French Reader to the Empress Augusta when in 1886 he met and took English lessons from Leah Lee (1861–88), an English girl from Teignmouth, Devon, who had served as governess to the Empress Augusta's children. They married in London on 31 December and moved to Paris, where Laforgue died penniless of tuberculosis in August 1887; Leah died of the disease in St Peter's Convent, Kilburn, the following June.

20–The first note on Laforgue in English was not by Gosse but by George Moore, whose 'Notes and Sensations' appeared in *The Hawk* of 23 September 1890 and was reprinted as 'Two Unknown Poets' in *Impressions and Opinions* (1891): 'Their names? – Arthur Rimbaud and Jules Laforgue, names for the first time printed in an English newspaper' (p. 112). TSE may have been thinking of Gosse's *French Profiles*, collected in 1904, but Gosse did not write on Laforgue until 1927, in an essay that elicited TSE's sharp response: 'Some protest ought to be raised first against his dismissal of Jules Laforgue and Francis Jammes and Tristan Corbière as "eccentrics" . . . and second against his statement that "the interesting French poetry of the end of last century . . . has had practically no influence at all on English metrical writers". The latter assertion goes to suggest that Sir Edmund Gosse is completely out of touch with modern poetry' (*Criterion*, September 1927, p. 195).

In 'The Perfect Critic' (1920) TSE had described his distance from his initial discovery of Laforgue in Symons's book (see p. 154, n. 45): 'After we have read Verlaine and Laforgue and Rimbaud and return to Mr. Symons' book, we may find that our own impressions dissent from his. The book has not, perhaps, a permanent value for the one reader, but it has led him to results of permanent importance for him' (*SW* 5).

were so much *felt* as to require a sensuous completion. They did not fit. Hence the metaphysicality of Laforgue reaches in two directions: the intellectualising of the feeling and the emotionalising of the idea. Where they meet, they come into conflict, and Laforgue's irony, an irony always employed against himself, ensues. This appears in the words of his Laertes to his Hamlet, in his curious prose version:

> – If (says Laertes meeting Hamlet at the grave of Ophelia) you were not a wretched madman, quite irresponsible according to the most recent investigations of medical science, you would be obliged to give me immediate satisfaction for the death of my honourable father and my sister – that highly accomplished young woman [. . .]
> – O Laertes, that's all one to me. But be sure that I allow for your point of view . . .
> – Good Heaven, what lack of any moral sense! [. . .]
> They sent to search for the corpse with torches of the best quality.[21]

Laforgue is the wholly self-conscious.

> Bref, j'allais me donner d'un "Je Vous Aime"
> Quand, je m'avisai non sans peine
> Que d'abord je ne me possédais pas [bien] moi-même.[22]

That "je m'avisai" is always interrupting, just as the disparity between the meaning of human lives and what they should mean is always driving his

21 – TSE's translation (and parenthetical intrusion) from 'Hamlet' in *Moralités légendaires*, included in volume 1 of the two-volume edition in his library (signed 'Thomas Eliot 1909') of *Oeuvres Complètes de Jules Laforgue*, quatrième edition (Paris: Mercure de France, 1909), pp. 69, 72.

   – . . . si vous n'étiez un pauvre dément, irresponsable selon les derniers progrès de la science, vous paieriez à l'instant la mort de mon honorable père et celle de ma soeur, cette jeune fille accomplie . . .
   – O Laertes, tout m'est égal. Mais soyez sûr que je prendrai votre point de vue en considération . . .
   – Juste ciel, quelle absence de sens moral!
   . . . . On envoya chercher le cadavre avec des flambeaux de première qualité.

TSE had written to Conrad Aiken on 21 August 1916 that Pound 'wants me to do the "Hamlet" to go to make a volume between us of the *Moralités Légendaires*, and I have done a few pages of it' (*L1* 145). The volume never appeared.
22 – 'Dimanches' (III), lines 1–3; minor mistranscriptions; from *Derniers Vers* (1890), in TSE's copy of *Oeuvres Complètes*, I, p. 297: 'In short, I was going to treat myself to an "I love you" when I realised, but not without trouble, that in the first place I was not really in possession of myself' (trans. Michael Collie, *Laforgue*, p. 116).

Hamlet back onto himself. But he is one who "ne croit à son Moi qu'à ses moments perdus",[23] in disaccord, and later in the same poem (*Dimanches* p. 297) he repeats the theme of Baudelaire and Emerson: "je ne suis qu'un faux accord" or "Seigneur, donnez-moi le force et le courage / De contempler mon corps et mon coeur sans dégoût".[24]

> Ah, que je te les tordrais avec plaisir,
> Ce corps bijou, ce coeur [à] ténor . . .
> Non, non; C'est sucer la chair d'un coeur élu,
> Adorer d'incurables organes . . .
> Et ce n'est pas sa chair qui me serait tout,
> Et je ne serais pas qu'un grand coeur pour elle . . .
> L'âme et la chair, la chair et l'âme
> C'est l'esprit édénique et fier
> D'être un peu l'Homme avec la Femme . . .
>
> – Allons, dernier des poètes,
> Toujours enfermé tu te rendras malade!
> Vois, il fait beau temps, tout le monde est dehors,
> Va donc acheter deux sous d'ellébore,
> Ça te fera une petite promenade.[25]

Later, in the same group of poems, he speaks of "les jeunes filles inviolables et frêles" going to church, and says of himself:

23 – Line 7: *translation*: 'only believes in his Self in moments of loss'.
24 – Misquoted from Baudelaire's 'L'Héautontimorouménos', line 13, 'Ne suis-je pas un faux accord' ('Am I not a dissonance'), and from 'Un Voyage à Cythère', concluding lines, 'Seigneur! donnez-moi la force et le courage / De contempler mon coeur et mon corps sans dégoût!' ('O Lord, give me the power and the courage / to regard my heart and my body without loathing!'; trans. C. F. MacIntyre, *One Hundred Poems from Les Fleurs du Mal*, p. 299). Emerson expresses Laforgue's theme of self-fragmentation and incompleteness in several essays, particularly in 'Circles' ('I unsettle all things') and in 'Experience' ('I am a fragment, and this is a fragment of me'). *The Collected Works of Ralph Waldo Emerson* (Cambridge: Harvard Univ. Press, 1971–), Vol. II, p. 188; vol. III, p. 83.
25 – 'Dimanches' (III), from stanzas 8, 9, 10 and 12, pp. 299–300; minor mistranscriptions. *Translation*: 'Oh, with what pleasure I'd wring them, this precious body and this tenor heart . . . No, no! That's to suck the flesh of a chosen spirit, to adore incurable organs . . . And it's not her flesh that would be everything for me. And for her I'd be more than a large-hearted man . . . The spirit and the flesh, the flesh and the spirit – it is the proud spirit of the Garden of Eden to be something of a Man with Woman . . . Come, last of poets, if you're always shut up, you will make yourself ill. See, it's a fine day, everyone's outside. Then go and buy a pennyworth of hellebore. It will give you a little walk' (trans. Michael Collie, *Laforgue*, pp. 116–17).

Moi, je ne vais pas à l'église,
Moi, je suis le Grand Chancelier de l'Analyse . . .[26]

It is noticeable how often the words "inconscient", "néant", and "L'absolu" and such philosophical terms from the vocabulary of Schopenhauer and Hartmann,[27] the Valkyrie, and such properties from the dramas of Wagner, recur.[28] Laforgue is the nearest verse equivalent to the philosophies of Schopenhauer and Hartmann, the philosophy of the unconscious and of annihilation, just as Wagner is the nearest music equivalent to the same philosophies, though apart from this approximation to a similar philosophic mood, it would be difficult to say what there is in common between Wagner and Laforgue. But in Laforgue there is continuous war between the feelings implied by his ideas, and the ideas implied by his feelings. The system of Schopenhauer collapses, but in a different ruin from that of *Tristan und Isolde*.[29]

The public cries recommence. Important notice! Redemption Loan has weakened, Panama Canal shares firm. Auctions, experts. Advances against securities quoted or unquoted, purchase of unencumbered properties or annuities; advances against expectations; time-tables, annuals, new-year's gifts. Circular tours at reduced prices. Madame Ludovic predicts the future, daily, from 2 to 4. Au paradis des Enfants: toys for children and cotillon favours for adults . . . Sole agency! . . . Cylinder machines Marinoni! Everything guaranteed, everything for nothing! Oh the rapidity of life also sole agency . . .[30]

26 – 'Dimanches' (IV), p. 301: 'The inviolable and frail Young Girls', and p. 302: 'I do not go to church not I! / I'm the High Chancellor of Analysis, in fact' (trans. Michael Collie, *Laforgue*, p. 114).

27 – After he went to Germany in 1881 Laforgue was influenced by Arthur Schopenhauer (1788–1860), and particularly by his disciple, Eduard von Hartmann (1842–1906), whose *La Philosophie de l'inconscient* (1869) became Laforgue's temporary Bible and provided the language for his personae, who, in the face of *le néant* in the external world, continuously seek *l'absolu* in the *l'inconscient*.

28 – In stanza seven of 'Dimanches' (III), immediately preceding the elided stanzas quoted above (see n. 23), the persona cries: 'A moi, Walkyries! / Walkyries des hypocondries et des tueries!'('Come to me Walkyries, Walkyries of hypochondria and slaughter!'). In Germanic mythology the Valkyries were warrior-maidens who presided over battlefields, selecting the victorious warriors and escorting the fallen to Valhalla. Wagner gave the Valkyries a prominent role in his *Die Walküre* (1854–6).

29 – Wagner's music drama, *Tristan und Isolde*, was first produced in Munich in 1865. TSE had quoted verses from Act I in Part I of *The Waste Land*, as indicated in his 'Notes' to the poem (*CPP* 76/50–51).

30 – TSE translates lines 41–51 from Laforgue's prose poem, 'Grande Complainte de la Ville de Paris', written in August 1884 and published in his first book, *Les Complaintes* (1885):

One would be inclined to date this 1919, school of Tristan Tzara's Dadaism.[31] No, it is Jules Laforgue in August 1884 deploring the existence of the state of affairs which we usually date from the Treaty of Versailles.[32] Only Laforgue is in revolt, not in acceptance; he is at once the sentimentalist day-dreaming over the *jeune fille* at the piano with her geraniums, and the behaviourist inspecting her reflexes.[33] What he wants, you see, is either a *Vita Nuova* to justify, dignify and integrate his sentiments toward the *jeune fille* in a system of the universe, or else some system of thought which shall keep a place [for and] even enhance these feelings and at the same time enable him to *feel* as intensely the abstract world. On the one hand he was fascinated by Miss Leah Lee, the English governess, and on the other hand by the Kantian pseudo-Buddhism of Schopenhauer and Hartmann.[34] What

---

Mais les cris publics reprennent. Avis important! l'Amortissable a fléchi, ferme le Panama. Enchères, experts. Avances sur titres cotés ou non cotés, achats de nu-propriétés, de viagers, d'usufruit; avances sur successions ouvertes et autres; indicateurs, annuaires, étrennes. Voyages circulaires à prix réduits. Madame Ludovic prédit l'avenir de 2 à 4. Jouets *Au Paradis des enfants* et accessoires pour cotillons aux grandes personnes. Grand choix de principes à l'épreuve. Encore des cris! Seul dépôt! soupers de centième! Machines cylindriques Marinoni! Tout garanti, tout pour rien! Ah! la rapidité de la vie aussi seul dépôt . . . [Laforgue's ellipsis] (*Oeuvres Complètes*, I, p. 178).

31 – The Rumanian-born poet Tristan Tzara (Sami Rosenstock, 1896–1963) was one of the founders and chief inspirers of the Dada movement in Zurich after the war. In 1919 Tzara sent TSE a copy of his *Vingt-cinq poèmes* (Zurich: Collection Dada, 1918), which TSE described in his review as 'a kind of something which has the odd distinction of being neither verse nor prose nor prose-poem . . . At least it is a symptom of "experiment," and ought not to be put in the hands of the young. Mr. Tzara's work does not appear to have very deep roots in the literature of any nation' (*Egoist*, July 1919, p. 39). The following year, in 'Modern Tendencies in Poetry', TSE declared that Tzara's verse represents 'the reductio ad absurdum of . . . the tendency of people of intelligence who have thought about art to the point of having become cynical about it, and of people who follow them without having thought about it at all . . . It is wholly unconstructive. It is in the end, unscientific. It is no more art than a postage stamp album' (*Shama'a* [Urur, Adjar, India], I, Spring 1920, p. 17). 'Dadaism', he wrote in 'The Lesson of Baudelaire' (see n. 4 above), 'is a diagnosis of a disease of the French mind; whatever lesson we extract from it will not be directly applicable in London. Whatever value there may be in Dada depends upon the extent to which it is a moral criticism of French literature and French life'.
32 – The treaty between the Allies and Germany that ended World War I, signed at the Palace of Versailles on 28 June 1919. TSE was to write in 'Dante' (1929): 'It is not particularly the Treaty of Versailles that has separated nation from nation; nationalism was born long before; and the process of disintegration which for our generation culminates in that treaty began soon after Dante's time' (*SE* 240/202).
33 – TSE alludes to the tenth (x) of the twelve poems in *Derniers Vers* ['O géraniums diaphanes, guerroyeurs sortilèges'], previously quoted in 'The Metaphysical Poets' as a poem that employs 'a method curiously similar to that of the "metaphysical poets", similar also in its use of obscure words and of simple phrasing' (*SE* 289/249).
34 – In their pessimistic philosophies. Schopenhauer and Hartmann uphold Kant's doctrine of will and the Buddhist ideal of desirelessness as a means of allaying the will. In the production of

is interesting in Laforgue is not his accomplishment; as an artist he is as much below Corbière and Rimbaud as he is above Verlaine as an intellect.[35] What is interesting and significant is the sacrifice of his art and his mind before an insoluble problem. Here is a poet genuinely occupied with the relation of feeling and thought, not, like Browning and Meredith, playing with their mechanical combinations. Baudelaire had the genius to attempt an insoluble problem and yet be a great artist; if Laforgue was not a great artist, it is not for us, who have dealt no better with the problem, to sneer at him.

If we can compare Laforgue, with very great differences, to Donne, so we can compare Corbière, with equal differences, to Crashaw. Not that Corbière is a religious poet: with these poets we have reached something which, for the nineteenth century, was more fundamental than religious devotion. Corbière is a finer poet, though a lesser intellect, than Laforgue; Laforgue was twenty-seven when he died, Corbière thirty; Laforgue died in 1887, Corbière in 1875. Also of lung trouble. In the work of Corbière there is less evidence of philosophic reading; he has less direct feeling of "the absolute", "the unconscious", and the other abstractions which aroused Laforgue's passion, but there is the same product of thought-feeling and feeling-thought. Like Crashaw, with Corbière the centre of gravity is more the *word* and the phrase, and he therefore has phrases which recall, in our comparison, the concentrated conceit of Crashaw. As we observed that Marvell, in his more conceited work, could concentrate more *wit* into a couple of words than is usual in Donne –

> Like a green thought in a green shade,[36]

or, of a spring,

> Might a soul bathe there, and be clean?[37]

———

intelligence, the will creates the possibility of its own negation in a calm, ascetic life of abstinence, though Schopenhauer and Hartmann find compensation for human suffering not in *nirvana* but in the Idea and in the Unconscious, respectively.

35 – The Symbolist poet Paul Verlaine (1844–96) was the mentor of Rimbaud, who recorded their turbulent relationship in *Une Saison en enfer* (1873). As a critic in *Art Poétique* (1884), and in his verse, Verlaine emphasized the musical quality of poetry: '*la musique avant toute chose*'. TSE had quoted a line ('*Et O ces voix d'enfants, chantant dans la coupole*'!) from Verlaine's sonnet, 'Parsifal', in Part III of *The Waste Land* (*CPP* 67/43).

36 – 'The Garden', line 48: *read* 'To a green thought in a green shade'; see p. 182, n. 57 and p. 199, n. 31.

37 – from 'Chlorinda and Damon', line 15; Muses' Library edition, p. 41. TSE had quoted the full interrogative lines ('Might a soul bathe there and be clean, / Or slake its drought?') in 'Andrew Marvell' (1921), where he finds that 'a metaphor has suddenly rapt us to the image of

where images are arbitrarily but felicitously yoked together, so Corbière at his best can find an image, a parallel, which in its way is as fine as Dante or Shakespeare.

From his greatest poem, *La Rapsode foraine*, the assemblage of crippled and diseased at a religious festival in Brittany –

> Là, ce tronc d'homme où croît l'ulcère,
> Contre un tronc d'arbre où croît le gui. . . .

"This trunk of a man on which the ulcer grows, (leaning) against this trunk of a tree on which grows the mistletoe": this sudden and surprising collocation of the animal and vegetable, with the added horror thrown back upon the human disease, is worthy of Dante.[38] Corbière's use of something resembling the conceit is more evident in his series of *Petits Rondels pour après*, exequies on the death of a poet, presumably himself (observe again how omnipresent is the Ego in metaphysical poetry of the nineteenth century). Here is one of them:

> Va vite, léger peigneur de comètes!
> Les herbes au vent seront tes cheveux;
> De ton oeil béant jailliront les feux
> Follets, prisonniers dans les pauvres têtes . . .
>
> Les fleurs de tombeau qu'on nomme Amourettes
> Foisonneront plein ton rire terreux . . .
> Et les myosotis, ces fleurs d'oubliettes . . .

---

spiritual purgation' (*SE* 300/259), and again in 'Andrew Marvell' (1923; see p. 123, n. 6), where he describes them as 'a conceit of the very finest order . . . Our pleasure is in the suddenness of the transference from material to spiritual water' (p. 809).

38 – TSE translates lines 137–8 from Corbière's 'La Rapsode Foraine et le Pardon de Sainte-Anne' ('The Wandering Singer and the Pilgrimage of Saint Anne'), which appeared in *Les Amours jaunes* (1873). TSE owned and quotes from (p. 200) the Edition définitive (Paris: Albert Messein, 1912), with a preface by Charles Le Goffic. He had chosen two preceding lines (113–14) in the poem as the original epigraph for 'Sweeney Erect' (Berg): 'Voici ton cierge:/ (C'est deux livres qu'il a coûté)', and he had sharply criticized an unnamed American critic, who 'appears to have studied at the graduate school of Chicago University', for having identified the poem 'as an exploration "of folk-religion" ' ('Contemporanea', *Egoist*, June–July 1918, p. 84). More pointedly, in 'Modern Tendencies in Poetry' (see n. 31 above) he had declared that Corbière's poem 'is as substantial in its way as Villon; when he describes the procession of mendicants and cripples to the shrine of the Virgin, and says: "Là, ce tronc d'homme ou croît l'ulcere, / Contre un tronc d'arbre ou croît le gui" the phrase burns itself in like the *cotto aspetto* of Dante's Brunetto Latini' (pp. 13–14).

Ne fais pas le lourd; cercueils de poètes
Pour les croque-morts sont de simples jeux,
Boîtes à violon qui sonnent le creux . . .
Ils te croiront mort – les bourgeois sont bêtes –
Va vite, léger peigneur de comètes![39]

I am much mistaken if this be not a sequence of modern *concetti*. There is much, and of the best too, in Corbière (for instance the *Lettre du Mexique*)[40] which is not metaphysical; just as Rimbaud altogether is nearer to Blake, the visionary, the *illuminé*; but the poem I have just quoted seems to me as near as possible a modern analogy to the conceited metaphysical. The satisfaction, when you analyse it, is due to the disparity between the idea and the image; so that what might be a cradle song for a baby becomes an elegy for a man of genius; there is the same yoking together of the dissimilar, which Johnson long ago noted in Donne and Cowley – with the effect of irony instead of wit. For the metaphysical poets of the seventeenth century were witty but not ironic – not ironic in so serious a way as this. Real irony is an expression of suffering, and the greatest ironist was the one who suffered the most – Swift.

It is impossible for me to enter upon further detail upon the metaphysical poetry of the nineteenth century. It has been impossible for me to do more than indicate, with the case of Laforgue and what is for our purpose the minor case of Corbière, that there is a type of metaphysical poetry existent

39 – 'Petit Mort Pour Rire' (Corbière's ellipses), one of six poems under the heading *Rondels pour après* in *Les Amours jaunes*, p. 293; minor mistranscriptions; trans. as 'A Little Death to Make One Laugh', C. F. MacIntyre, *Selections from Les Amours Jaunes*, p. 195:

> Go quickly, nimble comber of comets!
> The wind-blown grass will be your poll;
> elf-fires will flash from your hollow sockets,
> prisoners in the sorry skulls . . .
>
> the flowers of the grave called Amourettes
> will swell your earthy laughter full . . .
> and forget-me-nots, flowers of oubliettes . . .
>
> Don't make it heavy: coffins for poets
> are easy for hired mutes to follow,
> fiddle-boxes that sound hollow . . .
> they'll think you are dead – the bourgeois are fools –
> go quickly, nimble comber of comets!

40 – 'Lettre du Mexique', in which an old soldier reports to a relative in Toulon the death by fever of a young sailor in Veracruz, appeared in the section entitled *Gens de Mer* in the second edition of *Les Amours jaunes* (1891).

in the nineteenth century, and that these poets were preoccupied, like the poets of the *trecento* and the poets of the seventeenth century, consciously or unconsciously with the relation of thought and feeling. I am aware that I have left a gap; I should have proved that Baudelaire was occupied with the problem of Good and Evil, instead of merely assuming that he was, and traced the history of this idea throughout the nineteenth century; and I should have shown that the problem of Laforgue, instead of being, as it appears, more comprehensive than Baudelaire's, was a smaller and less mature version of it. But these gaps I must for the present leave to you to fill in. My theory of metaphysical poetry is, you will have seen, a heavy one for a mere man of letters to shoulder. It implies a theory of the history of belief, in which the thirteenth century, the seventeenth century, and the nineteenth century, all occupy their places in what I have called a process of disintegration.

You have understood that I take as metaphysical poetry that in which what is ordinarily apprehensible only by thought is brought within the grasp of feeling, or that in which what is ordinarily only felt is transformed into thought without ceasing to be feeling. My examples have been Donne for the former and Crashaw for the latter: in Crashaw by the substitution (an operation which is not easy or possible to many) of a divine object for a human. With the exception of Dante, my examples have been drawn from the restricted area of *merely* metaphysical poetry. At one time I was inclined to include Chapman with Donne and others amongst the metaphysicals;[41] I have withdrawn from this position by establishing a separate type for Chapman. Some of Chapman's most famous passages, as

Give me a spirit, that on life's rough sea . . .[42]

belong, I think, with the type of philosophical exposition which I illustrated in the first lecture with certain parts of Pope and incidental passages of Dante. The point which I have been blunderingly trying to reach is this –

Humanity reaches its higher civilisation levels not chiefly by improvement of thought or by increase and variety of sensation, but by the extent of co-

41–In 'Swinburne and the Elizabethans' (1919) TSE had been the first critic to point out the 'striking affinity' between Chapman and Donne as metaphysical poets (*SW* 23), an affinity he had reaffirmed in 'The Metaphysical Poets': 'In Chapman especially there is a direct sensuous apprehension of thought, or a recreation of thought into feeling, which is exactly what we find in Donne' (*SE* 286/246).

42–From the Duke of Byron's speech in *The Conspiracie and Tragedie of Charles Duke of Byron* (1608), III.iii.135: *read* 'Give me a spirit that on this life's rough sea' (from TSE's Mermaid edition, p. 372; see p. 152, n. 41).

operation between acute sensation and acute thought. The most awful state of society that could be imagined would be that in which a maximum condition of sensibility was co-existent with a maximum attainment of thought – and no emotions uniting the two. It would probably be a very contented state, and is all the more awful for that. It would not be necessary even that each individual should have both maximum sensibility and a maximum intellect: try to imagine a society in which everyone was either a Marcel Proust or an Einstein,[43] or an inferior grade of one *or* the other, and you have the thing itself. It is a worse nightmare than you think, and is more possible than you think; it is merely the existence of a highly perfected race of insects. Now it is the function of the metaphysical poet to transform thought into feeling and feeling into thought, as it is the function of other poets to fix and stabilise emotions as they exist. What I am insisting on is the role of the artist in the development and maintenance of the mind. It is difficult, certainly, and controversial, to decide what are the moments at which the human mind has attained its greatest range and unity. So many ages achieve perfection for themselves in certain details, while actually, and unobserved, living on the capital accumulated by apparently cruder but essentially more civilised ages. The eighteenth century was, I think, such an age which enjoyed the benefits, and wasted the stores, of preceding epochs. For some of the poetry of this age I have a great admiration. But it developed a petty intellect uncriticised by feeling, and an exuberant feeling uncriticised by thought. The nineteenth century paid for this debauch of Rousseau and the encyclopaedists.[44] Sensibility is always reaching after thought, and thought after sensibility. So the philosophies of the nineteenth century, whether of Kant, or Fichte, or Hegel,[45] of Schopenhauer, or James, or

43 – Einstein was then in Berlin at the Kaiser Wilhelm Institute, having received the Nobel Prize for Physics in 1921. He had evolved his special theory of relativity, had explained the photoelectric effect and Brownian movement, and was at work on his unified field theory. TSE was to translate and publish Charles Mauron's 'On Reading Einstein' (*Criterion*, October 1930, pp. 23–31).

44 – Rousseau was, with Quesnay, Montesquieu, Voltaire, Turgot and other *philosophes*, a contributor to the twenty-eight volume *Encyclopédie; ou, Dictionnaire raisonné des sciences, des arts, et des métiers* (1751–72) edited by Diderot and Alembert. The highly influential work, which championed rationalism and stressed scientific determinism, contributed significantly to the intellectual atmosphere that preceded the French Revolution of 1789. TSE had written in his first Extension lecture on Modern French Literature in 1916 that 'Romanticism stands for *excess* in any direction. It splits up into two directions: escape from the world of fact, and devotion to brute fact. The two great currents of the nineteenth century – vague emotionality and the apotheosis of science (realism) alike spring from Rousseau' (*RES* 1, 165).

45 – TSE had read Fichte and Hegel for his dissertation on F. H. Bradley, in which he concluded that Leibniz 'is nearer to the Middle Ages, nearer to Greece, and yet nearer to us, than are men

Bradley or Russell, are corrupted by feeling; the poetry of the nineteenth century, whether of Wordsworth, or Shelley, or Tennyson or Browning, is corrupted by thought. In this confusion a man like Laforgue was destroyed; for the philosophy which he endeavoured to feel was a philosophy already muddled by feeling – for what is more emotional than the philosophy of Schopenhauer or Hartmann? – his feelings required quite another system of thought.

It may be said that if the philosophies of the nineteenth century had not been so poetical, the poetry of the nineteenth century might have been more metaphysical. For a perfect art to arise, there must be a kind of co-operation between philosophy and poetry. I mean only the sort of happy coincidence that existed between Dante and Aquinas. But this was not a mere coincidence: thought and feeling developed in such harmony during the thirteenth century, that the lesser men of Dante's circle, men who dealt only, but adequately, with a part of metaphysics, in poetry, were perfectly consistent. And as far as he goes, Guido Cavalcanti deals with certain details of metaphysical poetry more satisfactorily and completely than does Dante. I have tried to show, especially in the third lecture, that in the poetry of the thirteenth century the human spirit reached a greater sum of *range, intensity* and *completeness* of emotion than it has ever attained before or since. I have tried to show that the philosophers – such as St. Thomas – were more simply philosophers, and the poets more simply poets, than have been at any time since. I have not in any way advocated a return to the thirteenth century, whatever that might mean, but only the eternal utility, in a world of change, of any achievement of perfection. I have tried to show that the chaos of the seventeenth century was a different chaos from that of the nineteenth century, and that it achieves a kind of unity in the strange ability of Donne to unite disparate thought in a continuity of feeling. A unity at the beginning of the century; later the world achieved a kind of specious unity by suppressing elements which afterwards burst out unpreparedly and without restraint.

---

like Fichte and Hegel' (*KEPB* 185). In 'The Perfect Critic' (1920) he had described Hegel as 'the most prodigious exponent of emotional systematization, dealing with his emotions as if they were definite objects which had aroused those emotions' (*SW* 9); and in 'Wordsworth and Coleridge' (1932) he was to remark: 'I have read some of Hegel and Fichte . . . and forgotten it' (*UPUC* 77/68). Later, however, in a discussion of the relative value and influence of certain 'one-man' philosophies, he was to describe how 'the colossal and grotesque achievement of Hegel may continue in concealed or derivative forms to exercise a fascination upon many minds' ('Introduction' to Josef Pieper, *Leisure The Basis of Culture* [London: Faber & Faber, 1952], p. 17). TSE's annotated copy of Hegel's *Lectures on the Philosophy of History* is in the Houghton Library.

And finally, I have tried to indicate that Belief was a different thing for the thirteenth, for the seventeenth, and for the nineteenth century. Donne does not "believe in" Anglican theology in the same way that Dante believes in Aquinas; and Laforgue does not "believe in" Schopenhauer or Hartmann in the same way as either.

The "disintegration of the intellect" of which I speak was, so far as I can see, an inevitable process. The process of knowledge and the process of history go on relentlessly, and it is always "up to" the human being to adapt himself to the alterations for which he is but partially responsible. Having achieved an unity on a basis which, so far as we can see, was partial and inaccurate, we can only go on and wait for luck to provide another. We cannot resist the alterations effected by scientific discovery; what is lamentable is that religious and artistic values cannot be separated from the flux of this development of knowledge and information. If they could be so separated by an astute theologian, psychologist, moralist, the world would be very different indeed.[46]

At the present phase of the world's process, we are at a stage where everyone is tempted to do everyone else's work. The poet or the novelist, even if he does not make such claim himself, is acclaimed or censured for his contribution to "thought", to what belongs to metaphysics, theology or psychology. Similarly the psychologist investigates, as if they were static or fixed, states of mind which it is for the poet to make or unmake. Frontiers are vague; a poet may analyse his own poetry, or a psychologist burst into dithyrambs. On the one hand it is supposed that the function of the poet is merely to amuse or to thrill; on the other he is expected to provide a gospel for the multitude struggling toward the light. Both views are wrong. Surely the thinking of the poet should be no more than transposing into poetry the

46– TSE was to address this conflict of values in 'Religion and Science: a Phantom Dilemma' (*Listener*, 23 March 1932, p. 429): 'And here is what I think you will find everywhere: that no scientific discovery influences people either for or against revealed religion, except so far as there already exists an atmosphere either favourable or unfavourable to religion . . . If what I suggest is true, that it is not science that has destroyed religious belief, but our preference of unbelief that has made illegitimate use of science, then it clearly follows that we should be ready to decline politely any support which a more modern science may offer to religion . . . For if we understand that religion has nothing to lose and nothing to gain by the progress of science, then we are at every moment prepared to give up some cherished belief, such as the belief in the movement of the sun round the earth, which we had previously thought belonged to religion and now find belongs only to science. There are certain dogmas which cannot be given up; it is possible that we still hold some beliefs as part of our faith which really belong only to immature science. We have had superstition in religion, and we have had superstition in science; we can do without both'.

thought of the time which he selects as important to him. Neither Dante nor Donne nor Laforgue did more. They were no prophets; they merely performed the work of integrating thought into life, and so did Lucretius. What happens to a poet who has an original philosophy? Does he not become the victim of those who want their philosophy cheap and without thought, and is he not, like Blake, perpetually a riddle to those who seriously would estimate his greatness as a poet?

We have not, with the so-called metaphysical poets of the seventeenth century, arrived at what many of you will have expected; a neat and comprehensive definition which shall include all of the poets of that century and none other, and which shall justify the title of "metaphysical". But I think that I warned you in advance, that I did not intend to define the seventeenth century, or the first half of it – for to do that I should have had to draw in the background much more completely, with the figures of James, and Charles, and Hooker,[47] and Laud, and Hyde and Strafford[48] – and an

47–Though TSE does not draw upon Hooker's *Of the Laws of Ecclesiastical Polity* after recommending it as a source book at the end of Lecture I (see p. 65, n. 48), he was to discuss its importance later in the year in 'Lancelot Andrewes', where he asserts that 'The intellectual achievement and the prose style of Hooker and Andrewes came to complete the structure of the English Church as the philosophy of the thirteenth century crowns the Catholic Church' (*SE* 343/301), and later he was to give a less formal account of Hooker's achievement: 'I think myself that the subject of Hooker's book is a very interesting one, and indeed very pertinent to some modern problems. For he set himself no less a task than a justification of the Church of England as against both Romans and dissenters, a task which involved a statement of the relation of the Established Church to the Civil Government . . . my point is that he was dealing with a problem which is as much ours as it was his, and dealing with it as a master' ('The Genesis of Philosophic Prose: Bacon and Hooker', *Listener*, 26 June 1929, p. 907).

48–The statesman and historian Edward Hyde, 1st Earl of Clarendon (1609–74), wrote *The History of the Rebellion and Civil Wars in England* (3 vols, 1702–4). In 'The Genesis of Philosophic Prose' (see previous note) TSE placed that work in the main line of the development of English prose: 'The style of Hooker, and the style of Bacon, have a stiffness due to their intellectual antecedents being Latin and not English prose; and this stiffness continues in the next generation into the styles of Thomas Hobbes in his *Leviathan* and Edward Hyde, Earl of Clarendon in his *History of the Great Rebellion*. But it is the stiffness of the first exercises of the muscles and joints of English prose: you have only to read a paragraph from one of the early Tudor writers, such as Elyot or Ascham, to find it supple and subtle in comparison' (pp. 907–8). Thomas Wentworth, 1st Earl of Strafford (1593–1641), Lord Deputy and then (1640) Lord Lieutenant of Ireland, had raised an army in Ireland to use against Scotland and had become, with Archbishop Laud, one of Charles's chief advisors. But when the Long Parliament convened in 1640 he was accused of planning to use Irish soldiers against English subjects, and Edward Hyde supported the impeachment proceedings that led to Strafford's eventual beheading. In 'Little Gidding' TSE was to allude to Charles and Strafford and Laud in thoughts 'of a king at nightfall, / Of three men, and more, on the scaffold' (*CPP* 195/143).

extraordinary period it is – but to arrive at a definition of metaphysical poetry which should justify or explain the attribution of this title to this period, and at the same time include other poets of other periods. We start, as I said, in literary criticism with a vague feeling of justice in a definition and of resemblances. Taking them in isolation from each other, those who are familiar with the poetry of the three periods I have treated will easily call any of them "metaphysical". I confess freely to having started from this experience: from having read in the three periods, and having thought of them all as "metaphysical", separately; and of having collocated them when I was obliged to consider the poetry of the seventeenth century. And the natural result follows. Any definition, such as mine, must be one as much imposed upon the material as derived from it. You must, in part, either cut your definition to suit the material arbitrarily selected or included, as I think does Mr. Saintsbury, or else you must cut your material to suit a definition, or else you must trim and compromise. I have chosen, considering that literary criticism is anything but an exact science, to trim and compromise. To those of you who arrived with a conception of "metaphysical poetry" as a phenomenon of the seventeenth century only, I shall seem to you to have excluded and included too much. Perhaps it is arbitrary to lay down that the seventeenth-century poetry is metaphysical only in so far as it approximates to Donne or to Crashaw or to both. I have taken a name which was hardly more than a collective sign, and I have endeavoured to give it a meaning. In doing so, I have had to neglect or exclude even, much that is assumed to be metaphysical. But bear in mind that I have not sought to define the poetry of the Jacobean and Caroline period as a whole; that would be another task, and would issue in a definition which would cut across mine of metaphysical poetry. My job has been to define metaphysical poetry in general; its place, past, present and future; by implication to define what may rightly be called metaphysical poetry of the present day in contrast to what may be called metaphysical but is merely conceited; and to establish the place of *some* of our seventeenth-century poetry in this conception. I have tried to distinguish, in the seventeenth century, the metaphysical from the conceited, and at the same time to indicate the way in which the metaphysical naturally tends to the conceited, and the conceited to the metaphysical – making clear, I hope, that I consider the Italian poetry of the age to be conceited without being metaphysical: the metaphysical at this moment flourished only in England. I have concentrated on Donne and Crashaw because I think that all the other poets usually included can be included under one or the other, or under some cross-breed of both: for these are the two great innovators:

the transmuters, the alchemists, of thought into feeling or of feeling into thought. And I have dealt with Cowley merely in order to show how easily the metaphysical poetry transforms itself into the Augustan; as I have tried to show in connection with Donne, how readily the Elizabethan poetical impulse, working on such a mind and with such a training and interest as Donne's, becomes the metaphysical. It is only a step from Chapman's *Ovid's Banquet of Sense* or *Hymn to Night* to Donne; but it is a very long and very important step.[49]

But I must call attention, in closing, to the dilemma which every honest literary critic, now and in the future, will have to face. On the one hand you cannot treat literary criticism as a subject isolated from every other subject of study; you must take account of general history, of philosophy, theology, economics, psychology, into all of which literary criticism merges. And on the other hand you cannot hope to embrace all of the various points of view implied by these various studies: for not only is such encyclopaedic knowledge impossible to any one man, but, even could you attain it, you would have lost the point of view of literary criticism in the process. The literary critic must remain a critic of literature, but he must have sufficient knowledge to understand the points of view of the sciences into which his literary criticism merges. You cannot know your frontiers unless you have some notion of what is beyond them. The only writer who has established a literary criticism which both sticks to the matter in hand and yet implies the other sciences, is of course Aristotle; and the comprehensiveness of Aristotle, in the expanse of modern science and knowledge, is impossible. The literary criticism of Horace, of Boileau,[50] of Dryden, is no longer

49–Chapman's 'Hymnus in Noctem' and its sequel 'Hymnus in Cynthiam' together form the one poem titled 'The Shadow of Night' (1594), which celebrates the intellectual and contemplative faculties as they are affected by the mysterious stimuli of night. It preceded 'Ovid's Banquet of Sense' (1595), an erotic poem that celebrates Ovid's feast of the five senses and their sublimation into spiritual ecstasy when he observes his Corinna bathing. In 'Wanley and Chapman' (see p. 152, n. 40), TSE had particularly recommended Janet Spens's essay ('Chapman's Ethical Thought'), 'dealing with Chapman's long, obscure and very beautiful poems, "Ovid's Banquet of Sense" and "The Shadow of Night",' both of which are included in TSE's copy of *The Works of George Chapman: Poems and Minor Translations*, A New Edition (London: Chatto & Windus, 1904), with an introduction by Algernon Charles Swinburne. In 'The Sources of Chapman' (see p. 73, n. 22), TSE asserts that Chapman is an 'illustrious example of that numerous tribe – very numerous in the Renaissance – for whom the value of a philosophy resides in the subjective emotion which they can relevantly or irrelevantly impose upon it'.

50–Nicolas Boileau-Despréaux (1636–1711), poet and critic, was the author of a verse treatise, *L'Art poétique* (1674), which aimed at teaching the craft of writing, and a critical dialogue, *Les Héros de roman* (1688). TSE had earlier discussed Horace, Boileau and Dryden

possible; it is too limited; the literary criticism of Coleridge or of Croce is no longer possible; it is too unlimited.[51] The task for the literary critic of the future is to co-operate with the workers on his frontiers, to understand their work well enough to be able to provide them with material, and to be able to resist the temptation to do their work for them.

> In eche estat is litel hertes reste;
> God leve us for to take it for the beste![52]

So far, therefore, as I have trespassed on the territory of history, social or political, of theology and religion, of psychology, my criticism of meta-physical poetry has been seriously at fault. What I have *tried* to do is to maintain literary values in the centre of the picture, to consider different periods of poetry by poetic values, and merely to indicate the extra-literary causes of the differences in literary value. In doing so, I have indicated a theory of what I call the "disintegration of the intellect". So far as *I* am concerned, this disintegration means merely a progressive deterioration of poetry, in one respect or another, since the thirteenth century. If I am right about poetry, then this deterioration is probably only one aspect of a general deterioration, the other aspects of which should interest workers in other fields. I have had to suggest causes, indicate alterations and tendencies. I

---

in relation to Aristotle in 'The Perfect Critic' (1920): 'It is far less Aristotle than Horace who has been the model for criticism up to the nineteenth century. A precept, such as Horace or Boileau gives us, is merely an unfinished analysis. It appears as a law, a rule, because it does not appear in its most general form; it is empirical . . . Dryden . . . displays much free intelligence; and yet even Dryden – or any *literary* critic of the seventeenth century – is not quite a free mind . . . There is always a tendency to legislate rather than to inquire, to revise accepted laws, even to overturn, but to reconstruct out of the same material. And the free intelligence is that which is wholly devoted to inquiry' (*SW* 11–12).

51 – The 'unlimited' quality of Coleridge's criticism had also been characterized in 'The Perfect Critic': 'Coleridge is apt to take leave of the data of criticism, and arouse the suspicion that he has been diverted into a metaphysical hare-and-hounds. His end does not always appear to be the return to the work of art with improved perception and intensified, because more conscious, enjoyment; his centre of interest changes, his feelings are impure. In the derogatory sense he is more "philosophic" than Aristotle. For everything that Aristotle says illuminates the literature which is the occasion for saying it; but Coleridge only now and then. It is one more instance of the pernicious effect of emotion' (*SW* 13). The philosopher and critic Benedetto Croce (1866–1952) had published his four-volume *The Philosophy of the Spirit* (1902–17), including a volume of aesthetic criticism, *Aesthetic as Science of Expression and General Linguistic* (1909). TSE had probably read Croce's *The Poetry of Dante* (1922) and had published an English translation of his 'On the Nature of Allegory' (1922) in the April 1925 issue of the *Criterion*.

52 – *Troilus and Criseyde*, Book v, lines 1749–50, as printed in TSE's annotated copy (Houghton) of *The Student's Chaucer*, ed. Walter W. Skeat (New York: Oxford Univ. Press, 1894), p. 323.

have had to refer certain qualities of thirteenth-century Italian poetry to what, working outward *from* the poetry, I believe to be the intellectual and emotional organisation of the age; I have had to refer certain peculiarities of phrase, image and poetic feeling of Donne and Crashaw to the political and theological background of their age. But I have criticised, or at least aimed to criticise, nothing but the poetry as poetry. If my observations on the poetic speech of different ages can have any interest for psychologists occupied with the history of the human mind, so much the better. My views can be utilised, justified, or discredited by students of the subjects which lie outside of literary criticism. Literary criticism cannot provide a gospel, an aesthetic, or a theory of the mind. If I have exalted the thirteenth century, that means only that I am convinced that it produced the best poetry. It does not mean that our best hope of producing great poetry in the future is to reinstate the conditions and beliefs of the thirteenth century. It does mean that if we are to acquire any conscious control over the quality of our poetry, we shall do well to study the conditions under which were produced the poetry of Dante, and of that greatest of English poets, who came soon after him. As I have not, in a series of lectures necessarily compressed and abbreviated, had occasion to mention Chaucer directly, I should like to pay him the tribute of ending with his own ending and invocation –

> Thou oon, and two, and three, eterne on-lyve,
> That regnest ay in three and two and oon,
> Uncircumscript, and al mayst circumscryve,
> Us from visible and invisible foon
> Defende; and to thy mercy, everychoon,
> So make us, Jesus, for thy grace, digne,
> For love of mayde and moder thyn benigne! AMEN.[53]

---

53 – The concluding stanza of *Troilus and Criseyde*, Book v, lines 1863–70, as printed in *The Student's Chaucer*, p. 325. In his review of R. K. Root's edition of *The Book of Troilus and Criseyde* later in the year, TSE was to illuminate his choice of Chaucer's poem to conclude his Clark Lectures: 'It may be said without exaggeration that "Troilus and Criseyde" is a document second in importance, in its kind, only to the "Vita Nuova." It is a pendant to the latter, and the two are perfectly consistent' (*TLS*, 19 August 1926, p. 547).

THE TURNBULL LECTURES

ENGLISH LION

An exclusive, unpublished sketch of T. S. Eliot, made from life by Theresa Garrett during the author's triumphal visit this year to the United States. T. S. Eliot is the idol of the younger literates of Europe and is considered by many the greatest living English poet.

From the *Chicago Daily Tribune*, 2 December 1933

EDITOR'S INTRODUCTION

Returning to America after an absence of eighteen years, T. S. Eliot disembarked from the *Ausonia* in Montreal on 25 September 1932 to begin his most intensive year of lecturing as Charles Eliot Norton Professor of Poetry at Harvard. The professorship, endowed by financier and Harvard benefactor Charles Chauncey Stillman (1877–1926) in 1925, required him to deliver a series of formal public lectures and to submit them for publication within the year. Though his appointment had been announced in December 1931, the complications of detaching himself from Faber and Faber and the *Criterion* for an extended period, including a planned separation from his wife, left him no leisure for preparation, and so he settled into lodgings at B–11 Eliot House under a pressure for lectures not experienced since he delivered the Clark Lectures six years earlier.

Between 4 November and 9 December Eliot delivered four of his eight Norton Lectures, which were to be published as *The Use of Poetry and the Use of Criticism* the following year. Meanwhile, there was the urgency of writing additional lectures for local groups and for a tour that would take him to California and back during the Christmas break. On 1 December he lectured in King's Chapel, Boston, on 'The Bible as Scripture and as Literature' (MS Houghton), and then on 'Two Masters' to the Boston Association of Unitarian Clergy (MS notes Houghton). On 26 December, hours before his departure for California, he wrote to Alida Monro that he had written five lectures during the past three weeks (Texas). More lay ahead, as invitations had been accepted from Johns Hopkins and Virginia, and he was obligated to give a course of lectures on modern poetry to Harvard undergraduates in the second term.

I

The invitation to give the Turnbull Lectures at The Johns Hopkins University evidently came late in November or early in December, but in the event it was a belated invitation in the eyes of Eliot's friend and fellow Faber editor, Frank Vigor Morley, a Hopkins graduate whose retired father had been a mathematics professor there for many years and whose home had welcomed Walter de la Mare as guest when he gave the Turnbull Lectures in 1924: 'As a Hopkins man I felt sore that the Hopkins had to wait upon Eliot's receiving an accolade from Harvard, but perhaps that was just as well. In 1924 an invitation from the Hopkins might have impeded Faber & Gwyer, might have impeded *The Criterion*'.[1] On 3 December 1932 Eliot received the invitation to deliver the Page-Barbour Lectures at the University of Virginia the following spring, and, as he negotiated dates and topics during the month, his Turnbull Lectures had become confirmed. On 26 December he wrote to Wilbur A. Nelson, Chairman of the Committee on Public Occasions at Virginia, proposing to give the lectures from 10–12 May:

> The decision of a subject is more difficult, when it is a matter of three consecutive lectures: you would not want me to repeat my three Turnbull lectures on Three Varieties of Metaphysical Poetry. May I let you know at the beginning of February, as I am just leaving. My address for the next fortnight will be c/o Scripps College, Claremont, California. (Virginia)

He left that night, having already agreed to be in Baltimore for the week beginning 30 January.

It was only incidental that Eliot was scheduled to lecture on 'The Formation of Taste' at Scripps College on 29 December, and on 'Edward Lear and Modern Poetry' a week later; the primary motive of the cross-country journey was a reunion with Emily Hale, his first love, who was now a member of the faculty there. Eliot had been sending her inscribed copies of his books since 1923, but on New Year's day 1933 he personally presented to her an inscribed copy of *Sweeney Agonistes*, which had been published by Faber and Faber in December. They had resumed correspondence in the late 1920s as Eliot's marriage declined, and their first reunion had come in the

---

1 – 'A Few Recollections of Eliot', in *T. S. Eliot: The Man and his Work*, p. 96. Faber & Gwyer, founded in 1925, became Faber and Faber in 1929.

summer of 1930 when Emily came to England. For Eliot, at forty-five, the journey to California was a momentous personal undertaking.[2]

Eliot lectured and read his poetry in San Francisco and in Los Angeles before beginning his cross-country return to Boston. His first stop was at his former home in St Louis. There on 16 January he lectured at Washington University on 'The Study of Shakespeare Criticism' before moving on to St Paul, Chicago, Detroit and Buffalo. He had taken manuscript material to write the Introduction for *The Collected Poems of Harold Monro*, but he scrapped the draft written in California before he returned to Boston. As he explained the tardiness of the Introduction to Alida Monro, her husband's editor, 'I caught a cold on the way from Buffalo, and had to spend two days in bed preparing for a lecture week in Baltimore' (Texas).

The typescript of the eight Clark Lectures, brought over from England with hopes of finding time to make revisions for publication, was at his bedside. He had obviously given some thought to synthesizing them when he provided his tentative title, 'Three Varieties of Metaphysical Poetry', but during these two days in bed he went carefully over the lectures, selecting, rearranging and altering the material for a more limited focus on the nature of metaphysical poetry in the thirteenth, seventeenth and nineteenth centuries. For his first Turnbull lecture he drew upon parts of Clark lectures I, II and III; for the second, upon III, IV and VI, with a brief summary of VII; for the third, upon VIII, with bits from I and III. He wrote the lectures on his typewriter, working directly from the Clark typescript. Some passages were incorporated unchanged; others were re-cast, revised, expanded; quotations were transcribed as previously typed, thereby carrying the errors, and some new ones, forward. Characteristically making corrections, additions and deletions in pencil as he progressed, he added new examples and contexts, particularly as the substance of his ongoing Norton Lectures came to bear upon the revisions – in the form of Coleridge and others. He had at hand his texts of Valéry and Mallarmé, both of whom had moved closer to the centre of his imagination. He had found new allies in Lautréamont and Christopher Dawson, new antagonists in Shaw and Renan, Anatole France and Aldous Huxley, Countess Russell and *Lady Chatterley's Lover*. At the end he exhausted his dwindling supply of Hammermill Bond: the last page had to be typed on the verso, up-side down, of his Eliot House stationery.

The revisions made, he went down to Baltimore on 29 January to spend

---

2 – For a full account of TSE's relationship with Emily Hale, see Lyndall Gordon, *Eliot's New Life* (Oxford: Oxford Univ. Press, 1988; New York: Farrar, Straus & Giroux, 1988).

most of the week as the guest of George Boas, who had been his admiring friend in graduate school at Harvard and who was now Professor of Philosophy at Johns Hopkins. Eliot had written ahead to Mrs Boas to advise of his bad cold and to ask her to refuse as many invitations as possible.[3]

Meanwhile, last-minute arrangements and announcements were being made by the chairman of the Turnbull Lectures Committee, H. Carrington Lancaster, Professor of French and chairman of the Department of Romance Languages. Lancaster had evidently acted unilaterally on Eliot's appointment during the long holiday break, for on 20 January, upon receiving the news, President Joseph S. Ames wrote to congratulate him on having secured Eliot as his Turnbull Lecturer, 'but I cannot find any action taken by the Academic Council, authorizing the selection. Please write me the proper kind of letter which I will bring before the Council' (Hopkins). While Eliot was being authorized by the Council, he was being mythologized by a student editor of the *Hopkins News-Letter*, Richard Feise, who announced Eliot as the leader of the 'Cerebralist Group' and as a poet-critic-editor whose 'conversion from republicanism to monarchism, from agnosticism to Anglo-Catholicism, from "modernism" to the stream in contemporary thought called "reactionary" makes him a figure of extraordinary interst in certain circles'. Mr Feise did his biographical as well as his critical homework, describing Eliot's family and educational background and capturing one of the fleeting 'legends' allegedly in circulation: 'One of the legends already in existence about his boyhood is that he did not speak a word until the age of 6 or 7, when he remarked one day to his mother that they were having a dreadful snow-storm'.[4] For the next fortnight the editors ceased publication for final examinations, and so there were no further student reports of Eliot's presence on campus.

II

The twenty-ninth course of the Percy Graeme Turnbull Memorial Lectures was scheduled for Monday, Wednesday and Friday at 5 p.m. in Latrobe Hall. The Lectureship had been endowed in 1889 by Mr and Mrs Lawrence Turnbull to commemorate the name of their gifted son, who had died in his ninth year in 1887. Lawrence Turnbull (1843–1919), a lawyer with

3 – This correspondence, now lost, was described to T. S. Matthews in an interview with Professor and Mrs Boas for *Great Tom*, p. 114.
4 – 'T. S. Eliot to Lecture on Puritan Poets', *Hopkins News-Letter* (27 January 1933), p. 1.

publishing interests, established an early reputation as an editor of two literary magazines, *The Land We Love* (1866–9) and *The New Eclectic* (1868–75). His wife, Frances Litchfield Turnbull (1844–1927) of New York, founded the Women's Literary Club of Baltimore and was the author of *The Catholic Man* (1890), a character study of her friend the Baltimore poet Sidney Lanier,[5] and of several historical romances. The original terms of their gift provided for an annual course of lectures on poetry 'by some one who has gained distinction as a writer or critical student of poetry'. The series was inaugurated in 1891 by the American poet-critic Edmund C. Stedman (1833–1908), who set an initial standard of eight lectures in speaking on 'The Nature and Elements of Poetry'. Stedman was succeeded by what was to become a roll-call of distinguished American, English and Continental authors, many of whom had played important roles in Eliot's own intellectual life: Jebb, Norton, Brunetière, Lanman, Kittredge, More, and others. Eliot's immediate predecessor, who upset traditional expectations with only two lectures, was George Russell (AE) in 1931 (see Appendix III).

Over 400 persons filed into Latrobe Hall to hear Eliot's opening lecture. 'Our English cousins', said Professor Lancaster in his introduction, 'are generous in sending us poets and other lecturers to help us in our war against Philistines and other barbarians. We are indebted to them, but we ask for no cancellation nor moratorium. Our debt is well re-paid, for we have given them Henry James and T. S. Eliot'. After the lecture a reporter from the Baltimore *Sun* asked Eliot how he could account for his success as both poet and critic 'in view of the general rule that a great poet is seldom a great critic'. 'Well, I don't know about that', Eliot replied, keeping to the practical side with his inquisitor. 'My chief reason for being a critic at present is the fact that you can make a little money out of an essay on criticism', a remark that earned Eliot a bold headline in the morning paper: '*T. S. Eliot Asserts Advantage Of Being Critic Is That It Pays*'. Asked if he found London conducive to the contemplative life, Eliot, perhaps increasingly ruffled by the rigorous invasion of his privacy during the last month on tour, replied: 'Perhaps so . . . In London you can always find some place where you can be alone. There people don't go out of their way to find you when you want quiet'.[6] An editorialist for the paper, probably John W. Owens (1885–

5 – Lanier (1842–81) was buried in the Turnbull family plot in Greenmount Cemetery.
6 – *Sun* (31 January 1933), p. 20. On 18 May 1933, a month before his departure, TSE wrote to Paul Elmer More: 'I am beginning to crave the anonymity that one enjoys in England' (Princeton).

1968), the outspoken editor of the *Sun* who won a Pulitzer Prize for his editorials, was himself unabashedly sceptical of the motives of the audience and the aims of the lecturer, though he had admittedly missed the second lecture. After noting in his Thursday editorial that the first lecture had drawn 'a vast array of earnest seekers after culture as well as a number of the more advanced thinkers of the community', he was moved, after excluding himself from the advanced thinkers, to share his conclusion 'that Mr. Eliot would never run afoul of the late C. E. Montague's rule against continuously unmistakable clarity in English prose. I did not find him at all guilty of obscurity of expression, but he appeared to be a master of what Mr. Montague called the "expression of obscurity" '.[7]

The editorialist did accompany a reporter to Eliot's Thursday evening lecture and reading before the Poetry Society of Maryland, where Eliot's topic was indeed the charge of obscurity against modern poetry. The Poetry Society, founded in 1923, hosted lectures and readings at the Emmanuel Parish House, 811 Cathedral Street, and existed primarily to bring distinguished travelling poets to Baltimore. Eliot had been preceeded by Stephen Vincent Benét, Padraic Colum, Walter de la Mare, Robert Frost, Vachel Lindsay, Amy Lowell, Edgar Lee Masters, Edna St Vincent Millay, Harriet Monroe, Carl Sandburg and, several weeks earlier, by W. B. Yeats, who told members of the Society 'that the Irish were great "appreciators of poetry, if not readers of it". They honored him as a personality, he admitted, even though they did not read his books'.[8] Eliot's appearance had been arranged by his host, Professor Boas, a member who introduced him to the Society.

Eliot explained to his audience that obscurity in verse 'is largely due, deliberately or not, to the suppression of one or more elements in order to emphasize the more essential poetical elements.' For the reader, he continued, it was a matter of getting used to a perspective or point of view that he had not previously experienced. Eliot chose a graphic example to illustrate his point:

'Suppose you went into a drawing room where the people were all without their skins,' he suggested. 'At first it would be hard to get used to seeing people like that . . . It would be so entirely new, seeing anyone

---

7–'Down the Spillway', *Sun* (2 February 1933), p. 10. The editorialist refers to an essay entitled 'Only too Clear' in *A Writer's Notes on his Trade* (1930), a posthumous collection of essays by Charles Edward Montague (1867–1928), the English journalist and drama critic who wrote for the *Manchester Guardian* from 1890 to 1925.
8–*Sun* (31 January 1933), p. 20.

without human skin . . . Then conceive that you found them more comfortable without their skins. You could then adjust yourself to the sight . . . Afterward you would find them, possibly, more interesting. Their eyes would be more expressive. The play of their muscles would be fascinating . . .'

As the reporter observed, 'By their squirming and peculiar expressions, a number of the women of the audience showed that they could not immediately accustom themselves to the picture.'[9] The editorialist, whose taste in poetry was more akin to Baltimore's Sidney Lanier than to London's T. S. Eliot, found the example 'too ghoulish to be relished' but accepted it as a basis for expressing his counter-view of modern poetry:

> Assume that Mr. Eliot intended to emphasize the importance of substance as opposed to superficial form. Assume that a great deal of the poetry which he sought to praise is all substance and no form and a great deal of the poetry he sought to condemn lies at what he called the 'cuticle level.' It is a matter of form and nothing more. It seems preposterous, however, to conclude, as Mr. Eliot seems to do, that modern poetry must of necessity be divided into these two sections and that we are forever condemned to be confronted with anatomical substance on the one hand and integumental brilliance on the other.
>
> May it not be possible that the true flowering of modern poetry will depend upon the reunion of flesh and cuticle in the noble and significant form which nature has evolved and which generations of beauty-loving people have enjoyed, whether in the human figure or in verse? Mr. Eliot does not appear to have envisaged this possibility in his assessment of the tendencies of modern poetry, but the illustration which he employed for his own purposes suggests its desirability.[10]

III

Eliot escaped the provincial press on the Turnbull estate, comprised of twenty-eight acres at Rodgers' Forge, Towson, on the northern perimeter of Baltimore. The estate was then in the keeping of Lawrence's son, Bayard Turnbull (1879–1954), an architect and Francophile, who with his wife Margaret Carroll Turnbull (1887–1981), the reader in the house, continued

9–'T. S. Eliot Talks on Modern Poetry', *Sun* (3 February 1933), p. 20.
10–'Reunion in Poetry', *Sun* (4 February 1933), p. 8.

his parents' tradition of entertaining the Turnbull lecturers. In 1925 Bayard had designed and built a new home, 'Trimbush', on the estate, leaving the fifteen-room Victorian cottage built by his father in 1885, 'La Paix', to let. By happy coincidence, the new tenant in La Paix was F. Scott Fitzgerald, who was then drying out from an alcoholic siege and working on *Tender Is the Night* (1934). Mrs Turnbull, knowing of his admiration for the author of *The Waste Land*, invited Fitzgerald to come in to a small dinner that evening after the final lecture. When Eliot arrived earlier in the day she introduced them, and Fitzgerald led Eliot off on the long walk that he frequently took when working out the scenes of his novel. Mrs Turnbull, later interviewed by T. S. Matthews, remembered

> seeing them start off across the lawn, toward the abandoned roadbed of a narrow-gauge railway track that ran for miles between woods and meadows. She wished she might have heard their conversation, which she was sure was 'immensely articulate' . . . When Eliot returned from his walk, Mrs. Turnbull showed him her copy of *The Divine Comedy*, and told him with some pride that she had read it. '*Begun* to read it,' he corrected her.[11]

In October 1925 Fitzgerald had sent Eliot a copy of *The Great Gatsby* from Paris, inscribed 'For T. S. Eliot / greatest of Living Poets / from his enthusiastic worshipper / F. Scott Fitzgerald'.[12] Eliot had not replied until 31 December, in the midst of preparing his Clark Lectures, thanking him for the 'charming and overpowering inscription' and explaining that though the book had arrived just as he was setting out on his sea voyage to France, he had now read it three times: 'In fact it seems to me to be the first step that American fiction has taken since Henry James'.[13] Fitzgerald prized the letter and carried it about for years to pull out at strategic moments. On this magical occasion of their first meeting Fitzgerald produced a copy of *Ash-Wednesday*, which was appropriately 'Inscribed to Scott Fitzgerald with the author's homage', signed and dated 'T. S. Eliot / 3.ii.33'.[14] After dinner that night, perhaps by pre-arrangement with his hostess, Fitzgerald seized the

11 – *Great Tom*, p. 115.
12 – *Correspondence of F. Scott Fitzgerald*, ed. Matthew J. Bruccoli and Margaret M. Duggan (New York: Random House, 1980), p. 180.
13 – Published in F. Scott Fitzgerald, *The Crack-up*, ed. Edmund Wilson (New York: New Directions, 1945), p. 310.
14 – *Correspondence of F. Scott Fitzgerald*, p. 305.

opportunity to read *The Waste Land* aloud to the poet. Mrs Turnbull later recalled the scene for her son, Andrew, who was to become a biographer of Fitzgerald: 'In the intimacy of a fire-lit room Fitzgerald was asked to read some of Eliot's verse, which he did without hesitation in that moving voice of his that could bring out all the beauty and hint at all the mystery of words'. Elated by the experience, Fitzgerald wrote to Edmund Wilson: 'I read him some of his poems and he seemed to think they were pretty good. I liked him fine'.[15]

On the Saturday morning train back to Boston, Eliot's eye may have caught the *Sun*'s brief report of his third lecture: '*Eliot Credits Laforgue / With Inspiring His Work*': 'Had it not been for Jules Laforgue, T. S. Eliot said yesterday that his own work would not have been written . . . Laforgue, finding his way out of a philosophy not satisfactory to himself, according to Mr. Eliot, pointed the path out for him'.[16] In the larger world little attention was paid to the lectures, but Eliot had been in correspondence with Frank Morley's brother, Christopher, the novelist and contributing editor of the *Saturday Review of Literature*, who, having received a printed invitation from the Hopkins Trustees, gave the lectures brief notice in his column, 'The Bowling Green'.[17]

Once Baltimore was behind him, Eliot turned immediately to his Introduction for Harold Monro's *Collected Poems*, sending it off the next day. Before him lay the first two lectures for English 26: 'English Literature from 1890 to the Present Day', limited to twenty selected students. After getting the course underway he wrote to Ottoline Morrell on 9 February to describe his recent activities: 'But I was very hardworked up to Christmas, and immediately after left for a prolonged tour . . . and I have only been back at work here since last Saturday; I am now lecturing to undergraduates (on Contemporary English Literature, a subject with which I have very little acquaintance) twice a week, as well as continuing my public lectures' (Texas).

In Baltimore, President Ames, delighted by Eliot's visit, was moved to inquire about the feasibility of publishing the lectures. On 13 February he sent a note to Professor Lancaster: 'I do not know what is customary to do in regard to publication of the Turnbull Lectures, but anything that Eliot

---

15–Andrew Turnbull, *Scott Fitzgerald* (New York: Charles Scribner's Sons, 1962), p. 230.
16–*Sun* (4 February 1933), p. 18.
17–(11 February 1933), p. 427.

writes is so good and so popular that the idea has been suggested to secure his lectures for the Johns Hopkins Press. Please let me know what you think of this idea' (Hopkins). Lancaster responded the same afternoon: 'In regard to Eliot, his first lecture was not worth printing, but I found the others quite interesting. If I may judge by the crowd he drew, I would say that, if published, they would pay, but he probably has in mind publication elsewhere. If the Press Committee, however, wishes to take the matter up with him I think it would be worth doing' (Hopkins). The following day President Ames asked C. W. Dittus of the Johns Hopkins Press to discuss the matter with Lancaster and Boas, and on 17 February Dittus informed the President that 'Doctor Boas has kindly offered to start the correspondence with the lecturer . . . If the response is favorable I will, with your approval, negotiate further with the lecturer and keep you informed' (Hopkins). Boas's correspondence with Eliot does not survive, but Eliot, who was already under obligation to publish his Norton and Page-Barbour lectures, would have politely but firmly declined. The refusal evidently did not sit well with Professor Lancaster.

As much as the Turnbulls enjoyed Eliot's presence, they had become concerned by the small number of lectures offered by him and AE. After a proper interval, they visited President Ames on 9 June to call his attention to the fact that the number of lectures had been getting rather small. Ames wrote immediately to Professor Lancaster: 'The family think that it would be better if we could have it understood that there is a minimum of six lectures to be given by any one individual' (Hopkins). Lancaster, who was negotiating the next course with Professor Raymond W. Chambers of the University of London, said he would try for six but thought it unwise to insist on that number, 'as we might not have money to pay for so many'. Seemingly put off by Eliot's rejection, he continued: 'It seems to me most fortunate that we did not have more than three from T. S. Eliot, though it was well enough to have him here for that many' (Hopkins). When Chambers agreed to give five lectures, President Ames wrote to Bayard Turnbull on 13 June to say that they were in sympathy with his point of view but that it was 'not always possible to get a man for a course of six, as I explained to you' (Hopkins). Thereafter, the standard of five or six lectures generally held until 1947, when the number rapidly dwindled to two or three. The age of the book-length lecture series was coming rapidly to a close: by 1950 a single lecture, or a group of lecturers, had become the norm; in 1985 the Turnbull Lectures became dormant when funds were administratively diverted elsewhere.

IV

As Eliot had disclosed to Ottoline Morrell, he was indeed still swamped with commitments for public lectures after returning from Baltimore. On 23 February he lectured at Yale on 'English Poets as Letter Writers'.[18] One of his earliest invitations had been to deliver the Spencer Trask Lecture at Princeton for $100, and though the amount, from which expenses were to be paid, was unattractive, he lectured there in March on 'The Bible and English Literature' in order to visit his friend Paul Elmer More. During the week of 20–27 April he was committed to giving three lectures and a reading at the New School for Social Research in New York ('The Verse of Milton', 'The Meaning of Poetry', 'Edward Lear and Modern Poetry'). Further on the horizon were his Page-Barbour Lectures at Virginia, but they too were to be written under great pressure at the wire: as late as 2 May the student paper announced that 'Professor Wilbur A. Nelson . . . has not yet learned Dr. Eliot's subject for this year's lectures'.[19] On the eve of the lectures the paper announced the general title, 'Tradition and Contemporary Literature', with individual lectures on 'The Meaning of Tradition' (10 May), 'Modern Poetry' (11 May) and 'Three Prose Writers' (12 May).[20] Fortunately, Eliot was able to draw substantially on his class lectures, particularly those on Thomas Hardy, D. H. Lawrence and James Joyce, for his Page-Barbour Lectures, which were to appear the following year under a new title, *After Strange Gods*. On 20 June 1934, after his two volumes of American lectures had been published, he wrote of their composition to Paul Elmer More:

Both of my sets of lectures in America had to be prepared under difficulties and at short notice; as this was for reasons which I would not want to make public account of, I desire and deserve no mitigation of severity therefor. But the subject of "The Use of Poetry" was undertaken merely because it seemed the one on which I could write with the minimum of new reading and thinking; the field of "After Strange Gods" was one to which my real interest had turned. I

18–Henry Ware Eliot made a few notes (Houghton) on this lecture, which was primarily on Keats and Lawrence, but TSE was not pleased with it and destroyed the manuscript after delivery. A passage from the lecture was published by F. O. Matthiessen in *The Achievement of T. S. Eliot*, p. 90, and a report, with quotations, appeared in the *Yale Daily News* (24 February 1933), p. 3.
19–*College Topics* (2 May 1933), p. 4.
20–*College Topics* (9 May 1933), p. 1.

therefore feel more regret at the inadequacy of the latter than of the former. (Princeton)

Fitzgerald had remarked to Wilson that Eliot had appeared 'very broken and sad + shrunk inside'.[21] There was indeed much weight on his mind as he wrote and delivered his various lectures: after returning from Baltimore he wrote to his solicitor in London to request a Deed of Separation from Vivien, and on 14 March he wrote to Ottoline Morrell about the matter: 'For my part, I should prefer never to see her again; for hers, I do not believe that it can be good for any woman to live with a man to whom she is morally, in the larger sense, unpleasant, as well as physically indifferent. But I am quite aware of putting my own interests first' (Texas). The happy prospect of meeting Emily Hale again in New Hampshire before his departure in June also had its dark side: as Lyndall Gordon has observed, in their meetings in 1933 Eliot experienced 'the germ of a conflict' that was soon to lead to 'the gravest moral crisis of his life from 1934 to 1938'.[22]

V

When Eliot arrived in England at the end of June, committed to a permanent separation from Vivien, he took guest lodgings at Frank Morley's seventeenth-century farmhouse in Surrey, Pikes Farm, where he was to spend the summer. On arrival, before turning to the preparation of his Norton and Page-Barbour lectures for required publication, he presented his Turnbull Lectures to Morley, inscribed in pencil at the top of the first page, '*FVM* Definitely *not* for publication but for your amusement'. Morley made a few marginal comments and queries, especially regarding one of his favourite authors, Matthew Arnold, and returned the typescript. Eliot, who was to have no real home for years, soon turned it over to John Hayward for preservation in the 'Archives'.

Hayward purchased a protective folder for the unbound typescript, elaborately inscribing the title on a paper label in his hand. In the spring of 1940, however, Eliot was moved to retrieve the typescript. Sir Hugh Walpole, who was collecting manuscripts and first editions for a series of 'Red Cross Sales' to benefit the war effort, had written to ask Eliot for a contribution. As Eliot explained to Elizabeth Drew in a letter of 7 October

21–Letter of March 1933 (Yale), quoted in Matthew J. Bruccoli, *Some Sort of Epic Grandeur* (New York and London: Harcourt Brace Jovanovich, 1981), p. 345.
22–*Eliot's New Life*, pp. 51–2.

1948, 'having nothing else I gave him this typescript . . . I have never ceased to regret it' (Smith). He presented the gift in Hayward's folder, inscribing and signing the top flap with the title and provenance of the lectures (see facsimile page). It finally came up for auction at Sotheby's over two years later, listed as lot 277 in the sale catalogue for 13 October 1942, two days before the publication of *Little Gidding* in the *New English Weekly*:

Given by T. S. Eliot, Esq.

Eliot (T. S.) The Varieties of Metaphysical Poetry, *the original script, typed by the author, on one side of 47 large 4to sheets, of three* UNPUBLISHED Lectures, delivered on the Turnbull Foundation at Johns Hopkins University in 1933, *a few MS. alterations in pencil and, on the first page, the superscription:* "F. V. M. [*i.e. F. V. Morley*] *Definitely not for publication but for your amusement", unbound in a lettered folder*

The three lectures were further described as having been abbreviated from the author's Clark Lectures, which 'were to have been the basis for a book that was never written'.[23] By good fortune, the lectures were purchased by a representative of Harvard University. On 24 November 1942 they were officially received at the Houghton Library, where they are now housed in Hayward's original lettered folder.

VI

When Eliot's year of lecturing in America finally came to an end, he was faced with months of preparing the Norton and Page-Barbour typescripts for press, finding some relief and joy in November 1933 by turning to his choruses for *The Rock*. Had he been placed under similar obligation by the Turnbull Foundation before he made his commitment to the Page-Barbour Lectureship Committee, he might have pushed the former lectures, or indeed a revised version of the whole Clark/Turnbull lectures, towards publication rather than leaving them for Morley's 'amusement'. As it was, by the end of 1933 he had had enough of turning lectures into books. The time and energy expended thereon broke his interest in returning to the Clark and Turnbull lectures, but he had not displaced the former from his

23—*Catalogue of the Manuscripts, Printed Books and Autograph Letters Presented to the Duke of Gloucester's Red Cross and St. John Fund Red Cross Sales* (London: Sotheby & Co., 1942), p. 43.

personal list of achievements, proudly and modestly singling them out for inclusion in the next Harvard class report: 'I was Clark Lecturer at Trinity College, Cambridge, in 1926; but the rules of that enlightened college do not require that these lectures be printed'.[24] As he wrote to More on 20 June 1934, concerning his reservations about sustained prose work, 'I depend upon intuitions and perceptions, and although I may have some skill in the barren game of controversy, have little capacity for sustained, exact, and closely knit argument and reasoning' (Princeton). The *Four Quartets* and five plays now lay before him, as did many named lectures on poetry and poets, but only once again – in his three Boutwood Lectures at Corpus Christi College, Cambridge – was he tempted to transform a series of lectures into a book, *The Idea of A Christian Society* (1939).[25]

Though Eliot chose to withhold the Clark and Turnbull lectures during his lifetime, we may be grateful that he was disposed to preserve them. They are now brought into the public domain as valuable documents of a major poet's critical life. The Turnbull Lectures rightly accompany the Clark Lectures from which they derive, for they are part of the history of that unfinished work. But the Turnbull Lectures themselves must be seen as much more than a rushed reduction of the Clark Lectures. Sitting in bed with a bad cold after his exhausting cross-country tour, his relationship with Emily Hale renewed, poring over the Clark typescript once again, his future life in London uncertain, Eliot seemed to relax among the transcriptions into some of his most personal moments of expository writing. There in Eliot House he allowed himself to make some of his most candid declarations about his conception of literary criticism, about his debt to nineteenth-century French poets, about the place of private emotion and subjectivity in poetry. There he was moved to make some of his most forthright statements about the function of the poet, the ultimate value of his work, the nature of greatness in poetry. There, at the midpoint of his academic year, he locked out the pensiveness of California and the sadness of London that a Fitzgerald would detect. In a sort of intellectual tranquillity, he found some two-day delight in clarifying anew the relation of the philosophical and the metaphysical in poetry, that constant delight of the younger Eliot.

24–*Harvard College Class of 1910. Seventh Report* (June 1935), p. 220.
25–TSE's final book of prose, *Notes Towards the Definition of Culture* (1948), was comprised of earlier essays and broadcasts, not lectures. Subsequent books, *On Poetry and Poets* (1957) and *To Criticize the Critic* (1965), were collections of essays and lectures.

THE VARIETIES
OF METAPHYSICAL POETRY

Three lectures delivered
at Johns Hopkins University
Baltimore, USA
[The Turnbull Lectures]
in January 1933

T. S. ELIOT

"The Varieties of Metaphysical Poetry"
Three lectures delivered
at Johns Hopkins University
Baltimore, U.S.A.
(The Turnbull Lectures)
in January 1933.

T. S. Eliot

[Toward a Definition of
Metaphysical Poetry]

It is not my intention, in three lectures, to cover the whole ground of what is ordinarily called "metaphysical poetry". Out of the group of poets commonly included under that term in extension, I shall only refer to the principal members. On the other hand, I shall have something to say about other poets, both more ancient and much more modern, who seem to me to have some relation to the subject; and in this way to support a tentative definition of metaphysical poetry. The purpose of these lectures is indeed to arrive somewhere near a definition. For there is an obvious difficulty about the term as we use it, most conveniently, to designate a number of poets more or less contemporary, or belonging to two generations which overlap, we will say from Donne to Cowley, in the seventeenth century. So long as we use the term "metaphysical poetry" merely as standing for the work of these poets, we get along well enough. But we cannot be content with that, and we try to discover what this "metaphysicality" is that they have in common. But the moment we define "metaphysicality" in any way at all satisfactory, we find that not all of these poets appear to share it, and that what they all have in common is something else, something local in time and place. What we have to do, in the end, is to *impose* a meaning, rather than to *discover* it.

We have on the one hand an idea, or a term which appears to stand for an idea; and on the other, a considerable mass of literature which appears to embody this idea. Nothing, at first sight, more easy. We have only to evolve from our own minds a definition of what metaphysical poetry ought to be, then apply it, separate the metaphysical authors from the non-metaphysical, and if we incline to be more analytical, the metaphysical from the non-metaphysical part of the former authors' writings. But consider the idea and the concrete product more closely. This term "metaphysical", used by Dryden and adopted by Johnson, was first used as a convenient term *pointing to* a certain number of poets; it was as much defined *by* its material, as defining it.[1] It was first used by persons who were not themselves metaphysicians, or of a very philosophical cast of mind, and they certainly did not employ the term with any thought of Lucretius or Dante in their heads. The more metaphysical branches of philosophy were neither much practised, nor in very high repute in England, either in the age of Dryden or in the age of Johnson. There is room also for asking whether the term may not somewhat have altered in meaning between the time of Dryden and that of Johnson. We have even to ask whether the term can remain in use, justifiably, for the poets to whom it was first applied. We must remember that we have been using it not only for a larger number of poets than that which Dryden and Johnson had in mind, but for these poets seen in a different order of merit. There is no evidence that Johnson had in mind, or would have included, many poets who seem to us to belong to this category: Crashaw, Marvell, King, the two Herberts, Vaughan, Benlowes, and of course Traherne who was not known, pass unmentioned.[2] Johnson speaks of Donne and Ben Jonson as setting the fashion (he makes a vague reference to Marino) and enumerates as their "immediate successors" who still wore some shreds of honour in his own time, Suckling, Waller, Denham, Cowley, Cleveland and Milton. Waller, Denham and Milton he presents only to withdraw instantly; Suckling he dismisses as negligible; there remain only Cowley and Cleveland, and these two, with Donne, are the poets from whose work he draws all the illustrations in his famous essay.[3] And remember that he attaches a higher value to the work of Cowley than to that of Donne. Dryden, in his "Preface to *Sylvae*", refers to Cowley with what seems to us unmeasured praise; and in his references to Donne, appears more impressed by the *Satires*, than by any other portion of that poet's work.[4]

It will be seen, accordingly, that there is something very accidental about the invention and use of the term "metaphysical poetry". To this race of authors, Dryden and Johnson, neither perhaps fully qualified to judge, conceded profundity of thought and learning; and thought and learning, dressed in outlandish and difficult imagery, seemed to Johnson "metaphysical". His description is perfectly just, and his criticism legitimate and

---

1–See p. 46, n. 5.
2–See p. 46, n. 7.
3–See p. 47, n. 8.
4–See p. 47, n. 9.

felicitous, when measured by the sort of passage that he quotes; but on the whole his use of the term "metaphysical" is rather libellous of metaphysics, than illuminating of his authors. And the qualities of profundity of thought and learning which Johnson respected in them, must be called into question and analysed: the profundity of their thought, and the use which they made of their learning.

At this point we might be tempted to make a fresh start. Let us begin, we might say, with those poets whom the whole world will admit to be concerned with metaphysics, and measure the metaphysicality of Donne and his school by them. If Donne and his school turn out not to be metaphysical at all, then we will find a new name for them. If we begin by assuming that "metaphysical" *ought* to mean something akin to "philosophical", then we must go to the poets – Lucretius, Dante and Goethe – discussed by Mr. Santayana in his brilliant and admirable little book *Three Philosophical Poets*. It is clear that for Mr. Santayana a philosophical poet is one with a scheme of the universe, who embodies that scheme in verse, and essays to realise his conception of man's place and part in the universe. Whether the philosophical system is one which he takes over from a philosopher, or whether it is one which he evolves himself in the process of writing his poetry, is not here important. I think that on the whole I accept Mr. Santayana's definition of "philosophical poetry". I think that neither Mr. Santayana nor I mean by philosophical poetry that poetry which may be given the sort of interpretation which finds "occult" meaning – the term *occult* including a wide range of types from the *Sortes Virgilianae* to certain interpretations of Shakespeare and Blake.[5] We have both, I imagine, a prejudice in favour of the clear and distinct; we mean a philosophy which is expressed, not one which is ineffable. And I should agree with Mr. Santayana that Shakespeare is not a philosophical poet; and should say that Coleridge, when he said he was, simply used the wrong adjective, even though I am not sure what the right one is.[6] And I would add one

5 – See p. 49, n. 13–14.
6 – Santayana does not actually say that Shakespeare is not a philosophical poet in *Three Philosophical Poets*; it is implicit in his definition of a philosophical poet. On the basis of that definition, TSE had himself argued that Shakespeare is not a philosophical poet in 'Shakespeare and the Stoicism of Seneca' (1927), an argument that he was to confirm in his Norton Lecture of 17 February 1933 on 'Shelley and Keats': 'Some years ago I tried to make the point . . . that Dante possessed a "philosophy" in a sense in which Shakespeare held none, or none of any importance. I have reason to believe that I did not succeed in making the point clear at all . . . Dante and Lucretius expounded explicit philosophies, as Shakespeare did not' (*UPUC* 98/89–90).

qualification. Under philosophical poetry we must, *a priori*, include Lucretius and Dante, poets whom we take to be poets and to be philosophical by immediate inspection and common consent. And we must not include *all* great poetry, for the adjective would become meaningless. And we must proceed from the side of poetry, not from that of philosophy. That is to say, we must restrict the inclusion to poetical work of the first intensity, in which the thought is so to speak fused into poetry at a very high temperature. Consequently we must leave out of account those works, even when very fine, such as Pope's *Essay on Man*, in which the fusion is less perfect, or made at a lower temperature, and some works of Blake in which we are not sure that it takes place at all.[7]

Now I am convinced that of "philosophy" in this legitimate sense, in the sense in which we can speak of Lucretius, Dante and Goethe as philosophical (though not so surely as "philosophers"), Donne and the poets whom we associate with him possessed not an atom. So far, we find no justification for using the term "metaphysical". Some years ago I had a correspondence with Mr. Saintsbury, both in *The Times* and privately, on this very point.[8] Mr. Saintsbury wished not only to keep the term – and in this we are in accord – but to give it, by what hardly seemed to me better than a *jeu de mots*, a further and more exact significance based on its etymology. Metaphysics was, of course, originally only that work of Aristotle's which came after his *Physics*. But the metaphysical, for Mr. Saintsbury, is that which comes after the natural; the metaphysical poets are those who seek something beyond or after nature, refinements of thought or emotion: ergo, they are metaphysical. Mr. Saintsbury's definition of metaphysical poets as those who have and are chiefly interested in "second thoughts", as he phrases it, is ingenious and worth considering. But it seems to me to have the usual inconvenience of applying to other poetry which we should not call metaphysical, and not applying to all the poetry which we call metaphysical, and still worse, of applying rather better to the second-rate than to the best. And when Mr.

In Coleridge's *Lectures and Notes on Shakspere* (London: G. Bell & Sons, 1908), to which TSE refers in the last of his Norton Lectures as a representative moment in the history of Shakespeare criticism (*UPUC* 121/113), Coleridge refers to Shakespeare on several occasions in noun form as 'a great Philosopher' (p. 487), but TSE may have had in mind Coleridge's attempt to link his recurring views of Shakespeare as both philosopher and aristocrat: 'He is always the philosopher and the moralist . . . If he must have any name, he should be styled a philosophical aristocrat' (p. 281).

7–See p. 50, n. 16.
8–See p. 62, n. 38.

Saintsbury chose to support his definition by claiming Swinburne as a metaphysical poet, the structure, so far as I was concerned, collapsed.

So I shall assert roundly that while metaphysical poetry has indeed something to do with philosophy, the connexion is not found through the *term* metaphysical. Its claim to the term comes only through one of the secondary, even whimsical meanings of "metaphysical", one of which is "oversubtle". I do not think that any of us would be satisfied by *meaning* "oversubtle poetry" when we speak of "metaphysical poetry". Subtle it usually is – but so is much other good poetry – and *over*subtle we will not allow the best of it to be. I think, however, that by its long association with the excellent society of Donne and others, the adjective is now entitled to a *tertiary* meaning, and that we proceed to discover or invent. I now proceed still more boldly to declare that I find something in common between Donne and two other groups of poets: Dante in his earlier poetry (as in the *Vita Nuova*) and his circle, and a few poets in the seventies and eighties of the last century, in France, particularly Jules Laforgue. My endeavour will be to persuade you that you find it too.

The Italian poetry of the time of Dante has a very significant background of ideas. Remy de Gourmont is not an authority whom one would often quote in matters of scholarship, but in his interesting, if not wholly satisfactory little book entitled *Dante, Béatrice et la poésie amoureuse*, he makes succinctly the distinction between Provençal and early Italian poetry.[9] Speaking of Provençal society, he says:

> Pour aimer, il fallait être marié et aimer en dehors du mariage. Pas plus qu'entre époux, entre jeunes gens libres l'amour n'était admis. Afin d'avoir droit aux hommages des chevaliers, il faut que la jeune fille se marie. Ce que nous laissent constamment entrevoir les poètes provençaux, c'est une dame noble, belle, puissante, entourée d'une cour de jeunes chevaliers, parmi lesquels il lui était permis, sinon dûment ordonné, d'en distinguer un et [de] se l'attacher. Le lien formé, ils [se] devaient mutuellement amour sous peine de déchéance; rien ne pouvait les séparer que, momentanément, la mort. C'était la fidélité dans l'adultère. . . . La dame provençale n'est nullement "angélisée". On ne la craint pas, on la désire.

He then draws the contrast between this system and the spirit of the Italian poets.

9–See p. 93, n. 3.

La nouvelle école florentine . . . devait modifier profondément la conception de l'amour, et par conséquent les moeurs. L'amour des poètes devient pur, presque impersonnel; son objet n'est plus une femme, mais la beauté, la fémininité personifiée dans une créature idéale. Aucune idée de mariage ni de possession [ne] les hante. . . . L'amour a tous les caractères d'un culte, dont le sonnet [et] la canzone sont les hymnes. [. . .] C'est une date dans l'histoire de l'évolution des sentiments humains; c'est un pas vers la vérité et un progrès social immense.[10]

More recent, and more scholarly writers – such as Señor Asin and Mr. Christopher Dawson – lead us to believe that this Dantesque conception of love is due, ultimately, to Arabic influences;[11] but I am not here concerned with its origins. My point is merely that in the poetry of Dante and his group we do find a philosophical passion – not a passion for philosophy but an alteration of human passion by philosophy. To us, as we first approach these poets, these may seem to be extremely abstract and rarified passions; but they are no more abstract than Crashaw's feeling towards the Magdalen.[12] It is true that contemplation, rather than enjoyment, is the state aimed at; but contemplation is probably the most ecstatic emotional state possible. When Cavalcanti says

> Chi è questa che vien, ch'ogni uom la mira,
> Chi fa tremar de claritate l'aere?

(or, *chi fa di clarità l'aer tremare*): "who makes the air all tremulous with light" in Rossetti's translation,[13] this is not a rhetorical and flattering flower

10–See p. 94, n. 4.

11–In *Islam and the Divine Comedy* (1919; Eng. trans. 1926), Miguel Asín Palacious (1871–1944), a Catholic priest and Professor of Arabic at the University of Madrid, delineated the general influence of Moslem philosophy on Dante's work and drew specific parallels between Dante's vision of love in the *Vita Nuova* and similar visions described by Ibn Arabi of the Spanish school of Arabic writers. In his influential article on 'The Origins of the Romantic Tradition', which had appeared in the *Criterion* (January 1932, pp. 222–48), Christopher Dawson (1889–1970), Lecturer in the History of Culture at University College, Exeter, argued that 'the new school of Tuscan poetry which arose in the second half of the thirteenth century, was equally indebted to the Provençal tradition and owes its peculiar character to its fusion of the art of the troubadours with the thought of Arabic philosophy. The poetry of Guido Cavalcanti and the other poets of the *dolce stil nuovo*, above all the youthful Dante, attains a deeper and more spiritual beauty than anything in the literature of northern chivalry or in that of Provence itself' (p. 245).

12–'Sainte Mary Magdalene or The Weeper' (1646). See pp. 171–2.

13–See p. 107, n.31.

of speech, but an exact statement of a visual impression produced by the beloved upon the lover for which I dare say some physiological account could be given. The *Vita Nuova* is no more a dry and lifeless allegory than it is a literal history; but of this I have already written what I have to say.[14]

Whether an Arabic influence was at work or not, there was certainly a background of mediaeval philosophy: the delight in ideas, the dialectical subtlety, the intensity with which ideas were felt, the clarity and precision of the expression, have this background. And one influence was surely the mysticism of the twelfth century. It is the antithesis of Bergsonism. Its origin is in Aristotle's *Metaphysics* 1072b and elsewhere, and in the *Nichomachaean Ethics*.[15] For the twelfth century, the divine vision could only be attained by a process in which the intellect took part; it was through and beyond discursive thought that man could arrive at beatitude. It is different from the way of approach of the Spanish mystics, and from that of the German mystics. It may be called the Scottish mysticism, since the Victorines, its ablest exponents Richard and Hugh of St. Victor, came from that country, and exhibit the analytical and dialectical abilities for which their race is renowned. This is the Riccardo of the *Paradiso*, Canto x:

> Che a considerar fu più che viro
>
> "Who in contemplation was more than man".[16]

His treatise *De Gratia Contemplationis*, called the *Benjamin Minor*, is concerned with the operations and stages of the mind in its progress towards the divine vision.[17] It shows some resemblance to the classifications of some Indian mystical treatises.[18] It is wholly impersonal, like a handbook of hygiene, and contains no autobiographical element whatever; and nothing emotional or sensational. Here he is distinguishing between the three stages

---

14–In Part III of 'Dante' (1929) TSE had turned from the *Divine Comedy* to the *Vita Nuova* in order to 'amplify what I have suggested about the mediaeval mind expressed in allegory' (*SE* 269/229). Recognizing that there are grounds for arguing that the work is entirely allegorical, 'for asserting, that is, that Beatrice is merely a personification of an abstract virtue, intellectual or moral', he had gone on to argue that it is 'a mixture of biography and allegory', that it 'can only be understood by accustoming ourselves to finding meaning in *final causes* rather than in origins', and that it is 'a very sound psychological treatise on something related to what is now called "sublimation"' (*SE* 274–5/234–5).

15–See p. 91, n. 12.

16–See p. 101, n. 17.

17–See p. 101, n. 19.

18–See p. 102, n. 20.

of mental progress: *cogitation, meditation* and *contemplation,* the three stages of the mind's pilgrimage.

> Cogitatio per devia quaeque lento pede, sine respectu perventionis, passim huc illucque vagatur. Meditatio per ardua saepe et aspera ad directionis finem cum magna animi industria nititur. Contemplatio libero volatu quocunque eam fert impetus mira agilitate circumfertur.[19]

He develops the distinction, with great anxiety not to be misunderstood, in several ways.

> Cogitatio est sine labore et fructu. In meditatione est labor cum fructu. Contemplatio permanet sine labore cum fructu. In cogitatione evagatio, in meditatione investigatio, in contemplatione *admiratio.* Ex imaginatione cogitatio. Ex ratione meditatio, ex intelligentia contemplatio. . . . Intelligentia obtinet supremum locum, imaginatio infimum, ratio medium.

(Incidentally, one may commend a comparison of this use of "imagination" with that of Coleridge).[20] The method seems to me to be essentially the same as that of Aquinas. CF. Aquinas: "It results evidently that it is only in the divine vision that intelligent beings can find the true felicity".[21]

Now in all of the three periods with which I am concerned – Florence in the thirteenth century, London in the seventeenth century, Paris in the nineteenth century, and in the poets of these periods whom I have most in mind, there is a background of philosophy *and* mysticism. Dante, as you will have become aware, I class *both* as a philosophical and as a "metaphysical" poet: we are occupied here with his metaphysicality, not with his philosophicality, though both are essential to the *Divine Comedy.* Among

19—See p. 102, n. 22.
20—Whereas Richard associates imagination with thinking and places it third in order of mental power to contemplation and meditation, Coleridge, in Chapter XIII of *Biographia Literaria,* holds the 'primary IMAGINATION' to be 'the living power and prime agent of all human perception, and as a repetition in the finite mind of the eternal act of creation in the infinite I AM'. The parenthetical invitation to comparison was prompted by the fact that on 9 December 1932 TSE had focused his fourth Norton Lecture ('Wordsworth and Coleridge') on Coleridge's 'doctrine of fancy and imagination', quoting the definitions of imagination in Chapter XIII and in Chapter I: ' "Repeated meditations led me first to suspect . . . that Fancy and Imagination were two distinct and widely different faculties, instead of being, according to the general belief, either two names with one meaning, or at furthest, the lower and higher degrees of one and the same power" ' (UPUC 76/67–8).
21—See p. 104, n. 23.

them all, ideas are felt, and feelings are transformed by ideas. Behind Dante and his friends, there is the mysticism of Richard and Hugh of St. Victor. Behind Donne and his period, is that of St. Ignatius and that of St. Theresa. Behind Jules Laforgue, is the mysticism of Hartmann and Schopenhauer. You will observe that not all these mysticisms are of the same quality. You will have to observe further that in these three periods we get a difference in kind and degree of penetration of the sensibility by the mystical philosophy. Nevertheless, I hope to establish some relationship. A strong bent towards theological and philosophical study, and no direction towards creative activity in these studies, is discernible in the three poets whom I have mentioned.

As a good deal has been written about Donne's *mediaevalism*, I am obliged in passing to try to dissipate that myth. The thesis has been most forcibly put by Miss Mary Ramsay in her valuable book *Les idées médiaé- vales chez Donne.*[22] Miss Ramsay maintains not only that Donne possessed a "very complete" philosophical system and a profound mysticism, but that his conception of the universe, and his philosophical technique, are essen- tially mediaeval. If this is true, it must follow that Donne is both a mediaeval and a philosophical poet; not only a metaphysical.

There is no doubt of Donne's natural turn of mind towards theology and the law: his extensive knowledge of law indeed suggests to us that there was an inclination to the more public and disputatious, rather than the more private and speculative, aspect of philosophy; as indeed was characteristic of his time. When we inspect the dreary index of his reading most usefully provided by Miss Ramsay, we recoil;[23] no man of Donne's ability and attainments ever seems to have read a greater quantity of solid rubbish. But we remark at once, how large a part of his reading was in authors contemporary with himself, or nearly so. True, he was familiar with the fathers of the Church, as any thorough student had to be, and with the most important of the mediaeval philosophers; but so was Hooker, as Miss Ramsay acknowledges, yet she does not go so far as to say that Hooker's conception of the universe was mediaeval.[24] Donne must have read Aquinas with care; he quotes Bonaventura, and of course Augustine influenced him. But he was equally at home among later theologians, both Roman and Protestant. Walton tells us that when Donne, at the age of nineteen, began to

22—See p. 63, n. 39, and p. 67, n. 1.
23—See p. 68, n. 3.
24—See p. 68, n. 4.

apply himself to the study of theology, he plunged into the work of Bellarmine – for the purpose of resolving his hesitation between the Roman and the Reformed Church – so thoroughly that a year later he was able to show the Dean of Gloucester all of Bellarmine's works annotated by his own hand.[25] Now Cardinal Bellarmine was a man some thirty years older than Donne, and still living when Donne studied his works. Donne made himself in time equally acquainted with the work of all his distinguished theological contemporaries, and also of a great many whose distinction has long since vanished. He knew the works of Luther, of Calvin, of Melanchthon, of Peter Martyr, among Protestant writers; of Cajetan, Valdez and Fra Victoria among the more philosophical of Roman commentators; he had the controversial literature of the Jesuits at the ends of his fingers; finally, he was acquainted with many of those writers of the Renaissance whose orthodoxy, from either a Roman or a Protestant standpoint, is doubtful, such as Nicholas of Cusa and the host of writers who exploited the Kabbalah, the hermetic writings and other compilations of the sort.[26] It is not irrelevant to remind ourselves that Donne's great grandmother was a sister of Sir Thomas More; and More wrote a biography of Pico della Mirandola, which was much admired by Donne. More admired Pico, and was also influenced by Colet, who translated that recension of neo-Platonic philosophy attributed to Dionysius the Areopagite. Donne's great grandfather, More's brother-in-law, was active in theological controversy, which led to his conversion to Protestantism. Donne's grandfather was John Heywood, the author of the Interludes; his uncle, whom he must have known, even though perhaps slightly, was the Jasper Heywood who made the first translation of three of Seneca's plays, and who subsequently became a Jesuit.[27] This is a remarkable family; and certainly one that kept up with the times; and the influences breathed on Donne's cradle do not seem to have been very mediaeval.

What Donne's reading does show is a pronounced taste, even a passion, for theology of the more controversial and legalistic type; for theology, in fact, as it was practised in his time; and I think that King James was perfectly right when he brought pressure upon Donne to make him take orders. His reading, and his tastes, were no more mediaeval than those of any other theologian or preacher of his time. What Miss Ramsay does however make

25 – See p. 69, nn. 8 and 9.
26 – See pp. 69–70, nn. 10–12.
27 – See pp. 70–71, nn. 13–18.

abundantly clear is the partiality, as well as the immensity, of his reading. He had no doubt been instructed in the Latin classics, if not in the Greek, by his tutors, but he makes little use of them. One allusion makes us believe that he read the *Divine Comedy*, or had the opportunity of so doing.[28] That there is no evidence of his appreciating his contemporary poets and dramatists, I count not against him; there is much to be said for a poet's not reading his contemporaries. And Donne was primarily a theologian; a poet, only [by] avocation. But the poet in a man does tend to spoil everything else; Donne could not have been a theologian of the type of Richard Hooker, or even of the type of Jeremy Taylor: his genius, his combination of gifts, is exhibited most fully in his magnificent sermons.[29] We must remember this in order to see him where he was, a little apart from his contemporary men of letters, even when he mixed among them. The speciality of his interests protected him from three great influences of his age: those of Montaigne, Machiavelli and Seneca the poet.[30] Donne is more Jacobean than Elizabethan; the century which was to be predominantly a century of ecclesiastical and theological politics was announced by the ascent of a Scottish theologian to the English throne, and this theologian made John Donne his private chaplain.[31]

The intellectual background of Donne, as I have tried to show, was thus very different from the intellectual background of Dante and his friends. There was a great deal of Jesuitism in it; and I do not think that anyone who has ever examined the origins and constitution of that remarkable order can fail to notice its great difference from any of the orders founded in the Middle Ages, or any of the more modern orders founded on their model. The founder of the Society of Jesus, that extraordinary man St. Ignatius

---

28–See p. 72, n. 20.

29–TSE had earlier distinguished among these types of theologians in 'The Prose of the Preacher' (1929; see p. 64, n. 41): 'In the classification of prose styles the theology of Hooker is nearer to the philosophy of Bacon than it is to the prose of Donne and other great preachers. The first represents an important step in the development of reasoning; the second represents a step in the development of oratory . . . They have a relation, on the other hand, to the more "decorative" or "poetic" prose in English; to Jeremy Taylor . . . In Hooker and Bacon we find what we may call "reasoning in tranquillity"; in Donne we find "reasoning in emotion" ' (p. 22). TSE declares that Taylor (1613–67), 'in the next generation, has a sweetness and purity of tone unknown to Donne', but observes that without the poetic qualities of Donne's sermons 'the more ornate types of English prose, of Sir Thomas Browne and Jeremy Taylor, would not have developed so rapidly' (p. 23). TSE had written of Taylor in his Introduction to Pound's *Selected Poems* (1928): 'To me, Pope is poetry and Jeremy Taylor is prose' (p. xix).

30–See p. 74, n. 26.

31–See p. 74, n. 28.

Loyola, seems to have been a reader of romances, before his vocation, an admirer of Amadis of Gaul, a sort of Don Quixote.[32] It has even been affirmed that in the formation of his order he adopted, in some particulars of practical organisation, Moslem rather than Christian models.[33]

Much of what I have been saying may seem to you to be very remote from my nominal subject. But in considering the three poets with whom I am chiefly concerned as "metaphysical", the philosophical background is very important; not so much for our purposes its abstract scheme, but its feeling [and] tone. As for the mediaeval philosophy behind Dante, we are now, I think, thanks to the devoted labours of Professor Etienne Gilson, and to his gifts of exposition and style, beginning to take a more enlightened view.[34] There was a time when we thought of the mediaeval philosophers as playing a futile game with a great many strict rules. They were not, we supposed, allowed to question the truth of dogma, and therefore their pursuit of truth was hopeless from the start; their thought was crushed by authority; and so they spent their time in dividing hairs and determining the specific gravity of angels – much as a man condemned to wait an hour in a country railway station with nothing to read might pass the time in casting up the figures on the timetable. We now look at them differently. Unlike modern philosophers, they held certain beliefs in common; they all wrote in the same language; it was therefore not impossible for them to some extent to understand each other – an attainment extremely difficult in our modern philosophy. Then, the Church could and did afford them great liberty of speculation; for the Church was one; when the Albigensian heresy was done away with, the Church was not occupied with defence or polemic.[35] The speculations of the philosophers were not dangerous; and they were men

32–See p. 76, n. 31.
33–See p. 76, n. 32.
34–See p. 77, n. 33.
35–The Albigensian religious sect, established in Provence during the 11th century, was based on the dualist Christian heresy of Manichaeism. In 1208, after local bishops and papal legates had been unable to contain the growth and political power of its religious centres, Pope Innocent III launched an Albigensian Crusade. After twenty years of war, which led to the Peace of Paris (1229), the religious effects on the Albigenses were negligible. In 1233 Pope Gregory IX established the medieval Inquisition to investigate their heretical religious practices, but it took another century before the Inquisition and various clerical reforms brought about the death of Albigensianism. TSE had written of the 'possibly maligned' sect in 'Dante' (1929): 'That mysterious people had a religion of their own which was thoroughly and painfully extinguished by the Inquisition; so that we hardly know more about them than about the Sumerians' (SE 275/235).

interested in the discovery of the truth who had no need to consider practical consequences.

Compare the situation of the thirteenth-century theologian, in the freedom of his university, unhampered, unhurried, unconcerned with wars and dynasties, with that of the theologian of either the Roman or the Reformed Churches at the time of the Counter-Reformation. The Society of Jesus was formed for the purpose of combating heresy; it was, in its first period, military, rather than meditative or charitable, in its purpose. And admirably did it do its work. It produced accomplished men of letters, erudite and subtle commentators; it was served perhaps by better brains, and certainly by a better organisation, than was Protestantism; it counted among its forces innumerable pious and devoted men; but it produced no great development in philosophic and theological thought. Neither, for that matter, did the Protestant Churches in the seventeenth century. There was no time. Politics cannot wait. One of the many disastrous effects of the Reformation was the theological war, the sectarian diplomacy, which reduced the Word of God to a business of armies, fleets and chancelleries. Theology which is bent to political agitation, orthodoxy and heterodoxy at bay, extinguishes the light of pure ideas, the Greek disinterestedness of mind, which the Middle Ages had revived: but it does not extinguish religious sentiment. On the contrary, the religious feeling of the sixteenth and seventeenth centuries burns with a fierce human heat which is itself alarming, as a rapid combustion in acceleration of nature. Human curiosity too, deflected from one direction, turns to another. Religion and theology, abandoning the pursuit of metaphysical truth, develop in the seventeenth century in the direction of psychology; an alteration which Mr. Mario Praz has well noted.[36]

It would seem as if now and then in history the human mind altered its categories of truth, ceased to be able to think in one way, and began a course of thinking in another. There is perhaps nothing mysterious about that. Often, it has been remarked, the state of mind appropriate to the development of a new science comes into existence before the science itself. Diderot in this way anticipated Darwin; the fancies of Leonardo were brilliant anticipations.[37] Certainly Donne, when we compare him to genuinely mediaeval poets, is in a sense a psychologist. And you will find this element too in his sermons, compared to earlier sermons. I am not qualified to

36—See p. 78, n. 34.
37—See p. 79, n. 35.

expose in detail how the change came about. It seems to me that the fine distinctions, the discussions of conduct and casuistry in which some orthodox theologians indulged, tend in the direction of a self-consciousness which had not been in the world before. It is clearly formulated, later, by Descartes, when he affirmed that what we know is not the world of objects, but our own ideas of those objects. The revolution is immense. Instead of ideas as meanings, as references to an outside world, you have suddenly a new world coming into existence inside our own mind and therefore, as we crudely fancy it, inside our own head. "Je conçois donc" [for dis-je], says Descartes,

> aisemént que l'imagination se peut faire de cette sorte, s'il est vrai qu'il y ait des corps; et parce que je ne puis recontrer aucune autre voie pour expliquer comment elle se fait, je conjecture de là probablement qu'il y en a; mais ce n'est que probablement; et quoique j'examine soigneuse-ment toutes choses, je ne trouve pas néanmoins que, de cette idée distincte de la nature corporelle que j'ai en mon imagination, je puisse tirer aucun argument qui conclue avec nécessité l'existence de quelque corps.[38]

Donne of course is not consciously of this way of thinking, or indeed of any way of thinking. He was not too nice about coherence: a notion of Maimonides or Averroes could exist in the mind of Donne alongside of the same notion in the form which St. Thomas had given it, or he will entertain a notion of the pseudo-Dionysius which St. Thomas would repudiate.[39] But his tendency is all in the new direction. In his poetry we often perceive his attention to be on the idea in his mind, rather than upon the object to which the idea refers. To contemplate an idea, because it is my idea, to observe its emotional infusion, to play with it, instead of using it as a simple meaning, may bring curious and beautiful things to light, though it lend itself, this petting and teasing of one's mental offspring, to extremities of torturing of language. It is not – as in the more bombastic Elizabethans – so much the vocabulary that is tortured, as it is the idea.

> I wonder by my troth, what thou and I
> Did, till we loved? Were we not wean'd till then?
> But sucked on country pleasures, childishly?

38–See pp. 81–2, n. 41.
39–See pp. 83–4, nn. 45 and 46.

Or snorted we in the seven sleepers' den?
'Twas so: but this, all pleasures fancies be.
If ever any beauty I did see,
Which I desir'd, and got, 'twas but a dream of thee.[40]

This is only one example, in Donne's lighter, though not frivolous mood, of what I have called teasing the idea. I shall pursue this subject in my next lecture.

40-'The Good-morrow', lines 1–9; partly modernized; minor mistranscriptions; see p. 85, n. 50 and p. 148, n. 27.

[The Conceit in Donne and Crashaw]

I want now to show, if I can, that the acceptance of an orderly system of thought results, with Dante and his friends, in a simple, direct and even austere manner of speech, while the maintenance in suspension of a number of philosophies, attitudes and partial theories which are enjoyed rather than believed, results, in Donne and some of his contemporaries, in an affected, tortuous and often over-elaborate diction.

If you examine the figure of speech used by Dante, or by Cavalcanti, you will find that the difference between their images and those of Donne lies in the focus of interest. The interest of Dante lies in the idea or the feeling to be conveyed; the image is there to make the idea more intelligible, the feeling more apprehensible, the vision more visible. In Donne, the interest is dispersed, it may be, in the ingenuity of conveying the idea by that image; or the image may be more difficult than the idea; or the interest may lie in the compulsion, rather than in the discovery of resemblances. Part of the pleasure may derive from the incongruity which is overcome; part of the feeling is the feel of an idea, rather than the feeling of a person who accepts that idea. Let us look first at one image of Dante's which I have quoted elsewhere.[1] He is attempting to express the feeling of entering the first heaven, at the beginning of the *Paradiso*.

> Pareva a me che nube ne coprisse
> lucida, spessa, solida e polita,
> quasi adamante che lo sol ferisse.

---

1 – TSE had previously quoted the following lines (31–6) from Canto II of the *Paradiso* in his first essay on 'Dante' (1920), where in discussing the complete scale of emotions expressed in Dante's poetry he includes the lines as 'a concrete presentation of the most elusive' (*SW* 169). See also p. 120.

Per entro sè l'eterna margarita
ne recepette, com' acqua recepe
raggio di luce, permanendo unita.

"It seemed to me that a cloud enveloped us, shining, dense, firm and polished, like a diamond struck by the sun. Within itself the eternal pearl received us, as water doth receive a ray of light, though still itself uncleft".[2]

This imagery is by no means simple: we have the rapid transition from cloud to diamond, from pearl to water; and the aim is to convey one kind of image, a supra-sensible imagery, by another kind familiar to us. It is directed by a purpose of strict utility. The imagery is not meant to be interesting in itself; like all of Dante's similes and metaphors, it has a rational necessity.

I do not want to draw my distinctions too sharply. I am aware that between the image of necessity and the extreme conceit there are infinite degrees; we could find many images from various sources of which it would be difficult to say whether they were serviceable or ornamental. One can, however, hardly define the "conceit", a kind of figure of speech character- istic of the English, Italian and some Spanish poetry of the age of Donne, better than by saying that it is the antithesis of the kind of imagery in the passage just quoted from Dante. Not all of Donne's imagery is "conceited". Let us take two poems which are variations on the same theme: "The Funerall" and "The Relique". The first begins:

Who ever comes to shroud me, do not harm
    Nor question much
That subtile wreath of hair, which crowns my arm;
The mystery, the sign you must not touch,
    For 'tis my outward Soule,
Viceroy to that, which then to heaven being gone,
    Will leave this to controule;
And keep those limbs, her provinces, from dissolution.[3]

This is typical of Donne's procedure. The first three lines are peculiarly simple. The adjective "subtile" is exact; the simple statement is perfect; the only possible blemish is the slightly distracting metaphor hidden in the verb "crown". But with line 5 Donne becomes wholly and characteristically

2—Translation slightly altered from *TC* III, 17. See p. 120.
3—See p. 124, n. 8.

conceited; you find yourself in a tangle of souls and deputy-souls, kings, viceroys and territories, and almost forget that this is all about a strand of a lady's hair around his arm. And yet, though it is distracting, though it diminishes the intensity, though it may represent some inward disintegration, it is pleasing. The ingenuity of the imagery, which is self-conscious and calls attention to itself, is "wit", and it is serious; it is what the word "wit" meant at that time. We turn to the first stanza of "The Relique".

> When my grave is broke up againe
> Some second ghest to entertain,
> (For graves have learn'd that woman-head
> To be to more than one a Bed)
>   And he that digs it, spies
> A bracelet of bright haire about the bone,
>   Will he not let us alone,
> And think that there a loving couple lies.
> Who thought that this device might be some way
> To make their soules, at the last busy day,
> Meet at this grave, and make a little stay?[4]

In this version we perceive that the order is not the same. The simplicity is put in the middle instead of at the beginning. In some ways this version is the more effective. To set the discovery of the token long after death and burial, instead of at the moment of shrouding, declares a more perdurable passion, makes more significant the "bright hair" which outlasts the flesh and now clings about the bone. But the notion of the violation of the grave for "entertaining a second guest", and still more, in a poem celebrating constancy, the analogy of the impermanence of graves to the fickleness of women is an association of ideas peculiar to Donne's idiom, of which you can only say that you either like it or you don't. I do like it; but I feel that it indicates that something was beginning to go wrong with civilisation about that time; the mind goes back to Propertius and to Persius to find a similarity. There is something ominous when such very dissimilar thoughts and feelings become yoked in one poem. In the next stanza he gives full rein to his fancy:

> If this fall in a time, or land,
> Where mis-devotion doth command,

4–See p. 125, n. 10.

> Then he, that digges us up, will bring
> Us, to the Bishop, and the King,
>   To make us Reliques; then
> Thou shalt be a Mary Magdalen, and I
>   A something else thereby;
> All women shall adore us, and some men;
> And since, at such time, miracles are sought,
> I would have that age by this paper taught
> What miracles we harmless lovers wrought.[5]

Here you see, Donne has become distracted from the meaning of the bracelet about the bone; he is occupied with fanciful consequences of the first assumption. His method is frequently like this, to proceed from the greater to the less, from the central to the peripheral, from the passionate to the reflective. And in this he is honest to his own feelings. For passion, unless of an astounding simplicity and intensity, or unless it be sustained by a high philosophy which transmutes it into something else, must always fade out. In Donne it fades into the play of suggested ideas; and Donne is the great ruler of that borderland of fading and change. In Dante we find complete coherence and integrity, in Donne disintegration, in Jules Laforgue the conscious irony of conflict between feeling, and the intellectual interpretation and dignity which feeling wishes to give itself, and reason. That is only another stage of disintegration.

Signor Mario Praz, in his admirable study of Donne, remarks shrewdly that "whilst in other singers the whole poem vibrates under the impulse of the first impetus, with Donne on the other hand the impulse is suddenly . . . broken by an anticlimax of ratiocination";[6] and I would suggest that one of the reasons why I find Donne so sympathetic is that we also, provided with no philosophy which can assign a serious and dignified place to the original impulse, take refuge in the anti-climax of ratiocination; only with us, the contrast is more conscious and complete. What I wish to make explicit is that there is no standard of *good writing* by which you can object to the kinds of figure of speech which Donne and other poets of his time employ. Even when they do not make sense, they have their own necessity. Let us examine a quatrain of the beautiful poem, "The Extasie".

> Where, like a pillow on a bed,
> A pregnant bank swelled up, to rest

5—See p. 126, n. 12.
6—See p. 127, n. 13.

The violet's reclining head,
Sat we two, one another's best.[7]

Now if you choose to look at it in that way, this is about as hideous a mixture of tropes as one could find. To compare a bank to a pillow does neither dignify nor elucidate; and it is surely superfluous to add "on a bed", since a pillow may be presumed to have much the same shape wherever it is disposed. This unhappy simile comes into collision with an equally forlorn metaphor: the bank is pregnant. Having already learned that the bank was shaped like a pillow, we hardly need to be informed that it was pregnant, unless an earthquake was preparing, which was not the case. The pregnant bank swells, which is a rather unfortunate type of ambiguity; it might be in the process of swelling, which is not what Donne ought to mean, as the whole scene is to be as static as possible; he means rather, "was swollen" or perhaps swells like a wave. We then learn at last why the bank had swelled: it did this in order to provide a pillow for the drooping head of the violet. But for this accommodating behaviour of the bank to be justified, the violet must be imagined as growing, not on the bank, but beside it; and if the bank swelled only just sufficiently to support the head of the violet, it was hardly of sufficient size to deserve the name of bank. Finally, it is a violation of the order of nature to conceive of the violet as antecedent to the bank, unless we affirm that the final cause of banks is the support of violets' heads. So here, as a critic like Dr. Johnson or Jeffrey might put it, are four lines wasted to let us know that the lovers sat upon a bank.[8]

Well, that is one way of looking at it. And it is often a useful exercise to take a figure of speech to pieces: if it can be put together again it is all right. Walter Pater observes that "the meaning" (of poetry) – I should say rather of some kinds of poetry – "reaches us through ways not distinctly traceable

---

7–See p. 108.
8– TSE refers to Johnson's criticism of the metaphysical poets in his *Life of Cowley*, where he is severely critical of their 'laboured particularities', 'false conceits', 'mixed wit', 'useless talk' and other 'inelegant applications' of poetic language, and to Francis Jeffrey (1773–1850), founder-editor of the *Edinburgh Review* (1802–29), a narrow critic who took Johnson as his master in attacking the stylistic excesses of the Romantic poets, including the 'metaphysical sensibility, and mystical wordiness' of Wordsworth and related flaws of rhetorical diffuseness and obscurity in Scott, Burns, Crabbe, Byron, Southey and Keats. In the *Criterion* of July 1924 (p. 373) TSE had applauded the announcement that a series entitled 'The Oxford Miscellany' would issue 'a volume of Jeffrey's criticism', but Professor D. Nichol Smith's edition of *Jeffrey's Literary Criticism*, originally published by Oxford University Press in 1910, did not appear in the series until 1928.

by the understanding";[9] and I think that there is a meaning to this stanza of
Donne, an emotive meaning, which could perhaps not be conveyed by less
confused imagery. You certainly will not get very much satisfaction out of
the poetry of this period unless you can receive the meanings expressed in
this way. Let me take an extreme specimen from Crashaw. He has a poem
called "The Tear". The tear is shining in the eye of the Blessed Virgin, and
each stanza deals with the tear under some new figure of speech – a form of
verse popular at the time in which Crashaw is specially adept.

> What bright soft thing is this?
> Sweet Mary thy faire eyes expence?
> A moist spark it is,
> A watry Diamond; from whence
> The very terme I think was found,
> The water of a Diamond.

"Soft thing" is good, for a tear; "Moist spark" is still better; "the water of a
diamond" is an excellent pass of pate.[10]

> O 'tis not a teare,
> 'Tis a star about to drop
> From thine eye its spheare,
> The Sun will stoop and take it up,
> Proud will his sister be to weare
> This thine eyes jewell in her eare.

Readers of Miss Sitwell's poetry should not find this difficult.[11]

> Faire drop, why quak'st thou so?

9–From 'The School of Giorgione' (1877), added to the third edition of *The Renaissance*
(London and New York: Macmillan, 1888), p. 143.
10–See p. 171, n. 32.
11–TSE had been increasingly critical of the verse of Edith Sitwell (1887–1964) since he first
described the 'weaknesses of technique' that undermined her poetry (*Athenaeum*, 11 April
1919, p. 171), and he soon found her excessive tropes to betray a 'poetry of perversity': 'The
paraphernalia of verse are the instruments of her disdain . . . With her "the fat leaves pat the
shrinking air" and "The candles weep and pry like living things" ' (*TLS*, 8 July 1920, p. 435).
The harshness of the present allusion to her poetry in relation to reading Crashaw is revealed by
way of reference to 'The Devotional Poets of the Seventeenth Century' (1930), in which TSE
had quoted these two stanzas from 'The Tear' as examples of Crashaw 'at his worst', citing the
final stanza in particular as 'the climax of absurdity' and asking 'who else would provide a
pillow stuffed with angel's down for the head of a tear?' (p. 553).

Cause thou straight must lay thy head
         In the dust? O no,
The dust shall never be thy bed;
A pillow for thee will I bring,
Stuft with down of Angels wing.[12]

This is better than Donne's pillow for the drooping violet; a pillow is to be
stuffed with angel feathers for the drooping head of a tear. Now this is not
really funny; it is perfectly serious poetry. Crashaw knew quite well what he
was about; it is for a serious effect, and an effect which could be got in no
other way. It is a mistake to suppose that a simile or a metaphor is always
something meant to be *visible* to the imagination; and even when it is meant
to be visible, that all its parts are meant to be visible at once. Examine a
sonnet by a modern poet – I say modern because I have had a friend[13] who
was a friend of his – Stéphane Mallarmé; *M'introduire dans ton histoire*,
and you will find in the fourteen lines four or five images which it is quite
impossible to imagine or conceive simultaneously, and at least one which
cannot be visualised at all:

            Dis si je ne suis pas joyeux
            Tonnerre et rubis aux moyeux
            De voir en l'air que ce feu troue

            Avec des royaumes épars
            Comme mourir pourpre la roue
            Du seul vespéral de mes chars.

"Thunder and rubies up to the wheel hub" is just as difficult to figure out as
the career of Crashaw's tear; and it is only when you have an impression of

---

12–See p. 172, n. 33.
13–The friend was Paul Valéry, the friend and disciple of Mallarmé (see p. 210, n. 11). TSE
wrote of their friendship after Valéry's death: 'Only as many meetings, I think, as could be
counted on the fingers: but these meetings were distributed at significant points in the twenty-
one years ending in July, 1945, twenty-one years during which Valéry, already recognized as a
great poet, came to be a figure symbolic of the Europe of our time . . . My impressions of him,
from our first meeting to the last, are of a personality, certainly not simple or easily
comprehended, but consistent throughout these years . . . Of some great men, one's prevailing
impression may be of goodness, or of inspiration, or of wisdom: I think the prevailing
impression one received of Valéry was of intelligence' (*Quarterly Review of Literature*, Spring
1947, p. 212).

the sonnet as a whole that it comes into place, and has meaning.[14] The poet's business is to know what effect he intends to produce, and then to get it by fair means or foul. There is the element of rationality, the element of precision, and there is also the element of vagueness which may be used; and we must remember that one distinction between poetry and prose is this, that in poetry the word, each word by itself, though only being fully itself in context, has absolute value. Poetry is *incantation*, as well as imagery. "Thunder and rubies" cannot be seen, heard or thought together, but their collocation here brings out the connotation of each word. You will find in Shelley or Swinburne tropical constructions that will no more bear analysis than what I have quoted from Donne and Crashaw.

> Violets that plead for pardon
> Or pine for fright[15]

are no more respectable than Donne's violet; and I confess that I myself do not like this use of the pathetic fallacy; but I can see that what Swinburne was after was a particular association of our feeling towards violets and our feeling towards small pathetic fragile human beings.

The Elizabethan lyric had been more truly *song* – verse meant to be sung – than any of the Jacobean or Caroline. The focus becomes shifted, if sometimes ever so little, from sound to sense; from the sound of the word to the sound of the sense of the word, so to speak; to the consciousness of the meaning of the word and a pleasure in that sound having that meaning. Parallel to this transition [was] the shift, of which I have spoken, from metaphysics to psychology; the word is not merely the sound with a

14 – 'M'introduire dans ton histoire' (1886), lines 9–14:

> Am I not (whose hub is
> All thunder and rubies)
> Glad to see the winged wheel

> With scattered realms fire-shot
> As though dying purple
> Of my one dusk-chariot.
> (trans. Keith Bosley, *Mallarmé: The Poems*, p. 191)

TSE was soon to adapt lines 10–11 as 'Garlic and sapphires in the mud / Clot the bedded axle-tree' and use them as the concluding lines in drafts (Houghton) of 'WORDS FOR AN OLD MAN', dedicated 'to Stéphane Mallarmé'. The poem was later published in *CPP* 143/95 as 'Lines for an Old Man' without the dedication and with line 9, 'Dis si je ne suis pas joyeux', adapted as 'Tell me if I am not glad!' for the concluding line. TSE then made them the opening lines (*CPP* 172/118) of Part II of *Burnt Norton* (1934).
15 – *Read* 'Snowdrops that plead for pardon / And pine for fright'; see p. 174, n. 39.

meaning; the word becomes interesting for its meaning elsewhere as well as for its meaning in the context; for its own meaning as well as what the writer means to mean by it. In its beginnings, the conceit as used by Donne is no more than the development in poetry of an expository device known to preachers from the earliest times: the extended, repeated, detailed, interminable simile. The Buddha used it in the Fire Sermon; Richard of St. Victor uses it in his interpretations of the Scriptures – as Noah's Ark, for instance; and Donne, in his own sermons, employed this device in a way very similar to that of Bishop Latimer in his sermons.[16] One of Donne's most successful extended conceits is in a beautiful poem, "A Valediction".[17]

> As virtuous men passe mildly away
> And whisper to their soules, to goe,
> Whilst some of their sad friends doe say,
> The breath goes now, and some say, no:
>
> So let us melt, and make no noise,
> No teare-floods, nor sigh-tempests move,
> 'Twere profanation of our joyes
> To tell the layetie our love.
>
> Moving of th'earth brings harmes and feares,
> Men reckon what it did and meant,
> But trepidation of the spheares,
> Though greater farre, is innocent.

Here is no flaw; no one has ever handled this quatrain movement better than Donne. The astronomical figure may give some trouble; but it has a legitimate effect of over-statement: it is to say, that so huge an event as this separation of lovers is like the immense but imperceptible movements of heavenly bodies.

> Dull sublunary lovers love
> (Whose soule is sense) cannot admit
> Absence, because it doth remove
> Those things which alimented it.[18]

16–See pp. 130–31, nn. 22–24.
17–See p. 131, n. 25.
18–*Read* 'Those things which elemented it'.

These lovers are (in modern language) "cosmic"; all others are "sublunary".

> But we by a love, so much refined,
> That our selves know not what it is,
> Inter-assured of the mind,
> Care lesse, eyes, lips, and hands to misse.

> Our two soules therefore, which are one,
> Though I must goe, endure not yet
> A breach, but an expansion,
> Like gold to ayery thinnesse beate.

The conceit here comes pretty near to the compliment. Donne is not here expounding or implying any theory of the soul in which he could be said to believe. At least, I feel confident that he is not, and hope that he is not; for his statement "our two souls . . . which are one" is directly controverted by St. Thomas, who, in combating a suggestion of St. Augustine by a reference to the *De Anima*, observes:

> Cum impossibile sit plurium numero differentium esse unam formam, sicut impossibile est quod eorum sit unum *esse*; oportet principium intellectivum multiplicari secundum multiplicationem corporum.[19]

It is impossible for two bodies to have one soul. But it is never quite certain what Donne believes, or whether he believes anything. The figure does make intelligible an idea, but there is properly no idea until you get the figure: if gold can be beaten out very thin, so love can be the same even if the two terms in the relation are at the opposite ends of the earth. When Guido Cavalcanti says

> Amor, che nasce di simil piacere,
> Dentro del cor si posa,
> Formando di disio nova persona,
> Ma fa la sua virtù 'n vizio cadere

he is speaking literally.[20] He is maintaining much the same theory as that of *Purgatorio* XVIII: "Then, even as fire moves upward by reason of its form, whose nature it is to ascend, there where it endures longest in its material; so

19—See p. 113, n. 41.
20—See p. 132, n. 26.

the enamoured mind falls to desire, which is a spiritual movement, and never rests until the object of its love makes it rejoice".[21]

It is not quite clear how much Spanish Crashaw knew. It is reported that he picked it up, with his first knowledge of Italian, by solitary study. That he knew Italian well is more probable than that he knew Spanish well. He may have read the *Life* of St. Theresa (Mother Theresa as she then was) in an English translation of 1612. Her autobiography is almost essential to an understanding of Crashaw. It is not only an interesting book, but a really great book, and also a feminine book (if I may be pardoned the adjective), by a woman who was an amazingly efficient organiser and administrator (she would have made a great University President); it is great because of the great beauty of character, and the transparent honesty and scrupulousness and profound piety of the writer. She is not the profound philosopher that is her disciple St. John of the Cross; she is more loveable, more human, and in that time much more influential. When, for instance, she tells us that the Lord took her crucifix from her, and returned it adorned with pearls, she adds conscientiously, that no one was ever able to see the pearls except herself.[22] Much seventeenth-century, or baroque poetry, reminds one of a crucifix ornamented with pearls, and they are too often cultured pearls. I must say emphatically that my view of St. Theresa is not that of modern psychologists, or of the psychologically minded laity who cannot read her innocent confessions without a titter; and when I say that her influence was towards the substitution of human for divine love for divine objects, I am not, as I may appear to be, giving away a trick to such people. I have in mind, here, rather the difference between the scholastic mysticism which is resumed, as is everything else, in St. Thomas Aquinas, and the Renaissance mysticism, at which I have already hinted. The earlier mysticism was more intellectual, more comprehensive, more Aristotelian – and for that matter more Spinozistic – Spinozistic without the artifice and pose of Spinoza[23] – and more balanced than Spinoza's. The later mysticism is less philosophical,

21 – *TC* II, 217, lines 28–33.
22 – See p. 165, n. 15.
23 – TSE had written in his review of Abraham Wolf's edition of *The Oldest Biography of Spinoza* (*TLS*, 21 April 1927, p. 275): 'The figure of Spinoza has been almost more important in the last hundred years than the philosophy of Spinoza. Few people have mastered the "Ethics," but everyone knows that Spinoza polished lenses; few people have read the "Tractatus Politicus," but the whole world has been impressed by his excommunication from the Jewish Church . . . So that the celebration of the 250th anniversary has a different meaning from the anniversary of an Aristotle, an Aquinas, or a Kant; it is the recognition not so much of a philosophy as of a personality in which certain human ideals seem to be realized.'

less cosmological, and far more psychological. Whatever modern psychologists may think of St. John of the Cross, he was a greater psychologist, in his analysis of the mind and the heart, than any of them. I am considering St. Theresa also, not as a clinical subject for psychologists, but as a psychologist herself: of the theology of the sixteenth and seventeenth centuries, St. Augustine, not St. Thomas, is the forerunner. The world of St. Thomas and of Dante is for me a world in which the real values, so far as I can apprehend them, are best arranged as I can understand them: with the sixteenth and seventeenth centuries my sympathies are more imperfect. Dante's sense of values, as illustrated in his sensibility, seems to me just right. His words before Beatrice appears to him in the *Purgatorio* put exactly his feeling toward Beatrice in heaven – the already sublimated still further sublimated feeling, but still human – as the fire runs through him – *Cognosco i segni dell' antica fiamma*;[24] and in the ultimate vision he is an exact trinitarian and no tritheist. But of the poetry of the *seicento* Signor Praz says truly that "the general tendency of the epoch was to make the divine passions a true mirror of the human passions".[25] But when I say that I insist that the *seicento* was still religious, I think that Praz will agree with me; and I am not to be disconcerted by your calling the baroque writers "erotic". Of course they are erotic; the love of God is erotic: that is only a tautology after all. The difference between human and divine love is much subtler than any of the distinctions which modern psychologists are able to draw. What I question is dependent upon the difference between ontology and psychology; and it is the psychologism, not the supposed eroticism, which lays a poet like Crashaw open to the charge of being a voluptuary of religious emotion. We may say, as a parallel, that Donne was a voluptuary of thought: the last two or three generations have suffered from voluptuaries of thought, such as Renan, Anatole France, André Gide, Bernard Shaw, and Mr. Aldous Huxley.[26] Crashaw has a more ingenious wit – and he is

24 – See p. 166, n. 18.
25 – See p. 167, n. 19.
26 – Provoked by Haakon Chevalier's study of Anatole France in *The Ironic Temper* (1932), TSE was preparing an attack on four of these 'voluptuaries of thought' for his 'Commentary' in the next issue of the *Criterion* (April 1933, pp. 468–73): Ernest Renan (1823–92), Anatole France (1844–1924), André Gide (1869–1951) – and his English contemporary, Aldous Huxley (1894–1963). Attacking them for their 'puny' intellectual sophistication, their 'arrested development' and their affected use of irony 'to give the appearance of a philosophy of life', TSE finds in France 'a kind of pretentiousness which is unendurable', and he looks upon Gide as a writer who has 'offered us the sophistication of the daring mind, freed from all prejudices and inhibitions (how that word fatigues one!) . . . willing to try anything – the slave, not of the past, but of the future . . . France is more sophisticated than Renan. Gide is more

very witty – he has stronger feelings, than his Italian models; of all the poets of the age, he is the one who is nearest to St. Theresa herself. Donne enters into his mind; the Italians into his language; but St. Theresa enters into and takes possession of his heart as she could not possess his more frigid Italian prototypes. The sensationalism which seems deliberated in Marino seems spontaneous in Crashaw. But as with Donne the thought is split up into thoughts, so with Crashaw the emotion is split up into emotions; instead of one emotion informing the whole poem, you get emotion piled on emotion, image on image – much as a man may go on drinking because he is terrified of becoming sober.

Let me compare one verse of Crashaw's paraphrase of the hymn *Vexilla Regis* (the Good Friday hymn)[27] with the original of Fortunatus. (This translating and paraphrasing [of] hymns and psalms was a frequent exercise of the epoch).

> Vexilla regis prodeunt,
> Fulget crucis mysterium,
> Quo carne carnis conditor
> Suspensus est patibulo . . .

which is humbly translated in our service:

> The royal banners forward go;
> The Cross shines forth in mystic glow
> Where he in flesh, our flesh who made,
> Our sentence bore, our ransom paid.[28]

---

sophisticated than France. For Mr. Huxley . . . the future is still open'. TSE had already declared that Huxley 'succeeds to some extent in elucidating how sordid a world without any philosophy can be' (*SE* 367/323), and on numerous occasions he had mocked the intellectual dexterity of the pacifist, socialist and dramatist, George Bernard Shaw (1856–1950): 'No one can grasp more firmly an idea which he does not maintain, or expound it with more cogency, than Mr. Shaw. He manipulates every idea so brilliantly that he blinds us when we attempt to look for the ideas *with which he works*. And the ideas with which he works, are they more than the residue of the great Victorian labours of Darwin, and Huxley, and Cobden?' (*Criterion*, October 1924, p. 4).

27–Hymn 106, '*Vexilla Regis prodeunt*' ('The royal banners forward go'), is found in the Anglican hymnal, *Hymns Ancient and Modern* (London: William Clowes & Son, 1909), p. 148. It has been in general use at Passiontide at least since the tenth century and is now sung in the Church of England 'From the Fifth Sunday in Lent to the Wednesday before Easter'. See *Historical Companion to Hymns Ancient and Modern*, ed. Maurice Frost (London: William Clowes & Sons, 1962), p. 187.

28–See p. 169, n. 26. TSE quotes the first stanza of the Revd John Mason Neale's translation in *Medieval Hymns and Sequences* (London: Joseph Masters, 1851), p. 6, as used in *Hymns Ancient and Modern*.

You will note the suggestion of wit in the line "quo carne carnis conditor" ("Where he in flesh, our flesh who made"). This is what Crashaw makes of it:

> Look up, languishing soul. Lo where the fair
> Badge of thy faith calls back thy care,
>   And biddes thee ne'er forget
>   Thy life is one long debt
> Of love to Him, who on this painful Tree
> Paid back the flesh he took for thee.[29]

You observe the exhortation to the "languishing soul" (in Crashaw's time souls readily languished and swooned), the introduction of the distracting conceit of debt and repayment. In his translation of the next stanza we get a "nest of loves", an "amorous flood", a "wedding" of water and blood.[30] And as in general, in Crashaw's poetry, we get a sequence of emotional disturbances, rather than any structure of emotion; it is, as with his Italian prototypes, a kind of radical empiricism.[31] The trouble is with the head, rather than with the heart, so far as those two organs can, in poetical criticism, be dissociated. The *trecento* had an exact statement of intellectual order; the *seicento* had an exact statement of intellectual disorder; the nineteenth century had a vague statement of intellectual disorder. The exactness of Crashaw is nowhere better illustrated than in the lines to the Saint:

> O thou undaunted daughter of desires!
> By all thy dower of lights and fires;
> By all the eagle in thee, all the dove;
> By all thy lives and deaths of love;
> By thy large draughts of intellectual day,
> And by thy thirsts of love more large than they;
> By all thy brim-filled bowls of fierce desire,
> By thy last morning's draught of liquid fire;
> By the full kingdom of that final kiss
> That seiz'd thy parting soul, and seal'd thee His;
> By all the Heaven thou hast in Him
> (Fair sister of the Seraphim)

29—See p. 169, n. 27.
30—For the second stanza, see p. 170.
31—See p. 170, n. 29.

By all of Him thou hast in thee;
Leave nothing of myself in me.
Let me so read thy life, that I
Unto all life of mine may die![32]

I should not like to quote anything more of Crashaw, or by anybody else, after reading that. A little acquaintance with the Italian and the English verse of the period enables us to recognise the lights and the fires, lives and deaths and thirsts; but here they are fused beyond analysis and perfected beyond criticism. It is the ultimate religious expression of that period of strange intellectual disintegration and religious intensity.

Anyone who has remembered the opening sentence of this lecture will at this point have noticed an apparent inconsistency. For I said "the maintenance in suspension of a number of philosophies, attitudes and partial theories which are enjoyed rather than believed, results, in Donne and some of his contemporaries, in an affected, tortuous and often over elaborate diction".

I did not wish to give the impression that John Donne was not, according to the sense of the words today, a Christian believer. We must keep in mind that not belief only, but the *meaning* of the word "belief", differs for different individuals and more certainly for different times; I hope still that Mr. I. A. Richards may some day throw some light upon the meaning of this word, for if he cannot, I do not know anyone else who can.[33] Donne was definitely a Christian believer; but the object of belief was not the same for him that it was in the thirteenth century. Crashaw was, if anyone ever was, a Christian believer; but for him again, the object of belief was not the same that it had been. The essential is of course always to be able to say *Credo*; but the objects of this verb vary a good deal in meaning from age to age. Jules Laforgue also was among the prophets, who say *Credo*, not among

32—See p. 179, n. 52; line 13: *read* 'By all of Him we have in thee'.
33—TSE and Richards had carried on their private and public dialogue on the problem of belief since Richards wrote in 1925 that Eliot had effected 'a complete severance between his poetry and *all* beliefs' in *The Waste Land* (see p. 81, n. 39). In February 1929 Richards prepared a lengthy notebook entitled 'Notes on Belief–Problems for T.S.E.', transcribed by John Constable in 'I. A. Richards, T. S. Eliot and the Poetry of Belief' (*Essays in Criticism*, July 1990, pp. 222–43). TSE had addressed Richards's theories in a special 'Note to Section II' of 'Dante' (1929), declaring, 'I deny, in short, that the reader must share the beliefs of the poet in order to enjoy the poetry fully' (*SE* 269/230), and in his first Norton lecture he had said of Richards: 'His ethics, or theory of value, is one which I cannot accept; or rather, I cannot accept any such theory which is erected upon purely individual-psychological foundations' (*UPUC* 17/7).

those lost people who say *Dubito*. But what were the objects of this nineteenth-century creed? When we have come to a conclusion on that matter, the stage is set for modern poetry.

[Laforgue and Corbière
in our Time]

It is not always true that the greatest poet of an age is the most representative of his age. All of the most interesting French poetry from the seventies of the last century to our own day is derivative from Baudelaire. Baudelaire was a great poet, and at his greatest is almost contradictory to his age; perhaps when a much longer span of time has elapsed, it will be possible to see him as representative, but certainly not of his own limited period of time as we can see it in this short perspective of the time since his death. "Whilst Verlaine and Rimbaud continued Baudelaire in the order of sentiment and sensation," says Paul Valéry, "Mallarmé prolonged his work in the domain of perfection and poetic purity".[1] We may add that Laforgue and Corbière prolonged his work in the domain of self-consciousness; and the disintegration and the strife between thought and feeling is more clearly visible in these minor men than in the master, who resisted the corrosion of his own time better than could the minor men.

Jules Laforgue was a young man who died at the age of twenty-seven in the year 1877. He was very poor, he became reader to a German princess, and during his residence in Berlin acquired the language and a good deal of German philosophy, especially Kant, Schopenhauer and Hartmann. He married a young English governess, and had, or acquired, some knowledge of her language and literature also. He was tuberculous, and died in poverty; I believe that his widow died not long after him.[2] I think that the first note about him in English was by Sir Edmund Gosse; though I was

---

1 – The concluding sentence of Valéry's 'Situation de Baudelaire' ('The Place of Baudelaire', 1924): 'Tandis que Verlaine et Rimbaud ont continué Baudelaire dans l'ordre du sentiment et de la sensation, Mallarmé l'a prolongé dans le domaine de la perfection et de la pureté poétique' (*Oeuvres*, I [1957], p. 613).
2 – See p. 212, n. 19.

indebted to the attractive study by Mr. Arthur Symons in his book *The Symbolist Movement*.[3] His poetry, and even his prose, is of course immature. He was a young man of ardent feelings, of an active intellect fascinated by abstractions, and with a remarkable gift for metaphysical emotion. He had a passionate craving for order: that is, that every feeling should have its intellectual equivalent, its philosophical justification, and that every idea should have its emotional equivalent, its sentimental justification. The world which could have satisfied his nature, therefore, was Dante's world; but there were no golden builders[4] of such a world in Paris or Berlin in the seventies. The disintegration of which I have spoken in connexion with Donne and Crashaw reached a much more advanced stage with Laforgue: for Laforgue, life was consciously divided into thought and feeling; but his feelings were such as required an intellectual completion, a *beatitude*, and the philosophical systems which he embraced were so much *felt* as to require a sensuous completion. The struggle of such a man as D. H. Lawrence might be expressed in somewhat the same terms, perhaps; though the two men were in themselves extremely different, and Lawrence's way of salvation, or what he thought the way of salvation, could never have been Laforgue's. It is only the world they lived in, and their affliction by it, that has any resemblance. The metaphysicality of Laforgue extends in two directions: the intellectualising of the sensibility and the emotionalising of the idea. Laforgue's irony, as in his fine prose *Hamlet* in the volume called *Moralités Légendaires*, an irony employed against himself, ensues from the conflict.

> — If (says Laertes when he meets Hamlet at the grave of Ophelia), you were not a wretched madman, and quite irresponsible according to the most recent investigations of medical science, you would be obliged to give me immediate satisfaction for the death of my honourable father and my sister — that highly accomplished young woman . . .
> — O Laertes, that's all one to me. But be sure that I allow for your point of view . . .
> — Gracious Heaven, (says Laertes) what lack of any moral sense! . . . .
> They sent to search for the corpse with torches of the best quality.[5]

His self-consciousness is of course partly adolescent, but is of a devouring intensity which renders it significant:

3 — See p. 212, n. 20.
4 — An allusion to Blake's 'To the Jews' in *Jerusalem*: 'What are those Golden Builders doing / Near mournful ever-weeping Paddington . . .?' See p. 205, n. 50.
5 — See p. 213, n. 21.

Bref, j'allais me donner d'un "Je Vous Aime"
Quand je m'avisai non sans peine
Que [d'abord] je ne me possédais pas [bien] moi-même.[6]

The "je m'avisai" is always driving him back to torment himself, just as the disparity between the meaning of human lives and what they ought to mean is always driving his Hamlet back upon himself. He is one who "ne croit à son Moi qu'à ses moments perdus"; but is yet haunted by the need of *living* some philosophy, if only the despairing abstractions of Hartmann's *Philosophy of the Unconscious*.[7] Had he been born later – and had he not been born a Frenchman – he might have fallen into the trammels of psychoanalysis; yet there is a masculine toughness and a keen ironic sense of humour essentially in his nature. He echoes sometimes the prayer of Baudelaire, "Seigneur, donnez-moi la force et le courage / De contempler mon corps et mon coeur sans dégoût".[8] His torments of sensibility, of body and soul, are expressed, for example, at the end of one of the poems which he calls *Dimanches*:

Ah, que je te les tordrais avec plaisir,
Ce corps bijou, ce coeur [à] ténor . . .
Non, non, c'est sucer la chair d'un coeur élu,
Adorer d'incurables organes . . .
Et ce ne'est pas sa chair qui me serait tout,
Et je ne serais pas qu'un grand coeur pour elle . . .
L'âme et la chair, la chair et l'âme
C'est l'esprit édénique et fier
D'être un peu l'Homme avec la Femme . . .

Allons, dernier des poètes!
Toujours enfermé tu te rendras malade!
Vois, il fait beau temps, tout le monde est dehors,
Va donc acheter deux sous d'ellébore,
Ça te fera une petite promenade.[9]

Later, in the same group of poems, he speaks of "les jeunes filles inviolables et frêles" going to church, and adds somewhat pompously:

6—See p. 213, n. 22.
7—See p. 215, n. 27.
8—See p. 214, n. 24.
9—See p. 214, n. 25.

Moi, je ne vais pas à l'église;
Moi, je suis le Grand Chancelier de l'Analyse . . .[10]

It is noticeable how often such words as "l'inconscient", "le Néant", "l'absolu", with similar terms from the vocabulary of the philosophers he had read recur, and such figures as the Valkyrie, and other images from the musical dramas of Wagner.[11] Laforgue gives the nearest verse realisation of the philosophies of Schopenhauer and Hartmann; it would be too much to say that he exactly believed them, but he certainly felt them, not in the way in which Wagner did, though he was influenced by Wagner too. His critical intelligence was incapable of drugging itself with emotion as Wagner seems to have done. The system of Schopenhauer does not work, but for Laforgue it collapses in a different ruin from that of *Tristan und Isolde* and *Parsifal*.[12]

Laforgue is surprisingly modern. As the *surrealistes*, in their peculiar mode of escape from life, look back to Rimbaud and Lautréamont[13] for their inspiration, so another type of poet is represented by Laforgue. Here is a piece of modern prose which might have been written in 1920, but which Laforgue wrote many years ago while Victoria was queen.

> The public cries recommence. Important notice! Redemption loan has weakened, Panama Canal shares firm. Auctions, experts. Advances against securities quoted or unquoted, purchase of unencumbered properties or annuities; advances against expectations; time-tables, annuals, new-year's gifts. Circular tours at reduced prices. Madame

10—See p. 215, n. 26.
11—See p. 215, n. 28.
12—See p. 215, n. 29. *Parsifal* (1877–82), Wagner's last work, is a religious festival play.
13—Isidore Lucien Ducasse (1846–70) assumed the name of Comte de Lautréamont upon publication of his *Les Chants de Maldoror* (1869), a montage of Gothic dreamscapes and fantasies in which the hero, Maldoror, revolts from God and discovers pleasure in evil and sadistic acts. In *Poésies* (1870), Lautréamont turned abruptly to a moralistic view of literature and denounced numerous romantic writers of doubt and despair. TSE may have discovered him through one of his earliest admirers, Remy de Gourmont, who introduced a new edition of *Les Chants de Maldoror* in 1920. In correspondence with Harry Crosby in September 1927 TSE expressed his familiarity with John Rodker's translation of Gourmont's edition for the Casanova Society in 1924, and on 27 October 1927 he wrote to thank Crosby 'for sending me the charming little book on Lautréamont which was entirely unknown to me' (*L2*). The Surrealist editors of *Littérature* – André Breton, Louis Aragon and Philippe Soupault – held Lautréamont in veneration during the 1920s, but it was André Gide who first associated Lautréamont with Rimbaud. In *Le Cas Lautréamont*, a special edition of *Le Disque vert* published in 1925, and evidently the book sent to TSE by Crosby, Gide proclaimed that Lautréamont, even more than Rimbaud, was to be 'le maître des écluses pour la littérature de demain'.

Ludovic predicts the future, daily from 2 to 4. The Children's Paradise: toys for children and cotillion favours for adults . . . Sole agency! Cylinder machines Marioni! Everything guaranteed, everything for nothing! Oh the rapidity of life also sole agency . . .[14]

There seems to have been something wrong with things even before the Treaty of Versailles.[15] Laforgue is certainly in revolt against something, a revolt which, as with D. H. Lawrence, is enacted on a deeper level of consciousness than that which deals with political and social notions. And he is at once the sentimentalist dreaming about the *jeune fille* at the piano or with her geraniums, and the pathologist commenting on her reflexes.[16] What he wants, of course, is some way of salvation in which both the mind and the feelings, the soul and the body, shall cooperate towards fulness of life; and I am afraid that it is neither the *jeune fille* of Laforgue's delicate and chaste imagination, nor Lady Chatterley who holds the key to that new world which is perhaps a very old one.[17] It was not Miss Leah Lee, the pretty English governess, or post-Kantian pseudo-Buddhism that could do the trick.[18]

If we can compare Laforgue to Donne, we can, with very great reservations, compare Tristan Corbière to Crashaw. Not that Corbière was a

14–See p. 215, n. 30.
15–See p. 216, n. 32.
16–See p. 216, n. 33.
17–In his Page-Barbour Lectures, delivered at the University of Virginia in May 1933, TSE was to point out 'the absence of any moral or social sense' in the relations of Lawrence's men and women before turning directly to *Lady Chatterley's Lover* (1928): 'In some respects, he may have progressed: his early belief in Life may have passed over, as a really serious belief in Life must, into a belief in Death. But I cannot see much development in *Lady Chatterley's Lover*. Our old acquaintance, the game-keeper, turns up again: the social obsession which makes his well-born – or almost well-born – ladies offer themselves to – or make use of – plebians springs from the same morbidity which makes other of his female characters bestow their favours upon savages. The author of that book seems to me to have been a very sick man indeed' (*ASG* 37, 60–1/39, 65–6). In a 1960 deposition (Nottingham) for the defence during the prosecution of Penguin Books for publishing the unexpurgated text of the novel, TSE was to disown his earlier statements as 'much too violent and sweeping': 'Perhaps I now understand better that Lawrence's vision concerned a spiritual morality for men and women which he regarded as so important that it entitled him to disregard ordinary social morality . . . It is my opinion now that Lawrence considered our society to be morbid and sick in its attitude to sex'. In 'To Criticize the Critic' (1961), further deploring the prosecution of the novel, he described it as 'a book of most serious and highly moral *intention*' but admitted that 'my antipathy to the author remains, on the ground of what seems to me egotism, a strain of cruelty, and a failing in common with Thomas Hardy – the lack of a sense of humour' (*TCC* 24–5).
18–See pp. 216–17, n. 34.

religious poet, any more than Laforgue; but the problems of poetry are not unrelated to the problems of theology. Corbière is a finer poet, at times, though a lesser and less interesting mind, than Laforgue. Laforgue was twenty-seven when he died in 1887; Corbière died in 1875 at the age of thirty; and they knew nothing about each other. In the work of Corbière there is less evidence of philosophic reading; he is less tormented by "the absolute", "the unconscious", but there is the same strange product of thought-feeling and feeling-thought. Like Crashaw, with Corbière the centre of gravity is more in the word and phrase, and he has phrases which recall, in our comparison, the concentrated conceit of Crashaw, but often with a savage humour, as when he calls Victor Hugo "Garde National épique";[19] and, with a savage concision worthy of Villon or Dante, two lines from a remarkable poem, *La Rapsode foraine*:

> Là, ce tronc d'homme où croît l'ulcère,
> Contre ce tronc d'arbre où croît le gui –

"This trunk of a man on which the ulcer grows, leaning against this trunk of a tree on which grows the mistletoe": that sudden collocation of the animal and the vegetable has a horror worthy of Dante.[20] Corbière's use of something approaching the conceit of Crashaw is more apparent in the series of *Petits Rondels pour après*, exequies on the death of a poet presumably himself; for instance:

> Va vite, léger peigneur de comètes
> Les herbes au vent seront tes cheveux;
> De ton oeil béant jailliront les feux
> Follets, prisonniers dans les pauvres têtes . . .

19–An allusion to Corbière's parodic portrait of Hugo in the twenty-first quatrian of 'Un Jeune Qui S'en Va', as printed in TSE's copy of *Les Amours jaunes* (p. 57):

> – Hugo: l'home [sic] apocalyptique,
> L'Homme-ceci-tuera-cela,
> Garde national épique!
> Il ne'en reste qu'un – celui-là! –

> – Hugo: apocalypse-man,
> the Man of This-will-end-that,
> . . . an epic national guard!
> There's only one Hugo – he's that!
> (Trans. C. F. MacIntyre, *Selections from Les Amours Jaunes*, p. 63)

20–See p. 218, n. 38; *read* 'Contre un tronc'.

Les fleurs de tombeau qu'on nomme amourettes
Foisonneront plein ton rire terreux,
Et les myosotis, ces fleurs d'oubliettes . . .[21]

only, as we notice in Laforgue, with much more sentimentality than we find in the seventeenth century.

In this very cursory survey of two French poets, I have had two things in mind. First to relate them to our present time, and second to relate them to "metaphysical poetry" in general, and so to arrive, if not at a definition, at least at a feeling of metaphysicality, and its relevance to our time. To take the first point first, what is the relevance of this French poetry of the seventies and eighties to us and our problems?

I perhaps am of all critics the most disqualified from judging. For I know that when I first came across these French poets, some twenty-three years ago, it was a personal enlightenment such as I can hardly communicate. I felt for the first time in contact with a tradition, for the first time, that I had, so to speak, some backing by the dead, and at the same time that I had something to say that might be new and relevant. I doubt whether, without the men I have mentioned – Baudelaire, Corbière, Verlaine, Laforgue, Mallarmé, Rimbaud – I should have been able to write poetry at all. This fact alone renders me unsuitable to be a critic of them. Without them, the Elizabethan and Jacobean poets would have been too remote and quaint, and Shakespeare and Dante too remote and great, to have helped me. I cannot but be aware, therefore, that in emphasising their importance for the present, I may be only defending myself. Yet I do think that they are important for our time; I do think that anyone who would understand contemporary literature should study that generation, not so much in England as in France; and not even so much the great progenitor, Baudelaire, as the minor epigoni. I conceive of literary criticism in the following way. The ideal literary critic should have both an intense concentration and an indefinite awareness. He should not be primarily concerned with sociology, or with psychology, or with politics, or with theology, or with any other ology; he should be primarily concerned with the word and the incantation; with the question whether the poet has used the right word in the right place, the rightness depending upon both the explicit intention and an indefinite radiation of sound and sense. He should differ from the practitioners of other sciences, not so much by what he needs to know and what he does not need to know – for indeed he needs to know everything – as by his centre of values: in the

21–See p. 219, n. 39; minor mistranscriptions.

beginning was the word. In speech is both the highest level of consciousness, and the deepest level of unconsciousness. By speech false values are maintained, or real values are revealed. The poet's first purpose is to amuse, and unless he can amuse, all else is vain; but he speaks in parables.

The ultimate purpose, the ultimate value, of the poet's work is religious. I mean, that every stage of society tends to harden into a set of purely social values. Society tends to exert a pressure, such that every poet is either accepted or rejected, according to his fitness to the set of social values of the time; contemporary criticism is thus largely irrelevant; it observes Procrustean principles. When Byron, in words which I have often been tempted to quote in extenuation of my own writings, remarks

> Some have accused me of a strange design
> Against the creed and morals of this land
> and trace it in this poem, every line;
> I don't pretend that I quite understand
> My *own* meaning when I would be *very* fine,
> But the fact is that I have nothing planned,
> Except perhaps to be a moment merry . . .[22]

he is, at bottom, affirming that the actual social values, whatever they are, are not the same as the poet's; for at any moment the practical and the theoretical values will differ. The artist is the only genuine and profound revolutionist, in the following sense. The world always has, and always will, tend to substitute appearance for reality. The artist, being always alone, being heterodox when everyone else is orthodox, and orthodox when everyone else is heterodox, is the perpetual upsetter of conventional values,

---

22 – Misquoted from Byron's *Don Juan*, Canto the Fourth, stanza v. TSE had memorized the stanza by 16 November 1914, when he misquoted several lines in a letter to Conrad Aiken (*L1* 69). He also misquoted the stanza, as above, in the 'Introduction' to his Norton Lectures on 4 November 1932, where he prefaced the quotation with the observation that 'the problem of what a poem "means" is a good deal more difficult than it at first appears. If a poem of mine entitled *Ash-Wednesday* ever goes into a second edition, I have thought of prefixing to it the lines of Byron from *Don Juan*' (*UPUC* 30/21; misquotation corrected in US edition).

> Some have accused me of a strange design
>> Against the creed and morals of the land,
> And trace it in this poem every line:
>> I don't pretend that I quite understand
> My own meaning when I would be *very* fine;
>> But the fact is that I have nothing plann'd,
> Unless it were to be a moment merry,
>> A novel word in my vocabulary.

the restorer of the real. He may appear at one time to hold one extreme opinion, at another period another; but his function is to bring back humanity to the real.

Now the critic has to be aware of all this, but to stick to his job. The more narrowly and closely he defines his job, if he is a man of wide and not pedantic sympathies, the better he will do it. I see no reason why sociologists should not scrutinise poetry, or why psychologists should not analyse it; but this is not literary criticism. There is no reason why one should not try to write great poetry, except that great poetry is not written in that way: I mean that if one cares enough about poetry, "greatness" is not the aim or the criterion. The aim is not to emulate Shakespeare or Homer or Dante or anybody else; for if and so far as one is a poet these criteria and ambitions are nonsense. Poetry is in this respect like science: the aim of the true poet is not to be a "great poet", but to make a contribution to poetry: merely to say the true thing at one's time; to say the thing to be said in the circumstances, in the right way. One positive contribution towards poetry is all that one can hope to make; beyond that it does not matter whether one is Shakespeare or Jules Laforgue; whether one is "original" or "derivative". Greatness is not a state that poets really seek; greatness is a matter, so far as we are concerned, of chance, of what happens afterwards when we are dead; and that depends upon a great many things outside of ourselves. It has often been said that no man is a hero to his own valet; what is much more important is that no honest man can be a hero to himself; for he must be aware how many causes in world history, outside of abilities and genius, have been responsible for greatness.

In looking at the history of poetry, accordingly, from – may I say – a poet's point of view – the values are not quite those which you will learn of from any history of poetry. They will be much more what is vaguely called "technical"; the important poets will be those who have taught the people speech; and the people had in every generation to be taught to speak: the function of the poet at every moment is to make the inarticulate folk articulate; and as the inarticulate folk is almost always mumbling the speech, become jargon, of its ancestors or of its newspaper editors, the new language is never learnt without a certain resistance, even resentment. *Donner un sens plus pur aux mots de la tribu*, Mallarmé said of Poe;[23] and

---

23–Line 6 of Mallarmé's 'Le Tombeau d'Edgar Poe' (1877), a line which TSE was to adapt in translation for Part II of *Little Gidding*: 'To purify the dialect of the tribe' (*CPP* 194/141). TSE had earlier quoted the line in 'Note sur Mallarmé et Poe' (1926) to suggest that Mallarmé's verse, which insists on the primitive power of the word, constitutes a brilliant critique of Poe.

this purification of language is not so much a progress, as it is a perpetual return to the real. I would have you understand, accordingly, that in talking about Dante, Donne and Laforgue as Three Metaphysical Poets I am not talking according to the, or any, scale of values which in a history of literature is deemed proper. But the scale of values in histories of literature is seldom the scale of values in life. I am aware that Dante deserves say ten pages, Donne one, and Laforgue a footnote. If I were a confessor of souls, would I give them that same rank in the confessional?

I ask for some revaluation of values in estimating the place of Laforgue and Corbière. I am all for considering literature by the pleasure that it gives, and I am aware that in the long run, Dante can give more pleasure than Laforgue. But we are not only concerned with pleasure; we are concerned, as historians, with what has made our present. The greatness of any artist depends upon the future; upon what he will do, upon his consequences. It seems to me that our present age has evolved a greatness for the French poets who have been the subject of this lecture. That is shown as much by the work of men who have never heard of them – like D. H. Lawrence – as by the work of men like myself who have been directly stimulated and affected by them.

The poet is not necessarily aware of all the implications of his own work. Indeed, he had better not be directly occupied with general questions at all. He is an accident, and should behave as such. That is to say, in writing poetry, we begin from our own immediate experience. That experience, in itself, has no relation to the experience of society as a whole. All that we are aware of doing, is expressing our own feelings about experience equally private; it simply happens, or it does not happen, that that private experience corresponds to a general state so that it both evokes the private experience, and expresses a public experience of the reader. Significant poetry occurs when there is a triple relation: that of the private experience of the poet to the general conditions, and that of the private experience of the poet *and* the general conditions to the private experience of the reader. There are two privacies, and one publicity; and there happens to be some point at which they all meet. Jules Laforgue was only occupied with his own private, and not representative emotions; he happened to be able to express them accurately, and it happened that thus expressed they were representative of the emotions of a larger number of persons. Dante, in attempting something on a much grander scale, managed to accomplish it by incorporating into it his private emotions, which, *qua* private, were no more significant than Laforgue's. First, the poet does not aim to be a great poet.

[290]

Second, he may happen to be what is called a "great poet". Third, there is a valuation of poets which can never be that of the general public, for its criterion is not "greatness" but "contribution".

I do not know whether I have seemed to approach anywhere near to a definition of metaphysical poetry. I began by pointing out that the term has two meanings, both of which must be retained, but which do not quite fit: it means the generation of poets between Donne and Cowley, though opinions may differ about minor individual poets; and also it means a *kind* of poetry not necessarily restricted to that period. I proceeded to the simple assertion that *I* find something in common between these seventeenth [-century] poets, or some of them, and such poets as Dante, Guido Cavalcanti, Guido Guinizelli, Cino of Pistoia, and such poets as Laforgue and Corbière; if you do not agree on this point, then everything I have said is pointless. Note that the difference between the two meanings of "metaphysical poetry" is not a simple difference of extension and intension. You cannot settle the matter so easily as that. To find out what metaphysicality is, in the seventeenth century, we must devote ourselves to the study of Donne. What the seventeenth-century poets had in common is primarily that they lived in the seventeenth century; and second, that they were influenced by Donne. Cowley is a metaphysical in so far as we can consider him in relation to Donne; but if we disregard this relation he is not metaphysical at all. When Cowley exclaims

> Now by my love, the greatest oath that is,
> None loves you half so well as I . . .[24]

we remember that he is a disciple of Donne; but we remember that we were told by Dr. Johnson, that however Cowley "may talk of his own inflammability, and the variety of characters by which his heart was divided, he in reality was in love but once, and then never had resolution to tell his passion".[25] It is easy to see why Dryden and Johnson deceived themselves about the importance of Cowley. Cowley was in his way a precursor of the style of Dryden, who in his earliest verse is merely a late conceited poet; Dryden and Johnson preferred his poetry for its likeness to their own, though they did not know that this was why they preferred it. Neither Dryden nor Johnson perceived how much a whole generation of poets owed to Donne, poets of very different tendencies: not only George Herbert and

24–See p. 188, n. 11.
25–See p. 188, n. 10.

Marvell, but Suckling and Lovelace;[26] not only the more crabbed and obscure, such as Benlowes,[27] but the more courtly and polished of the second generation, such as Rochester and Sedley.[28]

Accordingly we have, I think, to keep the two meanings of "metaphysical" in suspension in our minds: not so difficult as it sounds, for it is what we do anyway, and we are not ordinarily concerned with both meanings at once. The chief question is, whether you agree that the two other groups that I have mentioned, Italian and French, are just as metaphysical as the poets in the seventeenth century. If this is agreed by inspection, then what have they in common that can be formulated? It was capital here to distinguish between Dante as a philosophical poet and Dante as a metaphysical poet; and I do not mean that he had a metaphysical period and then a philosophical period; he began rather as a metaphysical, but he is in the *Divine Comedy* both metaphysical and philosophical according to Mr. Santayana's use of the latter word. I put forward that in each case, there was a philosophy and a mysticism in the background: for Dante, the philosophy of Aquinas and the mysticism of the Victorines; for Donne, there was a mixture of mediaeval philosophy – for there was only mediaeval philosophy for him to study – and the visual imaginative method of St. Ignatius – in whose *Exercises* any student of Donne must saturate himself;[29] for Crashaw, there was rather St. Theresa. And for Jules Laforgue the mystical

---

26 – In 'The Minor Metaphysicals' (1930; see p. 23, n. 36), TSE had ranked Suckling and Lovelace in the Donne tradition: 'In an age of rich poetic accomplishment we may expect to find a swarm of minor poets each of whom is the author of one or two noteworthy pieces of verse. Donne invented an idiom, a language which less original men could learn and talk . . . Herbert, Crashaw, Vaughan and Marvell, all made valuable variations on this idiom. Then come a third and a fourth class of poets: those who wrote a few good short poems without altering the idiom in any interesting way . . . Of those who wrote a few good poems, I recommend . . . Carew, Suckling, Lovelace. In a poet like Lovelace you observe an insensible and unconscious transition' (p. 641).

27 – See p. 137, n. 39.

28 – Rochester (see p. 138, n. 40) and his friend Sir Charles Sedley (1639–1701) both enjoyed notorious reputations as rakes and wits in the Restoration Court of Charles II, where they wrote amorous lyrics and satires. TSE probably became particularly interested in Rochester's indebtedness to Donne through Hayward's respective editions of the two poets in 1926 and 1929.

29 – See p. 105, n. 28. TSE had written of the importance of St Ignatius to Donne in 'Thinking in Verse' (see p. 23, n. 36): 'Now, if you read and study the *Spiritual Exercises*, you will find a stock of images which reminds you, and by no mere coincidence, of Donne . . . St. Ignatius works on the imagination, to make us realise the Passion as he realised it . . . And we shall find the visual imagery of St. Ignatius in Donne, whose childhood was passed under Jesuit influence' (p. 443).

philosophy of Hartmann and Schopenhauer, the same mystical philosophy which is infused into the music dramas of Wagner. Now philosophical poetry is written when a philosophical system is felt as a whole by the poet, when it affects the structure of his poem; when in fact it is *believed*. But metaphysical poetry can occur either with or without belief. It can occur either in the full possession of belief, or in the disintegration of belief, or in the conscious loss of belief and the search for it. What it makes manifest, and this is its great achievement, its great importance in the history of civilisation, is the intimate relation between our philosophical beliefs and our private feelings and behaviour. That is, indeed, one way of testing philosophical beliefs. The present Countess Russell has observed, in a book characteristically called *The Right to Be Happy*, that "animals we are, and animals we remain, and the path to our regeneration and happiness, if there be such a path, lies through our animal nature".[30] Whatever else is open to Lady Russell to be, it is quite certain that neither she, nor any of her regenerate and happy animal crackers will ever be metaphysical poets. Huysmans' hero of *En Route*, Durtal, observes after his excursion into happiness, *Mon Dieu, que c'est donc bête!*[31] and I cannot believe that D. H. Lawrence, in spite of superficial appearances, would have seen eye to eye with Lady Russell on this point. "The question is," as the late Lord Beaconsfield observed, "is man an ape or an angel?"[32] I think that Lawrence

---

30 – A quotation from Chapter VI, 'Modern Civilization', in Countess Russell's *The Right to be Happy* (London: George Routledge & Sons, 1927), p. 241. TSE had visited the Russells at their Chelsea flat, and she knew of TSE's strong reaction to the quoted sentence, writing in *The Tamarisk Tree* (London: Elek/Pemberton, 1975) that the remark had 'shocked T. S. Eliot, who evidently failed to understand what the book was about. Ecologists of today would find themselves in sympathy with many of my sentiments: I speak of the "quality" as opposed to the "quantity" in life; I suggest that a group of men and women who seek and find the "right road to conquering ourselves and our environments" could, by their speech and action, show that "this way of life can be practised by all and is capable of being the foundation of a society" ' (p. 194).

Dora Winifred Black Russell (1894–1986), a former student at Girton College and secretary of the Heretics, began her relationship with Bertrand Russell, 3rd Earl Russell, at Cambridge in 1919 and married him after his divorce in 1921, primarily to legitimate the birth of their impending child. As a feminist, social activist and author, she unsuccessfully resisted the use of her title until their marriage was dissolved in 1935.

31 – See p. 115, n. 46.

32 – Benjamin Disraeli (1804–81), novelist and then leader of the Tory Opposition, asked this famous question in 'Church Policy' (1864), his celebrated speech at the Oxford Diocesan Conference in defence of the Church Establishment: 'What is the question which is now placed before society with a glib assurance which to me is most astonishing? The question is this – is a man an ape or an angel? My lord, *I am on the side of the angels*. I repudiate with indignation and abhorrence these new fangled theories'. See Francis Hitchman, *The Public Life of the Earl*

was on the side of the angels; some reformers are certainly on the side of the Apes.

Now, there is a great deal of good poetry in the world that is not metaphysical. Indeed, some of the greatest. You only have metaphysical poetry, as I understand it, when you have a philosophy exerting its influence, not directly through belief, but indirectly through feeling and behaviour, upon the minute particulars[33] of a poet's daily life, his quotidian mind, primarily perhaps his way of love-making, but also any activity. There is nothing metaphysical about *Paradise Lost* or about *Faust*; and indeed a very great poet like Milton or Goethe may be much cruder in the way in which he feels his philosophy in daily life, than a smaller poet like Laforgue. Metaphysical poetry is highly civilised, and humanity is only highly civilised by fits and starts. Furthermore, the metaphysical poet must be subjective, or at least have a subjective side to him. It is not for nothing that the *Divine Comedy* is related in the first person. A poem like *Samson Agonistes*, however, is subjective in a very different and non-metaphysical way; it is in the way of *self-dramatisation*, a magnificent megalomania. Such egotism, however great the poetry may be which comes of it, is never metaphysical; the metaphysical poet, though much interested in his own feelings, whether in the way of Dante or in the way of Laforgue or of Donne, is interested in them in a cooler, detached way. Milton, in *Samson Agonistes*, expresses his feeling – largely a feeling of pride – towards the world through a dramatic figure; the metaphysical poet deals with his feelings directly, and more as if they were someone else's, only happening to be available to his inspection. One is the attitude of the theatre, the other that of the confessional. A poem like the great ode of Sappho, however acute its observation and statements of the feelings of a lover, is not metaphysical, because there is no definite philosophy behind it;[34] metaphysical poetry does not come early in the history of literature. A great philosophical poem like that of Lucretius is not metaphysical, because for instance the feelings of lovers

---

of *Beaconsfield* (London: Sampson Low, 1884), p. 359. In 1876, during his second term of office as Prime Minister, Disraeli was raised to the peerage, taking a name from his first novel (*Vivian Grey*, 1826) to become the 1st Earl of Beaconsfield.

33 – An allusion to a key concept in Blake's *Jerusalem*: 'He who would do good to another must do it in Minute Particulars: / General Good is the plea of the scoundrel, hypocrite & flatterer, / For Art & Science cannot exist but in minutely organized Particulars' (Plate 55, lines 60–62; *Blake: Complete Writings*, ed. Geoffrey Keynes [Oxford: Oxford Univ. Press, 1985], p. 672). TSE had earlier quoted these lines as an example of the 'formlessness' in Blake's marriage of poetry and philosophy (*SW* 156).

34 – See p. 51, n. 17.

which he describes are not coloured by philosophy, but are simply such as Countess Russell would have them be in the interest of happiness. And as I have said before, this tincture of human emotions by philosophy which is essential to metaphysical poetry as I conceive it, may or may not be accompanied by *belief* in that philosophy. In Dante we have the metaphysical development of feeling and also the cosmological belief. In Donne we still have a convinced Christian, but the belief is much narrowed in scope; his theological orthodoxy and his personal piety are corroded by a scepticism, not yet explicit, about philosophical truth in general: he has no accepted cosmology. In Laforgue we have the *entertainment* of German philosophical systems which are too abstract and skeletonised for the warm adherence of flesh and blood which is full belief, but which are powerful enough to disturb and afflict his personal emotions. I confess that I cannot see much prospect of metaphysical poetry issuing from the liberal or radical political cosmologies of the immediate future. A philosophy which lays under cultivation only the more social emotions and virtues, and which leaves the more private emotions to flourish or languish as weeds, could at best provoke the mental stress and tension of some more tortured Laforgue, but could not produce the harmony of the philosophical, the religious and the personal emotion which we find in Dante.

TEXTUAL NOTES

The Clark Lectures
The Turnbull Lectures

APPENDICES

INDEXES

TEXTUAL NOTES

The Clark Lectures

The following textual notes consist mainly of cancellations, insertions and other emendations made on the fair copy of the King's College typescript by TSE and others at various times after the lectures were delivered. Minor emendations without textual, editorial or substantive interest are excluded.

LECTURE I

The typing paper for the text of the lectures, 'Plantagenet/ British Make' (20.2 × 25.9 cm) was made and distributed by Spalding & Hodge, Ltd, Drury House, Russell St, London, WC; that for the preliminary pages, 'Colindia Parchment' (20.2 × 25.4 cm) by Strong, Hanbury & Co., Ltd, 196 & 197 Upper Thames St, London EC4.

43   title: '{INTRODUCTION: ...}': bracketed titles for the Clark Lectures are taken or adapted from TSE's projected titles, as pencilled on the verso of p. 183 of the typescript (Lecture VIII, p. 20). See below, following the note for p. 223.
      'even the eighteenth'; 'even' later cancelled in pencil.
      'Even the obscurer ... poems of Bishop King'; entire sentence later cancelled in pencil.

44   'attempted for eighteen years'; 'eighteen' changed in a later revision in pencil to 'twenty' in TSE's hand.

46   'and as much *defined* by the material'; 'by' later underscored in pencil.
      'Chamberlayne'; spelled 'Chamberlain' in the typescript.

47   'seems more impressed'; 'seems' later emended in pencil to 'appears' in TSE's hand.

48   'Mr. Santayana's'; Santayana is consistently mistyped 'Santavana' in the typescript, corrected at various times in pencil and ink by various unidentified hands.
      'or, for Goethe [the Faust legend,]'; words dropped by typist: text reads 'or, for

[299]

Goethe, which expresses'; TSE insertion mark in pencil after Goethe, with pencilled question mark in left margin. In 'Rhyme and Reason' (see p. 23, n. 36) TSE similarly described the philosophical poetry of the poets treated in *Three Philosophical Poets*: 'Lucretius wrote his poem to expound the philosophy of Epicurus in verse, and Dante expounded substantially the philosophy of St. Thomas Aquinas in verse – or else he makes his own system of philosophy and expresses that in verse; and the latter is more what Goethe did' (p. 502).

51   'the union of [things] hitherto'; 'things' inserted in pencil in TSE's hand, with pencilled question mark in left margin.
      'only existed'; circular pencil line indicating transposition to 'existed only' in unidentified hand.

52   'poets have a [feeling] more or less'; TSE insertion mark in pencil, with pencilled question mark in right margin; suggested insertion in pencil in an unidentified hand in the bottom right margin: '? meaning'.

54   'the *Word made Flesh*'; circled in pencil.

60   'and this is in the nature of'; 'in' later cancelled in pencil and changed to 'due to' in an unidentified hand.

61   'because we must assume'; 'assume' underscored in pencil.
      'admirable and almost impeccable anthology'; 'and' later cancelled in pencil and emended to 'admirable, almost impeccable anthology'.

63   'to those who think . . . the constant use of'; later cancelled in heavy pencil.
      'I would not like you'; 'you' circled in pencil.

64   'and you will find it a convenience . . . of a text'; later cancelled in heavy pencil.
      'Among other books' to end of lecture; later cancelled in pencil.

LECTURE II

67   In the top right hand corner of page [1] of Lecture II, TSE began numbering the pages of the eight lectures consecutively (26–184) in his hand, after cancelling page 26 (containing the list of recommended books) of the first lecture. Each separate lecture was consecutively numbered in type in the middle of the top margin by the typist, with page [1] of each lecture unnumbered.
      'I propose in this lecture'; 'lecture' later changed to 'chapter' in pencil in TSE's hand.

68   'whatever prospect of pleasure'; 'prospect of' later cancelled in heavy pencil.
      'seems to have read more positive rubbish'; 'more' later cancelled in pencil and changed to 'a greater amount of' in TSE's hand.

69   'Now this Bellarmine . . . great reputation'; all but 'Bellarmine' later cancelled in heavy pencil.
      'now unintelligible, if it ever existed'; 'if it ever existed' later cancelled in heavy pencil.
      'Melanchthon'; spelled 'Melancthon' here and on p. 258.

70   'It was the learned equivalent of the cross-word puzzle'; later cancelled in heavy pencil.

74   'But the century which was to [be] more'; 'be' inserted in pencil, apparently in TSE's hand.

75   'and it is on these grounds that he has advised me to take a spiritual director'; entire independent clause later cancelled in heavy pencil.

76   'and excessively Romantic'; later cancelled in heavy pencil.

     'Herrmann Müller'; spelled Hermann Mueller in the typescript.

     'There is some evidence . . . from Mohammedan examples'; question mark pencilled in right margin in unidentified hand.

     'Don Quixote'; spelled Don Quijote here and in the Turnbull typescript (p. 260).

77   'much as a man'; 'much' later cancelled in heavy pencil.

     'And [in] whatever degree of truth'; 'in' inserted in pencil, with question mark in left margin, in an unidentified hand.

78   'better organisation than did Protestantism'; 'did' later changed to 'had' in pencil in TSE's hand.

     'the detached and Olympian arbiter'; 'and' later cancelled in heavy pencil.

     'the same control over its own'; later changed to 'the same control over its own thought', inserted in pencil in TSE's hand.

79   'the fancies of Leonardo'; 'Leonardo' emended to 'Lionardo' in an unidentified hand.

83   'a different [form] of the old difference'; word dropped by typist; 'form' inserted in pencil by unidentified hand in carbon copy.

84   'are revived sometimes *tel quel*'; '*tel quel*' later emended (incorrectly) to '*telles quelles*' in pencil in TSE's hand.

86   'When Phaedra recalls'; Phaedra consistently typed 'Phedra'.

     'in my lecture of next week'; later circled in pencil.

86–7 '[a] far greater one than Donne'; the 'a' was later inserted in pencil in an unidentified hand.

89   'I believe that Jesuitism'; Jesuitism was consistently typed 'Jesuism' in the typescript, corrected in pencil throughout in an unidentified hand.

90   'my remarks on Donne *tel quel* to Browning'; the typescript incorrectly reads '*tels quels*'.

LECTURE III

97   'because [of] its meaning'; 'of' inserted in pencil in unidentified hand.

100   'the God, in short, of Mr. D. H. Lawrence'; 'in short' later cancelled in heavy pencil.

102   'Perhaps I should apologise . . . of Latin'; entire sentence later cancelled in heavy pencil.

103   'an allegory [which] causes no confusion'; words dropped or misread by the typist: typescript reads 'an allegory of the causes no confusion'; TSE later placed 'of the' in parenthesis, above which he inserted in pencil: '? which'.

104   'Incidentally . . . different things'; entire paragraph later cancelled in black ink.

     'of Cambridge, Massachusetts'; typescript reads 'of Cambridge Mass.', later cancelled in pencil.

109   'the violet would have to be imagined'; 'would have to' later cancelled and emended to 'must' in heavy pencil in TSE's hand.

111 'a mystes of Eleusis'; 'mystes' typed 'mustos', later emended to 'mustes'.
115 *'Donna è laggiù'*; later cancelled in black ink.

LECTURE IV

Pages 11–18 of the typescript (TSE's numbering 85–92) were mispunched (as was the carbon copy, which was repunched when received by his mother or brother); the top margins were consequently elevated 0.7 cm above the rest of the text in the original metal-clamp binder and were browned from exposure before being rebound. On the verso of page 20 (TSE's 94) are two columns of numbers in pencil in TSE's hand:

$$\begin{array}{c} 5.6 \\ 2.3 \\ \hline 7–9. \end{array}$$

122 'But in any case, the figure'; later partly cancelled and emended to read 'The figure' in heavy pencil.
123 'from *Antony and Cleopatra*'; spelled *'Anthony'* in the typescript.
125 'and our own precious wit'; 'precious' later cancelled in heavy pencil.
126–7 'an astounding simplicity and ingenuity'; last three letters of 'ingenuity' circled and queried '?' in pencil in unidentified hand; vertical pencil line-marker in right margin.

LECTURE V

Pages 9–22, through to page 1 of Lecture VI (TSE's 105–19), were mispunched, as in Lecture IV, and the protruding edges of the top margins were browned from exposure before being rebound.
142 'go [to] the formation'; 'to' inserted in pencil in an unidentified hand.
142–3 'a sharp-tongued satirist' (in quotation), followed by 'this sharp-fanged satirist'; 'tongued' and 'fanged' are circled and joined by a connecting line in pencil, with a question mark in the right margin in TSE's hand.
144 '("after gargling . . . by a liquid process of tuning")'; quotation misread and mistyped by the typist '("after gragling . . . by a bigger process of tuning")', corrected in ink in TSE's hand.
145 'though they have to the ear'; 'the' later cancelled in pencil and emended to 'our' in TSE's hand.
156 'requiring you see not a little'; 'you see' later cancelled in heavy pencil.

LECTURE VI

167 'this *substitution* of the divine passion'; the faulty construction in the text reads 'is this *substitution* . . .'
169 'the Italians [into] his language'; the typescript erroneously reads 'the Italians from his language'; 'from' has been cancelled and emended in pencil to 'into' in an unidentified hand.

LECTURE VII

187   'Would that his advice had been taken!'; later cancelled in heavy pencil.

188   'misinformation and cheap journalism'; later emended in pencil to read 'misinformation, ignorance and cheap journalism' in TSE's hand.

201   'This [has]'; typescript reads 'This is'.

202   'Wordsworth and Coleridge (Chamonix), in the last of whom'; words or phrase evidently dropped by the typist: typescript reads 'Wordsworth and Coleridge, Chamonix in the last of whom'. TSE later marked 'Chamonix' in parenthesis in ink for temporary clarification.

LECTURE VIII

209   'is, with the exception of Hawthorne and Henry James, who are almost equally unappreciated, although admired'; later cancelled in pencil.

216   'keep a place [for and] even enhance'; typist's error: typescript reads 'keep a place form even enhance'; 'form' was later circled in pencil and emended to read '? for and' in an unidentified hand.

220   'Humanity reaches its higher civilisation levels'; later emended in black ink in an unidentified hand to read 'Humanity reaches its higher levels of civilisation'.

223   'Donne does not "believe in" Anglican theology'; the typist typed 'Auguscan', corrected to 'Anglican' in black ink in TSE's hand.

On the verso of the penultimate page (20, TSE's 183), TSE later pencilled an outline of his proposed revision of the Lectures:

1. Introduction on the Definition of metaphysical poetry.
2. Donne & middle ages:
     a. Donne's supposed mediaevalism
     b. Contrast with Trecento
3. The Conceit in Donne
4. His longer poems.
5. The Religion of XVII Century.
        (D.' Relation to Elizabethan Drama?)
                           Chapman.
            Compare with
6. Crashaw.
7. A Note on Geo. Herbert
        Vaughan & Traherne
8. Cowley & the Transition
9. Summary & Comparison: XIX C.
        Appendix: the ultra-
           conceited: Cleveland
              and Benlowes.

On the verso of the final page (21, TSE's 184) there are three groups of lecture and page notes. The first group was evidently made by Herbert Read, as the page numbers for Lectures I and II, and possibly III, correspond to the queries and corrections made in his hand (see pp. 52, n. 18; 55, n. 27; 87, n. 55):

I p. 10, 14.

II p. 22

III p. 9

The second group is in TSE's hand, where he has made page notes on his theme of the disintegration of the intellect (see pp. 154–5, 158–9, 181, 186, 220, 223, 227):

"Disintegration"

V – 16, 17 & end   VIII. 14 &c

VI – 22

VII 2–3

The final entry is again in TSE's hand: a reference to his discussion of the fields of knowledge required of the literary critic (see p. 226):

VIII 19 as to the knowledge
         of the other studies required

THE CARBON COPY

The carbon copy (Houghton) of the Clark Lectures exists on unmarked paper (20.3 × 25.5 cm). A blank leaf of 'Plantagenet', used for the top copy, is inserted between lectures V and VI, with blank carbon leaves inserted between succeeding lectures. The copy has been numbered consecutively in pencil 1–188 in the lower left corner of each page, beginning with the title page but excluding the inserted blank leaves. Typographical errors have been corrected or marked in ink and in graphite and orange pencils by various hands, but there is insufficient evidence to determine whether TSE made any of the corrections before sending the copy to his mother. There are no textual or marginal comments by any reader, with the exception of one word, 'form', in an unidentified hand, to suggest a word dropped by the typist in Lecture II (p. 83, noted above).

The Turnbull Lectures

The typescripts of TSE's three Turnbull Lectures reflect the process of composition described in his letter to Harry Crosby of 8 September 1927: 'And of recent years I never have any manuscripts for the reason that I compose on the typewriter and the nearest approach to a manuscript I ever have is the first draft with pencil corrections' (L2). Unlike the fair copy of the Clark Lectures, these typescripts contain the characteristics of his first drafts: false starts; typeovers (xxxxx), with the emendation typed in the double-space above the line; slash-mark insertions typed above the line; slash-mark strikeouts of single letters, and no erasures. After completing the draft, he then pencilled in corrections, emendations, cancellations, and insertions. The printed text includes the revisions made before the lectures were delivered; the textual notes record the substantive typeovers and pencilled emendations of the composition process. Some passages in each typescript were typed directly from the top copy of the Clark Lectures, with errors and mistranscriptions carried forward.

The Turnbull Lectures were typed on 'Hammermill Bond / Made in USA' (21.7 × 28.0 cm), with the exception of the last page (15) of lecture III, which was typed on the verso, upside-down, of TSE's personal Eliot House stationery (also Hammermill Bond, 21.7 × 28.0 cm).

The illustration based on Theresa Garrett Eliot's drawing of TSE was published in the *Chicago Daily Tribune* (2 December 1933, p. 12). The drawing was made not from life, as the caption asserts, but from a photograph taken at Mountain View House, Randolph, New Hampshire, in June 1933, reproduced in Gordon, *Eliot's New Life*, facing p. 21. Though the original drawing has not been traced, Donald Gallup has a positive photostat (23.5 × 21.0 cm) of the original, which was evidently drawn on a leaf punched for a notebook. The artist presented another, larger drawing (49.0 × 37.5 cm; signed 'T. Garrett /33') from the photograph to Donald Gallup on 9 April 1949.

LECTURE I

249   The first page is inscribed above the title in pencil in TSE's hand: '*FVM* Definitely *not* for publication but for your amusement'.

251   'Lucretius, Dante and Goethe'; 'Virgil' typed over before 'Goethe'.

252   'And we must not include *all* great poetry'; 'great' above typeover 'good'.

253   'he makes succinctly'; 'he' inserted in TSE's hand in pencil.

254   'dont le sonnet [et] la canzone'; a linguistic slip: typescript reads 'dont le sonnet and la canzone'.

255   'Richard and Hugh of St. Victor'; 'Hugh' in TSE's hand above 'Adam', cancelled in pencil. Adam of St. Victor was evidently on TSE's mind, as he was to appear in the final Norton Lecture: 'the poetry of Villon is just as "Christian" in this way as that of Prudentius or Adam of St. Victor' (*UPUC* 136/129).

256   'Florence in the thirteenth century'; 'thirteenth' preceded by typeover 'twelfth'.

        'Dante, as you will have become aware,'; 'become aware' over typeover 'divined'.

258   'Now Cardinal Bellarmine'; 'This' cancelled and emended in pencil to 'Now'.

261   'the sectarian diplomacy'; 'sectarian' above typeover 'theological'.

262   'we often perceive his attention'; 'attention' preceded by typeover 'mind'.

LECTURE II

266   'some Spanish poetry of the age of Donne'; 'age' preceded by typeover 'seventeenth'.

268   'he is occupied with fanciful consequences of the first assumption'; 'fanciful' above typeover 'imaginary', 'assumption' preceded by typeover 'statement'.

        'What I wish'; preceded by typeover false start: 'The irony'.

269   'or perhaps swells like a wave'; in TSE's hand in top margin, with a pencilled line for insertion.

'as a critic like . . . Jeffrey might put it'; spelled 'Jeffries' in the typescript.

272 'The Elizabethan lyric had been'; 'had been' in TSE's hand over 'was', cancelled in pencil.

274 'for his statement'; 'statement' above typeover 'line'.
'Ma fa la sua virtú 'n vizio cadere'; circled in pencil.

275 '(she would have made a great'; 'made' in TSE's hand above 'been', cancelled in pencil.

276 'We may say, as a parallel . . . and Mr. Aldous Huxley.'; followed by a sentence cancelled in pencil: 'There have not been many voluptuaries of religious emotion in the same period.'.

LECTURE III

283 'psycho-analysis'; spelled with hyphen by TSE.

284 'the musical dramas of Wagner'; 'musical dramas' preceded by typeover 'operas'.

285 'some way of salvation'; 'salvation' above typeover 'life'.
'pseudo-Buddhism that'; 'that' in TSE's hand over 'which', cancelled in pencil.

287 'In this very cursory survey'; 'cursory' preceded by typeover 'rapid'.
'unsuitable to be a critic'; 'to be' in TSE's hand over 'as', cancelled in pencil.
'their importance for the present'; corrected slip: text reads 'presence'.

288 'or real values are revealed'; 'or' in TSE's hand over 'and', cancelled in pencil.
'but he speaks in parables.'; Frank Morley (FVM) has written '(Expand' in the right margin, with a wavy vertical line in pencil to indicate the preceding and succeeding sentences.
'he is, at bottom,'; FVM has circled 'at bottom,' with a pencilled line to the right margin: '? long way down v. Arnold'.
'The artist is the only'; FVM has circled 'artist', with a pencilled line to the right margin: 'don't see why you say the "artist" is the only. I don't agree'; he has circled 'the only', with a pencilled line to the right margin: 'Sometimes'.
'The artist, being always alone, being heterodox'; FVM has re-cast the first part of this sentence in pencil between the lines: 'When' [false start] 'The artist is always alone, and being an artist can persuade to etc'.

289 'bring humanity back to the real.'; at the end of this paragraph FVM has pencilled a bracketed note in the right margin: '[you oughtnt to mislead me old collegians FVM]'.
'outside of abilities and genius . . . responsible for greatness'; 'abilities' preceded by 'his own', cancelled in pencil; 'greatness' preceded by 'that', cancelled in pencil.

290 'Dante deserves say ten pages, Donne one'; 'one' in TSE's hand above 'three', cancelled in pencil.
'If I were a confessor of souls, would I give them that'; 'were' in TSE's hand above 'was', cancelled in pencil; 'souls' above typeover 'human beings'; 'that' above typeover 'the'.

291 'Dryden and Johnson preferred his poetry'; 'preferred' over typeover 'liked'.

292 'and we are not ordinarily concerned'; 'and' over typeover 'only'.
'in whose *Exercises* . . . himself'; 'in' inserted in TSE's hand; 'in' following 'himself' cancelled in pencil.

294 'some reformers are'; in TSE's hand over 'Lady Russell is', cancelled in pencil.
'because for instance the feelings of lovers'; 'for instance' inserted in TSE's hand in pencil.

295 'A philosophy which lays under cultivation only'; 'under cultivation only' above typeover 'emphasis only upon'.

APPENDIX I

French translation of Clark Lecture III

An edited version of Lecture III was translated into French by Jean André Moise de Menasce (1902–73) and published as 'Deux Attitudes Mystiques: Dante et Donne' in *Le Roseau D'Or* (Paris, 14 [1927], pp. 149–73). Born and educated in Alexandria, Menasce took his BA at Balliol College, Oxford, in 1924, and subsequently took a *Licence ès-Lettres* at the Sorbonne. In Paris, he was associated with the avant-garde periodicals *Commerce* and *Esprit* and translated several of Eliot's poems for French publications from 1926 to 1947. His translation of *The Waste Land* (*La Terre Mis à Nu*) was marked 'revue et approuvée par l'auteur', and as Eliot's most frequent translator in the 1920s he was largely responsible for making Eliot's poetry known in France as his reputation increased. A Catholic convert, Menasce joined the Dominican Order, French Province, and became an ordained priest in 1935.

For the following translation, Menasce worked from a shortened typescript, now lost. Eliot dropped the two opening paragraphs, deleted several sentences and paragraphs from the body of the text, and wrote an entirely new conclusion. Menasce returned the translation to Eliot from Alexandria on 15 October 1926, describing his few emendations in a cover letter (MS VE): the addition of a bibliographical note (see p. 313, n. 3); the reversal of sentence order on p. 312, where, after several paragraphs had been deleted between them (from p. 104 'In passing' to p. 106 'such prose as that of Richard of St. Victor'), the revised sentence beginning 'Elle pourrait servir' is made to precede that beginning 'Je note aussi' ('I find the present order more adequate and have ventured to introduce this change subject to your approval'); and the deletion of one sentence on page 6 of the missing typescript, evidently (see p. 100)'There is always some type of mysticism about' ('The sentence is explained by the lecture-context and clashes with the title of the essay as published separately'). Eliot's personal copy (Texas) of the printed translation, signed 'T. S. Eliot 1927' on the title page, is otherwise unmarked.

Deux Attitudes Mystiques: Dante et Donne

L'enrichissement de l'expérience humaine par la poésie peut s'accomplir selon deux modes, selon que la poésie perçoit et enregistre fidèlement l'univers de la pensée et du coeur, tel qu'il es présente à un moment donné, ou selon qu'elle en accroît le domaine. Le premier de ces modes (premier dans l'ordre chronologique, et je ne dis pas qu'il ne soit pas le premier dans l'order de la valeur) est celui de la poésie d'Homère. Un univers nouveau, plus vaste et plus élevé, comme celui de Dante, exige une base ferme à même le vieux monde visible; il ne descend pas des hauteurs comme l'échelle de Jacob. Entre les poètes qui ont procédé à cette expansion de la réalité – et j'avoue que ce sont ceux qui m'intéressent le plus – le plus grand me paraît être incontestablement Dante, dans l'ordre absolu, et Baudelaire dans les temps modernes. Quant à ceux qui ont présenté la réalité telle qu'elle est, il me paraît bien difficile, pour certaines raisons, de leur assigner des rangs; je n'hésiterais pas à mentionner Homère – même l'Homère de l'*Odyssée* – Catulle et Chaucer. Mais, comme toujours en critique, il importe de distinguer, lors même qu'on ne peut disséquer. On peut presque toujours considérer un poète sous des aspects contraires; tout poète participe, peut-être, des deux. Il est un poésie mixte, comme il est une poésie impure; car il ne faut pas confondre fusion et confusion.

Cette parenthèse tend avant tout à répondre à un préjugé qui domine l'étude de la poésie métaphysique de Dante et de son époque, et qui consiste à n'envisager toute cette littérature (la *Vita Nuova*, les sonnets, *canzone* et ballades des deux Guido) que comme pur jeu et pure fantaisie. Bien des gens n'admettent pas que c'est là le fond de leur pensée; mais il en est tant qui ont lu, et mal lu, l'épisode de Paolo et Francesca, et si peu qui aient lu, et bien lu, le *Paradis*, que cette attitude est peut-être celle de la majorité. J'entends montrer que cette poésie n'est nullement l'aimable divertissement d'une époque primitive, pré-raphaélitique, adonnée aux visions et aux processions célestes à la Benozzo Gozzoli, mais l'oeuvre d'hommes qui savaient à la fois penser et sentir clairement et dépasser les limites ordinaires de l'esprit. Hommes d'une haute formation intellectuelle, le pied solidement posé sur le sol quelque peu fangeux des intrigues politiques, des amours et des guerres de condottières, ils représentent, en un mot, une civilisation souvent supérieure à la nôtre, supérieure aussi à la civilisation du monde de Donne. Leur syntaxe et leur vocabulaire font foi de leur supériorité: car on ne vit guère sur un plan élevé quand on se livre au verbalisme.

Une des meilleures vulgarisations de la *Vita Nuova* est la plaquette de Remy de Gourmont intitulée *Dante, Béatrice et la Poésie amoureuse*. Gourmont s'y applique à montrer que la Béatrice de Dante n'est définitive qu'une construction, lors même que son nom n'aurait pas été choisi tout exprès pour le sens qu'il renferme. Argument propre à convaincre pleinement tous ceux pour qui la *Vita Nuova* est le récit fidèle d'une ancienne passion; mais je ne sache pas qu'un lecteur intelligent en ait jamais douté. Gourmont en souligne l'arbitraire et le symbolisme chronologique, et, à l'appui, compare la vision de Dante à d'autres visions de la littérature apocalyptique, entre autres au *Pasteur d'Hermas*. Mais Gourmont ne doit jamais être accepté sans réserves. Ce critique de talent n'était pas philosophe; et, n'étant pas philosophe, nourrissait quantité de préjugés philosophiques, notamment sur l'amour. Sa brochure pourrait nous faire accroire que la *Vita Nuova* n'est qu'une sèche allégorie, privée de toute vie. Il n'en est rien. A mon avis, la *Vita Nuova* rapporte une actualité vécue, moulée dans une forme particulière. Cela ne saurait se démontrer: il s'agit là d'un domaine de l'expérience particulier à une certaine catégorie d'esprits et que les êtres de cette nature reconnaissent immédiatement.

Ainsi, les émotions et les sentiments que Dante raconte avoir éprouvés à l'âge de neuf ans n'ont rien d'invraisemblable; ils pourraient même remonter à un âge plus tendre,[1] ce qui n'implique pas qu'un enfant de neuf ans est capable de les exprimer d'une manière aussi consciente. Je fais sa part à l'allégorie: ce n'est peut-être que le mode d'expression d'un esprit passionnément attaché à la recherche, dans l'univers, d'un ordre et d'un sens qu'il trouve, ou impose, d'une manière qui n'est plus la nôtre.

Le changement si profond et, semble-t-il, si brusque, de l'esprit provençal à l'esprit du *trecento* tel qu'il se révèle dans la *Vita Nuova*, a des causes si obscures que la plupart des historiens se bornent à le relever sans en donner une explication. Aussi est-ce avec beaucoup de circonspection que je hasarde l'hypothèse que les poètes du *trecento* participent au grand courant de la pensée européenne de leur temps alors que les Provençaux n'y participent pas. On est autorisé à croire que la meilleure noblesse provençale jouissait d'une culture d'un niveau très élevé, plus élevé sans doute que le reste de l'Europe à la même époque; et, d'ailleurs, une noblesse qui lit Ovide et Virgile est toujours digne de respect. Mais il semble bien que cette culture ait été toute classique, qu'elle ait eu pour base tous les classiques latins connus à cette époque. Il s'agit donc d'une petite renaissance latine au douzième siècle. Mais la source vive de la pensée de ce temps partait de L'Eglise; et c'est peut-être aux hérésies qui y florissaient que la Provence a dû d'être isolée du reste du l'Europe. La génération de Dante était nourrie d'une culture classique *médiévale*; et il suffit d'avoir abordé le latin du douzième et du treizième siècle pour voir dans ce fait l'origine de ce goût des idées, de cette subtilité dialectique, de cette intensité de pensée, de cette expression claire et précise.

Il est une mystique religieuse qui avait déjà trouvé à s'exprimer au douzième siècle, et qui fait corps avec le système que saint Thomas d'Aquin a formulé au treizième. Son point de départ est dans la *Métaphysique* d'Aristote (1072 B. et *passim*), dans l'*Ethique à Nicomaque*, et c'est l'inverse du bergsonisme. L'absolu de Bergson s'obtient, on le sait, en remontant le cours de la pensée, par un dépouillement spirituel de tout l'appareil de la distinction et de l'analyse, par un plongeon dans le courant de l'expérience immédiate. Au douziéme siècle, la vision divine, ou joussance de Dieu, exigeait un processus auquel l'intelligence devait participer; l'homme n'atteignait à la béatitude qu'à travers, par, et par delà la pensée discursive. Telle est la mystique de l'époque de Dante. Elle paraît très différente de la mystique de saint Ignace de Loyola, de sainte Thérèse et de saint Jean de la Croix.

L'examen de cette mystique du douzième siècle va nous permettre de distinguer certaines variétés de mystique qui faciliteront une confrontation de la *Vita Nuova* de Dante avec l'*Extase* de John Donne.

Richard de Saint-Victor est un des mystiques les plus intéressants du douzième siècle, et son cas éclaire Dante d'un jour considérable. Richard, comme le grand philosophe Hugues de Saint-Victor, était un Ecossais qui était devenu abbé du monastère de Saint-Victor. Ses oeuvres, assez volumineuses, occupent une bonne partie d'un volume de la Patrologie de Migne; mais elles paraissent peu connues, et j'avoue que je n'en connais moi-même qu'une partie. La plus intéressante pour nous

---

1—Je pense même, avec le psychologue, I. A. Richards, que cet ordre d'expérience est plus repandu à l'âge de quatre ou cinq ans.

est son *De Gratia Contemplationis*, qu'on désigne sous le nom de *Benjamin Mineur*. C'est un traité des opérations et des étapes de l'âme dans son progrès vers la vision béatifique. Il présente une analogie, d'ailleurs tout extérieure, avec les classifications de certaines mystiques hindoues. On y note aussi un ton aussi résolument impersonnel que celui d'un manuel d'hygiène, et l'absence de toute indication biographique, de toute apparence de sentiment ou d'émotion: cela suffit déjà à le distinguer des écrits des mystiques espagnols du seizième siècle. On conviendra enfin qu'il est écrit dans un style clair, simple et concis, si toutefois l'on veut bien admettre un latinité qui ne soit ni celle de Cicéron, ni celle de Tacite, ni celle de Pétrone. J'en cite un passage où il cherche à distinguer les trois étapes du progrès de l'esprit: la cogitation, la méditation, la contemplation:

Cogitatio per devia quæque lento pede, sine respectu perventionis, passim huc illucque vagatur. Meditatio per ardua sæpe et aspera ad directionis finem cum magna animi industria nititur. Contemplatio libero volatu quocumque eam fert impetus mira agilitate circumfertur. Cogitatio serpit, meditatio incedit, et tumultum currit. Contemplatio autem omnia circumvolat, et cum voluerit se in summis librat. Cogitatio est sine labore et fructu. In meditatione est labor cum fructu. Cogitatione permanet sine labore cum fructu. In cogitatione evagatio, in meditatione investigatio, in contemplatione admiratio. *Ex imaginatione, cogitatio, ex ratione meditatio, ex intelligentia, contemplatio. Ecce tria ista, imaginatio, ratio, intelligentia. Intelligentia obtinet supremum locum, imaginatio infimum, ratio medium. Omnia quæ subjacent sensui inferiori, necesse est ea etiam subjacere sensui superiore. Unde constat quia cuncta quæ comprehenduntur ab imaginatione, ea etiam aliaque multa quæ supra jam sunt comprehendi a ratione. Similiter ea quæ imaginatio vel ratio comprehendunt, sub intelligentia cadunt, et ea etiam quæ illæ comprehendere non possunt. Vide ergo contemplationis radius, quam late se expandat, qui omnia lustrat.*

Style monotone et diffus, semble-t-il; on voit bientôt cependant, que chaque phrase explicite quelque peu celle qui la précède, et qu'il n'y a pas un mot de trop. En outre, Richard est très avare de tropes et de métaphores, et son traité comporte une allégorie unique qui est une comparaison entre les étapes de l'esprit et les parties de l'Arche de l'Alliance, allégorie qui n'a rien de déconcertant. Sa prose me paraît répondre aux canons essentials du style: il écrit ce qu'il pense dans les termes mêmes qui servent à le penser, sans enjolivement, métaphores ou figures, et en faisant abstraction de tout sentiment (car le sentiment, s'il est assez fort, se fera jour de toute façon; et, sinon, n'est pas à sa place). Elle pourrait servir de modèle de style aux écrivains anglais, au même titre, à mon avis, qu'Aristote, *The Drapier's Letters* de Swift, *The Principles of Logic* de F. H. Bradley et le premier volume des *Principia Mathematica* de Bertrand Russell.

Je note aussi que la méthode et l'intention sont, en somme, les mêmes chez lui que chez saint Thomas et chez Dante: la contemplation divine, la sublimation et la subordination de l'émotion et du sentiment par l'intelligence dans la vision de Dieu. Saint Thomas dit en effect: 'Il apparaît clairement que la vision divine donne seule aux êtres intelligents la véritable félicité.'

Mais je ne m'occupe pas de l'influence de Richard de Saint-Victor sur Dante, encore que celui-ci parle de lui, dans une de ses lettres, comme d'un auteur qu'il connaît bien, et le place au Paradis. Je n'ai voulu, en le citant, que donner un spécimen de la pensée et du style qui ont contribué à la formation de la pensée et du style de Dante.

Gourmont note dans sa plaquette que, chez les *trecentisti*, l'amour n'implique point l'idée de possession; et, pour hasardée que soit cette généralisation, il est exact de dire que les *trecentisti* se soucient plus de la contemplation de l'object aimé que des sentiments et des sensations d'union; ce qu'ils rapportent, ce sont les sensations et les sentiments de l'amant qui contemple l'object de son amour.

> *Chi e questa che vien, ch'ogni uom la mira,*
> *Che fa tremar di claritate l'aere?*[2]

dit Cavalcanti dans son célèbre sonnet; et on constatera que ce vers n'est pas qu'une flatteuse hyperbole, mais la notation exacte de l'impression visuelle de l'être aimé sur l'amant. Ce fait est très significatif. Dans leurs meilleurs vers d'amour, Dante, Guinizelli, Cavalcanti et Cino ne se bornent jamais à faire acte de courtoisie ou d'hommage, à décrire l'object de leur amour, ou à noter complaisamment leurs émotions et leurs sensations, mais ils cherchent à suggérer la beauté et la dignité de l'objet contemplé en rapportant l'effet sur l'amant en contemplation. Nous allons voir que cette attitude est plus éloignée de celle de Donne et de Lord Herbert de Cherbury que de celle des Provençaux.

Cette différence n'est pas de celles que peut expliquer la biographie concrète de nos deux poètes; puisque aussi bien Donne est, en quelque sorte, le poète de l'amour conjugal, au même titre qu'un Coventry Patmore, tandis qu'à cet égard la vie de Dante est plutôt irrégulière. Mais la vie intérieure de Dante, plus vaste que celle de Donne, a atteint par ailleurs à une élévation de sentiment que celui-ci n'a pas connue.

Analysons l'*Extase* de Donne[3] et l'*Ode* de Lord Herbert de Cherbury.

> Sur la rive enceinte qui s'enfle
> Comme un oreiller sur un lit,
> Appui du chef penchant de la violette,
> Nous étions assis, deux amants.

C'est ainsi qu'un des plus beaux poèmes de Donne, qui est aussi un des plus beaux poèmes qui soient, s'ouvre par un des plus facheux mélanges de comparaisons.

Il n'est ni édifant ni particulièrement utile de comparer une rive à un oreiller, et il est bien inutile d'ajouter: sur un lit, car il est raisonnable d'admettre qu'un oreiller a

---

2–*Variante*: Che fa di clarita l'aer tremare.

3–On possède déjà deux versions françaises de l'*Extase* de JOHN DONNE (1573–1631), poème intraduisible entre tous: l'une de Miss RAMSAY, dans sa thèse intitulée *Les Idées Médiévales chez John Donne*. (Oxford, 1918, 2ᵉ édit. Paris, 1924); l'autre du présent traducteur, a été publiée, avec quelques autres traductions de DONNE, dans la *Nouvelle Revue Française* (avril 1923). C'est cette version qui est ici reproduite en partie, avec d'importantes modifications inspirées par le désir de serrer le texte de plus près. D'autres traductions de Donne ont été données par M. A. MOREL (*Le Navire d'Argent*, N° I), M. KOSZUL (dans son *Anthologie de la Littérature Anglaise*), et M. EMILE LEGOUIS (*Dans les Sentiers de la Renaissance Anglaise*). (Note de Traducteur.)

toujours la même forme. D'autre part la comparaison vient se heurter à une métaphore; la rive est enceinte; nous savions déjà que la rive avait la forme d'un oreiller, aussi n'avions-nous nul besoin de savoir qu'elle était enceinte, à moins que cet état n'ait été dû à un tremblement de terre, ce qui n'est pas le cas. Je m'abstiens d'apprécier la beauté des métaphores obstétriques en général: elles sont du goût de l'époque, qui n'est plus le nôtre. La rive enceinte s'enfle, et c'est précisément ce qu'elle ne doit pas faire, puisque toute la scène qui suit est donnée comme *statique*, sans quoi ce ne serait plus une extase. On nous dit maintenant pourquoi la rive s'est enflée: c'est pour servir d'appui au chef penchant de la violette. Mais cette attention délicate ne s'explique qui si la violette pousse à côté et non pas sur la rive; et, si cette rive ne s'est enflée que juste ce qu'il faut pour servir d'appui à sa tête, elle ne mérite guère le nom de rive. Enfin, c'est violer l'ordre de la nature que de nous faire accroire que la violette est antécédente à la rive, à moins d'admettre que la cause finale des rives est de servir d'appui aux violettes.

En somme, quatre lignes ont été gâchées pour nous faire savoir que les amants étaient assis sur la rive.

> Nos mains fortement cimentées
> Par un suc ferme qui provenait d'elles,
> Nos regards s'entrelaçaient, et enfilaient
> Nos yeux sur un même fil double

Voilà bien cette insistance, cette tendance à impressionner plutôt qu'à décrire, qui est la malédiction du dix-septième siècle, en Angleterre comme ailleurs. Les deux premiers vers sont plausibles, parce que l'on conçoit que les amants sentent comme un lien matériel entre leurs mains: ce serait donc comme la description d'une sensation. Quant à l'image des yeux enfilés comme des boutons sur un fil double partant de chaque oeil, elle ne rend nullement le sentiment d'extase d'amants qui se perdent dans leurs regards, et ajoute à la difficulté de comprendre ce dont il est question.

> Nos mains, ainsi entregreffées
> Faisaient notre seule union,
> Et les images procréées dans nos regards,
> Notre seule reproduction.

Cette strophe pèche tout d'abord en ce que l'image des mains cimentées, au lieu d'être isolée pâlit devant l'image plus complexe de la greffe; d'autre part, la procréation des images est une métaphore contre nature; enfin, le poète ne parvient pas à s'en tenir à l'extase et tend même à comparer cet état à l'union physique ordinaire.

> Comme entre deux armées égales
> Le sort suspend l'incertaine victoire,
> Nos âmes en reconnaissance
> Flottaient entre elle et moi.

L'intention de cette belle image n'est pas claire, en dépit du sentiment de frémissement et de suspens qu'elle communique. Je ne crois pas que le poète envisage un combat entre l'homme et la femme ou entre l'âme et le corps; mais il n'est pas d'autre interprétation, et celle-là semble confirmée par la strophe suivante.

> Et cependant que nos âmes négociaient,
> Nous sommes demeurés comme des statues funéraires:
> Tout le jour, notre pose fut la même,
> Et nous n'avons rien dit tout le jour.

Cette strophe m'a toujours paru singulièrement harmonieuse. Rien de plus heureux que l'usage du mot "négocier", ou que l'image des statues funéraires; et le "tout le jour" du début du troisième vers, auquel répond le "tout le jour" de la fin du quatrième vers, est une véritable trouvaille euphonique qui contribue à faire de cette strophe un des plus parfaits quatrains du genre que je connaisse. De même la simplicité *presque* affectée de "et nous n'avons rien dit", si caractéristique de Donne est une perfection. Les strophes qui suivent exhibent ce jeu de l'idée, cette manipulation de curiosité complaisante, qui est le fort de Donne et de son école. Elles nous mènent à l'introduction d'une idée nouvelle et très importante.

> Quand ainsi l'amour de deux âmes
> Les fait ainsi s'entr'animer,
> L'âme plus haute qui naît d'elles
> Remédie à sa solitude.

Donne s'avise parfois, avec beaucoup de succès, de placer un mot latin assez lourd et plus ou moins philosophique, parmi des mots saxons très simples. L'idée de ce quatrain est, peut-être, la clef de voûte de tout l'édifice: idée qui a pu lui être suggérée par le *Banquet* de Platon; l'isolement de l'âme, sa quête des rares moments où elle semble se fondre avec une autre âme. Et c'est là un sentiment auquel l'ancienne poésie amoureuse italienne ne présente rien d'analogue. Je doute même que, d'un point de vue strictement orthodoxe – et je n'ai à cet égard aucune competence – ou même du point de vue d'un mystagogue d'Eleusis, l'union de deux âmes humaines soit intelligible. Il n'en demeure pas moins que c'est là le thème fondamental de la littérature amoureuse des trois derniers siècles.

Cette idée si étrange et peut-être même hérétique, du point de vue du treizième siècle, est le prélude naturel au thème de la suite du poème.

> Mais, hélas, pour un temps si long,
> Pourquoi délaissons-nous nos corps?
> Ils sont nôtres sans êtres nous.
> Nous sommes les intelligences; ce n'en sont que les sphères.

> . . .

> Aussi doit s'incliner l'âme des purs amants
> Aux passions et aux affections
> Que le sens atteint et comprend:
> Autrement un grand Prince dépérit en prison.

> Alors c'est à nos corps que nous nous adressons
> Où les faibles pourront voir Amour révélé;

Les mystères d'Amour grandissent dans les âmes,
Mais le corps est son livre.

Et si quelque amant comme nous
A pu entendre ce dialogue d'un seul être,
Son attente sera déçue, car il ne verra guère plus
Quand nous serons devenus corps.

Ce qui nous est donné ici, de toute évidence, c'est une dissociation, une disjonction entre l'âme et le corps, que le *trecento* n'a, je pense, jamais exprimée et à laquelle vient s'opposer l'autorité de saint Thomas. Voyons d'abord ce que dirait saint Thomas de l'idée d'une fusion de deux âmes appartenant à des corps distincts. A la suite d'une réfutation de saint Augustin, où il invoque l'autorité du *De Anima*. il conclut:

"Comme il est impossible que plusieurs êtres numériquement distincts n'aient qu'une seule forme, aussi bien qu'il est impossible qu'ils n'aient qu'un seul et même être, il faut que le principe intellectif se multiplie suivant le nombre des corps."[4]

Et, de la différence de l'âme et du corps, il dit:

"L'âme diffère extrêmement du corps, si l'on considère séparément leur nature; si donc ils avaient une existence distincte et séparée, il faudrait une infinité de moyens pour les réunir. Mais en tant que l'âme est la forme du corps, elle n'a pas son *être* séparément de l'être du corps; c'est par son *être* au contraire qu'elle est unie au corps d'une manière immédiate. Il en est de même d'une forme quelconque, considérée comme acte; elle est extrêmement distante de la matière qui n'est un être qu'en puissance."[5]

Saint Thomas cherche évidemment à concilier les nécessités théologiques de sa théorie de l'âme avec la doctrine aristotélicienne, mais, même a défaut de cette préoccupation, il n'aurait jamais admis la possibilité de cette dissociation, qu'implique le poème de Donne, de l'animal humain en deux entités: l'âme et le corps, qui ne se distinguent qu'en ce que l'une est admirable et l'autre quelque peu honteuse. Mais saint Thomas ne nous intéresse ici que par rapport aux *trecentisti*, et je le répète, on ne trouve pas chez eux ombre de dualisme. Ils ne font de différence qu'entre le supérieur et l'inférieur, l'amour plus digne et l'amour moins digne: différence que Dante et ses amis sentaient et concevaient avec toute la plénitude de leur expérience.

---

4 — *Cum impossibile sit plurium numero differentium esse unam formam, sicut impossibile est quod eorum sit unum esse; oportet principium intellectivum multiplicari secundum multiplicationem corporum.* [Summa Theologica. Qu. LXXVI. Art. II]
5 — *Anima distat a corpore plurimum, si utriusque conditiones seorsim considerentur; unde si utrumque ipsorum separatim esse haberet, oporteret quod multa media intervenirent. Sed in quantum anima est forma corporis, non habet esse seorsim ab esse corporis, sed per suum esse corpori unitur immediate. Sic enim et quælibet forma, si consideretur ut actus; habet magnam distantiam a materia, quæ est ens in potentia tantum.* [Ibid. Art. VII.]

Ils n'imaginaient point de combat du corps et de l'âme, mais un effort identique des deux vers la perfection.

Ce dualisme de l'âme et du corps est une idée moderne: la seule analogie antique qui me vient à l'esprit serait l'attitude de Plotin d'après Porphyre. Mais, dans la forme qu'il prend chez Donne, il représente même un moment de la pensée philosophique bien plus grossier que celui de la pensée de saint Thomas. En réalité, la prétendue glorification du corps que tant d'admirateurs de Donne croient trouver chez lui se ramène à l'attitude des puritains. Et l'idée d'une extase d'union entre deux âmes est à la fois grossière, philosophiquement parlant, et étroite au point de vue affectif. L'idée de l'amour-contemplation, plus aristotélicienne, est aussi plus platonicienne, car c'est à la contemplation de l'absolute beauté et de l'absolute bonté que permet d'atteindre l'object humain, limité mais digne d'amour. Que pense Donne? L'extase est une union complète, et, en définitive, comme ils ne cherchent rien qui soit hors d'eux-mêmes, les deux êtres humains se maintiennent dans sa jouissansce. Mais le sentiment ne saurait se maintenir: pour ne pas déperir, il doit se depasser. Moderne, Donne est prisonnier de l'étreinte de ses propres sentiments. Aucun signe chez lui, ou presque, d'adoration. Et voici l'alternative qui s'offre à lui et à ses successeurs: le bon mariage à la Tennyson, qui n'est pas si différent du mariage même de Donne, et qui est une espèce de faillite; ou bien la débâcle du héros de *En Route*: "Mon Dieu, que c'est donc bête!" On retrouve en fin de compte le thème fondamental de la littérature moderne: il importe peu, en effet, que ce soit dans l'adultère et la débauche ou dans le mariage qu l'on cherche l'absolu: ce n'est pas là qu'il faut le chercher.

Cette même recherche du permanent dans la fixation de l'éphémère est reprise d'une façon admirable dans l'*Ode* d'un contemporain de Donne, Lord Herbert de Cherbury. Il m'arrive parfois de trouver cette *Ode* plus belle que l'*Extase* de Donne, quand elle me prend au dépourvu; quand j'y réfléchis je trouve plus de substance, plus de solidité, plus de perfection technique, et aussi plus de défauts impardonnables dans le poème de Donne. C'est le même cri:

> O vous où il est dit que les âmes demeurent
> Avant que de descendre en de célestes flammes,
> Votre graine immortelle mettra-t-elle sa grâce
> Sur la concupiscence et la chair du désir?

> Et notre amour si transcendant
> Au désir vil et moribond,
> Uni par de si chastes liens,
> N'est-il pas à jamais noué?

> . . .

> Car si les esprits imparfaits
> Font d'Amour ici-bas le terme de Sagesse,
> Quelle perfection n'attend pas notre amour
> Au jour où l'imparfait lui-même est purifié!

Et, en regard, je place un passage de la *Vita Nuova* (XVIII):

Certaines dames s'étaient réunies pour jouir d'une mutuelle compagnie. L'une d'elles, tournant son regard vers moi, et m'appelant par mon nom, me dit ces mots: "A quelle fin aimes-tu ta Dame, puisque tu n'en peux soutenir la présence? Dis-le-nous, car la fin d'un tel amour est, certes, digne d'être connue." Lors je leur dis ces mots: "Dames, la fin de mon amour n'a jamais été que le salut de la dame dont j'imagine que vous parlez, et c'est en cela qu'est toute la béatitude qui est la fin de tous mes désirs. Et puisqu'il lui a plu de me le refuser, mon seigneur Amour, dans sa miséricorde, a placé toute ma béatitude en un lieu où elle ne saurait m'abondonner." Alors ces dames commencèrent à parler entre elles, et comme j'ai vu tomber la belle neige parmi la pluie, ainsi il me semblait que leurs paroles étaient mêlées de soupirs. Et, après avoir conversé entre elles, celle qui m'avait parlé la première me dit ces mots: "Nous te prions de nous apprendre le lieu de cette béatitude." Et, en réponse, je dis seulement: "Elle réside en toute parole à la louange de ma dame."

En résumé j'ai cherché à poser le rapport entre la mystique de Richard de Saint-Victor et le poésie de Dante d'une part, et, de l'autre, la mystique du seizième siècle et la poésie de John Donne; et à indiquer que, de Dante à Donne, il y a une différence dans la conception de l'âme et du corps, qui correspond à une différence entre les philosophies des deux époques.[6]

6—Editor's note: This summary paragraph replaces the concluding and transition paragraphs of the original lecture (see pp. 116–17). *Translation*: In conclusion I have tried to give some idea of the rapport between the mysticism of Richard of Saint-Victor and the poetry of Dante on the one hand, and, on the other, the mysticism of the sixteenth century and the poetry of John Donne; and to indicate that, from Dante to Donne, there is a difference in the conception of the soul and the body, which corresponds to a difference between the philosophies of the two epochs.

APPENDIX II

Clark Lecturers

From Leslie Stephen in 1884 to T. S. Eliot in 1926, and from E. M. Forster in 1927 to Bernard Williams in 1993, the Clark Lectures at Trinity College may be the most prestigious lecture series continuous today from the late nineteenth century. The lecturers and their subjects virtually constitute an historical map of literary criticism and canon formation in the twentieth century.

1884   Leslie Stephen, 'Addison and Pope'
        [From 1885 to 1897 Lecturers were elected for a three-year period and could be re-elected; they were required to deliver twelve lectures each year over at least two terms.]

1885–9 Edmund Gosse – 1st series: 'English Prose in the Middle of the Eighteenth Century (1730–70)'; 2nd series: 'The Critical Literature of the Age of Anne'; 3rd series: 'The Development of Naturalism in English Poetry from 1780 to 1820'; selections published in *From Shakespeare to Pope* (1895)

1890–93 John Wesley Hales – 1st series: 'Spenser and Shakespeare'; 2nd series: 'Shakespeare's Tragedies'; 3rd series: 'Milton'; one lecture, 'Milton's Macbeth', published in *Folia Litteraria* (1893)

1893–6 Edward Dowden – 1st series: 'Latin, Greek and the Claims of Philology on English Literature'; 2nd series: 'The Influence of the French Revolution on English Literature'; 3rd series: 'The Effects of Puritanism on Literature'

1897   Duncan Crookes Tovey – 1st series: 'The Structure of Shakespeare's Plays'; 2nd series: '*Hamlet* and the Text of Shakespeare'; 3rd series: 'Some English Historical Plays of Shakespeare'

1898   Walter Raleigh – 1st series: 'English Letter Writers, 16th to 19th Centuries'; 2nd series: 'Courtesy Literature, 16th to 18th Centuries'; 3rd series: *Milton* (1900)

1899   H. C. Beeching – 1st series: 'The Study of Poetry'; partly in *Two*

	Lectures: Introductory to the Study of Poetry (1901); 2nd series: 'The History of Lyrical Poetry in England'
1900	Alfred Ainger – 1st series: 'The School of Ben Jonson'; 2nd series: 'The Lake Poets'; 3rd series: 'The Age of Victoria'
1901	Sidney Lee, 'Foreign Influences on Elizabethan Literature'
1902	Barrett Wendell, *The Temper of the Seventeenth Century in English Literature* (1904)
1903	——
1904	Frederick S. Boas, 'The Academic Drama'; adapted for *University Drama in the Tudor Age* (1914)
1905	Alexandre Beljame, 'Shakespeare Criticism in France from the time of Voltaire'
1906	——
1907	William Everett, 'The English Orators of the Eighteenth Century'
1908	——
1909	A. W. Verrall, 'The Victorian Poets'
1910	Walter Raleigh, 'Prose Writers of the Romantic Revival'; published in *On Writing and Writers* (1926)
1911	W. P. Ker – 1st series: 'Chaucer and the Scottish Chaucerians'; 2nd series: 'Forms of English Poetry'; published in *Form and Style in Poetry* (1928)
1912–13	——
1914	Adolphus Alfred Jack, *A Commentary on the Poetry of Chaucer and Spenser* (1920)
1915–20	——
1921	John Cann Bailey, 'Life and Art in English Poetry'; first lecture published in *The Continuity of Letters* (1923)
1922	Walter John de la Mare, 'The Art of Fiction'
1923	Lascelles Abercrombie, *The Idea of Great Poetry* (1925)
1924	John Middleton Murry, *Keats and Shakespeare* (1925)
1925	T. S. Eliot, 'The Metaphysical Poetry of the Seventeenth Century'; published as *The Varieties of Metaphysical Poetry* (1993)
1926	E. M. Forster, *Aspects of the Novel* (1927)
1927	André Maurois, *Aspects of Biography* (1929)
1928	Desmond MacCarthy, 'Byron'
1929	Herbert Read, *Wordsworth* (1930)
1930	Harley Granville Barker, *On Dramatic Method* (1931)
1931	Edmund Blunden, *Charles Lamb and His Contemporaries* (1933)
1932	——
1933	George Gordon, 'Shakespearian Comedy'; published in *Shakespearean Comedy and Other Studies* (1944)
1934	Ernest De Sélincourt, 'Wordsworth'
1935	R. W. Chambers, 'English Prose from Chaucer to Raleigh'
1936	(J. Dover Wilson – resigned)
	Herbert J. C. Grierson, 'Some of Shakespeare's Tragedies Considered in Relation to their Sources and to One Another'

1937   Harold Nicolson, 'Some Types of English Biography'

1938   W. W. Greg, *The Editorial Problem in Shakespeare* (1942)

1939   (Etienne Gilson – resigned)

1940   George Malcolm Young, 'Religious and Social Ideas in Nineteenth-century Literature from Wordsworth to William Morris'

1941   David Cecil, *Hardy the Novelist* (1943)

1942   J. Dover Wilson, *The Fortunes of Falstaff* (1944)

1943   C. S. Lewis, *English Literature in the Sixteenth Century* (1954)

1944   Raymond Mortimer, 'Five Dissident Victorians'

1945   C. Day Lewis, *The Poetic Image* (1946)

1946   H. B. Charlton, *Shakespearian Tragedy* (1948)

1947   (Etienne Gilson – resigned)

        R. W. Chapman, *Jane Austen: Facts and Problems* (1948)

1948   D. Nicol Smith, *John Dryden* (1950)

1949   Helen Darbishire, *The Poet Wordsworth* (1950)

1950   F. P. Wilson, *Marlowe and the Early Shakespeare* (1953)

1951   Humphry House, *Coleridge* (1953)

1952   Bonamy Dobrée, 'Public Themes in Poetry'; published as *The Broken Cistern* (1954)

1953   G. M. Trevelyan, *A Layman's Love of Letters* (1954)

1954   Robert Graves, 'Professional Standards in English Poetry'; published as *The Crowning Privilege* (1955)

1955   James Sutherland, *English Satire* (1958)

1956   Joyce Cary, *Art and Reality* (1958)

1957   C. V. Wedgwood, *Poetry and Politics under the Stuarts* (1960)

1958   Nevill Coghill, 'Shakespeare's "Know-how" as a Maker of Plays'; published as *Shakespeare's Professional Skills* (1964)

1959   E. M. W. Tillyard, *Some Mythical Elements in English Literature* (1961)

1960   Robert W. Birley, *Sunk without Trace: Some Forgotten Masterpieces Reconsidered* (1962)

1961   George Richard Wilson Bright, 'British Drama'

1962   Louis MacNeice, *Varieties of Parable* (1965)

1963   L. P. Hartley, 'Nathaniel Hawthorne'

1964   John Sparrow, *Mark Pattison and the Idea of a University* (1967)

1965   Stephen Spender, 'Aspects of British and American Imagination Since 1945'; expanded as *Love–Hate Relations* (1974)

1966   F. R. Leavis, *English Literature in our Time and the University* (1967)

1967   M. C. Bradbrook, *Shakespeare the Craftsman* (1969)

1968   V. S. Pritchett, *George Meredith and English Comedy* (1969)

1969   (Anthony Powell – resigned)

1970   L. C. Knights, 'Literature and Politics in the 17th Century'; published as *Public Voices* (1971)

1971   D. W. Harding, 'Forms and Uses of Rhythm in English Literature'; published as *Words into Rhythm* (1976)

1972   F. T. Prince, 'Makers and Materials: Shakespeare, Milton, Yeats and Eliot'

1973   William Empson, 'The Progress of Criticism'
1974   I. A. Richards, 'Some Futures for Criticism'
1975   (Jacob Bronowski – deceased)
        [In February 1976, the Council decided to elect Lecturers for a two-year period commencing 1978–80; the lectureship reverted to annual appointment in 1980.]
1976   Donald Davie, 'The Literature of Dissent, 1700–1930'; published as *A Gathered Church* (1978)
1977–8 David Piper, 'Poets and their Portraits'; expanded as *The Image of the Poet* (1982)
1979–80 Tom Stoppard, 'The Text and the Event'
1981–2 Charles Tomlinson, *Poetry and Metamorphosis* (1983)
1982–3 Geoffrey Hartman, 'The Poetical Character'
1983–4 Jonathan Miller, 'Limited Visibilities'; published as *Subsequent Performances* (1986)
1984–5 C. H. Gifford, 'Poetry in a Divided World'
1985–6 Geoffrey Hill, *The Enemy's Country* (1991)
1986–7 Richard Rorty, 'Irony and Solidarity'
1987–8 Jerome J. McGann, *Towards a Literature of Knowledge* (1989)
1988–9 Barbara Everett, 'Getting Things Wrong: Tragi-Comic Shakespeare
1989–90 Toni Morrison, 'Studies in American Africanism'
1990–1 Christopher Ricks, 'Victorian Lives: Aftersight and Foresight'
1991–2 ——
1992–3 Bernard Williams, 'Three Models of Truthfulness: Thucydides, Diderot, Nietzsche'

APPENDIX III

Turnbull Lecturers[1]

1891 Edmund C. Stedman, 'The Nature and Elements of Poetry' (8 lectures)
1892 Richard C. Jebb, 'The Growth and Influence of Classical Greek Poetry' (8 lectures)
1893 Robert Y. Tyrrell, 'The Growth and Influence of Latin Poetry' (8 lectures)
1894 Charles Eliot Norton, 'Dante' (6 lectures)
1896 George Adam Smith, 'Hebrew Poetry' (8 lectures)
1897 Ferdinand Brunetière 'French Poetry' (8 lectures)
1898 Charles R. Lanman, 'Poetry in India' (4 lectures)
1900 Charles H. Herford, 'English Poetry' (8 lectures)
1901 Hamilton W. Mabie, 'Poetry in America' (7 lectures)
1902 Emil G. Hirsch, 'Medieval Jewish Poetry' (8 lectures)
1904 Angelo de Gubernatis, 'Italian Poetry' (9 lectures)
1905 George E. Woodberry, 'Poetic Forms of Life' (8 lectures)
1906 Henry Van Dyke, 'The Service of Poetry' (6 lectures)
1907 Eugene Kühnemann, 'German Poetry' (8 lectures)
1908 A. V. Williams Jackson, 'The Poetry of Persia' (7 lectures)
1909 R. Menèndez Pidal, 'Spanish Epic Poetry' (7 lectures)
1911 Maurice Francis Egan, 'Typical Christian Hymns' (8 lectures)
1912 Paul Shorey, 'The Greek Epigram and the Palatine Anthology' (6 lectures)
1914 George Lyman Kittredge, 'The Poetry of Chaucer' (6 lectures)
1915 Sir Walter Raleigh, 'Poetry and Criticism of the Romantic Revival' (6 lectures)
1916 Paul Elmer More, 'Poets of America' (7 lectures)
1917 Edward Capps, 'Formative Influences in Greek Tragedy' (6 lectures)
1921 Charles Mills Gayley, 'Contemporary English Poetry' (6 lectures)
1922 Emile Legouis, 'The Poetry of Edmund Spenser' (6 lectures)
1924 Walter de la Mare, 'Three English Poets and Some Elements of the Poet's Art' (6 lectures)

1–This edited list was originally compiled by Professor Richard A. Macksay of The Johns Hopkins University for publication in Frank R. Shivers, *Maryland Wits & Baltimore Bards* (Baltimore: Maclay & Associates, 1985); reprinted by permission.

1927   Albert Feuillerat, 'Shakespeare and Poetry' (5 lectures)

1930   Edmond Faral, 'The Poetic Cycle of King Arthur' (6 lectures)

1931   George William Russell ('AE'), 'Some Personalities of the Irish Literary Movement' and 'A Poet and Artist Considers Dreams' (2 lectures)

1933   T. S. Eliot, 'The Varieties of Metaphysical Poetry' (3 lectures); R. W. Chambers, 'The Continuity of English Poetry, from the Beginnings to Tudor Times' (5 lectures)

1935   Lascelles Abercrombie, 'The Art of Wordsworth' (5 lectures)

1936   H. J. C. Grierson, 'Milton as Prophet and Artist' (5 lectures)

1937   Pedro Salinas, 'The Attitude toward Reality in Spanish Poetry' (5 lectures)

1938   Robert P. Tristram Coffin, 'New Poetry of New England' (6 lectures)

1939   Archibald MacLeish, 'Poets Now' (6 lectures)

1940   W. H. Auden, 'Poetry and the Old World' and 'America is where You Find It' (2 lectures)

1941   Joseph Warren Beach, 'A Romantic View of Poetry' (6 lectures)

1947   George Frisbie Whicher, 'Emily Dickinson: The Making of an American Poet' (6 lectures); Robert Frost, 'Precepts in Poetry' and 'Extravagances of the Spirit' (2 lectures)

1948   Donald H. Stauffer 'Studies in the Lyrics of William Butler Yeats' (3 lectures)

1949   C. J. Sisson, 'Shakespeare's Approach to Shakespeare' (3 lectures)

1950   Marie-Jeanne Dury, 'De Victor Hugo intime à Victor Hugo mythique' and 'La Poésie Française sous L'Occupation' (2 lectures)

1950   Henry Peyre, 'Baudelaire as Critic'

1951   E. W. M. Tillyard, 'The English Renaissance: Fact or Fiction?'

1952   F. P. Wilson, 'Elizabethan Drama'

1954   Pierre Emmanuel, 'Poetry, A Vocation'

1957   Richmond Lattimore 'Studies in the Poetry of Greek Tragedy'

1958   Poetry Festival, concurrent with First Bollingen Poetry Festival: R. P. Blackmur, 'The Poetry of Edwin Muir'; Yvor Winters, 'Poetic Styles, Old and New'; Marianne Moore, 'The Poetry of Dame Edith Sitwell'; Mark Van Doren, 'The Poetry of Thomas Hardy'

1961   'The Moment of Poetry': John Holmes, 'Surroundings and Illuminations'; May Sarton, 'The School of Babylon'; Richard Eberhart, 'Will and Psyche in Poetry'; Richard Wilbur, 'Round About a Poem of Housman's'; Randall Jarrell, 'Robert Frost's "Home Burial" '

1963   Yves Bonnefoy, 'La Poésie Française et L'Expérience de L'Etre'

1965–6   Roy Harvey Pearce, 'Whitman and our Hope for Poetry'; Arnold Stein, 'George Herbert's Lyrics: The Art of Plainness'; Wolfgang Clemen, 'The Spirits in Shelley's Poetry'; T. B. L. Webster, 'Euripides: Traditionalist and Innovator'; Jorge Guillén, 'A Portrait of Pedro Salinas'; John H. Finley, Jr, 'Pindar's Beginnings'; George E. Duckworth, 'The "Old" and the "New" in Virgil's *Aeneid*'; Viktor Pöschl, 'Poetry and Philosophy in Horace'

1966   Michel Deguy, 'Poésie et Connaissance'

1968   Margit Frenck and Antonio Alatorre, 'Poesia y musica del renacimento español', lecture and recital

1969   Northop Frye, 'Romantic Poetics and Myth'; Irving Singer, 'The Loves of

[324]

Dido and Aeneas: Variations on a Theme: Henry Purcell: *Dido and Aeneas*; Hector Berlioz: *Les Troyens à Carthage*

1970 A. Alvarez, 'The Savage God: Sylvia Plath and Contemporary Poetry'; David Ray, 'The Light-Bound Space of the Mind: Remarks on Contemporary Poetry and Painting'; Dámaso Alonso, 'Hijos de la ira: Children of Wrath'

1971 Paul Valéry Centennial: Jackson Mathews, Gérard Genette, James Lawler, Michel Deguy, Elizabeth Sewell, Jacques Derrida

1972 Kenneth Koch, 'Poetry and Children'

1973 Eric Segal, 'The Birth of Comedy'; Nathan A. Scott, Jr, 'Hope, History, and Literature'; William Heyen, 'On Richard Wilbur: An Experiment in Criticism'

1974 Conference on the Genealogy of the Epic: Gregory Nagy and Richard Macksey, chairmen; Joseph Russo, Albert B. Lord, David Bynam, Jenny Clay, Hugh S. MacKay, Jr, Douglas Frame

1975 Josephine Jacobsen, 'The Landscapes of the Imagination: Elliott Coleman at Hopkins'; Louis Zukofsky, 'Poetry and Poetics: An Objectivist Perspective'; Jacques Derrida, 'La Question de Style'

1976 Phillippe Lacoue-Labarthe, 'L'écho du sujet: sur la compulsion auto-biographique'

1977 Edwin Honig, 'The Poet's Other Voice: Spontaneous Exchanges on Translation'; Harold Bloom, 'The Sublime Crossing and the Death of Love'; Yves Bonnefoy, 'Que peut encore la poésie?' Symposium on John Ruskin, published as *The Ruskin Polygon: Essays on the Imagination of John Ruskin*: John Dixon Hunt, George L. Hersey, Jeffrey Spear, Marc A. Simpson, William Arrowsmith, Garry Wills, Richard Macksey

1978 Paul de Man, 'Baudelaire, Benjamin, and Translation'; Jean Starobinski, 'An Interpretation of Rousseau and Baudelaire'

1979 Ronald Paulson, 'Constable's Poetics: The Suppression of Literary Land-scape'; Frank Doggett, Stevens Centennial Lecture, 'Wallace Stevens: The Making of Poems'; Francis Fergusson, 'The Bathos of Experience: The Poetics of Edmund Burke'

1980 James Nohrnberg, 'Epic Comparison and Comparative Epic in *Paradise Lost*'; Michel Deguy, 'La poésie en question'

1981 Paul de Man, 'The Poetics of the Sublime'

1982 Arnold Stein, 'The Voices of the Satirist: John Donne'

1983 John Malcolm Wallace, '*Timon of Athens, De Beneficiis*, and the Three Graces'; J. Hillis Miller, 'The Difficulties of Reading William Carlos Williams' (Centennial Lecture)

1984 Joseph N. Riddel, 'An American Poetics'

INDEX TO THE LECTURES

The name, title and selected subject index to the text of the Clark and Turnbull lectures is supplemented by a separate Index of Editorial Material, p. 335

[327]

INDEX TO EDITORIAL MATERIAL